DIVINING THE ORACLE

DIVINING THE ORACLE

Monteverdi's *Seconda Prattica*

MASSIMO OSSI

THE UNIVERSITY OF CHICAGO PRESS
Chicago and London

Massimo Ossi is associate professor of musicology at Indiana University.

THE UNIVERSITY OF CHICAGO PRESS, CHICAGO 60637
THE UNIVERSITY OF CHICAGO PRESS, LTD., LONDON
© 2003 by The University of Chicago
All rights reserved. Published 2003
Printed in the United States of America

12   11   10   09   08   07   06   05   04   03   5   4   3   2   1

ISBN (cloth): 0-226-63883-9

Library of Congress Cataloging-in-Publication Data

Ossi, Massimo Michele.
    Divining the oracle : Monteverdi's seconda prattica / Massimo Ossi.
        p.   cm.
    Includes bibliographical references (p.   ) and index.
    ISBN 0-226-63883-9 (alk. paper)
        1. Monteverdi, Claudio, 1567–1643—Criticism and interpretation.
    2. Music theory—History—17th century.   I. Title.
ML410.M77 O78   2003
782'.0092—dc21

                                        2002153733

To Sally and Francesca

CONTENTS

Contents

ILLUSTRATIONS

PREFACE

In van la tento, et impossibil parmi.

"Oracolo della musica": with this epi-
thet in the dedicatory sonnet to the Venetian edition of the libretto of *Arianna*,
Benedetto Ferrari encapsulated Monteverdi's contribution to the musical culture of his time.[1] I must admit that, writing this book, I have indeed felt at
times that I was groping to interpret the hermetic verses of an inscrutable oracle. As important and seemingly extensive as they are, the sources that convey
the substance of Monteverdi's thinking about the transition from his Late
Renaissance training to his exploration of new forms, genres, and expressive
musical language are also laconic, confusing, and disjointed. This makes them
mesmerizing, and I confess to having fallen under their spell precisely because
they offer a peek at the rich and at times turbulent intellectual activity of a major composer at the forefront of his musical culture. What interests me about
them is not so much what they say about contrapuntal practice, but what they
imply, beyond the limitations of the written word, about the motivations behind the reevaluation of technique and expression.

In order to illuminate the implications of the various essays, letters, and
books that preserve Monteverdi's public and private thoughts about the changing aesthetic premises of composition during the late 1590s and early 1600s,
I have turned to his music. (The Italian texts, and one French one, of all but
the briefest prose extracts are gathered in an appendix, keyed to the footnotes

---

1. *Arianna* was revived in 1640 for the opening of the Teatro S. Moisè; reported in Paolo
Fabbri, *Monteverdi* (Turin: E.D.T., 1985), 323.

attached to the translations in the body of the book.) I do not claim that this is an original approach or a particularly surprising one—indeed I do not believe that my aim is to be original at all—but this intensely mined territory seems to me to be still productive, still capable of supporting yet another interpretation. Monteverdi scholarship has a long tradition of trailblazing scholars, from Henry Prunieres to Leo Schrade and Nino Pirrotta, and more recently to Gary Tomlinson, Silke Leopold, Ellen Rosand, and Eric Chafe; I hope to have entered into a continuing dialogue with this tradition, bringing together ideas that have been part of the conversation about Monteverdi and highlighting what seem to me to be fruitful approaches to his thought and his music.

In this spirit of evolving dialogue, I have emphasized from the very title the interpretative and of necessity partial nature of this study. Oracles are made to speak by those who strive to interpret them, and no single book can, in my view, illuminate all of Monteverdi's *seconda prattica:* the task itself, to borrow from Petrarch, "vince ogni stile."

"Monteverdi's *seconda prattica*": the fundamental assumption behind this study is that Monteverdi had a personal, perhaps idiosyncratic, view of the stylistic transition around the turn of the seventeenth century, and that this view was largely pragmatic. I do not believe that a single ideological point of departure drove his compositional solutions, and I am not sure he trusted his contemporaries' ideologies; in particular, I am not convinced that his view of modern music had much in common with that of the Florentine Camerata, although it is clear that he did feel the need to compete with the Florentines— not least for assignments at his own court in Mantua. Monteverdi's highly independent approach to solving compositional problems comes across in his letters to Giovanni Battista Doni written in the early 1630s, when he dismisses the writings of Vincenzo Galilei with barely concealed indifference. His independence also prompts the tone of surprise that permeates his first reaction to Artusi's criticisms, the *Lettera* introducing the fifth book of madrigals in 1605.

Thus the focus in the chapters that follow remains on a single practical problem from which all other aspects of Monteverdi's music seem to spring: the changing purpose behind musical composition. If he could state privately to Doni, and later publicly in the preface to the *Madrigali guerrieri et amorosi*, that he found no examples to imitate in the music of his predecessors and that indeed he could find no answer to the very question of what an "imitator" ought to be, it is largely because the composer's purpose behind the act of composition was changing. Choosing one style or another was not simply a matter of aesthetic allegiance but resulted from the compositional problem to be solved, which in turn was determined by the function the work would have in the social fabric that would surround it. It was to clarify this purpose and the compositional problem facing him that he asked Alessandro Striggio, in a letter dated 9 December 1616 concerning a dramatic commission from Mantua, "What does Your Lordship want the music to do?" It could be made to do whatever was required, but the problem had to be stated in a way that the composer could understand, and it had to be worth solving besides (in the case of the piece under discussion, it was not; see chapter 6).

Pragmatism does not imply a random wandering from problem to problem, and another assumption I have made is that Monteverdi's approach to the various problems he encountered was guided by certain preferences. Thus there is a consistent logic to the way he chose to organize his madrigal books, a similarly consistent logic to his development of a dramatic language, another to his approach to composing individual madrigals, and yet another to his theorizing about music. I am not sure that Monteverdi would recognize the aspects of his works that I see as manifesting these consistent preferences, but insofar as I am more comfortable assuming that there is a discernible logic, I have sought to demonstrate its presence.

The prologue to this book (so called because like the prologues of Baroque opera it establishes a road map by which to navigate the rest of the work) traces the logical threads that this study pursues across Monteverdi's output: the dramatic components of the *seconda prattica*, the establishment of style and genre categories as the means for constructing large-scale structures spanning entire madrigal books, the blurring of such categories in individual works to generate tension and meaning, and finally the realignment of text and music not so much into a servant–mistress hierarchy as into a position of expressive equality in which the two engage in a dialectic from which the audience can derive the meaning (or meanings) of the work.

The successive chapters approach these various elements in greater depth. Chapter 1 focuses on Monteverdi's recollections of the debate with Artusi, considers the much broader scope that the planned treatise on the *seconda prattica* had taken on by the 1630s, and reviews the Artusi texts in light of the aesthetic issues they raise as background to the music itself. Chapter 2 compares the organization of the fifth book of madrigals with that of the fourth by analyzing in detail the grouping of madrigals in each book and tracing the narrative strategy at work in the fifth.

Chapter 3 turns to the canzonetta, building on my *JAMS* article on *Un ordine novo bello et gustevole*[2] and surveying Monteverdi's continued interest in the genre as late as *L'Incoronazione di Poppea*. Chapter 4 looks at several individual pieces — "Con che soavità" from the seventh book of madrigals (1619), the *Lamento della ninfa* from the eighth, and the *Gloria a 7 concertata* from the *Selva Morale* (1640) — in which aspects of instrumentation, style, character, form, and genre either are superimposed and contrasted to create a musical meaning parallel to that of the text, or are used as building blocks to create larger forms.

Chapter 5 returns to Monteverdi's theoretical ideas, exploring the structure and content of the preface to the *Madrigali guerrieri et amorosi* in search of an overarching theoretical logic linking the three main functional categories of music (theater, dance, and chamber), the three main affective levels (high, middle, and low), and the rhetorical aspects of performance. I argue that Monteverdi's model for the essay is derived from the third book of Aristotle's *Rhetoric*, and that it is precisely from this rhetorical foundation that Monteverdi's entire system derives its coherence.

Chapter 6 focuses on the *genere concitato* and its use within the *Combattimento di Tancredi e Clorinda* (1624, but published in 1638 in the eighth book), analyzing the work from a literary and formal point of view and linking it to classicizing sources beyond Tasso's *Gerusalemme liberata* and *Gerusalemme conquistata*. The interpretation I propose de-emphasizes the violence of the battle scenes in favor of a more integrated view in which the power of the work derives from the extreme contrasts in affect to produce a sense of pathos and religious piety. This view is consistent with the iconography of canto 12 in the seventeenth century, which avoided the duel in favor of the conversion scene and other moments in the story leading to Clorinda's death.

The epilogue looks briefly at Monteverdi's later treatment of the *genere concitato* and closes with a brief synoptic view of Monteverdi as a self-conscious "modernist."

—✥—

Parts of chapter 3 appeared in "Claudio Monteverdi's *Ordine novo, bello et gustevole:* The Canzonetta as Dramatic Module and Formal Archetype," *Journal of the American Musicological Society* 45 (1992), 261–304.

2. "Claudio Monteverdi's *Ordine novo, bello et gustevole:* The Canzonetta as Dramatic Module and Formal Archetype," *Journal of the American Musicological Society* 45 (1992): 261–304.

Work on chapter 4 was completed while on a fellowship, made possible by a grant from the National Endowment for the Humanities, at the Harvard University Center for Italian Renaissance Studies at Villa I Tatti, Florence. The portion dealing with "Con che soavità" appears as "Between Madrigale and *Altro Genere di Canto:* Elements of Ambiguity in Claudio Monteverdi's Setting of Battista Guarini's 'Con che soavità,'"in *Guarini, la musica, i musicisti,* ed. Angelo Pompilio (Lucca: L. I. M., 1997), which records the proceedings of the international conference "Battista Guarini e la Musica," held in Ferrara in October 1991.

I presented a preliminary version of parts of chapter 5 at the 1993 annual meeting of the American Musicological Society in Montreal, Quebec. I am grateful to Barbara Russano Hanning for her insightful response to the paper, as well as for providing me with a copy of her remarks.

~

In the course of writing this study I have accumulated many debts to friends, colleagues, and institutions; indeed without them I might find myself paraphrasing Giambattista Marino's line, which I borrowed at the head of this preface, and write "in van la tentai, et impossibil divenne." I hope that the completion of the book itself may serve as partial validation and repayment for their encouragement.

The earliest stages of research were supported by a grant from the National Endowment for the Humanities administered through the Harvard University Center for Renaissance Studies at the Villa I Tatti in Florence. I am grateful to my colleagues at the Center, especially Michele Fromson and Ralph Hexter, for the many long conversations that helped to shape my thinking; to the Director, Professor Walter Keiser; and the wonderful staff of the Center, Kathryn Bosi-Monteath in particular, for providing a productive and nurturing environment in which to work. Subsequently, I was supported by a semester's leave from the University of Rochester.

The lion's share of my gratitude goes to those colleagues whose daily encouragement and gentle counsel have kept this book on the front burner of a slow stove: I am deeply in debt to Evan Bonds, Kim Kowalke, Ellen Rosand, and Kerala Snyder, who cajoled and nudged and questioned but never lost faith; as well as to Barbara Russano Hanning for her helpful and learned response to the paper I presented at the 1993 meeting of the American Musicological

Society in Montreal that eventually formed the core of chapter 5, and to Lorenzo Bianconi, who generously shared his reactions to the manuscript and offered suggestions for its improvement. Is there enough bourbon in Kentucky?

The readers of the original manuscript for the University of Chicago Press deserve particular thanks for their incisive and revealing readings, which made my own ideas apparent to me; for recognizing the good in the manuscript and not allowing its faults to obscure it; and for their support in the final stage of revision. And of course none of it would have mattered much had it not been for Kathleen Hansell's long-suffering and ever-gracious patience as I made my snail-like way through this project.

Finally, my greatest debt of gratitude goes to my family, Sally Gaskill and Francesca Ossi, who put up with this seemingly never-ending intrusion into our lives and remained steadfastly encouraging even when the going got to its toughest stages. Francesca was born just as this process was getting under way, and if she has perhaps contributed to slowing it down, she has also made it a more humane endeavor, with many pleasant and revitalizing interludes. It may not be much consolation to either of them to know that the next book will be a lot easier.

Inevitably this book, like all beginnings, is riddled with flaws, for it is but a tentative endeavor; this burden belongs to no one but myself. I apologize for its weaknesses in advance, in the hope that the reader will bear in mind my good will and will be kindly disposed toward my labors, for "omne principium est debile." I look forward to continuing the dialogue I have entered, and I await the sharpening of ideas that will inevitably come from the pens of my learned colleagues.

Vivete felici,
Bloomington, 2001

PROLOGUE

Divining the Oracle

*In the long run, I shall be happier to be moderately
praised in the new style, than greatly praised in the ordinary.*[1]

Few would not agree that Claudio
Monteverdi's genius lay to a great extent in his unfailing sense of drama, which
ranks him with the best operatic composers of the past four centuries. His surviving operas, which even today enjoy pride of place in the repertory, bear
ample witness to his keen instinct for timing, characterization, psychological
insight, and large-scale structure, as well as to his sophisticated ear for the
rhythms, meanings—whether ambiguous or forcefully direct—and sounds of
the texts he set to music. As with Mozart, his fundamentally dramatic musical
conception makes itself evident even in works not necessarily meant for the
stage: the air of the theater blows fair through most of his other compositions,
both sacred and secular.

Unlike Mozart, however, Monteverdi came late to opera, and this makes
his achievements as a dramatic composer all the more remarkable. The *favola
per musica* did not emerge as a courtly entertainment until he was a mature, accomplished composer who had seen five books of madrigals into press before
producing his first opera, *Orfeo*, in 1607 at the age of forty. From that point on
and for the next thirty-six years, he established himself among the earliest and
most influential practitioners of the new genre, helping to define its musical
and dramatic problems and developing the musical language to address them.

1. Monteverdi, letter 123, to Giovanni Battista Doni, 23 October 1633 (DS). *The Letters
of Claudio Monteverdi*, ed. and trans. by Denis Stevens (London: Cambridge University Press,
1980), 411. Throughout this volume, the translations are by me unless marked (DS).

Orfeo, as his first attempt at a genre that by 1607 had scarcely a half-dozen precedents, seems almost impossibly sophisticated. A great deal of ink has been spilled by modern scholars exploring its structure, symbolism, and musical language, far more than has been devoted to its predecessors, including Giulio Caccini's and Jacopo Peri's competing settings of Ottavio Rinuccini's *Euridice* (1600), which Monteverdi and his librettist, Alessandro Striggio, sought to emulate and surpass.[2] As a sequel, *Arianna* (1608), which followed *Orfeo* by about a year, again seems historically improbable, if not impossible: an almost instant, legendary success, it marks an enormous creative and expressive leap for both the composer and the genre. Its only surviving excerpt, the heroine's celebrated lament, circulated in manuscript for fifteen years before Monteverdi published it, achieving such a reputation that it was said that no cultured household in Italy lacked a copy.[3] Its popularity helped to establish the lament as a requisite element in most operas for the next sixty years or so and launched a new genre, the independent solo lament intended for chamber performance.[4] And, in an age of disposable operas, when revivals were extremely rare and musical fashion changed rapidly, *Arianna* may have been restaged at least twice, the last time in 1640 as the inaugural opera for the Teatro S. Moisè in Venice.[5]

The creative outburst that produced *Orfeo* and *Arianna* within the space of about two years, even had it remained an isolated event, would invite speculation about the composer's development in the years preceding 1607. Monteverdi's career between 1600 and 1607, however, had hardly followed the placid trajectory many others enjoyed under the protection of court employment. In 1600 and again in 1602, he found himself the target of critical censure at the hands of the Bolognese theorist Giovanni Maria Artusi, who took exception to a number of his madrigals as examples of the expressive excesses in which many "modern" composers indulged without regard for proper contrapuntal practice. As Claude Palisca put it, this much celebrated controversy forced

2. Gary Tomlinson, *Monteverdi and the End of the Renaissance* (Berkeley and Los Angeles: University of California Press, 1987), 131–36.

3. Severo Bonini, *Prima parte de' discorsi e regole sovra la musica* (1640-63c), quoted in Paolo Fabbri, *Monteverdi* (Turin: E.D.T., 1985), 145. Modern edition in MaryAnn Teresa Bonino, "Don Severo Bonini (1582–1663), His *Discorsi e Regole,*" Ph.D. diss., University of Southern California, 1971.

4. Massimo Ossi, "Lamento," in *Die Musik in Geschichte und Gegenwart, Sachteil* vol. 5 (1994), 903b–911a.

5. The first revival was planned for May 1620 in Mantua but was eventually abandoned: see Monteverdi, *Letters,* ed. Stevens, 194–210; *Arianna* was finally performed in 1640 at the Teatro S. Moisè; see Fabbri, *Monteverdi,* 323.

Monteverdi to explain himself and to raise the banner of the *seconda prattica* for his contemporaries to rally around, setting his historical position into bold relief.[6] In fact, it may have also considerably raised Monteverdi's stock with his contemporaries, for in 1600 he was still a relatively minor figure, with just three books of madrigals to his credit, and had been passed over in the succession to Jaches de Wert as *maestro di cappella* at Mantua in favor of the older, and more widely published, Pallavicino.[7] Nonetheless, Monteverdi's writings during this period—his "modernist" manifesto, the "Lettera" that introduces his fifth book of madrigals (1605), and his brother Giulio Cesare's gloss on the "Lettera" in the *Scherzi musicali* (1607)—together with Artusi's books, and a handful of contributions to the debate by other composers and theorists, have indeed provided a certain amount of light on his role as an exponent of a new approach to composition.

That light, however, does not reach either us or Monteverdi's music directly. It is refracted and filtered by ambiguities in his writings; by fragmentary thoughts left undeveloped; by Monteverdi's unfulfilled promise of a treatise to explain the methods, aims, and technical procedures of the *seconda prattica;* and finally by the incompleteness of the musical and historical records for the years preceding his first two operas. On the basis of what can be known, even an attempt to establish a reliable chronology of Monteverdi's compositional activities and courtly duties between 1592 (when the third book of madrigals was published) and 1607, the crucial fifteen-year period during which the new style was in its formative stages, raises as many questions as it settles.[8] All we know is that Monteverdi contributed four canzonettas to an anthology published in 1594; that he was named *maestro* of a reduced *cappella* that in 1595 accompanied Duke Vincenzo Gonzaga on a military expedition organized by Emperor Rudolf II against the Turks; and that he was passed over for a promotion to *maestro di cappella* at court after Jaches de Wert's death in 1596. One newly composed madrigal of his, "Ah dolente partita," and five others previously published in the second and third books, were included in an anthology, *Fiori del giardino di diversi eccellentissimi autori* (Nuremberg, 1597),[9] and at least

6. Claude Palisca, "The Artusi–Monteverdi Controversy," in *The New Monteverdi Companion*, ed. Denis Arnold and Nigel Fortune (London: Faber and Faber, 1985), 127.

7. Monteverdi finally attained the post of *maestro* in 1601, after Pallavicino's death.

8. On the question of the chronology of Monteverdi's works after the third book, see Tomlinson, *Monteverdi*, 98–113. On the problems of dating Monteverdi's works, see Silke Leopold, *Monteverdi: Music in Transition*, trans. by Anne Smith (Oxford: Clarendon, 1991), 216–20.

9. On the anthology and the possibility that "Ah dolente partita" may have appeared earlier see Fabbri, *Monteverdi*, 46.

four, and perhaps as many as six, of his compositions were performed at the now famous gathering hosted by the musician Antonio Goretti in Ferrara in 1597.[10] In 1599, he married Claudia Cattaneo, and later that year he traveled to Spa, in Flanders, with the Duke's retinue. He was at last named *maestro di cappella* at Mantua sometime between December 1601, after the death of Pallavicino, and 1 March 1603, when the dedication of his fourth book of madrigals refers to him as *maestro*. In 1607–8, he was by no means the obvious choice for composing the centerpiece of Mantua's most important public display of musical and theatrical patronage—the commission that would eventually produce *Arianna*.[11]

If this is more than we know about many of his contemporaries, it is also woefully little. Monteverdi's publications between the third and fourth books speak of his widening reputation, perhaps as a result of contacts made while traveling, but they account for all of a half-dozen compositions. The single reprint of the third book of madrigals (1594; the second came in 1600, probably on the wings of controversy, with others following it) is hardly evidence of great commercial success.[12] Just how influential, how visible, Monteverdi might have been in the late 1590s remains an open question, made all the more puzzling by the paucity of compositions around which to flesh out his career. Artusi's criticisms may well be evidence of Monteverdi's growing reputation (which would have made him a plausible target for public criticism), but the tale told by the reprints of his third book also suggests the polemic had a major role in establishing his reputation. Giulio Cesare in his "Dichiaratione" makes him out to be an influential and widely imitated innovator, but the question remains: If Artusi's invective was partly aimed at older established theorists like Ercole Bottrigari and perhaps even Vincenzo Galilei, why did he choose Monteverdi when other, arguably more visible, composers were available? Was his music so much more outrageous than Marenzio's, Luzzaschi's, Gesualdo's, or Caccini's? Was Monteverdi the only composer heard at Goretti's musical evening, and if so, was it simply a matter of his being in the right (or wrong) place at the right time? If Monteverdi was in fact the most notable, or

10. Four ("Cruda Amarilli," "Anima mia perdona," "Che se tu se' il cor mio," and "O Mirtillo") were criticized in the first volume of Artusi's treatise, and two more ("Era l'anima mia" and "Ma se con la pietà") in the second.

11. On the events leading up to the commission, see Fabbri, *Monteverdi*, 124–28.

12. Fabbri interprets the reprint history of the third book as a sign of the success the volume eventually attained, without speculating on the connection between the appearance of Artusi's book and Monteverdi's commercial viability. See *Monteverdi*, 43.

the most vocal, of a group of young "reformers," a kind of Mantuan-Ferrarese "camerata" (was Goretti their Bardi?), his companions have remained invisible or protected by the cloak of academic anonymity. (For example, Monteverdi's earliest known epistolary defender signed his letters to Artusi "l'Accademico Ottuso" [the Blockhead Academician]; his important statements regarding the avant-garde's aims survive only because Artusi, who was both a fair critic and well versed in his opponents' arguments, chose to include them in his books.)[13] If Artusi's mocking references to Monteverdi's claim of having coined the term "seconda prattica" suggest that it was inflated and that the composer was appropriating a term that had already been in general usage, there is also no evidence that anyone else (other than l'Ottuso, who was first to mention it in his letters to Artusi) was speaking of it.[14]

Monteverdi's response to the polemic itself also raises questions that have remained unanswered. Artusi issued his first criticisms in 1600 and returned to the subject with greater vehemence in 1602; Monteverdi's fourth book of madrigals of 1603 contained works relevant to Artusi's arguments against recent compositional trends, but the introduction makes no direct mention of the notoriety some of the contents had already achieved. In fact, he held his pen in check until the fifth book, and even then he remained relatively vague, so that the most elaborate statement of his aesthetic ideas came in the *Scherzi musicali* of 1607. Why he did not respond at the first opportunity remains open to speculation—perhaps he was hoping the controversy would die down (it intensified instead); perhaps he was planning a more extended reply and was not ready to commit his ideas to print, or lacked the theoretical background necessary to respond to Artusi's arguments; or, possibly, he had begun to consider other technical and aesthetic problems, and was waiting to produce some convincing examples with which to illustrate his notion of the "seconda prattica." In this book, I argue on the basis of his compositions and his later writings that even if the controversy was responsible for setting Monteverdi to the task of explaining what is likely to have been up to that point strictly a matter of compositional practice and not theory or even aesthetics, once he was on his way he quickly outstripped both his critic and his defenders. Monteverdi's conception of the *seconda prattica* by 1603 had evolved beyond mere dissonance

13. Artusi published part of Ottuso's first letter and the entirety of his second; for an extended discussion of these letters, see chapter 1, *The Artusi texts*.

14. For Giulio Cesare's claims, see his "Dichiaratione," in Monteverdi, *Lettere, dediche, e prefazioni*, ed. Domenico De' Paoli (Rome: De Santis, 1973), 401–2.

treatment, to which the "Lettera" of 1605 and the "Dichiaratione" modestly circumscribe it, and was already headed toward the "crisis" accompanying the composition of *Arianna* that Monteverdi later singled out as the most significant period in its formulation. If neither essay speaks of the *seconda prattica* as a still fluid concept, it is likely because its development to that point remained largely inchoate, waiting for a specific problem to bring it into focus; indeed, the very modesty of the two statements suggests defensive caution in the face of the unknown—not so much for lack of theoretical background, but for lack of a clear sense of the consequences that the new style would have for Monteverdi's views on music and composition.

In light of these larger questions, even what "seconda prattica" may have been meant to encompass cannot be postulated with any certainty. That it is characterized by the sorts of contrapuntal infractions to which Artusi points in his examples seems clear enough, and so does the justification, offered by Monteverdi and others, that these liberties arise from the expressive demands of the text, which must be followed by the composer above all other considerations. Beyond these points, however, its nature remains a matter of speculation. None of the texts specifies clearly to what sorts of textual cues the composer should react, or how broad a range of expressive liberties is acceptable; none of the texts distinguishes between the expressive aims of the madrigalisms common throughout the repertory of at least the previous two decades and those of the new style. Giulio Cesare Monteverdi's list of composers in the "Dichiarazione" brings into play a list of important precursors of the *seconda prattica*, but even with names in hand it is unclear exactly what aspects of their various styles he intends to link to his brother's development—especially when individual composers, like Cipriano da Rore, are claimed by both sides as representing their compositional ideals.[15] Nor is it evident what else besides the madrigal either Claudio or Giulio Cesare intended to include under the rubric of the *seconda prattica:* neither *Orfeo* nor *Arianna* had been written at the time of the "Dichiaratione," and nobody on either side mentions music for the theater. Finally, the question of what, if any, theoretical writings influenced Monteverdi's thinking remains very much open: To what degree was he aware of Florentine investigations into ancient music and of treatises like Galilei's *Dialogo della musica antica e moderna?* To what degree did the ideas formed by the Camerata influence his direction during the 1590s?

15. On the uses made of Rore as a seminal figure by the two sides, see Stefano La Via, "Cipriano de Rore as Reader and as Read: A Literary-Musical Study of Madrigals from Rore's Later Collections (1557–1566)" (Ph.D. diss., Princeton University, 1991).

In the end, it is difficult to define the boundaries of the *seconda prattica* as a critical term by which to explain the music of Monteverdi's predecessors and contemporaries or, more importantly, even for explaining his own. In spite of the similarities pointed out by Palisca between Galilei's theoretical writings and the contrapuntal freedom found in the madrigals of Monteverdi and others, it is still not clear that what Monteverdi was reaching for in the late 1590s and early 1600s was in fact the same end that Galilei had been seeking in the 1570s and 1580s.[16] Given Monteverdi's unequivocally contrapuntal compositional technique, which is evident in his continued cultivation of the ensemble madrigal long after the dispute with Artusi and which informs even such "monodic" works as the "Lamento" from *Arianna*, it is questionable whether his view of the *seconda prattica* had much in common with Galilei's treatises (which, in the 1630s, he claimed to have read at some—conveniently?—vague point in the past).[17] Even in the case of Monteverdi's own compositions, moreover, it is not clear whether the term can be applied to all his works beginning with those of the fourth and fifth books (and even in the fourth there are some madrigals that do not seem to fall within its purview), or whether indeed it lost its usefulness for characterizing his style after a certain point (following the sixth book of 1614? or the seventh of 1619? Are the dramatic works, especially *Arianna*, to be included? What about the *Combattimento* of 1624? Is there any validity to the term by 1638, when the *Madrigali guerrieri et amorosi* appeared?).

Nonetheless, it is evident from the canonical texts of the Artusi polemic that the term *seconda prattica* implied more than just dissonance treatment in conjunction with a handful of affective words, and Monteverdi's compositions—especially those of the fifth book itself—strongly suggest a broader interpretation. Finally, those writings in which Monteverdi revisited the events that defined his place among his contemporaries, particularly his correspondence of the 1630s with the theorist Giovanni Battista Doni, suggest that for the composer the *seconda prattica* remained a viable concept even some thirty years later, and that he himself associated it with a long process of experimentation and discovery that encompassed, and indeed was driven by, his earliest operatic experiences, especially *Arianna* and, specifically, the famous lament.

16. On this point, see Claude Palisca, "Galilei's Counterpoint Treatise: a Code for the 'seconda prattica,'" *Journal of the American Musicological Society* 9 (1956), 81; Leopold, *Monteverdi*, 42–45, draws a sharp distinction between the Florentine experiments and the contrapuntal tradition from which Monteverdi emerged.

17. Letter 124 of 2 February 1634 to Doni; *Letters*, ed. Stevens, p. 414.

Monteverdi's claim that the real work of the *seconda prattica* did not really begin until he was deep into the composition of *Arianna* points to the essential connection between musical drama and the new language that had come under attack from Artusi. But the historical record suggests other points of departure and highlights, once more, the composer's activities during the years preceding his earliest operatic experiments. In this connection, it is important to remember that the "Dichiaratione" itself, the most important and for a long time the only statement of Monteverdi's aesthetic premises, was drafted before and during the composition of *Orfeo*. If it does not mention the opera itself, its association with the *Scherzi* does point to one of the principal elements of the opera's dramatic structure and symbolism.[18] Coming as it does against the background of *Orfeo* and during the summer when preparations were under way for the wedding of Francesco Gonzaga and Marguerite of Savoy and when the commission for the celebratory opera was very much up in the air and in danger of going to a Florentine composer, the "Dichiaratione" takes on an added dimension as a political statement aimed at the Duke and his brother, at once answering Artusi's charges and addressing its courtly audience in support of Monteverdi's role in the upcoming celebrations of the wedding.

The intrinsic nexus between the *seconda prattica* and opera, although established by Monteverdi long after the fact, provides a framework for interpreting the aims of his *seconda prattica* during the crucial years around the turn of the seventeenth century. It has been argued that the performances of Battista Guarini's *Il pastor fido* at the Mantuan court in 1592 and later in 1598 must have left a strong impression on him; although nothing survives to suggest that he composed any of his *Pastor fido* settings for those performances, he likely participated in them in some capacity—either as an instrumentalist or as a singer.[19] Certainly it seems plausible that the whole experience proved formative for him and that it is reflected in the special prominence that excerpts from Guarini's play have in the structure of the fifth book. Tomlinson has recognized Wert's influence in Monteverdi's settings of Torquato Tasso's poetry published in his third book of madrigals (1592), and it is also evident in the *Pastor fido* excerpts of the fifth book (1605).[20] It seems likely, too, that in both

18. See my "Claudio Monteverdi's *Ordine novo, bello et gustevole*: The Canzonetta as Dramatic Module and Formal Archetype," *Journal of the American Musicological Society* 45 (1992), 282–91 and 301–2.

19. Tomlinson, *Monteverdi*, 114–18.

20. Tomlinson, *Monteverdi*, 58–72; also Nino Pirrotta, "Monteverdi's Poetic Choices," in *Music and Culture in Italy from the Middle Ages to the Baroque* (Cambridge: Harvard University Press, 1984), 279–80.

cases Monteverdi may have profited from the presence of the poets themselves, as he may have later with Gabriello Chiabrera and obviously did with Ottavio Rinuccini: Tasso was at court through most of 1591, and Guarini was there intermittently during 1591–92.[21]

As far as can be determined, Monteverdi had his first direct contact with the theater and with theatrical music during the Mantuan productions of Guarini's *Pastor fido*. Theatricality, however, was an integral aspect of the musical and literary world he had come to inhabit at the Mantuan court. The court dance tradition, important at Ferrara and imitated in Mantua, involved at least some staging and costumes, and it seems plausible that Monteverdi would have been acquainted with it, just as he would likely have heard about the 1589 *intermedii* for Bargagli's *La pellegrina* at Florence, in which the Pellizzari family, Mantua's answer to the Ferrarese *concerto delle dame*, had been involved and which the court had attended.[22] After the *Pastor fido* productions, moreover, he may have visited Florence, to which the court again returned in 1600 for the wedding of Henry IV of France and Maria de' Medici; if so, he would have had first-hand knowledge of *Euridice* and *Il rapimento di Cefalo*, the two musico-dramatic "experiments" of the wedding celebrations.[23] Certainly his librettist for *Orfeo*, Alessandro Striggio, was there, and it is clear that their *Orfeo* reflected the long-standing artistic rivalry between Mantua and Florence. In 1604, Monteverdi's correspondence bears evidence of his own earliest dramatic composition, a now lost *balletto* called *La favola di Endimione*, the first of a number of such works; another *balletto*, of uncertain date and possibly also authorship, is included in the *Scherzi musicali* of 1607.[24] Finally, the correspondence regarding *Endimione*, together with the compositions of the *Scherzi*, reveals Monteverdi's interest in using schematic forms and new, non-madrigalian forms of poetry, like the canzonettas of Gabriello Chiabrera, to build large structures that could be put to dramatic use.[25]

21. Fabbri, *Monteverdi*, 37.

22. Vincenzo Gonzaga and his party of forty retainers helped greet the bride, Christine of Lorraine, at the Florentine gates of Porta del Prato, and later he was, with Ferdinando de' Medici's brother Don Pietro, the presiding official at the Pitti parade of chariots, for which he made a triumphal entrance in the first *carro*; see James M. Saslow, *The Medici Wedding of 1589: Florentine Festival as Theatrum Mundi* (New Haven: Yale University Press, 1996), 40, 140, and 166.

23. Fabbri, *Monteverdi*, 97.

24. Fabbri accepts Monteverdi as author of the balletto "De la dolcezza le dovute lodi," (*Monteverdi*, 122), although Leo Schrade and others do not. See Schrade, *Monteverdi, Creator of Modern Music* (New York: Norton, 1950), 223.

25. *Letters*, ed. Stevens, 46–47.

The fifth book of madrigals, I argue, is a first point of arrival in Monteverdi's search for musical drama. Over the course of its nineteen madrigals, Monteverdi condenses the principal emotional and psychological tensions of *Il pastor fido*. The book opens with "Cruda Amarilli" and "O Mirtillo," a fictional conversation between the principal characters (the speeches come from widely separated parts of the play) and goes on to two real dialogue cycles, one between Dorinda and Silvio, and the other between, again, Amarilli and Mirtillo. The two couples are portrayed according to the nature of their interactions—the moment of dynamic change in which Dorinda and Silvio are brought together by her near death is set against the stasis of anger and recrimination that holds Mirtillo and Amarilli apart from one another until the end of the play. Following the *Pastor fido* excerpts, Monteverdi appends a commentary in the form of a madrigal cycle in which various unrelated poems, some by Guarini and some not, describe the emotional states of a lover who, having been hurt by a previous affair, contemplates falling in love again. The closing madrigal, the anonymous "Questi vaghi concenti," takes a last, generalized look at the ebb and flow of romantic pain and pleasure. Monteverdi, in the fifth book, seems to transcend the individual madrigal and indeed the madrigal book itself, reaching beyond the music to the play. The dramatic plan that emerges from the contrasting emotional states and narrative elements that make up the volume amounts to a critical interpretation of the play.

In light of Monteverdi's nascent awareness of, and eventual preoccupation with, the problems of dramatic music and large-scale organization, Artusi's focus on part-writing in the madrigals has thrown a perhaps unduly bright light onto the composer's activity as a madrigalist during the late 1590s and early 1600s. This is not to say that the madrigals are not important; indeed, they remain central to Monteverdi's musical language, which never really rejects counterpoint in favor of monody. If, however, the pairing of the *Scherzi* and the "Dichiaratione" was meant to point to new compositional concerns, as I have suggested, and if the "Lettera" introduces the fifth book and not the fourth because the contents of the volume are so radically different from those of earlier publications, then such associative arguments have not been heard across the span of history.[26] Artusi dominated the debate, and his particular light source—proper contrapuntal practice in the tradition of Zarlino and Willaert—has highlighted only one aspect of the *seconda prattica* but has done so with such brilliance that all others have remained hidden deep in the shadows.

---

26. See my "Claudio Monteverdi's *Ordine novo*," 301–2.

The music of the fifth book (1605) and of the *Scherzi* (1607), however, accomplishes what neither of the Monteverdi brothers could put into words. The madrigals strive for psychological insight and tension, building through a succession of dramatic contrasts developed over the course of the entire book; the *Scherzi* boldly sidestep the madrigal genre altogether, taking as their point of departure Gabriello Chiabrera's reformist poetry and responding to his literary innovations with a new handling of meter, melody, harmony, instrumental color, and form, all in the service of accessible simplicity. My purpose in the present study is to introduce at least a secondary light by which to bring into relief these dimensions, which seem to me to address some of the primary motivations behind the language of the *seconda prattica*.

If *Arianna* was not in fact the beginning of the process, it certainly altered its direction. It seems to have been its composition, and that of the lament itself, that led Monteverdi to identify the specific problems confronting him as he sought to give musical expression to the emotions of his characters and to do so in a language as close to "natural" as possible. By his own admission, the working out of this language became the central aim of the remainder of his career, and in the correspondence with Doni in the early 1630s, and later in the preface to the eighth book (1638), he made clear that the principal milestones in this journey were *Arianna*, the *Combattimento di Tancredi e Clorinda* (1624) with the introduction of the *genere concitato*, and then the *Madrigali guerrieri et amorosi* (1638). With these pivotal works he measured the progress of the "via naturale all'immitatione": a way of expressing changing emotions; the means for evoking truly violent affects and actions; and the means to define and deploy a musical language that, together with the words, could effectively represent not merely the letter of the individual words of the text, but their psychological meaning as well.

In the preface to the *Madrigali guerrieri et amorosi*, Monteverdi makes it a particular point to describe the circumstances of the first performance of the *Combattimento di Tancredi e Clorinda*, the work that stands at the center of the eighth book and of the preface itself. Conscious both of the importance of the *Combattimento* in his own development and of its innovative qualities, the composer devised a musical context intended to surprise the audience gathered at the country residence of Girolamo Mocenigo for the carnival of 1624 with the unexpected features of his new composition.

The evening began with a set of conventional *madrigali senza gesto* to make the spectators think that nothing out of the ordinary was about to happen. Then, Tancredi, mounted on a *cavallo mariano*, perhaps a horse caparisoned in a Christian coat bearing the symbol of the Virgin Mary, entered from a side door pursuing Clorinda; both were in armor. They began to pantomime the duel as offstage instruments provided the pacing and sounds of the fight and as the narrator began his recitation of Tasso's powerful epic text.

Gesture, pantomime, props, and hidden music—all elements of the theater suddenly brought to life in a chamber performance whose beginning had promised nothing out of the ordinary, and all calculated to astonish the audience. Monteverdi aimed to elicit that sense of wonder, or *meraviglia*, that since the middle of the sixteenth century had been considered essential to render an audience receptive to the aesthetic and ethical messages intended by composers, playwrights, and theatrical directors. In this case, the composer made sure that his patrons would not miss the novelty of his creation and that they would be overpowered by the extremes of affect the *Combattimento* was meant to explore.

Monteverdi's conception of the evening's entertainment transcended the limitations of the chamber setting—which had been invoked as a foil precisely to heighten the combined effect of Tasso's text and the new affective range made possible by the *genere concitato*. Thus the *madrigali senza gesto* became components in a theatrical event in which the stage-less chamber provided the stage setting for a semi-staged performance of a narrative epic which sought to construct an imaginary theater. The entire evening thus became a kind of play within a play in which the outer shell, populated by musicians as well as spectators, disguised itself as ordinary reality.

This blurring of distinctions between the non-theatrical madrigals and the clearly dramatic *Combattimento*, although an apparently routine strategy to maximize the cathartic value of his new composition, is indicative of a tendency evident in Monteverdi's work since at least the fifth book of madrigals. Such deliberate blurring, however, requires a firm command of such categories as style, genre, and function in order to be effective, and it is precisely in this area of musical thinking that Monteverdi made his most successful theoretical contribution. As with the *seconda prattica*, he seems to have "been there" as this approach gained currency and to have been the first to formulate its parameters.

It is impossible to tell whether Monteverdi's intellectual approach to music resulted from his dust-up with Artusi; nevertheless, his need to theorize about his work seems to have increased over the years. In spite of his much-lamented failure to write the treatise on the *seconda prattica* he had promised at the time of the polemic with Artusi, he did leave an influential if, again, somewhat enigmatic theoretical statement in the preface to the *Madrigali guerrieri et amorosi* of 1638; this is complemented and amplified by the group of letters written during the early 1630s to the Florentine theorist Giovanni Battista Doni. These, as private and personal reflections, lack the formality of the printed word—a medium that, it seems safe to say, did not suit Monteverdi, whereas his personality emerges vividly and forcefully from his correspondence—and thus provide a sketchy but frank and highly suggestive roadmap for bridging the gaps that separate his various essays from one another and from his compositions.

The preface establishes a classification of music based on its functions at princely courts: theater, chamber, and *ballo*. To these we can add ecclesiastical music, which Monteverdi does not include in his threefold division but which he does mention elsewhere in the essay as a separate type. These functional categories he links somewhat vaguely to elements of style (*guerriera, amorosa,* and *rappresentativa*)—all of which are represented in the compositions that follow the essay. Imprecise as it may have been, Monteverdi's formulation of a system that linked function and style found resonance among his contemporaries and his successors, most notably in the writings of Marco Scacchi, who refined the threefold organization into three principal styles, *Ecclesiasticus, Cubicularis,* and *Scenicus seu Theatralis.*[27]

Quite apart from its timeliness or its historical consequences, however, Monteverdi's system results directly from a preoccupation with stylistic boundaries that goes back to the beginning of the aesthetic "crisis" that led to the formulation of the *seconda prattica* as a stylistic alternative to the first. His penchant for classification seems to have been intrinsic to the formulation of his musical language, which rests in part on a keen sense for how different genres, forms, styles, and their intellectual and even social connotations could be exploited to generate meaning, affect, and drama. Evidence of Monteverdi's attention to precise genre designations, to the grouping of works according to scoring and other technical requirements, and to the particular poetic origins and currents represented by their texts abounds from at least his fifth book of madrigals (table 1). Already in that volume, Monteverdi seems to engage his audience in a dialogue about the nature of the madrigal: a cappella madrigals set theatrical texts in a largely discursive, almost recitative-like manner, even as continuo madrigals push to the fore "characters" like the voice of the beloved in "T'amo mia vita" but do so from within a more frankly polyphonic, florid

27. Palisca, "The Artusi–Monteverdi Controversy," 156–58.

Table 1 Structure of the fifth book of madrigals (1605)

Number	Scoring	Title	Poet	Literary source
A. A cappella madrigals				
1	A5	Cruda Amarilli	Guarini	*Pastor fido*, 1/2, 1–8
2		O Mirtillo		*Pastor fido*, 3/4, 1–13
3		Era l'anima mia		*Rime*
4a, dialogue cycle		Ecco Silvio		*Pastor fido*, 4/9, 100–13
b		Ma se con la pietà		*Pastor fido*, 4/9, 114–22
c		Dorinda, ah dirò mia		*Pastor fido*, 4/9, 123–30
d		Ecco piegando le ginocchia		*Pastor fido*, 4/9, 138–48
e		Ferir quel petto, Silvio?		*Pastor fido*, 4/9, 149–68
5a, dialogue cycle		Ch'io t'ami		*Pastor fido*, 3/3, 107–14
b		Deh bella e cara e sì soave un tempo		*Pastor fido*, 3/3, 143–57
c		Ma tu, più che mai dura		*Pastor fido*, 3/3, 158–66 and 170–73
6		Che dar più vi poss'io?	Anonymous	
7		M'è più dolce penar per Amarilli	Guarini	*Rime*
B. Madrigals with basso continuo				
8	A5 and BC	Ahi come a un vago sol cortese giro	Guarini	*Rime*, 110
9		Troppo ben può questo tiranno amore	Guarini	*Rime*, 108
10		Amor, se giusto sei	Anonymous	
11		T'amo mia vita la mia cara vita	Guarini	*Rime*, 70
12		E così poco a poco	Guarini	*Rime*, 112
C. Large-scale closing madrigal				
13	Two choirs, A5 and A4, BC, and A5 instrumental ensemble	Questi vaghi concenti	Anonymous	

Table 2 Structure of the sixth book of madrigals (1614)

Number and function	Scoring	Title	Text author
Part 1			
A. A cappella madrigals			
1a, lament cycle	A5	Lasciatemi morire (Lamento d'Arianna)	Rinuccini
b		O Teseo	
c		Dove, dov'è la fede	
d		Ahi che non pur risponde	
2, individual madrigal		Zefiro torna e 'l bel tempo	Petrarch
B. Madrigals with basso continuo			
3	A5 with BC	Una donna fra l'altre	Anonymous
4		A Dio, Florida bella	Marino
Part 2			
A. A cappella madrigals			
5a, lament cycle	A5	Incenerite spoglie (sestina: Lagrime d'amante)	Agnelli
b		Ditelo, o fiumi	
c		Darà la notte	
d		Ma te raccoglie	
e		O chiome d'or	
f		Dunque, amate reliquie	
6 individual madrigal		Ohimè il bel viso	Petrarch
B. Madrigals with basso continuo			
7	A5 with BC	Qui rise, o Tirsi	Marino
8		Misero Alceo	Marino
9		"Batto" qui pianse Ergasto, "ecco la riva"	Marino
C. Large-scale closing madrigal			
10, *Dialogo*	A7 with BC	Presso a un fiume tranquillo	Marino

style than the a cappella madrigals do—and the continuo madrigals set non-dramatic, independent lyric texts that the composer himself has grouped into a cyclic narrative that comments on the "dramatic" conversations of the a cappella madrigals—much as the choruses did that closed each act of Guarini's *Pastor fido.*

The dialogue continues in the next madrigal book, which picks up the thread after *Orfeo, Arianna,* and the *Vespers* of 1610. Like the fifth book, the sixth contrasts continuo and a cappella madrigals as well as literary genres, this time setting side by side Petrarch, Giambattista Marino, and Ottavio Rinuccini (table 2); but the sixth goes further in pointedly "mismatching" musical styles and poets (Marino's sonnet, "A Dio, Florida bella," set as a miniature dramatic scene on an instrumental strophic bass; Rinuccini's operatic lament from *Arianna*, "Lasciatemi morire," set as a cycle of a cappella madrigals). The architecture of the entire volume also relies on the different madrigal types, as had that of the fifth, but here the book is divided into two "parallel" halves. Each half opens with an a cappella lament cycle (Arianna's modern dramatic *versi sciolti* in the first, and its polar opposite, the retrospective *sestina Lagrime d'amante* in the second—one of Petrarch's favorite forms here invoked by the Mantuan courtier Scipione Agnelli) followed by an a cappella madrigal (in both halves setting a Petrarch sonnet) and a group of continuo madrigals (on texts by Marino). The two parts are not equal: a four-section cycle and three madrigals make up the first, and a six-part cycle and four madrigals the second; the symmetry is not rigid, but its presence is felt nonetheless. As with the fifth book, a large-scale madrigal (for seven voices plus obbligato instruments in addition to the continuo) closes the entire volume, introducing yet another poetic genre, a canzonetta by Marino set as a dialogue.

Not surprisingly, the dialectic stemming from the varied intersections of poetry, genre, function, and style continues in ever sharper terms in the seventh and eighth books. The seventh proclaims Monteverdi's terminological precision in its very title: *Concerto. Seventh Book of Madrigals for 1, 2, 3, 4, and Six Voices, with Other Genres of Song* (table 3). Unlike the approach taken by other composers in the first two decades of the century, whose *bizzarrie, stravaganze,* and *fioretti* seem at once to address the multiplicity of song types and to sidestep the terminological issue, Monteverdi's title offers a guide—however laconic and for historians problematic ("just what does he mean by 'Concerto'"?)—for approaching the contents of the book. Inside, the madrigals follow the organization advertised on the cover—with some notable discrepancies. The first item is an operatic prologue, built on a set of strophic variations and complete with sinfonia and ritornello, for solo voice; a duet follows. But the third piece is a *concertato* madrigal scored for six voices and instruments like the large-scale pieces that close the fifth and sixth books; after it, the duets, trios, and four-voice pieces follow one another without deviation until the unusual "Con che soavità" for solo voice and three instrumental groups—part madrigal, part monody, part canzonetta. Monteverdi leaves it unlabeled and follows it with a romanesca, two monodies in "genere rappresentativo," two canzonettas, and a *ballo*, "Tirsi e Clori," for voices and instruments—a gathering of "altri generi di canti," clearly not madrigals and individually identified as to their particular genres.

The larger outline was recognized thirty years ago by Nino Pirrotta: it is patterned on theatrical conventions, with strophic variations as the prologue addressing the source of the poet-composer-bard's inspiration and a *ballo* at the end — *Orfeo* opens and closes in just this way. Within this frame, the organization by vocal complement recalls scores of publications by Monteverdi's contemporaries. And the grouping of disparate, nonmadrigal pieces at the end goes back to the set of continuo madrigals relegated to the end of the fifth book (and of each "half" of the sixth). By 1619 this also was a generally accepted convention, but the placement of "Con che soavità" and "A quest'olmo" disrupts the neatness of the pattern: for one thing, the title promises madrigals for one voice — neither "Con che soavità" nor "Tempro la cetra" fits the bill comfortably. And the six-voice "A quest'olmo" belongs at the end of the progression of vocal ensembles instead of "Con che soavità," although the reverse is not true.

As in the sixth book, the organization is not necessarily true to a rigid model, and although the discrepancies might be explained away (a printer's error, or a purely practical decision regarding the placement of precisely the two most complex pieces in terms of parts, for example), their existence actually points to two pieces that represent important achievements: "A quest'olmo" is the first madrigal to incorporate obbligato upper parts (pairs of violins and of *flautini*) within the vocal fabric, not just in ritornellos or *colla parte* doublings (not counting very brief passages in two of the *Scherzi* of 1607, the extensive use of instruments in *Orfeo*, and the extraordinary instrumentation of the "Sonata sopra Sancta Maria" of the *Vespers*), an aspect of *concertato* composition that becomes integral to the language of the *Madrigali guerrieri et amorosi* and of some of the more spectacular psalm settings, spiritual madrigals, and mass movements of the *Selva morale* (1640) and of the *Messa et Salmi* (op. posth., 1651). And "Con che soavità" offers a glimpse into how a large continuo ensemble could be arranged to produce a variety of complex and subtle effects in supporting a solo voice. At the same time it also stands out because such an ensemble was well outside the norm for chamber music, into which Monteverdi imported it from theatrical practices. Although the placement of "A quest'olmo" remains baffling, that of "Con che soavità" seems less casual if one considers it as a sort of "crossover" piece, ambiguous because it draws from several genres and the styles associated with them, because it stands astride the divide between chamber and theater, and because it negotiates the transition between madrigals and "altri generi di canti."

Table 3 Structure of the seventh book of madrigals (1619)

Number and function	Scoring	Title	Poet
A. Prologue			
1	T and Basso Continuo, with A5 instrumental ensemble	Tempro la cetra	Marino
B. "Madrigal book" format			
2, S duet section begins	SS and BC	Non è di gentil core	Degli Atti?
3, misplaced?	A6, obbligato violins / flautini, and BC	A quest' olmo	Marino
4, S duets resume	SS and BC	O come sei gentile	Guarini
5	SS and BC	Io son pur vezzosetta	Incolto Accademico Immaturo
6	SS and BC	O viva fiamma	Anonymous
7, A duets	AA and BC	Vorrei baciarti, o Filli	Marino
8, T duets begin	TT and BC	Dice la mia bellissima Licori	Guarini
9	TT and BC	Ah che non si conviene	Anonymous
10	TT and BC	Non vedrò mai le stelle	Anonymous
11	TT and BC	Ecco vicine, o bella tigre, l'ore	Achillini
12	TT and BC	Perché fuggi tra' salci	Marino
13	TT and BC	Tornate, o cari baci	Marino
14	TT and BC	Soave libertate	Chiabrera
15, mixed duet	TB and BC	Se 'l vostro cor, Madonna	Guarini
16	TT and BC	Interrotte speranze	Guarini
17, Trios begin	TTB and BC	Augellin, che la voce al canto spieghi	Anonymous

18	Vaga su spina ascosa	TTB and BC	Chiabrera
19	Eccomi pronta ai baci	TTB and BC	Marino
20	Parlo, miser, o taccio?	SSB and BC	Guarini
21, Quartets begin	Tu dormi, ah crudo core	SATB and BC	Anonymous
22	Al lume delle stelle	SSTB and BC	Torquato Tasso
23, misplaced? Or transitional to *"altri generi"*?	Con che soavità, labbra adorate	S and three instrumental "chori"	Guarini
C. Altri generi			
24a, romanesca	Ohimè dov' è il mio ben?	SS and BC	Bernardo Tasso
b	Dunque ha potuto sol desio		
c	Dunque ha potuto in me		
d	Ahi sciocco mondo e cieco		
25, *lettera amorosa in genere rappresentativo*	Se i languidi miei sguardi	S and BC	Achillini
26, *partenza amorosa in genere rappresentativo*	Partenza amorosa	T and BC	Anonymous
27, canzonetta	Chiome d'oro	SS, 2 violins, and BC	Anonymous
28, canzonetta	Amor, che deggio far?	SS, 2 violins, and BC	Anonymous
D. Closing ballo			
29	Tirsi e Clori	A5 and doubling instruments, with BC	Anonymous

The eighth book sums up the organizational strategies of the preceding volumes (table 4). Like the sixth, it comprises two roughly symmetrical parts; here, however, the division is made explicit with the designation of the two sections as "madrigali guerrieri" and "madrigali amorosi." And, like the seventh, the eighth book opens with a sinfonia followed by a topical, prologue-like sonnet setting, "Altri canti d'Amor, tenero arciero," and closes with a *ballo*, the "Ballo delle Ingrate" from the 1608 wedding celebration for which *Arianna* was composed. In fact, both halves follow the same pattern, since the "canti amorosi" also open with a sonnet ("Altri canti di Marte," which parallels "Altri canti d'Amor" from a contrasting perspective), and the first half also closes with a *ballo*, the "Introduzione al ballo [Volgendo il ciel] e Ballo [Movete al mio bel suon]." The internal structure of the two halves is more or less symmetrical, as it had been in the sixth book: after the opening anonymous sonnets, each follows with a sonnet by Petrarch ("Or che'l ciel e la terra" and "Vago augelletto": the latter is incomplete, as the setting includes only the two quatrains); since there are no a cappella settings in the eighth book, both are for large vocal ensemble with continuo and obbligato violins. "Vago augelletto," however, departs radically from even the style of Monteverdi's large concertato pieces and almost assumes the character of a canzonetta, with a textual refrain imposed on the sonnet form. After the Petrarch selections, each half has a series of duets, trios, and larger madrigals leading up to a piece in *genere rappresentativo* (the *Combattimento di Tancredi e Clorinda* in the first half, and the three-part *Lamento della ninfa* in the second). In the second half, the *Lamento* is followed by three madrigalian trios before closing with the *Ballo delle Ingrate*; the *Ballo* follows the *Combattimento* directly in the first. And, again as in the sixth book, the eighth gathers contrasting poetic styles and genres and treats them freely: the mock high rhetoric of the opening sonnets in Petrarchan style is matched by similarly bombastic mock-military settings; the lyricism and tortured images of "Or che'l ciel" are followed by a comical canzonetta that evokes the onomatopoeic style of the *battaglia*, complete with trotting horses and panicked battle cries. The exaggerated language of the anonymous mock-Petrarchan "Ardo, avvampo, mi struggo, ardo: accorrete" is once again delivered by a ridiculously breathless deployment of almost-*concitato* confusion. And the powerful imagery of Tasso's *Combattimento* is matched, phrase by phrase and image by image, with Monteverdi's utterly earnest use of the *genere concitato* in addition to a panoply of sound effects. Finally, the impassioned musical language of the *Lamento della ninfa* masks its origin as a canzonetta, contrasting free declamation in the lament ("a tempo dell'affetto dell'animo" [to the time of the soul's affect] and strict metrical performance ("a tempo della mano") in the framing choruses. As with all three preceding books, the eighth juxtaposes and mixes chamber and theater genres, offering a practical illustration of the principal categories laid out in the preface, but also calling into question the distinction between *madrigali senza gesto* and *genere rappresentativo*, as the first performance of the *Combattimento* had done. Here, in *madrigali senza gesto* like "Ardo, avvampo" and "Gira il nemico," as in Mocenigo's villa some twelve years earlier, the line separating *teatro della mente* from "real" theater is very thin indeed.

Monteverdi's "invention" of the *genere concitato*, besides establishing yet another connection between the *seconda prattica* and theatrical music, provides a clue to the realignment of music and text that had taken place over the course of the preceding three decades or so. That crucial relationship had provided l'Accademico Ottuso with his chief justification for Monteverdi's violations of the rules of counterpoint—"The text made him do it!"—and was at the root of the second most often quoted motto of the polemic with Artusi after the term "seconda prattica" itself. Giulio Cesare's statement that "Music [is] the servant of the text, and the text [is] the mistress" has become almost synonymous with Monteverdi's "seconda prattica," in encapsulating the essential aesthetic shift that was taking place around 1600. But what does this pronouncement really mean in practical terms? Even if it is applied to the madrigals of the fifth book alone, which presumably is the closest of all of Monteverdi's collections to the new aesthetics of "modern music," Giulio Cesare's formulation needs to be interpreted very broadly to encompass both the austerely declamatory settings of the *Pastor fido* dialogues and the florid melismatic settings of the continuo madrigals at the end—so broadly, in fact, that it can be made to apply equally to the madrigalisms common to the pictorial madrigals of two decades earlier, the dissonances of "Cruda Amarilli," the recitative-like declamation of "Ecco Silvio," and the ornamented duet passages that open "E così a poco a poco." In truth, Giulio Cesare may have done his brother more a disservice than a favor with his famous encapsulation of the aims of the *seconda prattica*, because the notion of music being the servant of the text could not be further from the aesthetic ideal that Monteverdi was trying to achieve. In fact, one would be hard put to find much music by Monteverdi, especially from the fifth book on, in which Giulio Cesare's words can be said actually to hold true.

The answer to this paradox rests in part in the search for a psychologically realistic language that Monteverdi associated with Arianna's lament, which I discussed above: such a language reaches beyond individual words for the

Table 4 Structure of the eighth book of madrigals (1638)

Number and function	Scoring	Title	Text author
Canti guerrieri			
A. In two parts			
a) sinfonia to introduce the book as a whole	2 violins, viola da brazzo, and Basso Continuo	Sinfonia	
b) 1, prologue to *Canti guerrieri*	A6, 4 viole, 2 violins, and BC	Altri canti d'Amor	Anonymous
B. Madrigali senza gesto			
2a, large-scale madrigal opening the *madrigali senza gesto*	A6, 2 violins, and BC	Or che 'l ciel e la terra	Petrarch
b		Così sol d'una chiara fonte	
B'. Duets and trios			
3a	ATB and BC	Gira il nemico insidioso Amore	Giulio Strozzi
b		No'l lasciamo accostar	
c		Armi false non son	
d		Vuol degli occhi attaccar	
e		Non è più tempo ohimè	
f		Cor mio, non val fuggire	
4	TT and BC	Se vittorie sì belle	Testi
5	TT and BC	Armato il cor	Rinuccini
6a	TTB and BC	Ogni amante è guerrier	Rinuccini
b	B solo	Io che nell'otio nacqui	
c	T solo	Ma per quel ampio Egeo	
d	TTB and BC	Riedi, ch'al nostro ardor	
7, large scale madrigal, ending the *madrigali senza gesto*	A8, 2 violins, and BC	Ardo, avvampo, mi struggo	Anonymous
C. In genere rappresentativo			
8	STT, 4 viole da brazzo (SATB), and BC	Combattimento di Tancredi e Clorinda	Tasso
D. Closing ballo			
9a		Introduzione al ballo: "Volgendo il ciel"	Rinuccini
b		Ballo: Movete al mio bel suon	
Canti amorosi			
A. Prologue to Canti amorosi			
1a	A6, 2 violins, and BC	Altri canti di Marte	Marino
b		Due belli occhi	

(*Continued*)

Table 4 (*Continued*)

Number and function	Scoring	Title	Text author
B. Madrigali senza gesto			
2, large-scale madrigal opening the *madrigali senza gesto*	A7, 2 violins, and BC	Vago augelletto	Petrarch
B'. Duets and trios			
3	TT and BC	Mentre vaga angioletta	Guarini
4	TT and BC	Ardo e scoprir, ahi lasso	Anonymous
5a	TTB and BC; a: T solo	Ninfa che, scalza il piede	Anonymous
b	TT	Qui deh, meco t'arresta	
c	TTB	De l'usate mie corde	
6	A5, "a voce piena, alla francese"	Dolcissimo uscignolo	Guarini
7	A5, "a voce piena, alla francese"	Chi vol aver felice e lieto il core	Guarini
C. In genere rappresentativo			
8a, nominally still in trio category; modified canzonetta text	S, TTB, and BC a: TTB	Non avea Febo ancora	Rinuccini
b	S, TTB	Amor, dicea	
c	TTB	Sì tra sdegnosi pianti	
9, resume trios (*madrigali senza gesto*)	ATB and BC	Perché te 'n fuggi	Anonymous
10	AAB and BC	Non partir, ritrosetta	Anonymous
11	SSA and BC	Su, su pastorelli vezzosi	Anonymous
D. Closing *ballo*			
12, closes both the *Canti amorosi* and the book as a whole		Ballo delle ingrate	Rinuccini

essential affect of the text, which it expresses by any means necessary. The continuo madrigals of the fifth book, however, point toward yet another aspect of the relationship between music and text: music can contribute to the projection of the textual affect a battery of purely musical elements that are independent of the words themselves. In the continuo madrigals, the instrumental bass functions independently of the voices and of the text, contributing to the work a nontextual "musical" element that is most often abstract and structural but that can also take on greater significance as its workings intersect with the text. As I argue in chapter 2, parallel passages in the continuo help to establish correspondences between pieces that reinforce the cyclical design of the entire group. The *basso ostinato* is another example of the way in which a purely musical device can take on affective meaning: at its most abstract, it serves to define the building blocks of the musical form, but certain bass patterns can also become associated with specific affects (the descending tetrachord as the "emblem of lament"; the *ciaccona* as a dance).[28] In the fifth book, the ostinato patterns are not fully developed and serve primarily to underscore the sectional structure of the madrigals. But by the time of *Orfeo*, ostinatos can be seen as representing Music at its most powerful, as a dramatic agent capable of organizing the progress of the plot and determining its affective impact. In this sense, the opera's prologue ("Io la musica son") and Orfeo's "Possente spirto" express the power of music through identical means: both are strophic variations; in both, the singer-poet-composer appears as the mastermind who marshals music to his service and, through the simultaneous deployment of "spontaneous" rhetorical invention and strict formal organization, controls all aspects of the drama. Examples of such use of the ostinato abound in Monteverdi's music, from the transposed bass lines that unite and distinguish the lovers in the first two quatrains of Marino's dialogue sonnet "Addio Florida bella" in the sixth book, to the descending tetrachord in the *Lamento della ninfa*.

The ostinato was not the only musical element to carry specific connotations: genres, and the styles associated with them, could also convey meaning. The canzonetta, for example, seems to have taken on this associative role early on: in *Orfeo*, it is invoked to organize the celebrations of the first and second acts, and its highly rhythmic character and patterned structure are juxtaposed to the irregular rhythms and open-ended structure of the recitative in a musical contrast between life and death. After disappearing from the opera with Euridice's death, it is brought back to express Orfeo's triumph as he leads his wife from the underworld toward the world of the living. The character of "Qual onor," however, with its jaunty rhythms and walking bass (anachronistically, it might be thought of as having the character—or better, the *attitude*—of a jazz pianist's stride bass), also seems to point to his fatal hubris, the cause of Euridice's and eventually his own downfall. Canzonettas return in this symbolic role as late as the *Selva morale* (1640) and *Poppea* (1643), in pieces like the *canzonetta morale* "Chi vol che m'innamori" and in the scene between

28. Ellen Rosand, "The Descending Tetrachord: An Emblem of Lament," *Musical Quarterly* 65 (1979), 346–59, and also *Opera in Seventeenth-Century Venice: The Creation of a Genre* (Berkeley and Los Angeles: University of California Press, 1991), 369–77.

Seneca and his followers and household, in which the genre is invoked to represent foolish worldliness, superficiality, and transitory happiness.

In order for such symbolic correspondences to work, music cannot be the "servant" of the text: it must work alongside the text, as an expressive equal to it. This, ultimately, is the blueprint behind Monteverdi's new *prattica*—not only the intensification of the affective language he inherited from the Renaissance, but a thorough realignment of the materials at his disposal to reach a subtler, "truer," musical representation. At the core of the realignment lies a fundamentally dramatic impulse, which found its impetus in music for the stage beginning with *Il pastor fido* and which permeated all aspects of Monteverdi's compositional activity. As I seek to demonstrate in the chapters that follow, Monteverdi developed the tools by which he accomplished this realignment by taking available materials, such as the madrigal, the madrigal book, and strophic songs, and bending them to his needs, refining their application over the course of more than forty years through the subtlest pairing of text, musical declamation, and genre. Throughout, he was spurred in part by circumstances and in part by his own modernist motto: "In the long run, I shall be happier to be moderately praised in the new style, than greatly praised in the ordinary."

ONE

The Public Debate, I: *Prima* and *Seconda Prattica*

"È del poeta il fin la meraviglia" [1]

The year 1633 does not readily come to mind as an important date in the debate over the *prima* and *seconda prattica*. By then the principal texts around which the controversy had developed were over a quarter-century old, and much of the contested ground had long been settled, in practice if not in theory. And yet 1633 does mark a kind of milestone, albeit not a public one: it was only during 1633–34 that Monteverdi, revisiting the polemic in an exchange of letters with the theorist Giovanni Battista Doni, clarified aspects of the debate that had been left unsettled in his earlier writings and traced their continued significance over the ensuing twenty years.

Doni approached the composer in the early 1630s, having heard through the Paduan Bishop Marc'Antonio Cornaro that Monteverdi was working on a book about music theory.[2] The exchange seems to consist of only five letters:

1. Marino, *La Murtoleide*, "Fischiata xxxiii," 39. Although the line has been read in ironic terms (see Robert Holzer, "'Ma invan la tento et impossibil parmi,' or How *guerrieri* are Monteverdi's *madrigali guerrieri?*" in *The Sense of Marino: Literature, Fine Arts and Music of the Italian Baroque*, ed. Francesco Guardiani [Ottawa: Legas, 1994], 442 n. 27), Marino's continuation, "Parlo dell'eccellente, non del goffo," suggests otherwise. On the insertion of such an aesthetic pronouncement within a clearly comic text, see Marzio Pieri, *Fischiata xxxiii: Un sonetto di Giambattista Marino* (Parma: Pratiche, 1992), 129.

2. Cornaro was the *primicerio* of St. Mark's from 1619 until 1632, when he became Bishop of Padua. Monteverdi referred to him in a letter of 8 March 1620 to Alessandro Striggio, and, according to a subsequent letter of 17 March, the composer was engaged to provide weekly music for Cornaro's private oratory. See letters 48 and 50; *The Letters of Claudio Monteverdi*, ed. and trans. by Denis Stevens (London: Cambridge University Press, 1980), 184–85, 194–96, and 406–11.

three from Doni, the first conveyed to Monteverdi by the bishop sometime in October 1633, the others sent directly to the composer in December 1633 and January 1634 from Rome, where Doni was secretary to the College of Cardinals; and two from Monteverdi, the first in October 1633, the second in February 1634.[3] Apparently in response to the theorist's inquiries, the composer recounted the thirty-year-old dispute with Giovanni Maria Artusi and reported that he was still planning a treatise on the *seconda prattica;* this was the same work that, forced by the heat of controversy, he had promised in the preface to the fifth book of madrigals of 1605.[4] The project was never completed, and the preface, together with Giulio Cesare Monteverdi's "Dichiaratione" that was appended in 1607 to the first volume of *Scherzi musicali,* remained the composer's only public reply to the criticisms leveled against his works.[5]

On the face of it, the correspondence with Doni seems to suggest only that Monteverdi had a long memory for grudges, and that after nearly thirty years he was still embarrassed by not having lived up to his public promise;[6] but in fact it is vital to understanding the development of Monteverdi's thinking about the theoretical foundations of the *seconda prattica.* The letters show that it was only after the controversy with Artusi that the composer defined many of the problems central to the new aesthetic, and that at the time of Artusi's first

---

3. Letters 122 and 123 in Monteverdi, *Lettere, dediche e prefazioni,* ed. Domenico De' Paoli (Rome: De Santis, 1973); letters 123 and 124 in *Letters,* ed. Stevens. Both in Florence, Conservatorio di musica. On Doni see *Letters,* ed. Stevens, 406–11. The correspondence has been known to Monteverdi scholars since at least the 1920s, when both Prunières and Malipiero published Monteverdi's letters—the only ones to survive from the exchange—in their biographies of the composer. Letter 123: Gian Francesco Malipiero, *Claudio Monteverdi* (Milan: Treves, 1929), 291; Henry Prunières, *Monteverdi: His Life and Work,* trans. by Marie D. Mackie (London: Dent, 1926), 284; Emil Vogel, "Claudio Monteverdi," *Vierteljahrsschrift für Musikwissenschaft* 3 (1887), 438. Letter 124: Malipiero, *Monteverdi,* 294; Prunières, *Monteverdi,* 285; Vogel, "Monteverdi," 439.

4. Modern edition in *Lettere,* ed. De' Paoli, 390–92; English translation in *Source Readings in Music History,* ed. Oliver Strunk, rev. ed. By Leo Treitler (New York: Norton, 1998).

5. Modern edition in *Lettere,* ed. De' Paoli, 393–407; English translation in Strunk and Treitler, ed., *Source Readings,* 536–44.

6. Leo Schrade discusses it as evidence that the treatise never ceased to occupy Monteverdi's mind, but he does not connect it to his other theoretical writings and misinterprets some of Monteverdi's terminology (*Monteverdi, Creator of Modern Music* [New York: Norton, 1950], 204–5). Claude Palisca does not include them in his survey of the canonic texts of the Artusi–Monteverdi controversy ("The Artusi–Monteverdi Controversy," in *The New Monteverdi Companion,* ed. Denis Arnold and Nigel Fortune [London: Faber and Faber, 1985]. Paolo Fabbri reproduces excerpts from Monteverdi's letters and reports Doni's assessment of them but does so without exploring the significance of the exchange in the development of Monteverdi's theoretical ideas (*Monteverdi* [Turin: E.D.T., 1985], 290–93).

attacks, and even as late as the writing of the "Dichiaratione" around 1606, he was not yet fully aware of the theoretical implications of his ideas. Monteverdi continued to explore new compositional techniques in the years following the dispute with Artusi, and this exploration was coupled with a continued investigation of fundamental theoretical principles. As a result, the book he was considering in the 1630s was far more ambitious than the one he had proposed in 1605.

Perhaps most importantly, the letters of 1633–34 provide both a backward link to the writings of the turn of the century and a forward one to Monteverdi's final theoretical statement, published in 1638 as the preface to the *Madrigali guerrieri et amorosi*. In writing to Doni, Monteverdi connects his continued struggle with the problems of the *seconda prattica* to his study of the principles governing *immitatione*. A proper understanding of *immitatione*, indeed, was both the reason for his delay in publishing the treatise and the principal contribution he felt able to make with it. In establishing a connection between the development of the expressive resources needed for the "Lamento d'Arianna" and those needed for the *Combattimento di Tancredi et Clorinda*, the Doni correspondence allows us to see the continuity and growth of Monteverdi's theoretical ideas, which viewed through the more relaxed lens of private correspondence emerge as remarkably coherent, unified by consistent interests and method.

Monteverdi's first letter to Doni begins with a brief summary of the events that led up to the preface of 1605. He then details a plan for the book in progress:

> You should know therefore, that I am indeed at work—but under compulsion, however, inasmuch as the event which years ago spurred me to begin was of such a kind that it caused me unawares to promise the world something that (once I had become aware of it) my feeble forces could not manage. . . . The title of the book will be as follows: Melody, or the Second Musical Practice. I mean the second as regards numerical order, in modern style; first in order, in the old style. I am dividing the book into three parts corresponding to the three aspects of Melody. In the first I discuss word setting, in the second, harmony, and in the third, the rhythmic part.[7] I keep telling myself that it will not be unacceptable to the world, for I found out in practice that when I was about to compose the "Lamento d'Arianna"—finding no book that could show me the natural way

7. Monteverdi here refers to Plato's *Republic*, 398c. The passage is generally translated as "a song is a blend of three ingredients—words, music [*harmoniai*], and rhythm" (see for example Robin Waterfield's translation, (Oxford and New York: Oxford University Press, 1993). Plato's *harmoniai* may be better interpreted as "harmonic mode," taking into account the

of imitation, not even one that would explain what an imitator ought to be (other than Plato, in one of his shafts of wisdom, but so hidden that I could hardly discern from afar with my feeble sight what little he showed me)—I found out . . . what hard work I had to do in order to achieve the little I did do in the way of imitation.[8]

Four principal issues arise from this excerpt. First, Monteverdi acknowledges that he had indeed been forced by the events of 1600–5 to promise something he could not deliver. In the 1605 preface he had clearly exaggerated in suggesting that the treatise was only in need of rewriting before it could be published.[9] Second, between 1605 and 1633 he gave the book a new title, *Melodia overo seconda pratica musicale*. Third, the contents of the book were expanded significantly; and, finally, Monteverdi connects the development of the *seconda prattica* with the solution of new compositional problems raised by his pursuit of the "via naturale all'immitatione," of which the *locus classicus* was the "Lamento d'Arianna."[10] Each of these points sheds light on the evolution of Monteverdi's aesthetics after 1600.

The new title and organization of the treatise are especially telling. According to the preface to the fifth book of madrigals, Monteverdi's original title had been "Seconda pratica overo Perfettione della moderna musica." This not only betrayed the reactive nature of Monteverdi's statement—it was a paraphrase of Artusi's *L'Artusi, overo Delle imperfettioni della moderna musica*—but it also announced a modest theoretical agenda.[11] As Giulio Cesare explained in the "Dichiaratione,"

> he [Claudio] has called it "prattica" and not "Teorica" because he intends to focus on the ways of using consonances and dissonances in actual composition [nell'atto prattico], and he has not called it *Institutioni melodiche*,

---

broader implication of "mode" as encompassing both "scale" and "affect" as determined by tessitura and pitch frequency in direct relation to the text being used. See the translation by Tom Griffith (Cambridge: Cambridge University Press, 2000), as well as that by G. M. A. Grube, revised by C. D. C. Reeve, reprinted in Plato, *Complete Works*, ed. John M. Cooper (Indianapolis: Hackett, 1997).

8. *Lettere*, ed. De' Paoli, no. 122, 22 October 1633, pp. 320–21, = *Letters*, ed. Stevens, no. 123, p. 410 (DS).

9. "Tosto che sia riscritta uscirà in luce portando in fronte il nome di SECONDA PRATICA overo PERFETTIONE DELLA MODERNA MUSICA" [As soon as it is rewritten it will be published under the title of *Seconda prattica overo Perfettione della moderna musica*].

10. See Gary Tomlinson, "Madrigal, Monody, and Monteverdi's 'via naturale all'immitatione,'" *Journal of the American Musicological Society* 34 (1981), 86–95.

11. Giulio Cesare's explanation of his brother's title as derived from Plato's idea that music is concerned with perfection is clever but not convincing.

because he acknowledges that he is not up to such an imposing task, leaving the writing of such noble tomes to the Cavalier Ercole Bottrigari and to the Reverend Zerlino. . . .[12]

Giulio Cesare explicitly intended to distance his brother's proposed book from the kind of *musica Teorica* with which Zarlino's *Istitutioni harmoniche* was largely concerned, presenting Claudio's treatise instead as a new, second, *musica practica* that would replace that of Zarlino's third book—which represented, as Claudio put it, "the first [practice] in order, in the old style."[13] The new treatise would be concerned only with the use of consonances and dissonances—with what Zarlino had termed "armonia." In establishing the boundaries of Claudio's planned treatise, Giulio Cesare even parodied Zarlino's title, insisting that Monteverdi had no intention of writing anything that might aspire to the title of *Istitutioni melodiche*.

The title Monteverdi announced to Doni in 1633, however, transcends the boundaries Giulio Cesare had set in 1607. "Melodia overo seconda pratica musicale" no longer equates the *seconda prattica* with a new "armonia" but expands its purview to encompass all aspects of composition. By the 1630s, Monteverdi envisioned a treatise that dealt in separate sections with text, harmony, and rhythm.[14] This new *Istitutioni melodiche* was an enterprise that need no longer be left to theorists such as Bottrigari and Zarlino, as his brother had prudently done in the "Dichiaratione."

Monteverdi's account makes it clear that, at the time of the preface to the fifth book, his conception of the *seconda prattica* had been limited. He had simply sought to justify his new treatment of consonances and dissonances and had not yet begun to concern himself with the more profound problem of "immitatione." In the "Lettera" of 1605 he made no references to classical philosophers, no mention of any hierarchy involving text, rhythm, and harmony, and offered only a veiled promise of a defense on grounds that would appeal to "reason and the senses."[15]

12. Giulio Cesare Monteverdi, "Dichiaratione della lettera stampata nel quinto libro de' suoi madregali," in Monteverdi, *Lettere*, ed. De' Paoli, p. 399.

13. On the relationship between Monteverdi's proposed treatise and Zarlino's *Istitutioni harmoniche*, see Palisca, "The Artusi–Monteverdi Controversy," 152.

14. As Palisca has noted, Giulio Cesare used "melodia" to mean the entirety of a composition, taking his cue from Plato's definition of *melos* [song] as "melodia ex tribus constare, oratione, armonia, rhythmus" [a song consists of three [elements], text, harmony, and rhythm].

15. And, indeed, as Palisca points out in "The Artusi–Monteverdi Controversy," the greatest contribution of the "Dichiaratione" was to shore up the philosophical pedigree of the *seconda prattica*.

Furthermore, although in the preface Monteverdi takes credit for coining the term *seconda prattica*, the essay betrays his still limited awareness of its theoretical implications, allowing vaguely that, once the *seconda prattica* was made public, "men of intellect might . . . consider other second thoughts concerning harmony." It was perhaps in response to Claudio's own uncertainty that in the "Dichiaratione" Giulio Cesare had insisted on the limited scope of his brother's ambitions as a theorist.

The Artusi Texts

The exchange between Giovanni Maria Artusi and Monteverdi took place over a period of about ten years, beginning with *L'Artusi, overo Delle imperfettioni della moderna musica*, which Artusi had promised Cardinal Pompeo Arrigoni during the visit of Clement VIII to Ferrara in November 1598 (the main events of the "Ragionamento primo" take place on 16 November 1598). The treatise must have been drafted early enough in 1599 to be circulated in manuscript before its publication at the end of 1600.[16] Already in 1599 Artusi had received the first of two letters written by an anonymous academician, "L'Accademico Ottuso," in response to the *Imperfettioni*. Artusi followed his first treatise with the *Seconda parte dell'Artusi, overo Delle imperfettioni della moderna musica*, finished in 1602 (during "the most regrettable part of the summer" [i tempi più dell'estate rincrescevoli], according to the dedication) and published in March of 1603.[17] The *Seconda parte*, prompted in part by the exchange with L'Ottuso, contains a brief excerpt from the academician's first letter, as well as the second letter in its entirety and Artusi's replies to both.[18] The tone of the second book is considerably more acerbic than that of the first, suggesting that perhaps between 1600 and 1602 Artusi had come under fire from others besides Ottuso in what must have been a lively debate.

Monteverdi did not reply until after Artusi's second book, and then he did so only sketchily, in the preface to the fifth book of madrigals (1605). In dedicating the fifth book of madrigals to the Duke of Mantua, Vincenzo Gonzaga, Monteverdi pointedly placed the volume under the "protection of such a great Prince" [protettione di così gran Prencipe], in which "vivranno eterna vita ad onta di quelle lingue, che cercano dar morte all'opere altrui" [they will live forever in spite of those tongues that seek to bring death to the works of others].

16. (Venice: Vincenti). The dedication to Cardinal Pompeo Arrigoni is dated 20 November 1600.

17. The dedication is dated 25 March 1603 (Venice: Vincenti).

18. *Seconda parte*, 5 and 13–21.

That he was slow to defend himself is surprising, given how seriously both he and his brother, once they had made a public stand, took every offense they perceived in Artusi's various criticisms.[19] An explanation may rest in part with the tone of Artusi's original "Ragionamenti" in the first book, neither of which is particularly injurious to the composer, and with the subsequent escalation of the scholar's rhetoric in the *Seconda parte*. Monteverdi could have taken the opportunity to respond to the criticisms issued in Artusi's first book in the preface to his fourth book, which contains madrigals closely associated with Ferrara, at least some dating from before the 1598 performance at Antonio Goretti's house, and which is dedicated to the Ferrarese Accademia degli Intrepidi; but he did not do so.[20] It is possible that, at that point, he had not yet felt the sting of Artusi's vitriol and that he did not know what else the theorist had in store; either Artusi had not circulated the *Seconda parte* in manuscript (perhaps mindful of the prepublication reception accorded to his first volume), or Monteverdi had already committed the fourth book to press by the summer of 1602 and was not yet ready to issue a reply. In the event, the two publications are almost exactly contemporary, being dated within a few days of each other in March 1603.

Most surprising, perhaps, Monteverdi did not immediately publish all the works under discussion in the first *L'Artusi*: "Anima mia perdona" is included in the fourth book, but "Cruda Amarilli" and "O Mirtillo" had to wait until 1605 to be published. As we shall see in chapter 2, he had sound musical reasons for holding them in reserve and may well have been planning the fifth book at the same time that the fourth was in preparation. "Cruda Amarilli" and "O Mirtillo" open the fifth book, in what appears to be a defiant aesthetic gesture, and they are also integral to the overall structure of the volume, which, I shall argue, follows a boldly innovative narrative plan.

In retrospect, however, it is possible to detect perhaps a hint of the controversy even behind the traditional formulas of the dedication to the fourth book. In addition to remembering his many personal associations with the members of the Academy and "the many favors I received through their various shows of regard for me and my labors, such as they may be" [li molti favori ricevuti con diverse onorate loro dimostrationi verso di me, e dei miei

---

19. On Giulio Cesare's response to offensive language in da Todi's first *Discorso* see my "Claudio Monteverdi's *Ordine novo, bello et gustevole*: The Canzonetta as Dramatic Module and Formal Archetype," *Journal of the American Musicological Society* 45 (1992), 272–74.

20. On the dating of the madrigals in the fourth and fifth books see Tomlinson, *Monteverdi and the End of the Renaissance* (Berkeley and Los Angeles: The University of California Press, 1987), 98–113.

parti quali si siano], Monteverdi offers his madrigals to the Intrepidi so that they may enjoy the Academy's reflected glory, and—not coincidentally, per-haps—also its protection ("shedding light upon my pieces with the brilliance of their names, *and defending them with their serene protection*" [illustrando con la chiarezza dei lor nomi, e *diffendendo con la felice lor protettione,* questi miei canti] [emphasis added]).[21] Although it was founded too late to have been connected with the original event that sparked the controversy, the Accademia counted among its members at least some of the principals in the debate: Go-retti himself; Luzzasco Luzzaschi (who was present at the 1598 performance); and, later, Enzo Bentivoglio, to whom in 1606 the Intrepidi dedicated their theater and who is cited in 1612 as a "Principe dell'accademia."[22] Whether the elusive "Ottuso" was a member remains a mystery: Artusi criticizes a madrigal by him in the *Seconda parte* and reports only that L'Ottuso's academy had sent him several of his works.[23]

According to Giulio Cesare's account of the events that led to Monteverdi's "Lettera," it was sometime in 1603 that his brother had begun to speak of a *se-conda prattica* and to plan a response to Artusi's criticisms.

> My brother informed the world that this term is most certainly his, so that all may know and understand that when his opponent wrote in the sec-ond [volume] of *L'Artusi* these words, "*seconda prattica,* which can be called in truth the chaff of the first,"[24] that he intended to malign my brother's works, and that it was in 1603 that my brother resolved to begin writing to defend himself from his opponent, because this term "*seconda prattica*" had just left his mouth. This is an indication that his opponent would like to shred not only in writing, but in the very air, my brother's words to-gether with his music.[25]

On this point, Giulio Cesare's testimony conflicts with that of the other participants in the debate. Artusi's characterization of the *seconda prattica* as

21. Palisca notes that the Accademia degli Intrepidi was founded in 1600, too late for L'Ottuso to have been a member at the time of his first letter to Artusi. See Palisca, "The Artusi–Monteverdi controversy," 138. Stuart Reiner cites the original archival documents re-lating to the Accademia's founding by Francesco Saracini in his "Preparations in Parma—1618, 1627–28," *Music Review* 25 (1964), 285 n. 61 and 289.

22. Goretti and Bentivoglio remained connected with Monteverdi long after the turn of the century: the composer contributed to the wedding festivities of 1628 in Parma, which were organized by Bentivoglio, and Goretti served as his copyist (Fabbri, *Monteverdi,* 268).

23. *Seconda parte,* 47–52.

24. *Seconda parte,* 33.

25. "Dichiaratione," in Monteverdi, *Lettere,* ed. De' Paoli, 401–2.

"feccia della prima" had come in response to L'Ottuso's use of the term in his second letter, which as we have seen was probably written around 1600, in which he had referred to the new way of composing as "questa nova *seconda prattica*." [26] It may be that Giulio Cesare misremembered the sequence of events, and that Monteverdi had begun to plan for a rebuttal before 1603; it is just as likely that the term was "in the very air" around the turn of the century as part of the common language of the avant-garde. Artusi's introduction to the *Seconda parte* suggests that perhaps even the notion of a treatise establishing the compositional principles of the new style was part of a more generalized discourse, for he takes a passing shot at such an undertaking:

> They promise great things, philosophical arguments, new rules defended by the authority of Aristoxenus, Ptolemy, Zarlino, and Galilei, they enlarge the field with artful counterpoint, and I see that instead of improving it, they soil it. [27]

Following the "Lettera" of Book Five, Artusi responded with a now lost *Discorso musicale*, issued under the pseudonym of Antonio Braccino da Todi. Giulio Cesare makes reference to the *Discorso* in his "Dichiaratione," citing a brief comment in which the theorist appears to mock Monteverdi's claim to the term "*seconda prattica*" ("you appear so jealous of this term that you fear that it may be stolen from you"). The tone of the *Discorso*, if it may be judged by Giulio Cesare's reaction, seems to have been at least as acrimonious as that of the *Seconda parte dell'Artusi* and prompted Giulio Cesare to take the field in 1607 in his brother's defense with the "Dichiaratione" and the *Scherzi musicali*. To judge by its reference to the fifth book, which bears a dedication dated 30 July 1605, as having appeared "some months ago" [alcuni mesi addietro], Giulio Cesare's gloss on his brother's "Lettera" seems to have been drafted in late 1605 or early 1606. Braccino's *Discorso* must have come on the heels of the fifth book, suggesting that the pace of the debate quickened considerably after Monteverdi took a public stance in 1605. Artusi replied to the "Dichiaratione" in 1608 with a second pseudonymous *Discorso;* this, until 1633, remained the last word by any of the participants in the original debate. As Monteverdi remembered it (apparently only selectively, since he does not mention the second *Discorso*), Artusi eventually came to see the worth of the composer's innovations: "but on hearing of a certain difference of opinion published by my

26. *Seconda parte,* 16.
27. *Seconda parte,* 4–5.

brother," he wrote to Doni, "he calmed down in such a way that from thence-
forward not only did he stop overruling me — turning his pen in my praise —
but he began to like and admire me."[28] But of that, history has no record.

The Senses, Reason, and Musical Aesthetics

The principal texts of the controversy range quite widely beyond the well-
known details of contrapuntal technique that Artusi criticized in Monteverdi's
madrigals and that have become the hallmark of the *seconda prattica*. In their
epistolary debate, Artusi and L'Ottuso reflect on a broad spectrum of aesthetic
concerns that were the fodder of intellectual discourse during the closing
decades of the sixteenth century, from the rational basis for aesthetic judgment
to the proper relationship between invention and imitation. In their arguments, and more importantly in Giulio Cesare's reply to those arguments,
Monteverdi's modifications to contrapuntal practice emerge as a symptom of
an incipient process of experimentation that was leading him away from the
aesthetic principles of the Renaissance even as he produced the works that have
been taken to represent the crowning achievement of the Renaissance madrigal.

The fundamental question around which revolved much of the debate between Artusi and L'Ottuso dealt with the standards to be applied when judging the quality of a composition. Artusi refused to allow any argument that did
not start from a set of immutable natural laws, which were manifested in the
mathematical nature of intervals and in the way those intervals had come to
be treated by the composers whom he considered canonical and by the theorists who codified their practices. Music had reached its technical pinnacle in
Artusi's time, so that, as he says in the preface to his first book, "nothing can be
added to it" [non vi si può aggiungere cosa alcuna],[29] and Zarlino's writings on
counterpoint captured its perfection and the culmination of this tradition. This
powerful foundation led Artusi to certain inevitable conclusions about the
possibility of expanding the techniques of composition, the nature of aesthetic
judgment, the affective power of music, and how music is perceived.

Beginning with Monteverdi's "Lettera" of 1605 and still resonating in his
later comments to Doni, the question of the responsibility of the composer to
the accumulated wisdom of his predecessors was the most visible aspect of the
dispute. In order to argue for any kind of innovation outside the boundaries
determined by the canon, Monteverdi needed to establish at least a claim that

28. *Letters*, ed. Stevens, no. 123, p. 410; *Lettere*, ed. De' Paoli, no. 122, p. 321.
29. *L'Artusi*, "Agli amici lettori."

the authority of the models Artusi upheld was not unassailable. All of Artusi's respondents—the composer, Ottuso, and Giulio Cesare—insisted on the limitations of the tradition on which Artusi established his standards and on the degree to which innovation was possible. The "Lettera" makes one central point: that Zarlino could not be considered the only authority on the treatment of dissonances, and that there were other ways of thinking about counterpoint that, "with satisfaction to reason, and to the sense of hearing, defend modern composition" [con quietanza della ragione, e del senso diffende il moderno comporre].[30] In the "Dichiaratione," Giulio Cesare underscores this point, seeking to limit Zarlino's authority:

> Reverend Zarlino did not intend to treat of any other practice [than that of Willaert], as he indeed declares, saying: "It never was nor is it my intention to treat of the usage or practice according to the manner of the ancients, either Greek or Latins, even if at times I touch upon it; my intention is solely to describe the method of those who have discovered our way of causing several parts to sound together with various modulations and various melodies, especially according to the way and manner observed by Messer Adriano." Thus the Reverend Zarlino concedes (is it not true?) that is the only practice taught by him.[31]

Giulio Cesare also claimed that, just as Artusi appealed to the authority of principles codified and taught by Zarlino and embodied in the compositions of Willaert, his brother would base his writings on the reasons taught by Plato and on the solutions adumbrated in the music of Cipriano da Rore.[32]

The debate between Artusi and L'Ottuso brought to light one of the fundamental aspects of the aesthetic crisis facing Monteverdi: the inadequacy of past examples in addressing the compositional problems that confronted Monteverdi and others of his generation. In his letters to Doni, Monteverdi makes it clear that the past had been of no use in showing him the "*via naturale all'immitatione*, or even what an imitator should be," and in the preface to the *Madrigali guerrieri et amorosi* he notes that past masters had failed to produce

---

30. Monteverdi, *Lettere*, ed. De' Paoli, p. 392. This passage suggests that Monteverdi was not aware of Galilei's counterpoint treatise, which did just what he claims. On this point, see Palisca, "The Artusi–Monteverdi Controversy," 152 n. 71.

31. Monteverdi, *Lettere*, ed. De' Paoli, p. 400.

32. On the uses made of Rore as a seminal figure by the two sides, see Stefano La Via, "Cipriano de Rore as Reader and as Read: A Literary-Musical Study of Madrigals from Rore's Later Collections (1557–1566)" (Ph.D. diss., Princeton University, 1991).

examples of the *genere concitato*. Music, until the *seconda prattica*, had been, quite simply, "imperfetta."

This was a far cry from Artusi's view that music had achieved a state of time-less perfection. The problem of how to balance invention and tradition was in the background through much of the first "Ragionamento," and it was brought into the open in the second. From the beginning of the first "Ragionamento," Artusi's most damning comments about modern composers revolve around their gratuitous fascination with newness—with their search for "extravagant things, outside of reason" [cose stravaganti, fuori dalla ragione].[33] Modern composers, "to satisfy their whims" [per scapriciarsi], write things without rea-son, largely because of their ignorance of "the reasons of the Ancients, and of those many moderns who do not depart from their opinions" [la mente degli Antichi, et de' molti Moderni, che pur non si discostano dalla loro opinione].[34] Willful innovation leads to disregard for tradition, which in turn leads to er-rors—infractions against natural principles known since the time of the An-cients. This criticism is expanded and refined in the "Ragionamento secondo." Luca, introducing the problem of the new madrigals heard and discussed at Goretti's house, makes the claim that they introduce "new rules, new ways, and new phrasing" [nuove regole, nuovi modi, et nuova frase nel dire], but that they are "harsh, and little pleasing to the ear" [aspri, et all'udito poco piace-voli]. Such is inevitably the case, he goes on to say, when

> good rules, founded in part on experience, the mother of all things, in part derived from nature, and in part shown by demonstration, are vio-lated. We have to believe that these are aberrations of the nature and pro-priety of harmony itself.[35]

New composers, replies Vario, "are so enamored of themselves, that they think they can corrupt, damage, and ruin those good rules that they have in-herited from many excellent Theoreticians and Musicians" [tanto [sono] di sé stessi innamorati, che le pare di poter corrompere, guastare et rovinare quelle buone regole, che di già hanno lasciate tanti Teorici, e Musici eccellentis-simi].[36] At this point Luca broaches the question of progress and innovation:

> I will concede the truth of what you say. Tell me, however, if this science can be expanded with new methods: why do you not want it to be, or like

33. *L'Artusi*, 8v.
34. *L'Artusi*, 15v.
35. *L'Artusi*, 39v.
36. *L'Artusi*, 42.

it to be, or believe that it should be, expanded? The field is large, and everyone is concerned with new things, and musicians need to be able to enjoy themselves, since composing songs in a uniform manner annoys and disgusts the ear.[37]

Vario replies with a narrow definition of innovation. It is necessary to produce new works, but why, in order to do so, break the rules of counterpoint to which generations of respected composers have adhered? Dissonance is not new; study those composers who are considered canonical and who made liberal use of dissonances (Lasso, da Monte, Wert), and look for examples of the proper way to use them.[38] All of the arts and all of the sciences are

> governed by experts, and for each we have been given the fundamental elements, the rules, and the precepts on which they are founded, so that without straying from the principles and sound rules one can understand what others are doing.[39]

Artusi notes that there is no sculptor, painter, poet, or orator who does not try to imitate the ancient models, "che sono stati eccellenti" — except for Monteverdi. Innovation can only consist of the application, within a new context, of existing natural — and therefore definitive — rules. Artusi's aesthetic leaves no room for the formulation of new rules.

Ottuso's letters challenged the fundamental tenets of Artusi's aesthetic orthodoxy. It is telling that all that is left of his first letter is Artusi's brief quotation of a passage that strikes at the heart of the theorist's basic assumptions:

> This being a new song, it finds with its novelty new *concenti*, and new *affetti*, and without leaving reason in any way, it nevertheless departs in a certain way from some of the ancient traditions of some excellent musicians.[40]

Artusi devotes an entire letter to responding to L'Ottuso's errors.[41] The central problem — and the first that Artusi addresses — is the contradiction inherent in L'Ottuso's claim that the new compositions, while they "depart from the ancient traditions of some eccellent Musicians," do not at the same time depart

---

37. *L'Artusi*, 42.
38. *L'Artusi*, 41–41v.
39. *L'Artusi*, 41v.
40. *Seconda parte dell'Artusi*, 5.
41. Palisca has analyzed the terminological problems of this passage, and of L'Ottuso's other letter, in "The Artusi–Monteverdi Controversy," 140–42.

from the requirements of reason.[42] This is impossible. As Artusi had demonstrated throughout the first book, reason, together with the sense of hearing, founds its judgment on tradition: on natural laws expressed in the rules of counterpoint codified by such theorists as Zarlino and himself, and proven in the canonical works of past composers. To contradict the latter is to violate the former; L'Ottuso's claim makes no sense.

L'Ottuso's reply takes on the question of authority directly:

> And as for what you argue, that there is neither Painter, nor Sculptor, nor Poet or Orator who does not seek to imitate the Ancients, and especially those who excelled, I answer that there are, and there will always be, those who value invention more than imitation. In these madrigals, Signor So-and-so has made a particular effort in this direction, since in Music novelty is more valued than the other, especially since in this field there is no need to follow the Ancients, there being ample opportunity for progress through invention and this new *modulatione*.[43]

For L'Ottuso it was not a problem to state that "things that were forbidden by tradition" [cose per tradittioni proibite] were at times forbidden because there were matters that the canonical authors had not known about and that had been developed by composers of the most recent generations.[44] To counterbalance Artusi's notion of music as rooted in a set of unchanging and known natural laws, Ottuso brought to the debate a dynamic conception of music as a field in which knowledge was expanding.

Artusi's response to L'Ottuso's challenge emphasizes the imitation of models over the imitation of nature: invention may in some ways be superior to imitation because it comes first; but imitation is useful, according to Quintilian. L'Ottuso is mistaken in undervaluing imitation, and perhaps his mistake originates, surmises Artusi, with the Aristotelian principle that "ars imitatur naturam," on which Ottuso seems to base his disdain for those who follow earlier models. But in fact the imitation of models is a widespread practice, and this confirms its validity.[45]

The claim to novelty over imitation was one that Monteverdi himself, writing to Doni thirty years later, still made: "in the end, I am more pleased to be praised a little for what is new, than to be praised a lot for what is conventional

---

42. *Seconda parte*, 5.
43. *Seconda parte*, 19.
44. *Seconda parte*, 18.
45. *Seconda parte*, 42.

in my writing" [alla fine son per contentarmi d'essere piú tosto poco lodato nel novo, che molto nel ordinario scrivere].[46] By 1633, of course, Monteverdi's claim had only a distant echo of the revolution: composers and commentators had come to see innovation as an accepted goal of composition.[47]

Not surprisingly, Artusi and Ottuso also differ on how to build an aesthetic lineage by which to justify their ideas, and their organization of historical figures reflects their opposite views of tradition, one emphasizing continuity and oneness, the other fragmenting history into sharply defined periods.[48] Artusi's musical sources stay close to his own generation, ranging from Palestrina to Benedetto Pallavicino, Costanzo Porta, Claudio Merulo, Giovanni Croce, Giovanni Bassano, Baldassarre Donati, Andrea Gabrieli, Giovanni Giacomo Gastoldi, Giovanni Maria Nanino, Philippe da Monte, Giaches de Wert, Luzzasco Luzzaschi, Orazio Vecchi, and Cipriano da Rore.[49] These, and many others, are his "excellent musicians" [musici eccellenti] and "practitioners of the good school" [pratici della buona scola], whose work Artusi sees as belonging to an aesthetic continuum that collapses nearly a century of music into a single present, having begun with Josquin and Mouton, "who can be said to have lived in our own time" [che si può dire siano stati a' giorni nostri].[50] Only composers who lived five hundred or more years earlier could be called "ancient."[51]

---

46. *Lettere*, ed. De' Paoli, p. 321.

47. See, for example, Vincenzo Giustiniani's comment, from about 1628, that the new style of church music "demands great practical knowledge, quickness of invention, and effort to write rather than great maturity and knowledge of refined counterpoint" [ricerca gran pratica più tosto e vivacità d'ingegno e fatica di scrivere, che gran maturità e scienza di contraponto esquisita]. Less emphasis on training and more on invention made it possible for modern *maestri di cappella* to attain their positions at a younger age than ever before. Giustiniani cites the example of Vincenzo Ugolino, who at 40 had already been *maestro* in San Pietro "for some years" before moving to the same position in Parma. "Discorso sopra la musica de' suoi tempi," in *Le origini del melodramma*, ed. Angelo Solerti (Turin, 1903), 122–23.

48. Of the two, Artusi is the more learned but also the more eclectic: he cites sources ranging from Greek antiquity and the rhetorical tradition of Cicero to Petrarch and Tasso; all theoretical discussions, of course, turn on evidence derived from Classical philosophers (Aristoxenus, Aristotle) and, above all, Zarlino. Artusi even draws on a comprehensive knowledge of medieval treatises. See *L'Artusi*, 13v–14.

49. Artusi's lists of canonical authors in *L'Artusi* are on pp. 3, 42, 43v, and 67v; in the *Seconda parte* on pp. 5, 26, 41, and 56.

50. *L'Artusi*, 3 and 67v; *Seconda parte*, 41. Artusi's artistic "memory" is limited to a period spanning some 100 years, and in this regard he is typical of many writers on music. See Jessie Ann Owens, "Music Historiography and the Definition of 'Renaissance,'" *Notes* 47 (1990): 305–30, especially table 1 on pp. 320–21.

51. *Seconda parte*, 41.

L'Ottuso plays the "splitter" to Doni's "lumper." Taken to task for claiming that the new music departs from the traditions of the excellent musicians of the past, Ottuso groups composers by generation, expanding and dividing what Artusi had joined. To the generation of ancients belong "Josquin, Clemens non Papa, Mouton, Crecquillon, and others in their class, and after them our Divine Adriano" [Iosquino, Clemens non Papa, Mouton, Crequillon, et altri di quella Classe, et doppo loro poscia il Divino nostro Adriano].[52] These are the authors whose works established the rules of counterpoint that were eventually codified by Zarlino. Ottuso does not provide a comparable list of "moderni Autori," but the composers whose works he cites—Marenzio, Wert, Rore—are presented in opposition to this older "classe" for their departure from the rules, and it is they who make up Monteverdi's true aesthetic lineage.

Ottuso's construction of music history into two camps divided along generational lines was expanded and refined by Giulio Cesare Monteverdi in the "Dichiaratione." Ottuso's list of ancient composers becomes for Giulio Cesare synonymous with the *prima prattica*, "that which revolves around the perfection of the harmony; that is, which considers harmony not the servant, but the mistress." This first manner of composing was established

> by those who first composed their pieces for more than one voice using our notation. It was then continued and expanded by Ockeghem, Josquin des Pres, Pietro della Rue, Iouan Motton, Crequillon, Clemens non Papa, Gombert, and others contemporary with them, and it was perfected finally by Messer Adriano with his compositions, and by the Most Excellent Zerlino with most judicious rules.[53]

The *seconda prattica*, too, was to have its own lineage, claiming some of the same "eccellenti artefici" already enlisted by Artusi, most prominently Cipriano da Rore, whom Artusi both praises and criticizes,[54] Wert, and Marenzio. In addition, Giulio Cesare lists Gesualdo, Emilio de' Cavalieri, Alfonso Fontanelli, Giovanni Bardi, Giovanni Del Turco, Tomaso Pecci, Marc'Antonio Ingegneri, Luzzasco Luzzaschi, Jacopo Peri, and Giulio Caccini, all active in the latter part of the sixteenth century.[55]

52. *Seconda parte*, 18.

53. "Dichiaratione," in Monteverdi, *Lettere*, ed. De' Paoli, p. 399.

54. See *L'Artusi*, 15v–17, for a criticism of Rore's use of chromaticism. He is, however, generally praised—see for example 19v–20.

55. Although Ottuso and Giulio Cesare are not the first to divide the history of composition as they knew it into groups or periods—it is a practice that goes back at least as far as Johannes Tinctoris, who identified Dunstable [or, following the *New Grove*, Dunstaple] as

Such a clear-cut historical periodization, with Willaert as the culmination of the old generation (the end of the Renaissance?) and juxtaposed to the modernity of the younger composers, is quite alien to Artusi's view of history. There was no need for him to enumerate those who represent an older generation of "antichi" in opposition to the "moderni"—he simply did not formulate the problem in those terms. His "camps" were not historical but were simply defined in terms of those who, in his view, got things right and those who did not.

For Artusi, the body of natural laws and past examples was important because it formed the basis for aesthetic judgment—the means by which to evaluate a new composition. In a real sense, this can be considered the true core of the debate, because it defined not only what was permissible from a technical standpoint, but also the boundaries beyond which innovation was not possible. How each side construed the workings of aesthetic judgment determined what limitations could be imposed on a composer's, or a theorist's, imagination.

Throughout both volumes of the *Imperfettioni*, Artusi had forged a tight link between reason and the ear as the means by which to judge the worth of a composition.[56] He laid the foundations for this argument early in the "Ragionamento Primo" (which is couched, significantly, as a conversation between a listener and a theorist), in the course of a discussion of proper instrumental combinations. The listener, Luca, citing Francisco de Salinas's *De musica*, had raised the question of the primacy of the senses in judging a work of art. Was it not true, after all, that "the sense is never in error regarding that which triggers it and is properly its object" [il senso intorno al proprio sensibile, overo oggetto proprio mai non erra]?[57]

"novae artis fons et origo" and traced the progress of music through a generation of "contemporanei" (Dufay, Binchois) and "moderni" (Ockeghem, Busnois, Regis, Caron)—they appear to be the first to draw such sharp aesthetic distinctions between periods. Compare for example Ludovico Zacconi's more bland division into "vecchi" and "moderni," in which the "moderni" are merely either still alive or dead before their time. See Owens, "Music Historiography," 320–21.

56. Primarily in *L'Artusi*, "Ragionamento secondo," 44, but also the negative "Tutto il loro pensiero, è di soddisfare al solo senso; poco curandosi che la ragione, entri qua a giudicare le loro cantilene" [Their only concern is to satisfy the sense alone; they care little that reason may be called upon to judge their compositions], ibid. 43.

57. *L'Artusi*, 11v ff. The Spanish theorist Francisco de Salinas's (1513–1590) *De Musica libri septem* (Salamanca: Mathias Gast, 1577) had recently been reprinted (Salamanca: her. Cornelii Bonardi, 1592).

Vario, the theorist, noting the antiquity of the question, had set up a twofold categorization of objects capable of being perceived by the senses: those that could be perceived directly, as in the sense of touch; and those that needed a medium to reach the sense, as in music, which requires air in order to act upon the ear. Direct sensation was not a problem; in the case of indirect sensation, however, a number of factors, such as the patterns of light and shade that can seem to alter the color of an object, could interfere with perception.

Artusi's mechanism for musical perception places the sense of hearing as intermediary between the origin of the sensation and the intellect, introducing reasons to doubt the infallibility of the process. On this basis, he shows that the sense can be deceived by its object, especially by its "judicious deceptions" [inganni giudiziosi], and argues for the necessary coupling of reason and sense in reaching an aesthetic judgment:

> But if the intellect can make mistakes at times in the course of a conversation, as truly it does, will the senses not be even more susceptible to error? Therefore I say that sense without reason, and reason without sense, cannot render an accurate judgment of any object that involves learning [oggetto scientifico]. *They can only do so when they are joined together.* [emphasis added][58]

This argument returns when Luca raises the practice of "modulare accentato" and the way it masks harshness with pleasing harmonies. Vario explains:

> An excellent perceived object [eccellente sensibile] corrupts the sense. This simply means that the other parts distract the ear in such a way that it cannot hear in full the offense it has received, as it might were the composition in two or three parts. Reason, however, which knows and can discern good from bad, judges rightly that the sense has been deceived, since the sense only perceives matter in a slightly confused manner, however closely it may approach the truth.[59]

The ear applies itself to the physical phenomenon of sound, which can only be perceived imprecisely, and reason then considers in the abstract, against general principles of form, what the ear has gathered. The two processes are mutually dependent:

> I will tell you, therefore, that in matters pertaining to the harmonic faculty there are two judges: first, the sense of hearing; and second, reason. . . .

58. *L'Artusi,* 12.
59. *L'Artusi,* 41v.

The sense judges those things that pertain to matter; reason applies itself to form. From this one gathers that since matter is given perfection through form, so judgment makes it possible that the apprehension of any object is made perfect by reason. It is the province of the sense to find that which is closest to itself, and to receive perfection from reason. The reverse is true for reason, since it receives from the sense [information] regarding whatever is closest to the sense, and from itself it derives perfection. What the sense knows in a confused fashion from unstable matter, reason judges in the abstract, divorced from matter. For this reason not only these modern Theoreticians, but also the Ancients, conclude that the judgment of Harmony belongs not only to the sense of hearing, but to reason as well. . . . The sense of hearing is necessary because it is the first to receive unto itself those things that pertain to it, and without it reason cannot operate, but it is imperfect, because if reason does not come to its aid, it is evident that it is lacking, and weak and totally undependable.[60]

"Form," in this context, is the aggregate of the principles derived by theorists from the natural laws that determine the basic materials of composition (pitches, intervals, etc.) together with the examples gathered from the works of past masters who, through experimentation, have perfected the art of music. The understanding of this body of abstract rules and examples gives reason the tools to evaluate what the ear apprehends. Artusi returns to this same language in the second book, criticizing L'Ottuso's argument that dissonances can be mitigated by the context in which they are used. This Artusi again calls "the excellent perceived object that corrupts the sense," in which "the accompaniments can be said to have the effect of obfuscating the sense [of hearing] as I have always said, and confirm here."[61]

The denial of reason in favor of the irrational—a fleeting and erroneous effect that focuses on pleasing the ear—is at the foundation of Vario's criticism of the new compositions brought by Luca. Modern composers are so "enamored of themselves," he explains,

> that they think they can corrupt, damage, and ruin those good Rules, that have been passed on by so many Theorists and Excellent Musicians . . . they only think of satisfying the sense, caring little that reason may have a role in judging their Compositions.[62]

60. "Ragionamento secondo," 44.
61. *Seconda parte,* 37.
62. *L'Artusi,* 42–43. Mei had expressed a similar bias—albeit with a different intent—in 1572 when explaining to Galilei the reasons for the decay of ancient music. Composers had

Precisely because of its irrational nature, however, the sense of hearing is easily "corrupted"— or deliberately fooled, as happens when composers, as L'Ottuso suggests, mitigate the harshness of dissonances with clever accompaniments, which Artusi regards as having "the effect of clouding the sense" [gli accompagnamenti si potrà dire, che faccino effetto d'offuscare il senso].[63] In Artusi's view, the search for "cose stravaganti," whether in composition or in performance, is useless: such effects are "outside reason, and far from the experiences of our forebears, which have been reduced to clear rules embraced by the sense and confirmed by the intellect."[64]

It was Artusi's forceful insistence on this highly rational evaluation of all music that pushed the Monteverdi brothers to promise a defense of the *seconda prattica* that would satisfy (in the words of the "Lettera") both "reason and the senses." This was, I believe, a misjudgment on their part, and it may well have been the reason why Monteverdi never produced the treatise he promised. Weaned on the theoretical model of Zarlino, Monteverdi probably felt the need for, but could not really conceive the means to write, a treatise that was as radically different from its models as were the aims of the music he was to compose in the next twenty years. As he wrote to Doni, there were no models, only a general destination and the need to explore the means to move toward it, but although this was true for both music and theory, he was able to pursue only one of the two. This is why some of the most provocative early statements on the *seconda prattica* come not from the Monteverdis but from L'Ottuso, and also why neither Claudio nor Giulio Cesare seems to have been able to pick up on them.

Although L'Ottuso does not address the problem specifically, he seems most comfortable advancing precisely the kinds of irrational arguments Vario deems

---

begun to introduce new artifices that corrupted the purity of their formerly homophonic compositions: "From personal pride, they compete in seeking to please greatly the ears, forgetting to take into account the intellect, so that this new pleasure began to sway the soul away from the concepts and other imitations of the affects, almost weakening it [snervandolo] with these superfluous delicacies," Claude V. Palisca, *Girolamo Mei: Letters on Ancient and Modern Music to Vincenzo Galilei and Givanni Bardi: A Study with Annotated Texts* (Neuhausen-Stuttgart: Hansler, 1977), 114.

63. *Seconda parte*, 37. L'Ottuso's argument is given in *Seconda parte*, 16.

64. *Seconda parte*, 8v. See also Mei: "I see from the conclusion of your last letter that you believe that music should have as its purpose to please the ear with its harmonies. . . . Now if you mean the pleasure that arises from a sung air that is well conceived to espress appropriately the concepts [of the text] and which helps them by bringing out the affect of the text, it cannot be other than pleasing to hear. . . ." Mei's rhetorical bias is evident here, as is his emphasis on both hearing and intellectual understanding, necessary if a proper emotional effect is to be obtained. See Palisca, *Girolamo Mei*, 115, and also 132.

fallacious. A dissonance can please more than an expected consonance, not only because it is sweetened by the movement of the other parts, which mask its harshness, but also because its new sound will certainly please more than that which is expected. The novelty of sound produced in the new music will cause an *"affetto,* that is to say a desire"* to hear such new *concenti,* which will then be likely to move the soul. The ear is seduced, and the intellect, in Ottuso's view, is a willing accomplice. Desire, which in Artusi's aesthetic leads at best a marginal existence as the byproduct of a satisfied reason, is emancipated by Ottuso as an independent agent capable of operating in the pursuit of sensual pleasure, the very antithesis of reason.

Artusi's ideas regarding the expressive potential of music were bound up with his sense that music had achieved a state in which it was beyond improvement; they were rooted in his assumptions regarding the nature of music, beauty, and affect. His definition of affect was based on Cicero's: "If an affect is a passion, or a movement of the soul, or as Cicero put it in the second book of *De Inventione,* 'Est animi, aut corporis ex tempore aliqua de causa commutatio.'" [65] The mechanism by which the emotions could be moved was set in motion, according to Artusi, by the presentation of a beautiful object, which generates a disposition toward itself and in turn moves the soul toward the desired effect. [66] The only standard by which Artusi could measure such a "movement" was based on ancient accounts of the power of music:

> How could it be that the happy man for some reason could become melancholy; or that the infirm become healthy, and similar phenomena. Has the music of Signor So-and-so wrought such effects in the souls of men, or is likely to? Is there any real proof? Has this music caused some miracle, as we read that of the Ancient master musicians did? It has not, and therefore it cannot generate new affects, as Your Lordship maintains. Well, then; as I have said, it excites the ear, and strikes it harshly. [67]

There being no evidence that the new music had ever moved happy men to despair, or made the healthy sick, or moved the peaceful to wrath, it was therefore unlikely that it could create any new "affetti." L'Ottuso's claims on its behalf could be neither defended on the grounds of past authority nor proven by practical demonstration.

In Artusi's view, the affects were directly linked to the basic materials avail-

---

65. *Seconda parte,* 10.
66. *Seconda parte,* 52.
67. *Seconda parte,* 10.

able for composition—intervals, consonances, and dissonances—all of which
were fixed. Given that no new consonances or dissonances were likely to be
found, and that the mathematical nature of intervals could not be changed,
then the materials were lacking for the creation of new expressive combinations.
When a composer arranged these elements in an unorthodox way, as Monteverdi had done, the most he could claim was to have struck the sense of hearing with harsh sounds.[68] But harshness, for Artusi, did not constitute a new
concento, which, as he notes in the *Seconda parte*, could only result from sweetness. Monteverdi's use of dissonance between the outer parts in "Era l'anima
mia," although masked by the inner parts, could not be considered a new *concento*, as L'Ottuso might claim, because the necessary conditions of a *concento*
are "soavità et dolcezza." Were such a new *concento* to be found, then there
would also be a new affect associated with it.[69] Artusi's assessment of Monteverdi's composition clarifies his view:

> but I believe (and this is not to offend Your Lordship) that it would have
> been better if you had written: new discord, new air, new stimulus for the
> ear, which is stimulated and struck by the rapidity and slowness of the
> motion, now sweetly, now harshly, according to the air that Signor So-
> and-so has given to the parts of the song and to the arrangement of the
> consonances and dissonances. And this is the novelty introduced by this
> Music. And, in the end, new confusion.[70]

But the harshness of this novelty could not result in a new "concento," and
therefore also not in any new affect: "But if it cannot make a new *concento*, as
I have proven to Your Lordship, how will it create new affects?" [ma se non
può fare novo concento, come ho provato a V. S. come potrà fare novi affetti?]
Affects were associated with beauty, not harshness. Only a pleasing sound
could generate in the listener the desire to hear a particular composition again
and again.

"Affetto" equals "desiderio."[71] Music has as its primary goal to please [lu-
singare], and not "to act upon [the listener], nor to cause effects or move the
souls of others to different passions" [che operi, e facci effetti, né mova gl'animi
altrui a diverse passioni]. Music must be sweet, and it must soothe and please:
"Let these new Masters cease to bring to the ear annoying, sour, harsh, and

68. *Seconda parte*, 10.
69. *Seconda parte*, 7.
70. *Seconda parte*, 9.
71. *Seconda parte*, 40.

unbearable things; instead, let them bring forth works that are harmonious and sweet, the better to lead it toward their desired effect."[72] Beauty consists of the movement of natural intervals; all impediments to beauty must be avoided.[73]

For Artusi, the purpose of the musician was "giovare e dilettare," but evidently not "movere" and certainly not through novelty and the "meraviglia" produced by the "inganni giudiciosi" of the *seconda prattica*. That which is done against the proper nature of harmony is necessarily "far from the musician's purpose" [lontane dalla fine del musico].[74] New compositions that disobey the rules are such that "non si discernerà il bello e purgato stile; dal barbaro" [one cannot discern a beautiful and polished style from a barbaric one].[75] They are "cose impertinenti" that "offendono [l'udito] più tosto che lo dilettano" [impertinent things that offend the ear rather than please it], and they introduce confusion into the science of music, whose principal attribute must be "elegance" [gratia], from which the ear derives "enjoyment" [dilectatione]. This is the essence of the argument over the nature of dissonance that occupies much of both the "Ragionamento secondo" and the *Seconda parte*: Artusi criticizes the confusion introduced when modern musicians argue that some dissonances, in some situations, can be perceived as consonant. His rejection of the claims made on behalf of new compositions stems from his denial that any new emotions could be generated—especially not through the deliberate corruption of rules originating from natural principles—because the existing resources of composition already suffice to express what emotions there are.[76]

Artusi drew no distinction between the emotional and physical states upon which music could act; indeed, any new expression of "affect" had to manifest itself in the realm of the miraculous. He lacked a system, however rudimentary, for discussing human emotions, and although he never says so explicitly, it is quite clear that he considered the affective resources of contemporary composi-

72. *Seconda parte*, 52.

73. *Seconda parte*, 53. This echoes Zarlino's insistence that even in his search for expression, a composer should not cross the limits of good taste and must never offend the ear. On this point see Martha Feldman, *City Culture and the Madrigal at Venice* (Berkeley and Los Angeles: The University of California Press, 1995), 174–75.

74. *L'Artusi*, 4 and 39v.

75. *L'Artusi*, 40.

76. Enrico Fubini, in *A History of Musical Aesthetics* (London: Macmillan, 1991), 137–38, argues that it was Artusi's "unswerving abhorrence of the new tendency in music to become an 'expression of the affections,' that is, its tendency to become subjective and appeal to individual sensibilities. This is why he defended polyphony. . . ." This is an oversimplification of Artusi's position.

tion adequate to their task—anything beyond them was magic. Perhaps surprisingly, in spite of his Ciceronian bent, he ignored the problem—common in rhetorical treatises of the time—of how the representation of certain passions acted upon the listener.[77]

The closest Artusi comes to a description of how music affects its audience occurs in the response to L'Ottuso's second letter. He explains the process in the following terms:

> For some, according to their disposition, this new air and new modulation will surely cause them to want to hear the song more than once, provided that it is beautiful and has *gravitas* and artful counterpoint. But this should not lead us to say that this is a new kind [specie] of affect, because this has been felt many times before for compositions written by good composers. . . . This desire can be understood in two ways. It arises in man because the ear derives pleasure [from the music] and the intellect enjoys it . . . or the ear wants to hear it again because it finds it in some way enjoyable, and leads to laughter and mockery. . . . It is true that the two reactions, which are opposites of one another, cannot be heard in the same way. Taste does not crave in the same way, and with the same desire, both sweet and bitter. . . .[78]

This sets on its ear L'Ottuso's argument that novel sounds would make the listener want to hear a composition over and over again: it may be true, but only because the piece is more burlesque than seductive. Only through the pursuit of natural effects—those sanctioned by the laws of harmony—can a composer hope to achieve any effect on an audience, but even then only to the extent that the listeners are receptive:

> We seek things that are natural, that are in conformity with nature, we want nature to move, and make natural effects, but we also need a subject who is ready to receive such emotions. These effects however will not be of a new kind, but ones that have been deployed thousands of times before. And when Modern music obtains such effects, are these the results of such intervals, and through other things used against nature? They are born of Harmony, and number and Rhythm, which are the servants of the Text, and these operate on the listener [soggetto] according to his predisposition to receive such passions, as the Rev. Zarlino has shown at length

77. Bernard Weinberg, *A History of Literary Criticism in the Italian Renaissance* (Chicago: University of Chicago Press, 1961), 129 [and elsewhere].

78. *Seconda parte,* 26.

in the Institutioni cited above and in the eighth chapter of the eighth book of the Sopplimenti.[79]

The senses, being natural, are better moved by things natural than by artifices that go against nature. The ear, therefore, will naturally prefer "intervalli naturali" to those that are "accidentali."[80]

Artusi's theory of the passions is closely related to that articulated by Zarlino in the second part of the *Istitutioni harmoniche*.[81] Chapters 4–9 of the *Istitutioni* are devoted to the problem presented by Classical accounts of the power of music to move listeners, sometimes to a miraculous extent. Zarlino begins from the premise that this may well appear doubtful to a modern observer, since modern music, having reached an unprecedented degree of perfection, is nevertheless incapable of anything even approaching the effects of ancient music. The discussion focuses on four principal areas: how ancient music was used, and how it differs from modern practice; who the ancient musicians were, and how their subjects differ from those of the moderns; how human passions work, and by what means music can affect them; and finally, what types of music produced certain effects. Zarlino proceeds from the premise that modern and ancient musical practices differ greatly in all respects, and that modern music is indeed capable of achieving powerful affects of its own—it can move to tears, laughter, or anger.[82]

Four elements, operating together, produce affect: harmony, rhythm or meter, text ("oratione, overo il parlare"), and the presence of a subject predisposed to the affect being presented. The first three make up what Zarlino calls *melodia*.[83] Taken alone, none of the three fundamental components is sufficient on its own to produce a proper affect; in the absence of one or more, the result may be, as with instrumental dance music, enjoyable at best, but it certainly will not produce a "movement of the soul."[84] The question of the text is especially important: not only does Zarlino emphatically insist that its presence is

---

79. *Seconda parte*, 31. Zarlino, *Sopplimenti musicali* (Venice, 1583; repr. Gregg Press, 1966), book 8, chapters 7 and 8, pp. 305–11.

80. *Seconda parte*, 33.

81. Gioseffo Zarlino, *Istitutioni harmoniche* (Venice: 1558; repr. New York: Broude, 1965), 62–77.

82. Palisca, *Girolamo Mei*, 42–43, views Zarlino's position as one of indifference to ancient models.

83. On the use of this term by Artusi and L'Ottuso, see Palisca, "The Artusi–Monteverdi Controversy," 141.

84. *Istitutioni*, 84.

crucial, but in his original definition he intimates that the rhythm or meter imposed upon the harmony derives from the verse—that whatever life the composition may have is given it by the text. This produces a powerful effect: speech moves human passions; musical speech is all the more effective at doing so.

As important as the three components of *melodia* are, they nevertheless require, for Zarlino, the presence of a receptive listener [soggetto] on whom they can act. In his analysis of Classical examples he emphasizes that the recipient is already predisposed to the musician's subject matter—as was Alexander, a military hero, who was moved to battle by music.[85] This is refined when he discusses the mechanism by which the passions are aroused. Emotions are "located in the corporeal and organic sensorial appetite" [poste nell'appetito sensitivo corporeo, et organico], each consisting of two components in different proportions: temperature (hot or cold) and humidity (wet or dry). In anger [ira], heat and wetness predominate; fear is characterized by cold dryness. Changing the relationship between the ingredients produces a change in emotion. Certain harmonies are associated with the various emotions, and their deployment either mitigates or accentuates the intensity of the affect:

> Given that the Harmonies and Numbers are similar to the passions of the soul, as Aristotle maintains, we can say that to adapt oneself to Harmonies and Numbers is nothing more than to adapt and make oneself receptive to different passions and different Moral habits and customs of the soul. Therefore those who hear Harmonies and Numbers are transported, according to the disposition of their soul, at times toward love, at others toward anger, and at others still toward courage. This only happens . . . as a result of the similarity between these passions and certain Harmonies.[86]

Thus the Phrygian mode excites anger, the Mixolydian produces sadness, and the Dorian, being balanced between the others, is more appropriate to strong and temperate characters. Harmonies of the same affect as the emotions of the listener, because they are joined by similitude, will intensify his emotions; exposure to a harmony of contrary affect will on the other hand weaken the listener's passions and "purify" him of his predominant affect.[87] Different emotions, therefore, result from different motions of the spirit, and the closer

---

85. *Istitutioni,* 84–85.

86. *Istitutioni,* 88.

87. The stricture against the mixing of conflicting affects recurs both in Girolamo Mei's writings and, under his influence, in Galilei's. See Mei's discussion of affects in the first letter to Galilei, and also in his sixth, in Palisca, *Girolamo Mei,* 169.

a work's affect to that natural to the listener, the easier it will be for it to take effect.[88] Knowledge of the characteristics of each affect and of each harmony should make it quite easy for the composer to move an audience at will.[89]

In the *Sopplimenti musicali,* Zarlino returns to the nature of the "affettioni, o costumi dell'animo, e quello che ciascuna sía da per sé" [affections or habits of the soul, and what characterizes each alone].[90] Here he sets up three categories or *generi:*

> We must therefore realize, that the Affections or Customs were called by the Ancients *ethoi,* because through them one could direct and know human Qualities or Constitutions, which we might call, without being in error, the Passions of the Soul. These were of three kinds. The first was that called *sustaltikon,* that is to say *intervallare,* in which by the means of speech was acted and shown an action carried out with strong and manly soul, such as the actions of Heroes. Tragedy is concerned with this type above all others. . . . The second was called *hesuchastikon,* that is, restrained or constricted, in which by narrating some matter, either contemporary or past, the soul was represented as shrunken and withdrawn into humility. It was represented as subject, in an effeminate way, to any passion or affection, and as not very manly, lacking in all resolve. . . . But the third, called *hexukastikon,* or Quiet, was reserved for quiet and free actions, and peaceful dispositions of the soul, with a moderate mind.[91]

Whereas the heroic *genere* was best suited for tragedy, the others were each appropriate to a range of compositions: the *genere ristretto o contratto* was used for "lullabys, laments, weeping, moaning, sighing, and other similar things; an example of this appears in the fourth book of the *Aeneid* of Virgil, where he tells of Dido"; to the *genere quieto* belonged "hymns, wedding songs [*Imenei*], songs of parting, of praise, of counsel, and other similar things." Their effect resulted not only from the "movement of the intervals and from the way the

---

88. Mei expressed similar ideas regarding the ease with which certain passions are imitated and instilled in the audience: "One must consider that natural emotions and affects all occur without effort, such as those that result from inclinations and tendencies [inclinazioni e principi] originating within ourselves and that are suited to them [i. e., to those inclinations and tendencies]. It is therefore easy to imitate them and to express them, and therefore to move [the listener], nor is there need for much other than an aptitude and disposition suited to their nature [quello che sono]." Letter of 8 May 1572 to Vincenzo Galilei, in Palisca, *Girolamo Mei,* 101.

89. *Istitutioni,* 87.

90. *Libro settimo,* chap. 11.

91. *Sopplimenti,* 270–71.

strings were touched (so to speak) and stroked, which can be many, but also by the various purposes and functions to which such genres were put. Thus there were many different kinds of songs." [92] Zarlino's division of the *affetti* into three *generi* corresponds to the three styles of Ciceronian rhetoric: a high style appropriate for magnificent and lofty subjects; a middle style characterized by moderation and elegance of language; and a simple, ordinary, or low style. [93]

The *affetti* are not the passions themselves, which Zarlino does not attempt to organize into any kind of system. Rather, they are the means by which human emotions [costitutioni o qualità] may be "directed and known" [indricciare et conoscer]. Zarlino's *affetti* refer to musical styles, "which brought together in compositions, according to the Subject of the Text, may, in the aggregate [that makes up] the Melodia, move the Soul and make it conform to various habits and passions." [94] In light of Zarlino's use of the term, Artusi's insistence that the creation of new *affetti* could only result from the creation of new *concenti* becomes clear. As expressive tools of musical artifice, the *affetti*—that is, the means of representing human emotions—are tied to the available resources of musical grammar, and these were in his and Zarlino's view finite and already fully developed. For Monteverdi, by the time of the preface to the *Madrigali guerrieri et amorosi* (and perhaps as early as the fifth book of madrigals), the *affetti* were real emotions, psychological states to be evoked, and not merely stylistic labels.

L'Ottuso's own definition of affect was not very different from Artusi's and Zarlino's; after noting that the word could have numerous meanings, he argued that "it could be taken to mean a passion of the soul" [può torsi come passione d'animo]. Like Zarlino, he maintained that modern music need not demonstrate magical powers, and like Artusi he linked affect and desire. He differed from Artusi and Zarlino, however, on what could move the spirit to desire a particular object: novelty attracted as much as beauty. To be successful, music

> will, with the novelty of its *modulatione*, engender *affetto*, that is, the desire to hear frequently such a manner of *concento*, which is more likely to move our soul with its novelty in this new practice than was the old, for the new [practice] is the one that strikes the sense more effectively. [95]

92. *Sopplimenti*, 271.
93. On the Ciceronian framework of Zarlino's *Institutioni*, see Feldman, *City Culture*, 171–76.
94. *Sopplimenti*, 270.
95. *Seconda parte*, 17.

Ottuso's idea that the novelty of the sounds employed by modern composers stimulates the intellect and disposes it favorably toward their compositions provides the foundation for his perhaps most interesting observation. One of the novel effects introduced in Monteverdi's "Era l'anima mia" is the substitution of one interval (a dissonant seventh) for another (a consonant octave). Artusi had argued at length that, since the two intervals were mathematically different, it was illogical to propose that one could function in place of the other. L'Ottuso conceded that the two intervals were not the same; but, he argued, that was precisely what made the substitution effective: the ear, expecting an octave, is surprised when the seventh is struck instead. It is not their identity that creates the effect, but their difference: the novelty of such a device is pleasing, appealing to both the ear, which is delighted by the sound, and the intellect, which recognizes the substitution for what it is. In defense of this new effect, L'Ottuso appeals to Artusi to consider the offending passage and, "as a good poet," to "remember in this connection the metaphor, and therefore to replace the seventh with the octave, which is done very easily."[96]

Dissonance, in L'Ottuso's "nuova pratica," is treated as a figure of speech, transcending the limitations of contrapuntal practice to create more abstract effects.[97] Just as in poetry one image may be used to signify another, surprising the reader and enriching the poem not by concealing the intended object entirely but by veiling it with one that by its difference calls it to mind, so in music the ear and the intellect know what is intended by the context of a passage and are stimulated upon hearing another sound instead.[98] Unlike a true metaphor, however, in which the effect depends on distant similarity, sometimes at the level of individual words, in music it is not the distant similarity between the seventh and octave (there is none) that causes the effect, but the comparison between the entire passage in which the substitution is effected and its ideal counterpart, in which the rules of counterpoint are not violated. The "real" passage, then, is the "similar object" of the metaphor, which "suggests" the "ideal" passage that is triggered in the listener's mind. The mechanism

96. *Seconda parte*, 16.

97. On this point, see Palisca, "The Artusi–Monteverdi Controversy," 149, who notes that L'Ottuso fails to develop this potentially productive idea.

98. The substitution functions like Tesauro's metaphor, as a "parola pellegrina, velocemente significante un oggetto per mezzo di un altro" [floating word that quickly signifies one object by means of another]. *Il cannocchiale aristotelico* (Turin, 1670), 302, excerpted in James V. Mirollo, *The Poet of the Marvelous: Giambattista Marino* (New York: Columbia University Press, 1963), 119.

invoked is the same as that which underlies Artusi's relationship between the ear and the intellect, in which the intellect provides the abstract "form" against which to measure what the ear has gathered. The difference is that the composer's target has shifted from approximating as closely as possible this abstract "ideal form" to creating an intentionally distorted version of it, and that the listener's satisfaction results not from matching the two exactly but from recognizing just where and how the distortion has been effected. Like the poet's, the composer's end is *meraviglia*.

L'Ottuso may have failed to pursue the implications of his literary analogy,[99] but his comparison is significant because it points toward a new way of conceiving the relationship between text and music. In L'Ottuso's example, the composer no longer strives for the immediate identity between words and setting, in which the music is understood through the text and, requiring no independent scrutiny, is secondary to it (as in the pictorial vocabulary of the sixteenth-century madrigal). Rather, music and text are heard as separate components, each of which is to be understood in terms of the rhetorical operations that are proper to it; the meaning of the setting as a whole results from the juxtaposition of the two. In this process, each individual event is therefore heard not in isolation (as it could be in the Renaissance madrigal, in which meanings were isolated by the one-to-one correspondence of word and setting) but as part of a larger context, in which the immediate relationship between words and music is subordinated to the behavior of the two over a larger span — the phrase, as in the case described by L'Ottuso, or even the entire piece. In this new interaction, rather than the one being subordinate to the other, music and text become equal participants.

The radical realignment of music and text adumbrated in L'Ottuso's comparison between composer and poet remained largely inchoate until Monteverdi's preface to the *Madrigali guerrieri et amorosi*, but it was nevertheless fundamental to the composer's development in the decades following the exchange with Artusi. Although neither Claudio nor Giulio Cesare took up L'Ottuso's point, and although their famous claim that music should become the servant of the words may sound in fact like a relatively modest expansion of the Renaissance madrigal aesthetic, in which the music molds itself even more tightly to the text, Monteverdi's works, beginning around 1600, suggest otherwise. As I have argued, the apparently incongruous pairing of the *Scherzi*

99. Palisca, "The Artusi–Monteverdi Controversy," 149, notes that L'Ottuso is one of the few Italian writers on music to associate musical license with rhetorical figures.

musicali with the "Dichiaratione" can be read as a subtle indication that the terms of the debate had already shifted in a very different direction; even the fifth book of madrigals, long heralded as the finest expression of the classic madrigal, shows signs that the familial hierarchy that had governed text – music relations was undergoing analysis in light of Monteverdi's changing interpretation of "oratione."[100]

100. On the relationship between the *Scherzi* and the "Dichiaratione," see my "Claudio Monteverdi's *Ordine novo*," 301–2; for an analysis of the social structures invoked by Giulio Cesare's terms "serva" and "padrona," see Suzanne G. Cusick, "Gendering Modern Music: Thoughts on the Monteverdi – Artusi Controversy," *Journal of the American Musicological Society* 46 (1993), 1–25.

T W O

Toward a New Conception of the Madrigal Book: Aspects of Large-Scale Organization in the Fourth and Fifth Books

If the story of the early development of Monteverdi's thought regarding the *seconda prattica* remains almost entirely shrouded in the mists of a few laconic and imprecise texts, his fourth and fifth books of madrigals offer a glimpse of his changing aesthetic direction around the turn of the seventeenth century. Seen against the backdrop of the Artusi texts, these books may well offer evidence of the composer's initially tentative response to the theorist's criticisms, as well as a practical demonstration of the expressive freedom with which he treated contrapuntal technique. But considered in light of the works that precede them, and more importantly in comparison with one another, they attest to the enormous distance Monteverdi traversed in exploring not only the stylistic potential of the Renaissance madrigal, but also the possibilities offered by the madrigal book itself as a narrative and dramatic medium.

That the contents of the two volumes appear to look in opposite directions has long been recognized: the fourth book has a retrospective air and gathers a broad cross section of madrigals that fill the gap between it and the third, which preceded it by eleven years; the fifth contains forward-looking continuo madrigals as well as Monteverdi's pithy and almost recitational settings of selections from Battista Guarini's play *Il pastor fido*, which had held the interest of the Mantuan court throughout the 1590s, beginning with the earliest abortive attempts to produce the play in 1591.[1] As Tomlinson has argued, Monte-

---

1. For a summary of the history of *Il pastor fido* in Mantua, see Gary Tomlinson, *Monteverdi and the End of the Renaissance* (Berkeley and Los Angeles: The University of California Press, 1987), 114–18.

verdi's madrigals were not likely to have been used in the productions of the play itself; nonetheless, they have a strong "theatrical orientation" that makes them the natural forebears of the dramatic language that was to find its mature expression in *Arianna*. This is indeed convincing in light of the supple declarative language of the *Pastor fido* settings. But looking beyond the flexibility with which the music adapts itself to Guarini's speech rhythms, these madrigals also suggest ways in which Monteverdi's theatrical conception led him to transcend the boundaries of the single madrigal, deriving from the play not only the grouping of madrigals into cycles of adjacent texts, but also the juxtaposition of cycle against cycle and, breaking outside the given plot, even gathering disparate texts to create cycles whose coherence depends on a narrative continuity of the composer's own devising. From such an expanded perspective, the madrigal book no longer functions as a repository of unrelated pieces; rather, it acquires a central topic developed by a progression of "chapters," each comprising several individual madrigals, according to a dramatic logic.

I argue in this chapter that Monteverdi imposed this narrative coherence on the fifth book, selecting passages from the play that represent the essential psychological conflicts that drive its plot and expanding his subject with a group of lyric poems, also arranged as a narrative cycle. The suppleness of the musical language of the *Pastor fido* settings, essential to the psychological naturalism of *Arianna*, springs from precisely this larger conception of the madrigal not as an isolated unit but as a means to an end, as a component in an unfolding drama, just as the language of Arianna's lament finds its impetus in her story. It is in this sense that the fifth book belongs to the world of the theater and of the operas it precedes more than to that of the classical madrigal, represented by the fourth book. And in the same vein, the florid style and incipient formalism of the continuo madrigals prefigure the formal structures and style of *Orfeo* and parallel Monteverdi's contemporaneous experiments with canzonettas and other dramatic genres, the topic of the next chapter.

Narrative and Form in the Continuo Madrigals

Much has been written about the sudden appearance of schematic formal structures in Monteverdi's continuo madrigals. The refrains of "T'amo mia vita" and "Ahi come a un vago sol cortese giro" and the patterned organization of "Troppo ben può" have typically been viewed as a natural consequence of the introduction of the instrumental bass in the ensemble madrigal. But the presence of schematic form—at some times, as in "Troppo ben può," congruent with the poetic shape, and at others, as in both "T'amo" and "Ahi come a un vago," imposed upon it—has drawn widely divergent interpretations. It is seen as a sign of expressive sterility or of the loss of the musico-allegorical potential of the classical madrigal; or, more positively, as a harbinger of Baroque trio textures, concerto-ritornello technique, and rondo form.[2] The presence of semidramatic and schematic elements poses little problem in the continuo madrigals of the sixth book, where their intent seems clear, especially if they are read against the backdrop of similar techniques in *Orfeo*. In the fifth book, however, these more "modern"-sounding structures coexist with typical madrigalian elements in a relationship that clouds the distinction between the two.

The group of madrigals that concludes the fifth book is distinguished from the rest by technique—the basso continuo obbligato—and by poetic source: while the bulk of the collection is excerpted from Guarini's *Il pastor fido*, the texts for the last five are taken, with one anonymous exception, from the poet's *Rime* (table 1 in the prologue).[3] Their nondramatic origin stands in contrast to the dramatic context of the a cappella madrigals that precede them. In addition to their shared technical innovations and common literary origin, these five madrigals also form a continuous narrative group, unified by theme, textual connections, tonal center, melodic returns, and common aspects of texture and structure.[4]

Unlike the two *Pastor fido* cycles that form the core of the book, "Ecco Silvio" and "Ch'io t'ami," in which cyclical continuity originates with the play itself, the narrative unity of the continuo madrigal group results from the arrangement of texts that do not belong together in the poetic sources: Monteverdi reorders four madrigals from the *Rime*, nos. 110, 108, 70, and 112 in the

2. For the various interpretations, see for example Henry Prunieres, *Monteverdi: His Life and Work*, trans. by Marie D. Mackie (London: J. Dent, 1926, repr. Westport, Conn.: Greenwood Press, 1974), 41–46; Leo Schrade, *Monteverdi, Creator of Modern Music* (New York: W. W. Norton, 1950), 217–19; Alfred Einstein, *The Italian Madrigal*, trans. by Alexander H. Krappe, Roger H. Sessions, and Oliver Strunk (Princeton: Princeton University Press, 1971), 850–72; Nino Pirrotta, "Scelte poetiche di Monteverdi," *Nuova rivista musicale italiana* 2 (1968), 226–29; Nigel Fortune, "Monteverdi and the 'seconda prattica' ii: from Madrigal to Duet," in *The New Monteverdi Companion*, ed. Denis Arnold and Nigel Fortune (London: Faber and Faber, 1985), 203–10; Paolo Fabbri, *Monteverdi* (Turin: E. D. T., 1985), 90–94; Tomlinson, *Monteverdi*, 151–56; and Eric Chafe, *Monteverdi's Tonal Language* (New York: Schirmer, 1992), 117–25.

3. *Rime del molto illustre Signor Cavaliere Battista Guarini* (Venice: Ciotti, 1598); modern ed. in Battista Guarini, *Opere*, ed. Marziano Guglielminetti (Turin: U.T.E.T., 1971), 189–318.

4. The melodic similarities between the lines "Ah che piaga d'amor" and "Ah che piaga d'amore" in "Ahi come a un vago sol" and "E così a poco a poco" have been noticed, as have the formal parallels between the settings of the madrigals "Ah come vago sol cortese giro" and "E così a poco a poco": see Fabbri, *Monteverdi*, 93.

1598 edition, and inserts a text of unknown origin in the middle of the set. In the *Rime,* madrigals 110 and 112 belong to a group of three that treat the same subject ("Recidiva d'amore" [Relapse into love]), and 108, which bears the title "Fuga restia" [Reluctant escape], follows another poem on a similar topic, "Chi vuol aver felice e lieto il core," titled "Fuggasi amore" [Flee from love].

The narrative that results from Monteverdi's rearrangement forms a balanced scheme in which the outer madrigals, "Ahi come," "Troppo," and "E così," introduce, comment on, and bring to a close the main topic of the group, the poet's ambivalence upon considering a new love while still smarting from the wounds of an old one. The remaining two, "Amor, se giusto sei" and "T'amo mia vita," treat separately the causes of that ambivalence—the lover's suffering in the face of his lady's aloofness, and his delight at her declaration of love. The cycle is framed by the first sentence of "Ahi come a un vago sol cortese giro," which recalls a past love and introduces a new one, and, at the other end, by the closing gesture with which the last poem opens, "E così a poco a poco torno . . ." [And thus, little by little, I return . . .].

1

Cruda Amarilli, che col nome ancora
d'amar, ahi lasso! amaramente insegni;
Amarilli, del candido ligustro
più candida e più bella,
ma de l'aspido sordo
e più sorda e più fèra e più fugace;
poi che col dir t'offendo,
i' mi morrò tacendo.

> Cruel Amaryllis, who with your very name
> You teach, alas, bitterly to love;
> Amaryllis, whiter than white jasmine,
> and more beautiful,
> But more deaf than a deaf asp,
> and more cruel and fleeting;
> Since I offend you with my words,
> I will die silently.

2

O Mirtillo, Mirtillo, anima mia,
se vedessi qui dentro
come sta il cor di questa
che chiami crudelissima Amarilli,

so ben che tu di lei
quella pietà che da lei chiedi, avresti.
Oh anime in amor troppo infelici!
che giova a te, cor mio, l'esser amato!
che giova a me l'aver sì caro amante!
Perché, crudo destino,
ne disunisci tu, s'Amor ne strigne?
e tu, perché ne strigni,
se ne parte il destin, perfido Amore?

Oh, Mirtillo, Mirtillo my soul,
If you could see within me
How fares the heart of her whom
You call most cruel Amaryllis,
I know well that you would feel
For her the pity that you ask of her.
Oh, souls most unhappy in love!
What good is it, my heart, that you are loved?
What good is it for me to have such a dear lover?
Why, cruel fate, do you separate us, if Love brings us together?
And you, cruel Love, why do you bring us together, if Fate separates us?

3

Era l'anima mia
già presso a l'ultim'ore
e languia come langue alma che more;
quand'anima più bella, e più gradita
volse lo sguardo in sì pietoso giro,
che mi mantenne in vita.
Parean dir que' bei lumi:
"Deh, perché ti consumi?
Non m'è sì caro il cor, ond'io respiro,
come se' tu, cor mio;
se mori, ohimè, non mori tu, mor'io."

My soul was already
Near its final hour,
And languished as do dying souls;
When a soul more beautiful and more welcome
Turned its gaze with such a merciful turn
That it kept me alive.
Those lovely eyes seemed to say:

"Come, why do you languish?
The heart that keeps me breathing is not so dear to me,
As you are, my heart;
If you die, alas, it is not you, but me who dies.

4

Ecco, Silvio, colei che 'n odio hai tanto,
eccola in quella guisa
che la volevi a punto.
Bramastila ferir: ferita l'hai;
bramastila tua preda: eccola preda;
bramastila alfin morta: eccola a morte.
Che vuoi tu più da lei? che ti può dare
più di questo Dorinda? Ah garzon crudo!
Ah cor senza pietà! Tu non credesti
la piaga che per te mi fece Amore:
puoi questa or tu negar de la tua mano?
Non hai creduto il sangue ch'i' versava dagli occhi:
crederai questo, che 'l mio fianco versa!

Here she is, Silvio, the one whom you hate so much,
Here she is, just
As you have wanted her.
You wanted her wounded: you have wounded her;
You wanted her at last dead: here she is about to die.
What more do you want from her? What more can
Dorinda give you? Ah, cruel youth!
Ah, pitiless heart! You did not believe
That Love had wounded me for you:
Can you now deny this wound from your own hand?
You did not believe that I wept blood,
Now you will believe the blood that flows from my side!

5

Ma, se con la pietà non è in te spenta
gentilezza e valor, che teco nacque,
non mi negar, ti prego,
anima cruda sì, ma però bella,
non mi negar a l'ultimo sospiro
un tuo solo sospir. Beata morte,
se l'adolcissi tu con questa sola
dolcissima parola

voce cortese e pia:
"Va' in pace, anima mia!"

> But, if your native kindness and valor are not extinguished
> Within you along with mercy,
> Do not deny me, I beg you,
> Cruel but beautiful soul,
> Do not deny me, with my last breath,
> A single sigh from you. Blessed death,
> Were you to sweeten it with this single,
> Sweetest word,
> Gentle and pious utterance:
> "Go in peace, my soul!"

6

Dorinda, ah! diro "mia" se mia non sei
se non quando ti perdo e quando morte
da me ricevi, e mia non fosti allora
ch'i' ti potei dar vita?
Pur "mia" dirò, ché mia
sarai mal grado di mia dura sorte;
e, se mia non sarai con la tua vita,
sarai con la mia morte.

> Dorinda, alas! will I say "mine" even if you are not mine
> Except as I lose you, and as from me
> You receive your death, and as you were not mine
> When I could give you life?
> But "mine" I will call you, because mine
> You will be in spite of my harsh fate;
> And, if you will not be mine in life,
> You will be upon my death.

7

Ecco, piegando le ginocchia a terra,
riverente t'adoro
e ti cheggio perdon, ma non già vita.
Ecco gli strali e l'arco;
ma non ferir già tu gli occhi o le mani,
colpevoli ministri
d'innocente voler; ferisci il petto,
ferisci questo mostro,

di pietade e d'amore aspro nemico;
ferisci questo cor che ti fu crudo:
eccoti il petto ignudo.

> Here, bending my knee to the ground,
> I adore you reverently,
> And ask forgiveness, but yet not life.
> Here are the arrows and the bow;
> Do not wound the eyes, or the hand,
> Guilty agents
> Of an innocent will; wound the breast,
> Wound this monster,
> This harsh enemy of mercy and love;
> Wound this heart that was cruel to you:
> Here is my bare breast.

8

Ferir quel petto, Silvio?
Non bisognava agli occhi miei scovrirlo,
s'avevi pur desio ch'io tel ferissi.
O bellissimo scoglio,
già da l'onda e dal vento
de le lagrime mie, de' miei sospiri
sì spesso invan percosso,
è pur ver che tu spiri
e che senti pietate? o pur m'inganno?
Ma sii tu pure o petto molle o marmo,
già non vo' che m'inganni
d'un candido alabastro il bel sembiante,
come quel d'una fèra
oggi ingannato ha il tuo signore e mio.
Ferir io te? te pur ferisca Amore,
che vendetta maggiore
non so bramar che di vederti amante.
Sia benedetto il dì che da prim'arsi!
benedette le lagrime e i martíri!
di voi lodar, non vendicar, mi voglio.

> Wound that breast, Silvio?
> You should not have bared it to my gaze
> If you wanted me to wound it.
> Oh, most beautiful rock,

Once uselessly lashed by the waves and winds
Of my tears and my sighs,
Is it true that you breathe
And that you feel mercy? Or am I deceived?
Be you a soft chest or marble,
I must not be deceived by your resemblance to white alabaster
As your and my lord was today deceived by
My resemblance to a wild beast.
That I should wound you? Let Love wound you instead,
For greater revenge
I cannot imagine than to see you become a lover.
Let the day be blessed on which I first became enflamed!
Blessed be my tears and sufferings!
I want to sing your praises, not be avenged of you.

9

Ch'io t'ami, e t'ami più de la mia vita,
se tu nol sai, crudele,
chiedilo a queste selve,
che tel diranno, e tel diran con esse
le fère loro e i duri sterpi e i sassi
di questi alpestri monti,
ch 'i' ho sì spesse volte
inteneriti al suon de' miei lamenti.

That I love you, and love you more than my own life,
If you do not already know, cruel one,
Ask these woods,
And they will tell you, and along with them
The wild beasts and harsh brambles and stones
Of these craggy mountains will tell you,
Which I have so often
Softened with the sound of my laments.

10

Deh! bella e cara e sì soave un tempo
cagion del viver mio, mentre a Dio piacque,
volgi una volta, volgi
quelle stelle amorose,
come le vidi mai, così tranquille
e piene di pietà, prima ch'i' moia,
che il morir mi sia dolce.

E dritto è ben che, se mi furo un tempo
dolci segni di vita, or sien di morte
que' begli occhi amorosi;
e quel soave sguardo,
che mi scorse ad amare,
mi scorga anco a morire;
e chi fu l'alba mia,
del mio cadente dì l'espero or sia.

    Come, beautiful and beloved, at one time,
    As pleased God, reason for my life,
    Turn at least once, turn
    Those loving eyes
    Such as I never saw them, so tranquil
    And filled with mercy, before I die
    So that my death may be sweet.
    And it is right that, as once they were
    Signs of life, now they should signify death,
    Those beautiful loving eyes;
    And that sweet glance,
    Which saw me love,
    Should now see me die;
    And she who was my dawn,
    Should now be the sunset of my ebbing day.

11

Ma tu, più che mai dura,
favilla di pietà non senti ancora;
anzi t'inaspri più, quanto più prego.
Così senza parlar dunque m'ascolti!
A chi parlo, infelice? a un muto marmo!
S'altro non mi vuoi dir, dimmi almen: "Mori!"
e morir mi vedrai.
Questa è ben, empio Amor, miseria estrema,
che sì rigida ninfa
né mi risponda, e l'armi
d'una sola e sdegnosa e cruda voce
sdegni di proferire
al mio morir.

    But you, harsher than ever,
    Still feel no spark of pity;

Rather, you become harsher the more I beg.
Thus you listen to me without responding!
With whom am I speaking, wretch? With silent marble!
If you have nothing else to say to me, say at least: "Die!"
And you will see me die.
This is, cruel Love, extreme misery,
That such an unbending nymph
Should not answer me, and that
She should disdain to use the weapon of a single
Scornful and cruel word
Upon my death.

12

Che dar più vi poss'io?
Caro mio ben, prendete; eccovi il core,
pegno della mia fede e del mio amore.
E se per darli vita a voi l'invio,
no'l lasciate morire;
nudritel di dolcissimo gioire,
che vostr'il fece amor, natura mio.
Non vedete, mia vita,
che l'immagine vostr'è in lui scolpita?

What more can I give you?
My dear beloved, take it: here is my heart,
Token of my faith and of my love.
And if I send it to you to give it life,
Do not let it die;
Nourish it with sweetest joy,
For love made it yours, and nature mine.
Do you not see, my life,
That your image is sculpted upon it?

13

M'è più dolce penar per Amarilli,
che il gioir di mill'altre;
e se gioir di lei
mi vieta il mio destino, oggi si moia
per me pure ogni gioia.
Viver io fortunato
per altra donna mai, per altro amore?
né, volendo, il potrei,

né, potendo, il vorrei.
E, s'esser può che 'n alcun tempo mai
ciò voglia il mio volere
o possa il mio potere,
prego il cielo ed Amor che tolto pria
ogni voler, ogni poter mi sia.

It is sweeter to suffer for Amaryllis,
That to enjoy a thousand others;
And if fate
Forbids me to enjoy her, let today
All my joys die as well.
Should I ever
Live in the good fortune of another woman, another love?
I could not, were I willing;
I would not, were I able.
And, if it ever happened that at some point
I should desire such a thing,
Or that I could manage it,
I pray to heaven and to Love that I lose
Well before then all my desires and all my powers.

14

Ahi, com' a un vago sol cortese giro
de due begli occhi, ond'io
soffersi il primo, e dolce stral d 'amore,
pien d'un nuovo desio,
sì pronto a sospirar, torna il mio core!
Lasso, non val ascondersi ch'omai
conosco i segni, che'l mio cor m'addita
de l'antica ferita,
ed è gran tempo pur che la saldai:
Ah, che piaga d'amor non sana mai!

Alas, just as it was from the lovely single gentle glance
Of two beautiful eyes that I
Suffered my first sweet arrow of love,
Now, full of a new desire,
My heart is once again ready to sigh!
Wretch, there is no point in taking cover, for
I know the signs that my heart points out
Of the ancient wound,

And it has been a long time since I healed it:
Alas, for love's wound never heals.

15

Troppo ben può questo tiranno Amore,
poiché non val fuggire
a chi no'l può soffrire.
Quando i'penso talor com'arde, e punge,
i' dico: "Ah core stolto, non l'aspettar; che fai?
Fuggilo sì, che non ti prenda mai."
Ma non so com'il lusinghier mi giunge,
ch'io dico: "Ah core stolto,
perché fuggito l'hai?
Prendilo sì, che non ti fugga mai."

This tyrant Love is far too powerful,
For it is useless to flee from it
For those who cannot abide it.
When I think, at times, how it burns and stings,
I say: "Ah, foolish heart, do not wait for it, what are you doing?
Flee from it so that it may never catch you."
But I have no idea how that flatterer reaches me,
So that I say: "Ah, foolish heart,
Why did you flee from it?
Catch it, so that it may never flee from you."

16

Amor, se giusto sei,
fa che la donna mia
anch'ella giusta sia.
Io l'amo, tu il conosci, e ella il vede,
ma più mi strazia e mi trafigge il core,
e per più mio dolore
e per dispregio tuo, non mi da fede.
Non sostener, Amor, che nel tuo regno
là dov'io ho sparta fede mieta sdegno,
ma fa, giusto signore,
ch 'in premio del amor io colga amore.

Love, if you are fair,
Make it so that my lady
Be fair, as well.

I love her, as you know and as she can see,
But all the more she wounds and pierces my heart,
And to my greater suffering,
And with disrespect for you, she is not faithful to me.
Do not allow, Love, that in your kingdom
Where I have sowed my faith I should reap scorn,
But make it so, fair lord,
That in return for love I should reap love.

17

"T'amo, mia vita" la mia cara vita
dolcemente mi dice, e'n questa sola
sì soave parola par che trasformi lietamente il core,
per farmene signore.
O voce di dolcezza, e di diletto!
Prendila tosto, Amore;
stampala nel mio petto.
Spiri solo per lei l'anima mia;
"T'amo, mia vita" la mia vita sia.

"I love you, my life" my beloved life
Sweetly tells me, and with this single
Sweetest word she seems happily to transform her heart
And make me master of it.
O word of sweetness, and delight!
Catch it at once, Love;
Imprint it upon my heart.
Let my soul breathe for her alone;
Let "I love you, my life" be my life.

18

E così a poco a poco
torno farfalla semplicetta al foco,
e nel fallace sguardo
un'altra volta mi consum'e ardo:
Ah, che piaga d'amore
quanto si cura più tanto men sana.
Ch'ogni fatica è vana,
quando fu punto un giovinetto core
dal primo, e dolce strale;
chi spegne antico incendio il fa immortale.

And thus, little by little,
I return, simple-minded butterfly, to the flame,
And in the deceiving glance
Am once again consumed and burned:
Alas, for love's wound
Is least likely to heal when it is tended to.
For all efforts are in vain
When a youthful heart is pierced
By the first sweet arrow;
One who tries to put out an ancient fire makes it immortal instead.

19

Questi vaghi concenti
che l'augellett'intorno
vanno temprando a l'apparir del giorno
sono, cred'io, d'amor desiri ardenti;
sono pene e tormenti;
e pur fanno le selv'e'l ciel gioire
al lor dolce languire.
Deh! se potessi anch'io così dolce dolermi
per questi poggi solitari e ermi,
che quell'a cui piacer sola desio
gradiss'il pianger mio,
io bramerei sol per piacer a lei
eterni i pianti miei.

These lovely harmonies
That the birds all around
Temper to the rising dawn
Are, I believe, burning desires of love;
They are pain and sufferings;
And yet they gladden woods and air
With their sweet languishing.
O, were I able to suffer sweetly thus
Among these lonely remote hills,
So that she whom alone I wish to please
Were to appreciate my weeping,
I would wish, just to please her,
That my tears might be eternal.

The narrative structure is reinforced by textual parallels between madrigals. The strongest occur between the outer two, both titled "Recidiva d'amore" [Relapse into love] by Guarini. These two texts, and "Troppo ben può" as well, emphasize the poet's helpless return to love's perils (*"torna il mio core"* [my heart *returns*] in "Ahi," and "E così a poco a poco *torno* farfalla semplicetta al foco" [And thus, little by little, I *return*, simple-minded butterfly, to the flame]); in both it is the lover's look, the "vago sol cortese giro di due begli occhi" [lovely single gentle glance of two beautiful eyes], characterized in the last poem as a "fallace sguardo" [deceiving glance], that lures the poet back. In both, the love recalled is the youthful poet's first ("primo" [first] in "Ahi," and "giovinetto core" [youthful heart] in "E così"); and in both, love's arrow and its incurable wound are described in the same terms—as the "primo e dolce stral d'amore" [first sweet arrow of love] and "piaga d'amor non sana mai" [love's wound never heals], which becomes, in "E così," "piaga d'amore quanto si cura più tanto men sana" [love's wound is least likely to heal when it is tended to].

The continuation of the narrative, "Troppo ben può," expands on the ambivalence of the first text: although the poet may have wished to hide from love ("lasso, non val ascondersi" [wretch, there is no point in taking cover], in the first poem), there is no escaping it ("non val fuggire" [it is useless to flee from it]), and his "nuovo desio" [new desire] brings him back to it. Textual correspondences are less pronounced between "Troppo" and the other poems, although love's stinging and burning ("Quando i' penso talor com'arde, e punge" [when I think, at times, how it burns and stings]) recur in "E così" as the consuming flame to which the moth is drawn, as the piercing arrow that wounds the young man ("fu punto un giovinetto core dal primo, e dolce strale" [a youthful heart is pierced by the first sweet arrow]), and finally as the "antico incendio" [ancient fire] that becomes eternal. The "stral d'amore" [arrow of love] that wounds in "Ahi" may be presumed to be the same that had stung, and will sting again, in "Troppo ben può."

Whereas both "Ahi come a un vago" and "Troppo ben può" are first-person narratives with embedded passages of direct speech (the poet's own words to himself in "Troppo"), "Amor se giusto sei" and "T'amo mia vita" shift entirely to direct speech (with quotations of remembered speech in "T'amo"). "Troppo ben può" introduces Amore as a tyrannical agent who overpowers human judgment and coaxes the ambivalent poet back to love, and it is Amore whom the poet addresses in the third and fourth poems. "Amor se giusto sei" and "T'amo mia vita" together form a central block that may be read, within the narrative, as illustrating the more generalized assessments of the lover's condition offered in the other three poems—it is to these two madrigals that the

Table 2.1 Tonal characteristics of the continuo
madrigals in Book Five

Madrigal	Tonal characteristics
Ahi, come a un vago sol cortese giro	D-*durus* throughout
Troppo ben può	D-*durus*, plagal g-*mollis* close
Amor, se giusto sei	G-*durus* throughout
"T'amo mia vita"	D-*durus*, plagal g-*mollis* close
E così a poco a poco	d-*mollis* to g-*mollis*
Questi vaghi concenti	G-*durus* throughout

resigned opening, "E così a poco a poco" [and thus, little by little], of the last refers as a case in point. These madrigals exemplify the two conditions that engender the poet's ambivalence: the piercing torture of the beloved's rejection (recalling the wounds of the other poems in the line "ma più mi strazia e mi trafigge il core" [but all the more she wounds and pierces my heart]), and the complete pleasure, unmarred by the thought of consequences, with which he savors her profession of love and urges Amore to imprint it on his heart.

This web of narrative and textual connections is reflected in the way the group is unified by common modal features, in the distribution of formal and textural elements, and in melodic correspondences between two pairs of madrigals, "Ahi come a un vago" and "E così a poco a poco," and "Troppo ben può" and "T'amo mia vita" (table 2.1). The tonal layout of the cycle focuses on D and G and emphasizes the distinction, within these modal centers, between the *mollis* (flat) and *durus* (natural) forms.[5] The cycle moves from D-*durus*, the stable tonal center of "Ahi come," toward G, on which "E così" closes. Three of the madrigals, "Ahi," "Troppo," and "T'amo," center on D; "Amor, se giusto sei" is unambiguously in G-*durus* throughout; and "E così" opens in D but quickly abandons it in favor of G. Within the D madrigals G, and especially g-*mollis*, plays an important role; this is particularly true of the second and fourth, which end with plagal cadences (g–D) preceded by g-*mollis* pedals (example 2.1). In "Troppo," the plagal close at the end of the repeat of the second half of the last line, "che non ti prenda mai" [so that it may never catch you], comes after the true final cadence (at m. 77) as a cadential extension; in "T'amo" there is no double close, only the threefold reiteration of the last line, "'T'amo mia vita' la mia vita sia" [Let "I love you, my life" be my life], articulated by cadences on G, a, and the plagal close to D. As Eric Chafe has argued, the final section in "T'amo" recapitulates the harmonic structure of the entire setting

5. Chafe's analysis is laid out in *Monteverdi's Tonal Language*, 1–55.

Ex. 2.1. Bass parts, final cadences, "Troppo ben può" and "T'amo mia vita"

and reinforces the structural fourth and fifth degrees of the scale in a way that is remarkably modern. It also, equally importantly, brings back the bass part of the plagal cadence at the end of "Troppo." Monteverdi rarely uses closing plagal cadences in the fourth and fifth books (I count only two instances, in "Ah dolente partita" and "Era l'anima mia"), although they occur more frequently in his earlier publications, and "Troppo" and "T'amo" are the only cases in which he uses this particular bass formula.

The connection between the ambivalence of "Troppo ben può" and the apparently unclouded sweetness and delight of "T'amo mia vita" draws a parallel between "prendilo sì, che non ti fugga mai" [catch it, so that it may never flee from you] and "prendila tosto, Amore" [catch it at once, Love], highlighting the poet's earlier optimistic mood. It also undermines the ecstatic contemplation of the beloved's words by recalling that the object of attraction also engenders fear.

"T'amo mia vita" is framed by the poet's closing plea in "Amor se giusto sei," "that in return for love I should reap love" [ch'in premio del amor io colga amore], and by the opening line of the last poem, "And thus, little by little, I return, simple-minded butterfly, to the flame." The less than final quality of the cadence to D, which lacks melodic closure and cadential ornamentation, leads into the opening sonority of "E così," also on D, and suggests that this particular chapter of the narrative is not closed. Taken in context, the disembodied female voice in "T'amo" may be seen as the poet's wish come true—but also as a figment of his imagination, which conjures it and revels in it (she does not truly speak in the first person but only in his recollection).[6] Ultimately, of

6. The poem itself is of course gender-neutral. Among other female voices that are "mediated" by a male chorus speaking as narrator are those of the nymph in "Amor, dicea," the middle section of the "Lamento della ninfa" from the *Madrigali guerrieri et amorosi* (1638); and perhaps the most extreme case, Ergasto's lover in "Eccomi pronta ai baci" from the seventh book (1619), who is "represented" by three low male voices (two tenors and bass). The

course, it proves as fleeting as the "fallace sguardo" [deceiving glance] in which the poet consumes himself in flames of ecstasy.

The balanced tonal organization of the cycle, with its symmetrical arrangement on either side of the G-*durus* setting, is reinforced not only by direct quotations between madrigals, but also, in a more general way, by the distribution of vocal combinations over the span of the entire group. The most obvious parallel, again, occurs between the first and last pieces, both of which alternate long declamatory duet sections (tenors in "Ahi" and soprano–tenor in "E così") with commenting trios (two sopranos and bass in "Ahi"; and alto, tenor, and bass in "E così") (figure 2.1). Although the last madrigal does not employ the refrain technique of the first, the return of "Ahi, che piaga d'amore" [Alas, for love's wound], complete with its opening rhythmic motive, sequential repetition, and general melodic contour, can be seen as an extension of the earlier refrain that obviates the need for further reiteration (example 2.2a–b).

The three inner madrigals all incorporate solo passages within the polyphonic context. "Troppo" and "T'amo" do so in highly schematic fashion, although in the former the scheme is dictated by the text, and in the latter it is imposed upon the original poem by the composer (figure 2.2). "Amor, se giusto sei" is divided into two halves; the text does not suggest any particular pattern for the setting, and Monteverdi's division of it, while congruent with its

---

Fig. 2.1. Formal structure of "Ahi, come a un vago" and "E così a poco a poco"

"Ahi, come a un vago"		"E così a poco a poco"	
Duet (2T)	— mm. 1–23	Duet (ST)	— mm. 1–26
Trio (2S, B)	Refrain — mm. 24–32	Trio (ATB)	— mm. 27–35
Duet (2T)	— mm. 33–45	Duet (ST)	— mm. 36–57*
Trio (2S, B)	Refrain — mm. 46–51	Trio (ATB)	— mm. 57–62
Duet (2T)	— mm. 52–61	Tutti	— mm. 62–77
Tutti	Refrain — mm. 62–73		
Duet (2T)	— mm. 74–77		
Tutti	Refrain — mm. 78–91	*Opens with "Ahi" refrain.	

---

representation of female characters in Monteverdi's madrigals remains essentially unexplored in spite of recent studies devoted to the women in his operas: see Susan McClary, "Constructions of Gender in Monteverdi's Dramatic Music," in *Feminine Endings: Music, Gender, and Sexuality* (Minneapolis: University of Minnesota Press, 1991), 35–52; Suzanne G. Cusick, "There was not one lady who failed to shed a tear: Arianna's Lament and the Construction of Modern Womanhood," *Early Music* 21 (1994), 21–41; and, more recently, Wendy Heller, "Arcangela Tarabotti and Busenello's Octavia: Defending Women in The Opera in Venice," paper presented at the 1993 annual meetings of the Society for Seventeenth-Century Music in St. Louis and the American Musicological Society in Montreal.

Ex. 2.2. *(a)* "Ahi, come a un vago sol," mm. 24–29 and 65–71;
(b) "E così a poco a poco," mm. 36–41

syntax, seems to find little logical connection with it. His assignment of various solo voices and, later, of the entire ensemble to the poet's first person utterances is entirely in keeping with the aesthetics of the Renaissance madrigal, in which there is no attempt at character portrayal.[7] The apparently anomalous structure of this madrigal and its greater reliance on solo singing, however, seem to set it apart from the others and to reinforce its pivotal position within the cycle (figure 2.3 and example 2.3).

The balanced arrangement of this five-part commentary on the poet's "desiri ardenti" [burning desires] and their attendant "pene e tormenti" [pain and sufferings] (to paraphrase the summary offered in the last piece of the collection, "Questi vaghi concenti") reflects a concern with abstract musical architecture that is evident in such patterns as the refrain structures of "Ahi" and

7. Fabbri, *Monteverdi*, 92–93.

Fig. 2.2. Formal structure of "Troppo ben può" and
"T'amo mia vita"

A	ens	Troppo ben può questo tiranno amore	a
		poiché non val fuggire	b
		a chi no'l può soffrire.	b
B	solo	Quando i'penso talor com'arde, e punge,	c
		i' dico: "Ah core stolto,	d	5
	ens	non l'aspettar, che fai?	e
	T-refr	Fuggilo si che non ti prenda mai."	e
B'	solo	Ma non so com'il lusinghier mi giunge,	c
		ch'io dico: "Ah core stolto,	d
	ens	perché fuggito l'hai?	e	10
	T-refr	Prendilo sì che non ti fugga mai."	e
A	S¹*/	"T'amo mia vita" la mia cara vita	a
	ATB	dolcemente mi dice,* e'n questa sola	b
		sì soave parola*	b
		par che trasformi lietamente il core	c
		per farmene signore.*	c	5
B		O voce* di dolcezza e di diletto!	d
		Prendila tosto, Amore,	c
		stampala nel mio petto.	d
		Spiri solo per lei l'anima mia,	e
	R-Tutti	"T'amo mia vita" la mia vita sia.	e	10

* = refrain

Fig. 2.3. Structure of "Amor, se giusto sei"

S		Amor, se giusto sei	a
		fa che la donna mia	b
		anch'ella giusta sia.	b
B		—^Io l'amo, tu il conosci, e ella il vede	c
T		^ma più mi strazia e mi trafigge il core,	d	5
		e per più mio dolore	d
		e per dispregio tuo, non mi dà fede.	c
a5		Non sostener, Amor, che nel tuo regno	e
		là dov'io ho sparta fede mieta sdegno,	e
		ma fa, giusto signore,	d	10
		ch' in premio del amor io colga amore.	d

^ = strophic bass

Ex. 2.3. Bass pattern, "Amor, se giusto sei," mm. 13–32

∧ = beginning of strophic bass

"T'amo" and the symmetrical construction of "Troppo ben può." In addition to these large-scale and easily perceived formal elements, however, Monteverdi introduces another, less obvious, form-generating device: the strophic bass. In later works, such as "Addio Florida bella" and "Misero Alceo," from the sixth book, the bass helps to lend coherence to quasi-recitative sections by establishing a rigorous structure against which the vocal line can develop freely (figure 2.4 and example 2.4).[8]

Ex. 2.4. Bass pattern, *(a)* "Addio Florida bella"; *(b)* "Misero Alceo"

8. In *Orfeo* as well, the strophic bass plays a structural and allegorical role, both in the prologue and in the various canzonettas distributed throughout the rest of the opera. See,

Fig. 2.4. Structure of "Addio Florida bella" and
"Misero Alceo"

I (D)	⌐ "Addio Florida bella, il cor piagato	
	nel mio partir ti lascio, e porto meco	
T solo	la memoria di te, sì come seco	
	⌐ cervo trafitto suol lo strale alato."	
II (A)	⌐ "Caro mio Floro, addio; l'armato stato	5
	consoli Amor del nostro viver cieco:	
S solo	che se'l tuo cor mi resta, il mio vien teco	
	⌐ com'augellin che vola al cibo amato."	
	⌐ Così sul Tebro, allo spuntar del sole,	
Tutti	quinci e quindi confuso un suon s'udio	10
	⌐ di sospiri, di baci, e di parole.	
A2	⌐ "Ben mio, rimanti in pace." "E tu, ben mio,	
	⌐ vattene in pace, e sia quel che'l ciel vole."	
Tutti —	"Addio Floro (dicean), Florida addio."	

Tutti	⌐ Misero Alceo, dal caro albergo fore	
(D-A)	⌐ gir pur convienti, e ch'al partir t'apresti	
	⌐ "Ecco Lidia, ti lascio, e lascio questi	
	poggi beati, e lascio il core.	
	Tu, se di pari laccio e pari ardore	5
	meco legata fosti e meco ardesti,	
solo	fa che ne' duo talor giri celesti	
(E)	s'annidi e posi ov'egli vive e more.	
	Sì, mentre lieto il cor staratti accanto,	
	gl'occhi lontani da soave riso	10
	⌐ mi daran vita con l'umor del pianto."	
	⌐ Così disse il pastor dolente in viso:	
Tutti	la ninfa udillo: e fu in due parti intanto	
(A-D)	⌐ l'un cor da l'altro, anzi un sol cor, diviso.	

In "Addio Florida bella," the lovers' parting words are divided symmetrically between the two quatrains of the sonnet; in the first tercet, the narrator interrupts their dialogue, setting the stage for their encounter and mediating the remainder of their exchange. Monteverdi follows Marino's exploitation of

among the more recent studies, my "Claudio Monteverdi's *Ordine novo, bello et gustevole:* The Canzonetta as Dramatic Module and Formal Archetype," *Journal of the American Musicological Society* 45 (1992), 281–91, and Chafe, *Monteverdi's Tonal Language,* 126–58. On the concertato madrigals of the sixth book, see Schrade, *Monteverdi,* 284–86; Nino Pirrotta, "Monteverdi's Poetic Choices," in *Music and Culture in Italy from the Middle Ages to the Baroque* (Cambridge: Harvard University Press), 298–304; Chafe, *Monteverdi's Tonal Language,* 191–94 and 204–6; and Tomlinson, *Monteverdi and the End of the Renaissance,* 159–64.

the sonnet's dramatic potential, setting the dialogue as a small-scale *scena* consisting of a pair of strophic variations for solo voice (tenor first, then canto), introducing the five-part ensemble for the narrative voice, and retaining the identity of the two characters even in the closing tercet. The connection between musical and dramatic structure is emphasized by the deployment of the strophic bass in the two quatrains only, as well as by the transposition of the pattern from D to A for Florida's words, which introduces an element of harmonic tension between the lovers' statements and binds the musical architecture to the text. In "Misero Alceo," the solo lament, which unlike the dialogue in "Addio Florida bella" cuts across the sonnet form, unfolds freely over three statements of the bass. The central section is framed by symmetrical narrative choruses scored for the entire ensemble; and, as in "Addio Florida bella," the harmony revolves around a symmetrical circle-of-fifths arch from D to A and E and back to D, underscoring the dramatic and formal structure.

In the fifth book the most extensive bass patterns occur in "Ahi, come," where they provide a structural underpinning for the first three declamatory phrases of the opening duet but are abandoned for the continuation of the madrigal (example 2.5). A faint echo of this organization returns in the first two phrases of "E così": although there is no repeated bass part, both phrases occur over static harmonies that oscillate between D and A in the first, and between D and G in the second. In "Amor," the only other member of the group in which Monteverdi uses a strophic bass, the pattern is not central to the structure—it occurs in a highly modified form only for the solo bass and tenor sections in the first part, and not for the opening soprano solo. In the second half there is an abundance of revoiced text repetitions, but there is no particular schematic structure.

Ex. 2.5. Strophic bass pattern, "Ahi, come a un vago sol," mm. 1–19

∧ = beginning of strophic bass
* = break from strophic bass

The strophic basses of Book Five are put to limited use, and they do not provide the structural backbone for entire compositions. Nevertheless, their use does point toward the more fully worked out strophic variations of *Orfeo*, such as those of the prologue and of "Possente spirto," and toward the madrigals of the sixth and later books. The use of strophic variations as structural foundations also aligns the continuo madrigals of the fifth book with similar developments in the canzonettas and other works of the first decade of the century. The continuo madrigals share with the canzonettas of the *Scherzi* both a concern with block forms and ritornello structures and an overarching formal plan that relates corresponding elements on either side of a central section, a scheme that returns in parts of *Orfeo*, in "Misero Alceo," and, in what is perhaps its most famous occurrence, in the "Lamento della ninfa" from the *Madrigali guerrieri et amorosi* of 1638.[9]

The cyclical organization of the continuo madrigals fits within a larger narrative structure that spans the entire book. On the simplest level, the structure of Book Five depends on the progressive arrangement of madrigals for five, six, and nine voices; this is reinforced by their grouping according to scoring—a cappella madrigals first, then the works with continuo, and finally one double-choir madrigal that requires an instrumental *sinfonia*. Congruent with these categories is the division of the texts into two contrasting groups, the first dominated by excerpts from Guarini's *Pastor fido*, and the second, which corresponds to the continuo madrigals, consisting entirely of short, independent *madrigali*. The consistent exploration of amorous suffering, the ambiguity it engenders, and the helplessness of men and women in the face of Love's torments bridges all of these formal and genre-based groupings, establishing dramatic continuity over the entire volume.

The principal material for the a cappella madrigals is taken from Battista Guarini's *Il pastor fido*.[10] As table 2.2 shows, the composer selected from the play two extended continuous excerpts, one from the fourth act beginning at "Ecco Silvio" (scene 9, lines 1237–1305), and another, "Ch'io t'ami," from the third (scene 3, lines 296–362). In addition, Monteverdi also set three isolated

9. See Ossi, "Claudio Monteverdi's *Ordine novo*," 292–301, and Schrade, *Monteverdi*, 219–23.

10. Monteverdi was among the first composers to rely so heavily on Guarini's play; in 1600 Filippo di Monte devoted to it his entire second book for seven voices, which he titled *Musica sopra Il pastor fido*. Monte had set texts from the play as early as 1590, when he included a setting of "Cruda Amarilli" in his fourteenth book for five voices. See Brian Mann, *The Secular Madrigals of Filippo di Monte, 1521–1603*, Studies in Musicology, no. 64 (Ann Arbor: U.M.I. Research Press, 1983), 60–61.

Table 2.2 Tonal Groupings of the a cappella madrigals in Book Five

Madrigal	Source	Characters	System	Finals
⌐ Cruda Amarilli	act 1/2, 272–79	Mirtillo/Amarilli	durus	g
└ O Mirtillo	act 3/4, 506–18			d
⌐ Era l'anima mia	*Rime*, no. 65	[none]	mollis	
⌐ Ecco, Silvio	act 4/9, 1237–1305	Dorinda/Silvio	mollis	d
│ Ma, se con la pietà				d
│ Dorinda, ah! dirò "mia"				g
│ Ecco, piegando le ginocchia				g
└ Ferir quel petto, Silvio?				g
⌐ Ch'i' t'ami, e t'ami più de	act 3/3, 296–362	Mirtillo	mollis	g
│ la mia vita				
│ Deh! bella e cara e sì soave			mollis	g
⌐ Ma tu, più che mai dura			mollis/	g
¦			durus	
∟ Che dar più vi poss' io?	anon.	[none]	durus	d
└ M' è più dolce il penar	Act 3/6, 930–43	Mirtillo	durus	g

passages: the famous pair "Cruda Amarilli" and "O Mirtillo" (respectively from act 1, scene 2, lines 272–79; and act 3, scene 4, lines 506–18), and "M'è piú dolce il penar per Amarilli" (act 3, scene 6, lines 930–43). Punctuating these selections from *Il pastor fido* are two independent *madrigali*, the anonymous "Che dar piú vi poss'io" and "Era l'anima mia" from Guarini's *Rime* (no. 65). These thirteen madrigals fall into a balanced three-part arrangement that opens with a dialogue between Mirtillo and Amarilli, turns to Dorinda and Silvio for the central five-part group "Ecco Silvio" (introduced by "Era l'anima mia"), and closes with Mirtillo's three-part cycle "Ch'io t'ami" (which forms a unit with "Che dar più vi poss'io" and "M'è più dolce il penar"), returning to the themes introduced in the opening dialogue.

Narrative in the A Cappella Madrigals

Like the continuo madrigals, the a cappella pieces are arranged in a logical progression that explores various aspects of love's "pene e tormenti." Monteverdi's selections encapsulate the principal themes of Guarini's play: unwavering devotion, represented by Mirtillo, Amarilli, and Dorinda; and the moment of epiphany, brought about by fate, that unites two lovers, seen in the fateful hunting accident that brings Dorinda and Silvio together. The narrative structure focuses on the contrasts presented by the two main couples of the play: throughout Book Five, Mirtillo and Amarilli remain in a state of seemingly hopeless alienation, while Dorinda and Silvio, kept apart by Silvio's indifference toward love, are seen just at the cathartic moment that unites them. The complications of the plot are kept entirely in the background, although they could have been supplied by anyone familiar with the play, which had been the subject of widespread debate and was lavishly produced at Mantua in the late 1590s. Similarly, Monteverdi avoids the comic aspects of the play, embodied by Corisca, who pursues Mirtillo, and by Satiro, her lover. Rather, the passages excerpted focus on the psychological states of the principal characters: Mirtillo and Dorinda are obsessed lovers, whose passion is beyond rationality, even to the point of relishing their amorous suffering; Silvio's guilt at having wounded Dorinda brings him out of his childishly self-indulgent preoccupation with the hunt, humanizing him and making him realize his love for her (figuratively at least, he becomes a man at this point); and Amarilli represents love tempered by reason and duty.

Although "O Mirtillo" appears to be Amarilli's response to her lover's "Cruda Amarilli," the exchange is actually a composite dialogue whose components are drawn from widely separated parts of the play. Their juxtaposition, however, does no effective violence to Guarini's treatment of the characters or to the dramatic function of the two texts.[11] Throughout much of the play, Mirtillo and Amarilli mirror one another: on the one side, a blindly passionate Mirtillo pursues Amarilli, remaining devoted to her but unaware of her love and uncomprehending of the circumstances that prevent her from reciprocating his advances; on the other, an equally helpless but knowing Amarilli, in love with Mirtillo but, unlike him, aware that her feelings are reciprocated and yet prevented by fate from revealing them to him. In the original context for the two opening madrigals, neither character addresses the other directly: both excerpts are taken from monologues, and this heightens the alienation of Monteverdi's artificial dialogue, in which the lovers speak past one another and which stands in contrast to the real dialogue that occurs between Silvio and Dorinda.

Monteverdi selects Mirtillo's lines primarily for his impassioned righteous anger at Amarilli's perceived cruelty ("Cruda Amarilli" and "Ma tu, piú che mai dura"), but also for the range of his emotions, which run from tender

11. In a different reading of these two pieces, Suzanne G. Cusick, in "Gendering Modern Music: Thoughts on the Monteverdi–Artusi Controversy," *Journal of the American Musicological Society* 46 (1993), 22, argues that Monteverdi's juxtaposition of the two excerpts is a "misreading" of Guarini's play that enables him to represent modern music as a "union of opposites."

recollection (as in the entreaties of "Deh! bella e cara") to steadfast resolution and resignation (in "M'è più dolce il penar").[12] "Cruda Amarilli" is Mirtillo's first entrance and sets the tone for his condition through most of the play: his desire for Amarilli is unfulfilled, and he cannot approach her; in the words of his companion Ergasto, "in chiuso foco e' si consuma e tace" [he is silently consumed by an inner fire]. When he voices his feelings for the first time, he does so out of necessity, because he has heard of her impending marriage to Silvio. Mirtillo's opening monologue on what he perceives as Amarilli's cruelty sets the tone for his later expostulations: she is comparable to jasmine in purity, and yet more cruel, deaf, and fleeting than an asp. The woods and the mountains pay more heed to his suffering and offer more sympathy than she does, and they will bear testimony to his pain. His condition has not changed by the time he confronts her in the third scene of the third act, from which Monteverdi excerpts "Ch'io t'ami." He has no idea that she loves him, and he addresses her in terms that are a variation on "Cruda Amarilli": she is silent as stone, still cruel and deaf, and he again invokes the woods and the mountains as his witnesses.

"O Mirtillo" opens Amarilli's monologue after he confronts her during the *gioco della cieca.* Face to face, Amarilli rebukes him: she rejects his advances and sends him away, telling him that he should take consolation from the knowledge that unhappy lovers are legion. After his departure, however, her long soliloquy, beginning with "O Mirtillo," is a full-fledged declaration of love and reveals the hidden drama that Mirtillo cannot see.

The connection between "Cruda Amarilli" and "O Mirtillo," however distant the two texts may be in the play, is therefore not so far-fetched as a superficial glance might suggest. "O Mirtillo" is indeed a response to "Cruda Amarilli," the refrain that Mirtillo has sung in nearly unaltered form since his first appearance. By bringing the two together, Monteverdi has in essence collapsed the plot, representing the essential nature of their relationship.

Before shifting to the dialogue between Dorinda and Silvio, Monteverdi inserts "Era l'anima mia," which introduces its principal themes. Guarini's *madrigale* draws on a familiar *topos:* the poet's soul, overcome with amorous suffering, lies *in extremis* when the object of her desire, an "anima più bella, e più gradita" [a more beautiful soul, and more pleasing], turns his gaze upon her

---

12. In the play, Mirtillo fulfils a sometimes ambiguous role, taking on the characteristics of a comic character (as in his subterfuges to steal a kiss from Amarilli during the "gioco della cieca"). See Angelini, *Il Seicento,* 31. This is in keeping with his double identity as a low character of hidden noble birth.

and is moved to declare his own love. The sight of the lover's impending death precipitates the beloved's epiphany, and his love revives her moribund spirit.[13]

The incident in act 4, scenes 8 and 9, in which Dorinda is wounded by Silvio's arrow, elaborates on this theme. Silvio is alone in the woods, where he has gone hunting; Dorinda, in order to follow him, has dressed herself in a wolf's skin. Silvio, seeing a movement in the bushes, mistakes her for a real quarry and shoots her with an arrow. When he realizes that it is not a wolf that he has shot, he assumes he has wounded a shepherd, and his first reaction is guilt at having spilled another man's blood ("Io dunque reo de l'altrui sangue? Io dunque cagion de l'altrui morte?" [Am I thus guilty of spilling someone else's blood? Am I the cause of someone else's death?]). He then recognizes Dorinda and is horrified. He is tempted to run but cannot, held back by an impulse he does not understand:

> Fuggi la pena meritata, Silvio,
> di quella vista utrice;
> fuggi il giusto coltel de la sua voce.
> Ah! che non posso; e non so come o quale
> necessità fatale
> a forza mi ritegna e mi sospinga
> più verso quel che più fuggir devrei.

>   Flee from the well-deserved punishment, Silvio,
>   of that reproachful look;
>   flee the righteous knife of her voice.
>   Alas, I cannot; and I know not how, or what
>   fateful urge
>   forcefully holds me back and pushes me
>   toward that which I most should flee.

Linco, who has come to Dorinda's rescue and has recognized Silvio's arrow, is quick to draw the moral of this "accidente sì mostruoso e novo" [accident so monstrous and unprecedented]:

> Credi tu, garzon vano,
> che questo caso a caso oggi ti sia
> così incontrato? Oh come male avvisi!
> Senza nume divin, questi accidenti
> sì monstruosi e novi
> non avvengono agli uomini. Non vedi

---

13. The text is actually gender-neutral.

che 'l cielo è fastidito
di cotesto tuo tanto
fastoso insopportabile disprezzo
d'amor, del mondo e d'ogn'affetto umano?

> Do you think, vain youth,
> that this has befallen you today
> by accident? You are much mistaken!
> Without divine will, such accidents,
> so monstruous and unprecedented,
> do not happen to people. Do you not see
> that the heavens are displeased
> with your
> haughty and unbearable disdain
> for love, the world, and every human emotion?

Dorinda then addresses Silvio, reminding him of his power over her in life and death. It is at this point that Monteverdi picks up the dialogue with "Ecco, Silvio, colei che 'n odio hai tanto." Dorinda's physical wound reflects Love's wound; her blood is a vivid counterpart to the tears that Silvio had ignored. On the point of death, she asks for one last kind word from him:

> *Beata morte,*
> *se l'addolcissi tu con questa sola*
> *voce cortese e pia:*
> *"Va in pace, anima mia!"*

> Blissful death,
> if you were to sweeten it with this single
> blessing, kind and pious:
> "Go in peace, my soul!"

Silvio is overcome by guilt; his mind has been prepared by his unsettling "dialogue" with Echo in the the first part of scene 8 that foretold his impending capitulation to Love, and Linco's admonishments have driven home the idea that a divine will, displeased with his disdainful attitude toward human emotions, is behind his fateful error. He is ready to declare his love for her, and he does so, offering his own breast for her to strike; she refuses. Silvio then takes her home and cures her wounds, transformed from indifferent youth into lover.[14]

14. See Jackson I. Cope, *The Theater and the Dream: From Metaphor to Form in Renaissance Drama* (Baltimore: The Johns Hopkins University Press, 1973), 261–66, for an interpretation

The parallels between "Era l'anima mia" and this brief excerpt are evident not only in the way the situation itself develops, but also in some textual correspondences between the play and the *madrigale*. Dorinda addresses Silvio as "anima cruda, sì, ma però bella" [cruel soul, but beautiful nonetheless], just as the lover in "Era l'anima mia" was described as an "anima più bella, e più gradita" [a more beautiful, and more pleasing, soul]," and in both the madrigal and the play the indifferent lover's sudden change of heart is expressed using similarly chiastic constructions.

> *Non m'è sì caro il cor, ond'io respiro,*
> *come sei tu, cor mio;*
> *se mori, ohimè, non mori tu, mor'io.*

>> The heart with which I breathe is not so dear to me
>> as you are, my heart;
>> if you die, alas, it is not you who dies, but me.

> *Pur mia dirò, che mia*
> *sarai mal grado di mia dura sorte;*
> *e, se mia non sarai con la tua vita,*
> *sarai con la mia morte.*

>> I will call you mine, since
>> you will be mine in spite of my hard fate;
>> and, if you will not be mine with your life,
>> you will be mine with my death.

Monteverdi contrasts this moment of catharsis and rapid development with the stasis of the other couple's alienation. Mirtillo's three-part cycle, "Ch'io t'ami," extends the themes set forth in "Cruda Amarilli." Unlike "Cruda," Mirtillo's opening soliloquy "Ch'io t'ami" addresses Amarilli directly. What passes between the two in act 3, however, cannot be said to be properly a dialogue comparable to that between Silvio and Dorinda. Mirtillo's lines are excerpted from a longer speech in which he pleads his case after Amarilli has, in essence, told him that it is useless for him to speak:

> *Per levar te d'errore e me d'impaccio,*
> *son contenta d'udirti;*
> *ma ve', con queste leggi:*
> *di' poco, e tosto parti, e più non torna.*

---

of the incident as a "fortunate fall," drawing on a tradition of miraculously cured wounds from Homer to Ariosto.

To cure you of your error, and to extricate myself,
I'll be glad to hear you out;
but, be warned, these are the rules:
say little, leave immediately, and don't come back.

As far as he knows, Mirtillo might as well still be speaking to the woods and the mountains; his terms remain those of "Cruda Amarilli." In reality, of course, Amarilli has just given him the opportunity to make his case and thus to begin turning the events toward their inevitable conclusion. In this regard, the "Ch'io t'ami" cycle occupies a comparable position to that of "Ecco Silvio": both are pivotal in the development of the situations surrounding their characters; and because the fates of the two couples are intertwined, the two events bear directly on one another.

After Mirtillo's impassioned pleas, the opening rhetorical question of the madrigal "Che dar più vi poss'io?" [What more can I give you?] may be taken in several ways. Like "Era l'anima mia," it may function independent of the dramatic texts as a commentary on the lovers' condition in the face of their mutual demands. It may also be seen as an extension of the characters's words, either as another expression of Mirtillo's frustration, or as a reiteration of Amarilli's unspoken feelings, recalling her "O Mirtillo"—"I may appear more cruel than ever, but what more can I give you? Here is my heart." Although not derived from the play, its apparent response to what precedes it suggests a parallel with the dialogue that opens the book and lends an element of symmetry to the first and third units in the collection.

> *Che dar più vi poss'io?*
> *Caro mio ben, prendete; eccovi il core,*
> *pegno della mia fede e del mio amore.*
> *E se per darli vita a voi l'invio,*
> *no'l lasciate morire;*
> *nudritel di dolcissimo gioire,*
> *che vostr'il fece amor, natura mio.*
> *Non vedete, mia vita,*
> *che l'immagine vostr'è in lui scolpita?*

> > What more can I give you?
> > My dear love, take it; here is my heart,
> > token of my faith and of my love.
> > And if, in order to give it life, I send it to you,
> > do not let it die;
> > let sweetest joy nourish it,

because love made it yours, and nature mine.
Do you not see, my life,
that your image has been carved into it?

The impression of continuity between the *Pastor fido* excerpts and this anonymous text is reinforced by the next madrigal, "M'è più dolce il penar per Amarilli," which brings to a close both the Mirtillo–Amarilli sequence and the *Pastor fido* portion of the book by summarizing Mirtillo's resolve to continue loving Amarilli regardless of the hopelessness of his situation. In the scheme of Monteverdi's condensed plot, this excerpt carries multiple significance. First, it is taken from a conversation between Mirtillo and Corisca, the wanton nymph who pursues him. Corisca makes no appearance in Monteverdi's book, so this excerpt introduces, if only obliquely, the other important plot line and theme in the play. Second, it confirms Mirtillo's constancy: he rejects Corisca's advances, and the purely sensual aspect of love that they represent, in favor of an unfulfilled, but higher, love. Finally, the excerpt establishes the dual nature of love — its sufferings bring a kind of pleasure that makes amorous pain inflicted by one's beloved preferable to satisfaction with another. This mood of "dolce penare" [sweet suffering] connects the *Pastor fido* cycles to the ambivalent view of love that is presented in the continuo madrigals and is eventually summarized in "Questi vaghi concenti."

The dramatic plan of the a cappella madrigals is supported by their grouping according to modal characteristics (table 1 in the prologue). Eric Chafe has noted the overall modal symmetry of the entire book, in which the only madrigals in which Monteverdi shifts from one system to the other (the cycle "Ch'io t'ami," which shifts from *mollis* to *durus*) are also placed roughly at the center of the collection, flanked by eight pieces on either side. In the first eight, *mollis* settings predominate (six); in the second, the lion's share (seven) goes to *durus* pieces.[15] Although such a symmetrical scheme is indeed one aspect of the design of the collection, considerations of dramatic structure seem equally, if not more, likely to have governed the distribution of modal finals. The first pair is in *durus* modes (g and d); this is justified by Mirtillo's harsh tone and by the apparently unbridgeable distance between him and Amarilli. The change of system from *durus* to *mollis* introduced by "Era l'anima mia" defines the transition from one couple to the other, and the Silvio–Dorinda cycle is entirely in *mollis* (d for the first two, then g), reflecting the conciliatory tone of their interaction. The shifting quality of Mirtillo's three madrigals reflects the shift in

15. Chafe, *Monteverdi's Tonal Language*, 105–6.

his tone, from the opening entreaties of "Ch'io t'ami" to the indignation of "Ma tu più che mai dura," which returns to the g-*durus* of "Cruda Amarilli." The last two pieces, "Che dar più" and "M'è più dolce," are both *durus*, on d and g. Although their texts return to an apparently conciliatory tone (already seen in "Ch'io t'ami"), their modal finals parallel, in reverse order, those of the opening dialogue. The d-*durus* mode of "Che dar più" reinforces the impression that it functions similarly to Amarilli's "O Mirtillo," as a response to his entreaties and accusations. And, in spite of the difference in emotional quality, Mirtillo's original grimly steadfast resolve echoes throughout "M'è più dolce." Its *durus* setting recalls his impassioned opening madrigal and underscores his rejection of Corisca. The hint of "sweet suffering" [dolce penar] foreshadows the ambivalent eroticism of the continuo madrigals, in which G figures prominently, and looks to "Questi vaghi concenti," with which "M'è più dolce il penar" shares the g-*durus* tonality that Monteverdi after Book Five increasingly associated with the lighter side of amorous pursuit.[16]

Direct textual connections similar to those found among the continuo madrigals are less necessary in the a cappella madrigals because most are set within continuous dramatic units. A number of textual and musical correspondences do, however, strengthen the unity of the entire volume. In the most general terms, the last piece of the collection, "Questi vaghi concenti," looks back over the madrigals that precede it and summarizes their themes. Its rather mechanical form (two seven-line clauses, with the identical rhyme schemes *abbaacc, deeddff*) and derivative imagery suggest that, unlike the rest of the texts, it was written as *poesia per musica* specifically to fulfill its function as the *envoi* of the collection.

> *Questi vaghi concenti*
> *che l'augellett'intorno*

16. Chafe, *Monteverdi's Tonal Language*, 116, makes this point. Cleffing follows a pattern that is similar to, although not exactly congruent with, the modal grouping. The entire "Ecco Silvio" cycle is in *chiavette*, and Mirtillo's entire set, from "Ch'io t'ami" through "M'è più dolce il penar," is in ordinary clefs. The clefs of the opening pieces, however, are not so clearly distributed: "Cruda Amarilli" is in high clefs; "O Mirtillo" follows the standard disposition of c- and f-clefs. The difference in characters may account for the change, although Monteverdi does not follow the same pattern for Dorinda and Silvio and it is not reflected in Mirtillo's later pleas. More troubling, however, is the disposition of "Era l'anima mia," which follows the same pattern as "O Mirtillo." This may reflect the introductory function of the *madrigale* "Era l'anima," and it may also provide an element of continuity across the various cycles. In this regard, the shared cleffing functions similarly to the d modal final that "Era l'anima" has in common with "O Mirtillo" and, later in the volume, to the g-*mollis* of "Ferir quel petto?" that is carried over into the "Ch'io t'ami" cycle.

vanno temprando a l'apparir del giorno
sono, cred'io, d'amor desiri ardenti;
sono pene e tormenti;
e pur fanno le selv'e'l ciel gioire
al lor dolce languire.
Deh! se potessi anch'io
così dolce dolermi
per questi poggi solitari e ermi
che quell'a cui piacer sola desio
gradiss'il pianger mio,
io bramerei sol piacer a lei
eterni I pianti miei.

> These lovely harmonies
> that the songbirds all around
> are creating as daylight appears
> are, I believe, burning, amorous desires;
> they are pains and torments;
> and yet they make the woods and sky rejoice
> with their sweet languishing.
> Ah, if I too were able
> to lament so sweetly
> on these solitary and deserted hills
> that the one woman whose pleasure I have at heart
> took delight in my weeping,
> I would desire, only to please her,
> that my sorrows were eternal.

Its opening line, "Questi vaghi concenti" [these lovely harmonies], looks at once backward and forward, seemingly referring to the pieces that precede it and at the same time to its own modern *concento* of instrumental and vocal forces. The sylvan imagery of the first half recalls the *selve* that bear witness to Mirtillo's sufferings and that are the setting for much of *Il pastor fido*. The lovers' desires and sufferings, heard in the preceding madrigals, are echoed by those of the songbirds, whose erotic expression enlivens the woods and the sky and is, just like the madrigals themselves, a source of pleasure. In the second part, the composer-narrator adds his own voice to those heard earlier, taking up the themes of sweet lamenting (his "dolce dolermi" [sweet pain] recalls Mirtillo's "dolce penar" [sweet suffering]) and eternal suffering devotion ("io bramerei sol per piacer a lei eterni i pianti miei" [I would desire, only to please her, that my sorrows were eternal]) that form the backbone of the entire collection. The large vocal requirements of Monteverdi's setting (two ensembles, for four and five voices, from which various soloists are drawn), as well as the instrumental *sinfonia* that opens the piece and returns to separate the first part from the second, give it the character of a chorus closing a theatrical performance, like those that close each act of Guarini's play.

Other correspondences, like the well-known parallel between the setting of "ferisci" in "Ecco, piegando" and "ferir" in "Ferir quel petto, Silvio," which follows it, function on a more localized level.[17] Although in the *Pastor fido* excerpts such textual parallels originate in the dramatic continuity of the dialogue, there are other instances in which the similarity between two texts is the result of Monteverdi's own design; as we have seen, this is the case for the continuo madrigals, where narrative continuity may have been the main criterion guiding the selection and placement of the individual poems.

Elsewhere Monteverdi seems to have taken a stronger hand, intervening in the texts themselves to establish correspondences where none existed. Such is the case with the insertion, in "Ma, se con la pietà," of the antepenultimate line, "dolcissima parola" [sweetest word]. It has been noted that the added verse disrupts the syntax and adds an unnecessary rhyme;[18] the alliteration it introduces (*addolcissi—dolcissima*) may make up for its awkwardness. More importantly, however, the insertion looks forward to a similar passage in "T'amo mia vita," which the modified version of "Ma, se con la pietà" parallels almost exactly.

Beata morte,	*"T'amo mia vita" la mia cara vita*
se l'addolcissi tu con questa sola	*dolcemente mi dice, e'n questa sola*
dolcissima parola,	*sì soave parola*
voce cortese e pia:	*par che trasformi lietamente il core,*
"Va' in pace, anima mia!"	*per farmene signore.*
O voce di dolcezza e di diletto!	

Blissful death,	"I love you my life" my dear life
If you were to sweeten it with	sweetly tells me, and in this single
this single	sweet word
sweetest of words,	she seems to transform happily her
kind and pious blessing:	heart
"Go in peace, my soul!"	to make me its master.
O words of sweetness and delight!	

17. Fabbri, *Monteverdi*, 84.

18. Stanley Appelbaum, preface to *Madrigals, Books IV and V,* by Claudio Monteverdi (New York: Dover, 1986). Although it is possible that the line belongs to a now lost version

The added rhyme *(sola / parola)* links an *endecasillabo* with a *settenario,* just as it does in "T'amo mia vita," and in both poems this couplet is followed by another on a different rhyme. Other similarities reinforce the connection between the *Pastor fido* excerpt and the madrigal: "dolce" pervades both *(addolcissi— dolcissima;* and *dolcemente—soave—dolcezza),* and in both passages "parola" [word] and "voce" [voice, but also utterance] refer to an imaginary quotation, the lover's words, remembered in "T'amo" and hoped for in "Ma, se con la pietà."

Monteverdi reinforces this textual parallel with similar settings. The melodic lines resemble one another, the two passages share a similar rhythmic shape, and, although in "Ma, se con" the line in question is given to the high voices and in "T'amo" its counterpart is assigned to the low-voice ensemble that functions as narrator, the corresponding sections resemble one another in texture (example 2.6). Finally, in both pieces Monteverdi makes extensive use of structural refrains, "beata morte" [blessed death] in the second half of "Ma, se con la pietà" and "T'amo mia vita" throughout the continuo madrigal. The climactic closing sections of the two madrigals grow out of these refrains, and both end with the beloved's words.

The likelihood that the emendation of the *Pastor fido* excerpt was modeled on the madrigal text raises the possibility that the composition of the two pieces may have been linked. Thus, either the continuo madrigal predates its counterpart, or the two were conceived at the same time, possibly with a view to their eventual placement within the fifth book. Artusi's second volume, finished as we have seen by summer 1602, provides a *terminus ante quem* for "Ma, se con la pietà," which the theorist criticizes along with "Era l'anima mia." [19] Unlike the latter, "Ma, se con la pietà" was not discussed in the exchange of letters between Artusi and Ottuso, which had taken place by 1599, but only in the main body of the treatise, which was drafted after the correspondence. This leaves open the dating of "Ma, se con la pietà," but it seems probable that it, together with "T'amo mia vita," was written sometime between 1599 and the completion of the treatise. [20] The connection between them also places Monte-

---

of Guarini's play, the hypothesis that it is Monteverdi's is consistent with its awkward placement and with the composer's willingness to modify the poetic material to suit his needs. On this point see Pirrotta, "Monteverdi's Poetic Choices," and Tomlinson, "Via naturale all'immitatione."

19. *Seconda parte dell'Artusi* (Venice: Vincenti, 1603), 25.

20. This range of dates is consistent with those proposed by Tomlinson for the entire "Ecco Silvio" cycle. See *Monteverdi,* 111.

Ex. 2.6. (a) "Ma, se con," mm. 49–55; (b) "T'amo mia vita," mm. 11–17

verdi's interest in incorporating continuo technique within the ensemble madrigal as early as 1602, when the composer had already been experimenting for a couple of years with similar techniques in the canzonettas of the *Scherzi musicali*.[21] That "T'amo mia vita" might be the earliest of the continuo madrigals is consistent with its style, which differs from the others in the relatively restricted role of the solo voice, whose presence is limited to repeating the same short cadential formula with minor embellishments. In the other continuo madrigals, Monteverdi writes more extended soloistic sections, including both duets and true solo passages, and makes greater use of ornamentation.

21. Such an early date for the development of Monteverdi's continuo technique is entirely in keeping with the chronology I proposed in "Claudio Monteverdi's *Ordine novo*," 275–77. On the question of dating these works, see Tomlinson, *Monteverdi*, 111 n. 22, who argues (111 and 152 n. 2) that the continuo madrigals were composed after the a cappella works of Books Four and Five, on the grounds that they represent a stylistically coherent group, significantly different from the other works in the fifth book, and that Artusi does not comment on the continuo works in either of his volumes. It is of course possible that Artusi was not aware of these pieces.

The Fourth Book of Madrigals: Organization

The existence by 1602 of a common stock of pieces from which both the fourth and fifth books were drawn raises the vexing question of why Monteverdi did not publish all of the Artusi madrigals together in the fourth book. It is of course possible, as Tomlinson has proposed, that Monteverdi simply hoped that the controversy would die down after Artusi's first book.[22] The nearly contemporaneous publication of the fourth book and the *Seconda parte dell'Artusi* does indeed suggest that the composer may have assembled the collection of 1603 without concern for the ongoing debate, of which as we have seen only a faint echo may be discerned in the language of the dedication. Nevertheless, it would have been logical for Monteverdi to have issued, for example, "Anima mia perdona" and its *seconda parte*, "Che se tu se' cor mio," together with "O Mirtillo," with which they form a nearly continuous cycle (all three are taken from Amarilli's soliloqui in Act 3, scene 4: lines 506–18, 539–47, and 548–55, respectively, and all three are criticized in Artusi's first book). Instead, they are divided between the fourth and fifth books, suggesting that perhaps the two volumes were planned at nearly the same time and that a tentative outline for Book Five may have influenced the choice of works included in Book Four.

The possibility that Monteverdi conceived Books Four and Five during a period of profound change in his compositional technique may help to explain the differences between the two collections. Book Four is largely retrospective and covers a wide variety of styles: its earliest material is thought to have been composed as early as 1590, and several pieces may date from as late as 1602.[23] Unlike the fifth book, which focuses on Guarini, the fourth draws on a variety of poets, ranging from Guarini and Tasso to Maurizio Moro, as well as such local Ferrarese poets as Ridolfo Arlotti and Aurelio Gatti.[24]

The fifth book overlaps the fourth slightly, reaching only as far back as the first group of pieces criticized by Artusi (to sometime around 1597–98) and taking those works as a starting point for a decidedly forward-looking collection. Together, the two volumes account for Monteverdi's development over a period spanning more than a decade, illustrating a variety of stylistic currents and putting in perspective the new techniques of the *seconda prattica*. Book Four

22. Tomlinson, *Monteverdi*, 111 n. 22.

23. Ibid., 98–111.

24. Ibid., 102; see also Anthony Newcomb, *The Madrigal at Ferrara, 1579–1597* (Princeton: Princeton University Press, 1980), 113–53.

provides the necessary background to Book Five, and it may be for that reason that in it the works criticized by Artusi are not given greater prominence.

In addition to focusing on different aspects of Monteverdi's output, the two volumes were assembled according to very different plans. Narrative does not play a part in the fourth book as it does in the fifth; rather, the collection follows a more conventional outline for a madrigal book, grouping pieces by mode and only loosely according to topic. Certain elements do prefigure techniques that in Book Five take on structural significance (such as the manipulation of unrelated texts to create continuity between them, or the recurrence of musical structure to link two madrigals), but here their deployment takes on a more limited significance.

The twenty madrigals fall into five sections, alternating between the *durus* and *mollis* systems (table 2.3). Monteverdi limited his tonal choices to a narrow range of finals: primarily a and d in the *durus* system, and g in *mollis*; only one madrigal, "Sfogava con le stelle," was set in d-*mollis*, and one, "Longe da te cor mio," is in g-*durus*. The only other final is represented by the lone madrigal in F, "Non più guerra."[25] The distribution of finals within the five sections suggests smaller subsections (indicated with braces in table 2.3), but these groupings are not consistently supported by either musical or textual connections between madrigals.

Although no single subject dominates Book Four, several themes are interwoven throughout the collection. The anguish of parting and of the lover's absence recur at the beginning, the midpoint, and the end, providing the structural foundation for the entire volume. Against this backdrop, the madrigals fall into smaller topical groupings: the lover's hope for mercy from his beloved; the devastating effect of the beloved's eyes; and the lighter aspects of love, sexual play and flirtatious banter. Some of these themes are reflected in the contrasting modal systems—*durus* pieces tend to deal with the harsher aspects of love (all of the texts about separation are in the *durus* groups) and to be characterized by one-sided statements; whereas those cast in the *mollis* system set dialogue texts (either direct, as between the lovers of "Volgea l'anima mia soavemente," or indirect and at cross-purposes, as are Amarilli's "Anima mia perdona" and Mirtillo's "Che se tu se'l cor mio") and are as a rule more hopeful in character. Such subjects as the "pietosa amante" [merciful lover] and amorous banter occur primarily in the *mollis* groups. However, these correspondences are not meant to underscore the division of the volume into alternating

25. Chafe, *Monteverdi's Tonal Language*, 76–77.

Table 2.3 *Il Quarto libro de madrigali* (1603), showing tonal groupings and literary sources

Madrigal	Incipit	Final	System	Poet	Sources
1	*Ah dolente partita	a		Guarini	*Pastor fido* 3/3, 498–05
2	†Cor mio mentre vi miro	d	*durus*	Guarini	*Rime*
3	‡Cor mio non mori	d		anon.	
4	Sfogava con le stelle	d		[Rinuccini]	
5	Volgea l'anima mia	g	*mollis*	Guarini	*Rime*
6	Anima mia perdona	g		Guarini	*Pastor fido* 3/4, 539–47
7	Che se tu se 'l cor mio	g		Guarini	*Pastor fido* 3/4, 548–55
8	Luci serene e chiare	d		[Arlotti]	
9	La piaga c'ho nel core	d	*durus*	[Gatti]	
10	*Voi pur da me partite	a		Guarini	*Rime*
11	A un giro sol	a		Guarini	*Rime*
12	†Ohimè, se tanto amate	g		Guarini	*Rime*
13	Io mi son giovinetta	g	*mollis*	[Guarini]	
14	Quel augellin	g		Guarini	*Pastor fido* 1/1, 175–86
15	Non più guerra	F		Guarini	*Rime*
16	†Sì ch'io vorrei morire	a		[Moro]	
17	‡Anima dolorosa	d		[Guarini]	
18	Anima del cor mio	d	*durus*	anon.	
19	Longe da te cor mio	G		anon.	
20	*Piagn' e sospira	d		T. Tasso	*Gerusalemme conquistata* 8.6

*, † and ‡ show madrigals linked by common themes.

Brackets show groups of related madrigals.

blocks of madrigals but spill beyond the modal boundaries (as does "Sì ch'io vorrei morire," which has more in common with the preceding *mollis* madrigals than it does with the other *durus* pieces that follow it).

In general terms, the central piece, "Voi pur da me partite," which represents the book's high point of scornful recrimination, serves as a pivot for the entire collection. The first half is dominated by love's "pene e tormenti" [pain and suffering]; after "Voi pur," anger gives way to either playful texts or to the self-pity and melancholy sentimentality of the last four madrigals. Finally, the arrangement of poems suggests that Monteverdi sought to emphasize textual connections between them, whether by grouping madrigals with similar *capoversi* ("Cor mio, mentre vi miro" and "Cor mio, non mori? e mori!") or works with internal images in common (as in "Luci serene e chiare" and "La piaga c'ho nel core," in which the "piaga" [wound], as well as the look, link the two texts).

The anguish of separation is the subject of the opening madrigal, "Ah dolente partita," in which parting is likened to a kind of death, whose sting revitalizes the heart and condemns it to eternal suffering; as well as of "Cor mio, non mori? e mori!" (no. 3), in which it is coupled with betrayal.[26] In the latter, the beloved's departure for another's arms robs the heart of hope, leaving death as the only alternative ("ch'esser non può che ti riserbi in vita / senza speme e aita. Su, mio cor, mori!" [for it cannot be that you should be kept alive / without hope or help. Come, come, my heart, die!]). Only one other text in the collection, "Anima dolorosa che vivendo" (no. 17), approaches the despair of "Cor mio non mori," paralleling in its closing line, "Mori, meschina, al tuo morir morendo" [die, unfortunate one, upon your death], the hopeless exhortations that mark the earlier text ("Cor mio, non mori? e mori!" [You do not die, my heart? Die at last!] . . . "Deh spezzati, mio core!" [Break, my heart, at last!] . . . "Su, mio cor, mori! Io moro" [Come, my heart, die! I die] . . .). In several places ("Ancor dimori in questa viva morte?" [Do you still dwell in this living death?] . . . "Perché, morta'l piacer, vivi al martire? Perché vivi al morire?" [Why, dead to all pleasure, do you live by suffering? Why do you live even as you die?]) "Anima dolorosa" also recalls the oxymorons of "Ah dolente partita" ("e sento nel partire un vivace morire, che da vita al dolore" [And I feel, in parting, a living death, that gives life to my pain]).

At the midpoint of the book, Monteverdi recapitulates "Ah dolente partita" with "Voi pur da me partite" (no. 10). Just as Mirtillo could not understand how he could leave Amarilli and not die, and how the pain he felt could stimulate life within his soul, in "Voi pur" the poet considers how the beloved is able not to feel the pain of separation even as the lover is near death.

> *Quest'è vicino aver l'ora suprema,*
> *e voi non lo sentite.*
> *O meraviglia di durezza estrema:*
> *esser l'alma d'un core*
> *e separarsi, e non sentir dolore.*

> He is near the final hour,
> and you do not feel it.
> O what a marvel of extreme cruelty:
> To be a heart's soul,
> and be separated from it without feeling pain.

---

26. As an opening theme, parting had found favor with other composers, most notably Jaches de Wert, whose eleventh book opens with a setting of "Ah dolente partita" that served as a model for Monteverdi's. See Fabbri, *Monteverdi,* 72. On Monteverdi's possible reasons for opening the fourth book with this text, see Tomlinson, *Monteverdi,* 101.

Finally, the last three poems, "Anima del cor mio," "Longe da te cor mio," and "Piagne e sospira," balance the book's opening, focusing, rather than on the parting itself, on the longing that follows the lovers' separation. This group is introduced by "Volgea l'anima mia," which as we have seen establishes a parallel with "Cor mio non mori? e mori!" In "Anima del cor mio," the lover begs to be allowed to remain with his beloved after she has left him, even if only in the form of a sigh to remind her of his true faith. In "Longe da te," the poet longs for her return so that he may suffer contentedly near the object of his desires. The closing madrigal, Tasso's "Piagne e sospira," excerpted from the *Gerusalemme conquistata,* summons one of the best-known of all scorned lovers, Erminia, whose compulsive and fruitless pursuit of Tancredi parallels the Christian hero's own obsession with Clorinda.[27] Her presence here, at the end of the volume, balances that of Guarini's Mirtillo in the first madrigal—both are emblematic of unrequited love, although their stories, temperaments, and literary origins justify the polarity of their placement.[28] Monteverdi's treatment of Guarini's and Tasso's texts creates a powerful parallel between the opening and closing of the book, drawing attention to the recurrence of the "partita" [parting] as a structural theme: both settings are contrapuntal showpieces whose complexity is well beyond that of any of the other works in the volume.[29]

"Pietà" [mercy] replaces the pain of separation as the connecting thread of the four madrigals that follow "Cor mio non mori." "Sfogava con le stelle," the opening piece in this first *mollis* section, appears to look at once backward and forward. As in the two preceding madrigals, its final is d, although in *mollis* rather than *durus.* Its text seems to comment on the condition of the betrayed lover in "Cor mio non mori," who might aptly be described as being terminally "infermo d'amore" [ill with love]. The continuity between the two texts is reinforced by the common reference to the beloved as "idolo mio" [my idol]: "L'idol tuo, ch'è tolto / a te" [your idol, who is removed / from you] in "Cor mio" returns in "Sfogava" as "'O immagini belle / de l'idol mio ch'adoro'" [O

---

27. To judge by the number of paintings inspired by her adventures, Erminia's pursuit of Tancredi seems to have occupied a more prominent place in the imagination of sixteenth- and seventeenth-century readers than her rival. See Rensselaer W. Lee, *Poetry into Painting: Tasso and Art* (Middlebury, Vt.: Middlebury College, 1970), and Andrea Buzzoni, ed., *Torquato Tasso tra letteratura, musica, teatro, arti figurative* (Bologna: Nuova Alfa, 1985).

28. The three pieces involved also allude to three different literary genres: Guarini's *tragicommedia,* his lyric madrigals, and Tasso's epic.

29. See Tomlinson's discussions of these two pieces in *Monteverdi,* 99–101.

beautiful images / my adored idol].[30] The alienated, solipsistic outbursts of the previous madrigal also continue with the suffering lover's address to the stars, his mute and remote interlocutor. The presence of the narrator, however, gives the whole poem a tone of objective detachment that is absent in the first-person directness of the first three madrigals and that extends to the next piece, "Volgea l'anima mia soavemente." This is another mixed-mode text, in which the poet remembers the urgency of his own suffering and the mercy shown him by his beloved. The brilliance of the night sky of "Sfogava" ("O immagini *belle . . .* mentre così *splendete .. la fareste col vostr'aureo sembiante . . .*" [O beau-*tiful* images . . . as you *shine . . .* you might make her with *your golden visage . . .*]) continues to shine in the beloved's luminous look in "Volgea":

> *Volgea l'anima mia soavemente*
> *quel suo caro, e* <u>lucente</u>
> *sguardo, tutto* <u>beltà</u> *tutto desire,*
> *verso me* <u>scintillando</u>

> My soul turned sweetly
> her dear and <u>luminous</u>
> look, full of <u>beauty</u> and desire,
> <u>sparkling</u> toward me

The lover's prayer for a compassionate response from his beloved in "Sfogava" seems to find its fulfilment in "Volgea," and the tone of conciliation continues in the two excerpts from *Il pastor fido,* Amarilli's "Anima mia perdona" and "Che se tu se' 'l cor mio." As in the fifth book, Amarilli and Mirtillo stand as emblems of erotic alienation; and their one-sided statements, which reflect the frustration of their situation at the same time that they express their mutual affection, pose a direct contrast to the lovers' dialogue in "Volgea." This is reminiscent of the contrast between Mirtillo and Amarilli and Silvio and Dorinda in Book Five, and the texts are derived from the same sources. "Ah dolente partita" marks Mirtillo's exit after being rebuked by Amarilli for confronting her during the *gioco della cieca;* like "O Mirtillo" in the fifth book, "Anima mia" and "Che se tu se'" are drawn from the extended soliloquy in which, after he has left, she reveals her secret love for him. In the play, Amarilli recalls in the last lines of "Che se tu se'" ("quel dolor, che senti, / son miei, non tuoi,

---

30. Appelbaum, preface to *Books IV and V,* standardizes the second line as "l'idolo tuo," although both "tuo" and "mio" occur in the text underlay and both work reasonably well in the syntax.

tormenti" [that pain you feel / is my torment, not yours]) Mirtillo's own closing "e sento nel partire / un vivace morire, / che da vita al dolore / per far che
moia immortalmente il core" [and I feel in parting / a living death, / that gives
life to pain / so that the heart may die immortally]. In Book Four, her "anima
mia perdona / a chi t'è cruda sol dove *pietosa* / esser non può" [my soul for-
give / one who is cruel to you only because / she cannot be *merciful*] also looks
back to the lover's plea in "Sfogava," that the stars make his beloved "*pietosa sí*
come me fate amante" [*merciful*, just as you make me her lover]; and, like his
futile address to the heavens, her words cannot be heard by the ears for which
they are intended.

The beloved's look in "Volgea l'anima mia" had conveyed her invitation to
love, and three of the four texts in the middle *durus* section (nos. 8, 9, and 11)
focus on the eyes as love's devastating weapons. After the dialogues of the *mollis* madrigals, this group returns to the first-person utterances of the first *durus*
pieces. In the first two, "Luci serene e chiare" and "La piaga c'ho nel core," the
eyes wound and set the heart ablaze; these effects are, however, pleasant in-
ducements to love, and the resultant sufferings fall into the category of "dolce
doler" [sweet suffering]. As elsewhere, the juxtaposition of these unrelated
texts (they are tentatively attributed to Ridolfo Arlotti and Aurelio Gatti, respectively) seems to have been motivated by their textual connections: the welcome wound inflicted by the beloved's words in the middle strophe of "Luci
serene" ("prova il petto non dolor ne la *piaga*, ma diletto" [the heart feels no
pain from the *wound*, but pleasure]) looks forward to the topic of the next poem
("La *piaga* c'ho nel core" [the *wound* I have in my heart]). The third poem, "Voi
pur da me partite," appears out of place, changing subject and separating "A un
giro sol de' begl'occhi lucenti" from the first pair of madrigals, but the painful
parting of which it speaks marks the change from the "dolce penare" [sweet
suffering] of the first two texts to the despondent tone of "A un giro." In the
latter, the beloved's gaze no longer engenders pleasure, but only sadness, and
the poet represents her in harsh terms that echo the *durezza* of "Voi pur da me
partite."

> *Certo quando nasceste*
> *così crudel e ria,*
> *nacque la morte mia.*

> Certainly when you were born,
> so cruel and treacherous,
> my death was born.

One more text, "Non più guerra, pietate" (no. 15), returns to the subject of the lover's glance. In it, the eyes are once more love's weapons, to which the poet surrenders. The separation between "Non più guerra" and the earlier madrigals on the same subject undermines any claim of continuity between them; rather, the lighthearted tone of the poet's request for peace fits in with the more playful mood of the surrounding madrigals.

Beginning with "Ohimè se tanto amate" (no. 12), the first madrigal in the second group of *mollis* pieces, the mood of the collection turns from love's "pene e tormenti" [pain and suffering], with various degrees of suffering, toward the sporting aspects of love. These manifest themselves in two different kinds of amorous play: disguised (and not-so-disguised) references to lovemaking, and the banter of seduction. Already in "Cor mio, mentre vi miro" (no. 2), death had figured as a metaphor for sexual play and fulfillment ("O bellezza vitale, / poiché sì tosto un core / per te rinasce e per te nato more" [O living beauty, / since so quickly for you a heart / is reborn and once born dies again]), but there it was cloaked in the poem's emphasis on romantic love. In "Ohimè se tanto amate" (no. 12), this conceit is extended, taking on a more playful tone.

> *Ma se, cor mio, volete*
> *che vita abbia da voi, e voi da me,*
> *avrete mille e mille dolci "Ohimè."*

> But if, my heart, you want
> me to receive life from you, and you from me,
> you will then have a thousand sweet "Alas."

Pure eroticism is then exaggerated in the well-known sexual imagery of "Sì ch'io vorrei morire" (no. 16), which reaches a level of intensity unmatched in any of the preceding texts. This metaphorical death affords the opportunity for the most abrupt mood change in the collection when it is juxtaposed to the prospect of real despairing death in "Anima dolorosa," the madrigal that follows "Sì ch'io vorrei morire."

Playful banter is the subject of "Io mi son giovinetta" and "Quel augellin" (nos. 13 and 14). The former is a *madrigale* of uncertain origin; the latter is yet another excerpt from *Il pastor fido*, in which Linco attempts to teach Silvio about love by pointing to the behavior of the birds.[31] Both poems revolve

31. Fabbri attributes "Io mi son giovinetta" to Guarini (*Monteverdi*, 72), and Appelbaum, preface to *Books IV and V*, xv, accepts his attribution.

around a symmetrical call-and-response between two lovers, and in both it is the "augellin" [little bird] that mediates the dialogue. In the first poem, the poet's heart is likened to the bird as it responds to the shepherdess's song, and the two echo one another in a pattern of double parallels. He picks up her opening ("io mi son giovinetta" [I am young]) with "son giovinetto anch'io" [I, too, am young], imparting an A–A' form to the main body of the poem, and turns her celebration of spring ("canto la stagion novella" [I sing of the new season]) into an invitation to love ("canto alla gentil e bella primavera d'amore che ne' begl'occhi tuoi fiorisce" [I sing of gentle and lovely Spring of love that blossoms in your eyes]). She, in turn, dashes his hopes, denying him access to the springtime he sees in her eyes.

> *"Io mi son giovinetta,*
> *e rido e canto alla stagion novella,"*
> *cantava la mia dolce pastorella,*
> *quando subitamente*
> *a quel canto il cor mio*
> *cantò quasi augellin vago e ridente:*
> *"Son giovinetto anch'io*
> *e rido e canto alla gentil e bella*
> *primavera d'amore*
> *che ne' begl'occhi tuoi fiorisce." Ed ella:*
> *"Fuggi, se saggio sei," disse, "l'ardore;*
> *fuggi, ch'in questi rai*
> *primavera per te non sarà mai."*

> "I am young,
> and laugh and sing to the new season,"
> sang my sweet shepherdess,
> when suddenly
> my heart responded to her song
> like a lovely cheerful bird:
> "I, too, am young,
> and laugh and sing to the gentle and lovely
> springtime of love
> that flowers in your lovely eyes." To which,
> "Flee, if you are wise," she replied, "your desire;
> flee, for in these eyes
> you will never find springtime."

Quel augellin, che canta
sì dolcemente e lascivetto vola
or da l'abete al faggio
ed or dal faggio al mirto,
s'avesse umano spirto,
direbbe: "Ardo d'amore, ardo d'amore."
Ma ben arde nel core
e chiam'il suo desio
che li risponde: "Ardo d'amor anch'io."
Che sii tu benedetto,
amoroso, gentil, vago augelletto.

That little bird that sings
so sweetly, and flies provocatively
now from fir to birch
and now from birch to myrtle,
if it had human spirit
it would say: "I burn for love, I burn for love."
But its heart does burn,
and he calls the object of his desire,
which answers: "I too burn for love."
May you be blessed,
you amorous, gentle, and lovely little bird.

The conclusion of "Quel augellin," however, differs from Guarini's original. The alteration eliminates the reference to Silvio, decontextualizing the poem; and the addition of the weak but entirely conventional closing couplet rounds out the form, allowing the madrigal to stand as an independent piece. Guarini's two sentences are collapsed into one, eliminating the repetition of "il suo dolce desio" [his sweet desire] and strengthening the parallel construction of call and response ("ardo d'amore, ardo d'amore" and "ardo d'amore anch'io") that illustrates Linco's point.

Ma ben arde nel core
e parla in sua favella,
sì che l'intende il suo dolce desio.
E odi a punto, Silvio,
il suo dolce desio
che gli risponde: "Ardo d'amore anch'io."

But its heart does burn,
and [the bird] speaks in its own tongue,
so that the sweet object of its desires may understand it.
And now hear, Silvio,
its sweet beloved's
answer: "I too burn for love."

Monteverdi reinforces the textual link with closely parallel settings, even reusing the closing bass part of "Io mi son" at the end of "Quel augellin," much as he does with "T'amo mia vita" and "Troppo ben può" in the fifth book. Both madrigals are in g-*mollis*, are similar in character and texture, and follow similar outlines. Both open with melismatic, canzonetta-like trios for two sopranos and alto, and, having completed the first syntactic unit, contrast the opening texture with declamatory passages for the entire ensemble ("Quando subitamente" and "S'avess'umano spirto"). In both madrigals these homo-rhythmic passages are repeated, and the restatements close with a brief return to the melismatic passagework of the opening trios. In "Io mi son giovinetta," Monteverdi exploits the dialogue by assigning the male and female characters to low and high trios. The second half of the madrigal underscores the ex-change between them by alternating between the two sonorities and returning to the melismatic style of the opening before bringing in the entire group for the closing repetition of the last three lines. "Quel augellin" affords no such opportunity for character representation; but for the closing couplet, Monte-verdi, as he had done in "Io mi son giovinetta," returns to the melismatic trio writing before bringing in the entire ensemble for the final peroration.

The two madrigals, furthermore, follow nearly identical harmonic plans, with structural cadences on G, B-flat, D, and G occurring at similar points of articulation (figure 2.5). Prominent textural details are also treated similarly, as at the transition between the opening section and the first full ensemble, which is elided by letting an inner voice (the alto in "Io mi son giovinetta" and the tenor in "Quel augellin") introduce a new motive while the cadence is still being formed, and then having it imitated by the rest of the ensemble (ex-ample 2.7).

Finally, the closing sections of both madrigals are built on nearly identical bass lines (example 2.8). Although the musical device is the same as that used in the continuo madrigals of the fifth book, in "Io mi son" and "Quell'au-gellin" the musical parallel reinforces the connection between two texts that are already very similar, whereas in the fifth it links two pieces that might not oth-erwise be seen as related. In the fourth book, the musical device has its origin

Fig. 2.5. Structure of "Io mi son giovinetta" and "Quel augellin, che canta"

"Io mi son giovinetta, e rido e canto alla stagion novella,"	⎤ a3 Canzonetta-like ⎦ (CCA)
cantava la mia dolce pastorella, [G] quando subitamente a quel canto il cor mio [Bb]	⎤ Tutti, homorhythmic ⎦ close of melismatic texture
cantò quasi augellin vago e ridente: [D] "Son giovinetto anch'io e rido e canto alla gentil e bella primavera d'amore [D]	⎤ a3 ⎦ (ATB)
che ne' begl'occhi tuoi fiorisce." Ed ella: "Fuggi, se saggio sei," disse, "l'ardore; fuggi, ch'in questi rai primavera per te non sarà mai." [G]	⎤ a3 ⎦ (CCA); Tutti second time

Quel augellin, che canta sì dolcemente e lascivetto vola or da l'abete al faggio ed or dal faggio al mirto, [G]	⎤ a3 Canzonetta-like ⎦ (CCA)
s'avesse umano spirto, direbbe: "Ardo d'amore, ardo d'amore." [Bb], they [D] Ma ben arde nel core e' chiam'il suo desio che li rispond': "Ardo d'amor anch'io." [D]	⎤ Tutti, ⎦ homorhythmic
Che sii tu benedetto, amoroso, gentil, vago augelletto. [G]	⎤ a3 ⎦ (CCA); Tutti second time

Ex. 2.7. *(a)* "Io mi son giovinetta," mm. 12–16;
(b) "Quel augellin, che canta," mm. 17–20

in the surface of the texts, in their similar wording and structure. In the pair from the fifth book, it acts independently of the texts, overlaying an interpretation that reaches beyond their apparent differences to construct a new meaning out of their connection.

In spite of the presence of techniques that are common to Book Five as well, Book Four was conceived according to very different principles. Whereas

Ex. 2.8. Bass patterns, closing measures, *(a)* "Io mi son giovinetta";
(b) "Quel augellin, che canta"

the fifth book follows a narrative outline in part provided by the *Pastor fido* and in part imposed by Monteverdi, the fourth, as we have seen, is more loosely organized according to primarily topical considerations. The modal arrangement recalls (in spirit if not in letter) the sixteenth-century practice of ordering collections according to a progression of finals and remains largely tangential to the poetic groupings. In the fifth book, the harmonic and dramatic dimensions are brought more closely in line to create a large-scale cyclical structure.

As I argue in the next chapter, Giulio Cesare's "Dichiaratione" makes for an odd pairing with the canzonettas that fill the pages of the *Scherzi musicali;* music and essay point in very different directions. Similarly, the madrigals of the fifth book point to a wider context for the *seconda prattica* than Monteverdi's "Lettera" makes apparent: the brief introductory essay to the volume is limited to addressing only the main issue raised by Artusi's treatises, dissonance; the music points toward the composer's concern with dramatic music. It is likely that the seeds of Monteverdi's interest in the problems of dramatic representation were sown at the time of the Mantuan productions of *Il Pastor fido,* to which he must have contributed in some way. However, his earliest known dramatic composition was the ballet "Gli amori di Diana ed Endimione," which occupied him during 1604 and coincides with the gestation of the fifth book. In the next chapter we shall see that his correspondence regarding the ballet attests to Monteverdi's primarily formal response to the problems of organization that confronted him in this first staged work, and that this formalist tendency was probably inspired by his experience with Chiabrera's strophic poetry.

In the fifth book, however, large-scale structure results from the juxtaposition of emotionally and psychologically contrasting situations. Alongside this dramatic conception, born in part from his reading of Guarini's play, Monteverdi deployed structural elements that are similar to those of the *Scherzi:*

- balanced form, both large-scale (as in the three-part organization of the a cappella madrigals and in the structural parallels spanning across the continuo pieces) and small-scale (in the formal schemes of the continuo madrigals);
- contrast between solo and ensemble passages, made possible by the presence of the basso continuo; and
- contrast between instrumental and vocal ensembles.

In the fifth book, the text-dependent musical devices of the classical madrigal were augmented with purely musical elements—form, scoring, and the like—which were deployed alongside the text to reveal its hidden implications. This established a new relationship between music and text that transcended the superficial one-to-one resemblances achieved by the perfect match of words and music in the classic madrigal. The dramatic potential of the *Scherzi musicali* and of Book Five found its first full expression in the large-scale architecture of *Orfeo*, which blends form, genre, scoring, and small-scale musical structure not only to create a full-blown allegory of the power of music, but also to bring to life realistic, three-dimensional characters ("Mosse Orfeo per essere uomo" [Orfeo moved because he was a man]). As Monteverdi indicated to Doni thirty years later, his goal during the composition of *Arianna* had been the creation of a language capable of meeting the needs of the *via naturale all'immitatione,* and the evidence of the works leading up to 1608 suggests that his main concern throughout this period had been to find the means by which to represent human emotion as realistically as possible.[32]

32. In "Madrigal, Monody, and Monteverdi's 'via naturale all'immitatione'" (*Journal of the American Musicological Society* 34 [1981], 60–108), Tomlinson argues that the *via naturale all'immitatione* was the search for a perfect match of poetic and musical rhetoric *(immitatione delle parole)*. Although it is true that in Rinuccini's *Arianna* Monteverdi found a text that was perfectly suited to the particular musical rhetoric with which he had experimented in *Orfeo,* and which he had to impose on Striggio's text, his real goal lay beyond the "parole" themselves. The more enduring legacy of the lament, evident in such later landmark works as the *Combattimento di Tancredi et Clorinda* and *L'incoronazione di Poppea,* is its emphasis on the accurate representation of the character's emotion and the flexibility with which the musical language responds to it. The perfection of the musical rhetoric is that it transcends the text itself to reveal the human condition that lay beyond it.

THREE

The Canzonetta

"Ciascuno dee poter cantare" [1]

By 1600, when Artusi issued his first criticisms, Monteverdi had already embarked on the exploration of compositional techniques that departed radically from those of the madrigal and that were to influence his works for the rest of his career.[2] In 1599 he accompanied the Duke on a trip to the baths at Spa, in Flanders, and, according to Giulio Cesare Monteverdi's "Dichiaratione," came into contact with French music, elements of which he introduced into Italy to reportedly excellent effect. The "Dichiaratione" itself, as we have seen, was probably drafted in 1605–6, and its report that the previous "three or four years" had seen the rising popularity of Monteverdi's "canto alla francese" in both sacred and secular compositions suggests that the new style had begun to spread by about 1601 or 1602. Its introduction, therefore, must have taken place sometime between 1599 and 1601, and Giulio Cesare points to the canzonettas collected in the *Scherzi musicali* as evidence of his brother's early efforts.

In light of the controversy surrounding Monteverdi's madrigals, the pairing of the "Dichiaratione" with the *Scherzi musicali* is significant for a number of reasons. First, although Giulio Cesare's essay addresses Artusi's criticisms of Monteverdi's contrapuntal infractions, the *Scherzi* had very little in common

---

1. Gabriello Chiabrera, "Il Geri: dialogo della tessitura delle canzoni," in *Opere*, ed. Marcello Turchi (Turin: U.T.E.T., 1973), 574.

2. Ossi, "Claudio Monteverdi's *Ordine novo, bello et gustevole*: The Canzonetta as Dramatic Module and Formal Archetype," *Journal of the American Musicological Society* 45 (1992), 270–76.

with the madrigals that had attracted the wrath of the Bolognese theorist. In the canzonettas, contrapuntal technique is replaced by homorhythmic textures, simple part-writing, straightforward (but as we shall see by no means trivial) harmonic language, schematic form, instrumental ritornellos, and dance-like rhythms.[3]

Second, by pointing to the *Scherzi musicali* as the primary musical evidence of his brother's preeminence as a composer, Giulio Cesare sought to position Claudio as an innovator widely imitated by his contemporaries:

> The *canto alla francese* in the modern manner that is found in publications of the last three or four years, now for motet texts, now madrigals, now canzonettas, now arias; who before him [used it until he] brought it back to Italy when he returned from the baths at Spa in 1599? And who began to use it for Latin and Italian texts before he did? Did he not at that time compose these *scherzi*?[4]

Third, the pieces Giulio Cesare either chose or was given for the *Scherzi musicali* focus on texts by Gabriello Chiabrera, who was closely allied with Giulio Caccini and the development of the new Florentine *favole per musica*. Chiabrera had already been singled out in the preface to Caccini's *Le nuove musiche* as being particularly attuned to the needs of the new musical style:

> Therefore . . . considering that at that time musicians used for their canzonettas mainly texts of very poor quality, which I felt were not appropriate, and which men of sound judgment did not hold in any esteem, I had the idea, as the means of giving solace to languishing souls, to compose some aria-like canzonettas to be performed to the accompaniment of an ensemble of string instruments. Having let a number of gentlemen in the city know that this was my intention, I was courteously favored by them with many canzonettas in a variety of verse types. Among them was signor Gabriello Chiabrera, who gave me a large number of them, quite differ-

---

3. Monteverdi was not new to strophic forms: his first secular publication, the *Canzonette a tre voci* of 1584, had consisted of twenty-one strophic compositions for three voices, all a cappella, in homorhythmic style, and setting verses of eleven syllables. This first effort was wholly within the sixteenth-century tradition of canzonetta composition; Paolo Fabbri, *Monteverdi* (Turin: E.D.T., 1985), 14, identifies the origins of the texts chosen by Monteverdi for this collection in Orazio Vecchi's *Canzonette. Libro primo a quattro voci* (Venice, 1581), as well as in collections by Stefano Lando, Gian Domenico da Nola, Alessandro Romano, and Giovanni Zappasorgo.

4. In Claudio Monteverdi, *Lettere, dediche e prefazioni*, ed. Domenico De' Paoli (Rome: De Santis, 1973), 402.

ent from one another. He gave me the opportunity to compose a great variety of them, and, over time, they have found favor all over Italy.[5]

And Lorenzo Fabri, writing in defense of Chiabrera's mixture of verse forms, had cited in the preface to *Le maniere de' versi toscani* (1599) the favor with which such mixtures had been received by composers. He notes in particular Caccini's effective, and very successful, settings of such poetry:

> Nor will I deny that since lyric poetry is especially suited to being sung, musicians find it easiest and most pleasing to others to vary the rhythm of verses that are not all the same. Giulio Romano is proof of this, and his authority is to be believed, because all of Italy admires him.[6]

By 1600, Chiabrera's credentials as an avant-garde poet were well established. He had written the text for Caccini's and Buontalenti's spectacular *Il rapimento di Cefalo*, the centerpiece of the wedding festivities between Maria de' Medici and Henry IV of France, as well as for a number of arias and other shorter works set by Caccini.[7] The Mantuan court, including Alessandro Striggio, who was to write the libretto of Monteverdi's *L'Orfeo*, and possibly Monteverdi himself as well, had been in attendance and had met the poet.[8] Subsequently, Chiabrera developed close ties with Mantua: he visited the duchy in 1602, remained in contact with the Duke in the years following his visit, and eventually was engaged to contribute to the Mantuan wedding festivities of 1608.[9]

5. Giulio Caccini, *Le nuove musiche* (Florence: Marescotti, 1601; repr. SPES, 1983), [v].

6. Lorenzo Fabri, in Chiabrera's *Opere*, 215.

7. On *Il rapimento di Cefalo*, see my "*Dalle macchine . . . la meraviglia*: Bernardo Buontalenti's *Il rapimento di Cefalo* at the Medici Theater in 1600," in *Opera in Context: Essays on Historical Staging from the Renaissance to the Time of Puccini*, ed. Mark Radice (Portland: Amadeus Press, 1998), 15–35. For an assessment of the importance of the celebrations of 1600, see Tim Carter, "A Florentine Wedding of 1608," *Acta Musicologica* 55 (1983), 89–107.

8. "Provandosi alcune musiche nella sala dei Pitti, vennervi ad udirle la serenissima sposa, madama la gran duchessa, la duchessa di Mantova, il cardinal Monti, ed altro numero di chiari personaggi . . ." Chiabrera, *Opere*, 516; see also Tim Carter, review of *The New Monteverdi Companion*, ed. Denis Arnold and Nigel Fortune, and *Monteverdi*, by Paolo Fabbri, *Music and Letters* 67 (1986): 170.

9. Chiabrera characterized his relationship with Mantua in his autobiography as follows: "Vincenzo Gonzaga, Duke of Mantua, also availed himself of his services [Chiabrera writes about himself in the third person], and for the wedding of his son Francesco brought him in, and gave him the responsibility of devising both the machines and the verses for the intermedii to be staged. In this way, he was always honored by this sovereign, who housed him and paid all his expenses while he stayed at his palace, and who allowed him to keep his head covered in his presence. When they went fishing on the lake, he had him ride in his carriage,

Chiabrera also provided a model for self-conscious modernism. He styled himself in the mold of a literary explorer (in perhaps the most often quoted line of his autobiography, the poet described himself as "following his countryman Christopher Columbus, *in that he would either find the new world or drown*" [dicea ch'egli seguia Cristoforo Colombo suo cittadino, *ch'egli voleva trovare nuovo mondo, o affogare*]).[10] Chiabrera's ideas on versification were strongly influenced by French poetic models, Ronsard in particular, whose works he had come to know from Marc-Antoine Moret, a friend of Paolo Manuzio, who was a neighbor of Chiabrera's when the poet was growing up in Rome; he knew the French models through the works of the poet Sperone Speroni as well.[11] The preface to *Le maniere de' versi toscani,* written by Fabri but based on Chiabrera's own ideas, staked out a modernist position regarding the principles of Italian versification, introducing verse forms not normally used by his predecessors and comparing Italian versification with French and Spanish practices. It seems more than coincidental that Giulio Cesare, writing for his brother, should have connected Claudio so prominently with the importation of French style into Italian music just at the time of Chiabrera's presence in Mantua.

Most importantly for the debate with Artusi, the style of the *Scherzi* shifts away from the refined compositional techniques of the classical madrigal, with its connotation of learned art, and toward Chiabrera's more common aesthetic, aimed at simpler sensibilities and more direct expression. As Chiabrera explained in one of his dialogues on poetry, "Il Geri,"

---

and fish from his boat, and at dinner he had him sit at his table. Then, once the festivities were over, he sent him back to Savona and, without servile obligation, had him draw a salary from the treasury of Monferrato. Thus was done, and every time Gabriello visited his court, he always held him dear." *Opere,* 517–18. On Chiabrera and Mantua, see also Nino Pirrotta, "Monteverdi's Poetic Choices," in *Music and Culture in Italy from the Middle Ages to the Baroque* (Cambridge: Harvard University Press, 1984), 292 n. 50; Fabbri, *Monteverdi,* 116; and A. Neri, "Chiabrera e la corte di Mantova," *Giornale storico della letteratura italiana* 7 (1886), 317–75.

10. *Opere,* 521. The figure of the discoverer of new worlds as the poet's ideal recurs in his characterization of Galileo Galilei, another of Chiabrera's heroes. On Chiabrera and the canzonetta, see Giovanni Getto, "Gabriello Chiabrera poeta barocco," in *Barocco in prosa ed in poesia* (Milan: Rizzoli, 1969), 137–42, and Robert Holzer, "'Sono d'altro garbo . . . le canzonette che si cantano oggi': Pietro della Valle on Music and Modernity in the Seventeenth Century," *Studi Musicali* 21 (1992), 277–81.

11. Speroni had written a letter in *endecasillabi sciolti* to Ronsard, titled *Au Seigneur Pierre de Ronsard,* shortly after receiving a book of the Frenchman's poems in 1582. See Mario Pozzi, ed., *Trattatisti del Cinquecento,* vol. 2 (Milan: Ricciardi, 1996), 488. On the importance of French poetry, and in particular of Ronsard, whose influence on Chiabrera he describes as "explosive" for Chiabrera's development, see Getto, "Gabriello Chiabrera." On Muret and Speroni, see Chiabrera's autobiography in *Opere,* 513.

Take a young man, or young woman, in love, in whose breast passion
rages beyond reason and the speculation of philosophy. Of what would
they sing? Surely of everything they feel in their hearts, and this would be
nothing other than those emotions, happy or sad, that naturally fill all persons who are in love. In my opinion, out of one hundred persons ninety
would forget what Socrates divinely taught Phaedrus, and everything that
Plato includes in his dialogue. . . . I believe you read French poetry: recall
their amorous coquetries, their flatteries, their tender [gestures], such that
every woman and every man can and knows how to express, and that
everyone, once they are expressed, understands easily. Do you not obtain
solace from seeing such coquetries [*scherzi*] represented, which require
neither art, nor comment, nor explication? On the other hand, sing a *canzone* by Dante or Petrarch to a group of young women, and then ask them
what they have heard. You will say that it is true, that those are superhu-
man poems, that they require an audience of the subtlest intellect, and
that they deserve admiration. I will not deny it, but humankind includes
the subtlest intellects, as well as pedestrian ones, and all have to be able
to sing. Therefore one wants to give them verses that take into good account the subjects to which they are accustomed and that they can sing.[12]

In light of Chiabrera's prominence in Mantuan court circles, it is not coincidental that eleven of the seventeen canzonettas and one *balletto* that make up
the *Scherzi musicali* set texts by Chiabrera (see table 3.1).[13] Of the remaining
seven canzonettas, two are by Ansaldo Cebà, like Chiabrera a Genoese and a
follower of his; and the *balletto* has been attributed, at least tentatively, to Ferdinando Gonzaga.[14] The poet for three of the remaining canzonettas is still un-
identified, although stylistically they are in the same vein as those by Chiabrera.
The only text that looks back to the style of the sixteenth-century canzonetta is
Jacopo Sannazaro's "La pastorella mia spietata e rigida," written in hendecasyllabic *terza rima sdrucciola*, although it is set in the same musical style as the
others. Indeed, the homogeneous musical and literary style of the volume

---

12. Chiabrera, *Opere*, 573–74.

13. Two of the canzonettas are by Giulio Cesare, and the authenticity of the *balletto*
has been questioned. See Leo Schrade, *Monteverdi, Creator of Modern Music* (New York: W. W.
Norton, 1950), 223, according to whom "stylistic evidence points to Giulio Cesare as the
composer."

14. Sartori attributes two of the anonymous texts, "Amorosa pupilletta" and "Lidia spina
del mio core," to Cebà; Fabbri, *Monteverdi*, 116, does not. On Ansaldo Cebà, see Marcello
Turchi, *Opere di Gabriello Chiabrera e lirici del classicismo barocco* (Genoa: U.T.E.T., 1974), 38–
39 and 735–40.

Table 3.1 Poetic texts in the *Scherzi musicali* (1607)

Title	1st setting*a*	Publication*b*	Author
I bei legami	1602	1599	Chiabrera
Amarilli	1607	1606	Chiabrera
Fugge il verno	1606	—	anon.
Quando l'alba	1607	1599	Chiabrera
Non così tosto	1607	1599	Chiabrera
Damigella	1607	1603	Chiabrera
La pastorella			Sannazaro
O rosetta	1602	1599	Chiabrera
Amorosa pupilletta	1600		Cebà [?]
Vaghi rai	1607	1606	Chiabrera
La violetta	1607	1599	Chiabrera
Giovinetta	1607	—	anon.
Dolci miei sospiri	1607	1599	Chiabrera
Clori amorosa	1607*c*	—	anon.
Lidia spina	1607	—	Cebà [?]

a. All items dated 1607 first appeared in the *Scherzi musicali.*

b. 1599: *Maniere dei versi toscani;* 1603: *Vendemmie di Parnaso;* 1606: *Delle poesie.*

c. Both in the *Scherzi musicali* and in Amante Franzoni's *Secondo libro delli fioretti musicali a tre voci.*

points to a deliberate effort by the two Monteverdis to position Claudio at the forefront of the court's current tastes.

It is unclear whether Monteverdi worked from published sources or had access to manuscript copies of the poetry originating from Chiabrera's visits to Mantua. Nine of the texts set in the *Scherzi* had already appeared in Chiabrera's own poetic collections, and none of Monteverdi's texts differs significantly from Chiabrera's published versions. In view of the poet's presence, however, it is significant that Monteverdi was the first to set all but four of the poems included in the *Scherzi.*[15]

15. "Fugge il verno" and "Amorosa pupilletta" had already been set to music: the former by Domenico Brunetti in *L'Euterpe . . . opera musicale di madrigali, canzonette, arie, stanze, e scherzi diversi, in dialoghi, e echo, a una, due, tre et quattro voci* (Venice: Amadino, 1606) and by Giulio Santo Pietro del Negro in *Gl'amorosi pensieri: Canzonette villanelle et arie napolitane a tre voci da sonare et cantare su'l chitarrone, clavicembalo, et altri stromenti. Libro secondo* (Venice: Gardano, 1607); and the latter by Simone Molinaro, *Il secondo libro delle canzonette a tre voci* (Venice: Amadino, 1600) and Giovan Domenico Montella, *Primo libro de' madrigali a quattro voci* (Naples: Sottile, 1604). "I bei legami" had been set by Domenico Maria Melli in *Le seconde musiche . . . nelle quali si contengono madrigali, canzonette, arie, et dialoghi, a una et due voci* (Venice: Vincenti, 1602), which also included the earliest known setting of "O rosetta," and by Amante Franzoni in *I nuovi fioretti musicali a tre voci* (Venice: Amadino, 1605).

In addition to the *Scherzi musicali*, three other collections attest to the popularity of the canzonetta at the Mantuan court in the first decade of the seventeenth century, preserving some fifty-one canzonettas for three voices as well as a number of solo settings of canzonetta texts. These three volumes, Amante Franzoni's first and second books of *I nuovi fioretti musicali a tre voci* (the first was published in 1605 and reissued in 1607, and the second appeared in 1607), and Francesco Rasi's *Vaghezze di musica per una voce sola* of 1608, like the *Scherzi musicali*, are closely tied to court circles and appeared within the span of just three years.

Franzoni served at Mantua, with minor interruptions, from sometime before 1605 until his death in 1630. Both of his volumes of *Fioretti* were, like Monteverdi's *Scherzi*, edited on his behalf by others. The first book, which was seen into print by Fulvio Gonzaga, contains, besides Franzoni's own works, one canzonetta each from the Monteverdi brothers, as well as others by composers active around Mantua (Giovanni Giacomo Gastoldi, Giovanni Leite, and Giulio Cesare Bianchi).[16] Francesco Dognazzi, who must have been at the beginning of his long Mantuan career, was responsible for the second set of *Fioretti*, which appeared almost simultaneously with Monteverdi's *Scherzi* late in the summer of 1607.[17]

Francesco Rasi, who earlier in 1607 sang the title role in Monteverdi's *Orfeo*, was one of the most highly prized singers in the Gonzagas' musical establishment, and the *Vaghezze*, edited by the Duke's *vice-maestro di cappella*, Bassano

16. Regarding the strong Mantuan flavor of *I nuovi fioretti*, see Fabbri, *Monteverdi*, 94. The 1607 reissue has a new introduction by Franzoni himself, who mentions that the reprint includes a newly composed *basso generale*—either the original one mentioned in the title was never included, or it was in some way defective. On Franzoni, see Iain Fenlon, "Franzoni, Amante," in *The New Grove Dictionary of Music and Musicians*, 2d ed. (New York: Grove, 2001), 9, 213.

17. Dognazzi's dedication to Bonaventura Grignano closely recalls the Chiabreresque images of Giulio Cesare's dedication to the *Scherzi* ("These sweet flowers, which [were] born and nurtured in your household" [Questi soavi fiori, che per esser nati, et nodriti in casa sua]). His activity in Mantua seems to have lasted for over forty years, and he eventually came to direct the music at both the court (by 1619) and the church of Santa Barbara (by around 1643). His relations with Monteverdi appear to have been relatively close, and he is mentioned in four of Monteverdi's letters (*The Lettesrs of Claudio Monteverdi*, ed. and trans. by Denis Stevens [London: Cambridge University Press, 1980], no. 21, 9 December 1616; no. 48, 8 March 1620; no. 62, 21 October 1620; and no. 63, 31 October 1620); he may also have visited Monteverdi in Venice in 1619. See Jerome Roche, "Dognazzi, Francesco," in *The New Grove Dictionary of Music and Musicians*, 1st ed. (London: Macmillan; New York: Grove's Dictionaries, 1980), 5, 521–22, and Susan Parisi, "Dognazzi, Francesco," in ibid., 2d ed. (2001), 7, 423–24.

Casola, presumably reflects at least in part the repertoire he performed at court. It includes a setting of Chiabrera's "Dolci miei sospiri," as well as an "aria francese," "Or ch'a noi rimena l'alma primavera," "translated into Italian by [ridotta in italiano da] Francesco Rasi." The latter underscores the Mantuan taste for French music that Rasi himself had noted as early as 1600, when he complained that his sister Sabina was in danger of ruining her training by learning to sing in the French manner at the request of the Duke.[18]

Not surprisingly, Chiabrera's poetry does figure in these collections, but it is not so pervasive as in the *Scherzi musicali*. In comparison to the eleven texts by him in Monteverdi's volume, only four are found in Franzoni's *I nuovi fioretti musicali* of 1605 and none in the sequel of 1607; six are among Francesco Rasi's *Vaghezze di musica* of 1608.[19] Most of the other texts are anonymous and cannot be accounted for, although some appear to have originated in Mantua. The two earliest settings of the anonymous "Clori amorosa" are found in Monteverdi's *Scherzi* and in Franzoni's *Secondo libro*, and "Lidia spina," also anonymous, survives only thanks to Monteverdi's setting.

In the "Dichiaratione," Giulio Cesare reminded Francesco Gonzaga (in language that recalls Chiabrera's preoccupation with gardens and flowers) that the *Scherzi* were "flowers that my brother Claudio sowed, and then plucked, in the lovely garden of Your Highness's royal chambers" [fiori, che nel bel giardino delle regie camere di V. A. furono da mio fratello seminati, e colti].[20] That the duke did indeed need reminding became apparent barely two months later, when at the end of summer the court prepared for the wedding celebrations of 1608 by turning to Florentine composers and poets for the central opera, and

18. Rasi's letter is in Pietro Canal, "Della musica in Mantova: Notizie tratte principalmente dall'archivio Gonzaga," *Memorie del R. Istituto veneto di scienze, lettere e arti* 21 (1881), 740; see Fabbri's discussion of it in *Monteverdi*, 117. It is possible that Monteverdi's two pieces "alla francese" among the *Canti amorosi* of the eighth book (1638), "Dolcissimo uscignuolo" and "Chi vole aver felice e lieto il core"—both, perhaps significantly, on madrigal texts by Guarini—are either distant reminiscences or actual documents of the French taste at the Mantuan court.

19. The first volume of *Fioretti* was later (1610) copied into a manuscript anthology by the Parmense "Mich[ele] Parius." In addition to the *Fioretti*, the anthology also includes works from Monteverdi's *Scherzi* and a number of unica by Monteverdi, Gesualdo, Pomponio Nenna, Orazio Vecchi, Salomone Rossi, and Victoria, and many of the pieces are contrafacted with sacred texts (Bologna, Civico Museo Bibliografico Musicale Q. 27). See Jeffrey Kurtzman, "An Early 17th-Century Manuscript of *Canzonette e Madrigaletti Spirituali*," *Studi musicali* 8 (1979), 149–71.

20. Plants and gardens figure prominently in Chiabrera's works—see for example his "Il vivaio di Boboli" (Turchi, *Opere*, 400–5), in addition to the flower images of "O rosetta" and other poems.

Monteverdi found himself nearly shut out of the opportunity to compose the work that eventually solidified his reputation—*Arianna*.[21] Seen against the political background of the commission and flanked by publications addressing the latest fashions at court, the *Scherzi* appear to fulfill a double function, publicly addressing Artusi's criticisms but also privately positioning Monteverdi among his competitors, both local and Florentine, as a home-grown but broadly influential modernist. Giulio Cesare's "Dichiaratione," stressing Claudio's adoption of French style elements as well as his use of Chiabrera's verse, strives hard to establish his brother's achievements and to cement his claims as an innovator capable of embracing the latest literary trends and exploiting them to new and pleasing ends—in short, as the logical alternative to those Florentine imports to which the court was drawn. In light of Monteverdi's complaints that he was treated poorly during the ensuing festivities of 1608, when Marco da Gagliano was paid handsomely for doing "almost nothing" in comparison with his own extensive "labors" [fatiche], the tone of the "Dichiaratione" suggests that that document stemmed, at least in part, from the composer's insecurity, whether real or perceived, regarding his position at court just as a commission was about to be awarded that would bring its recipient "the highest degree of fame a man can garner on earth."[22]

Three Analyses

Commentators have paid little attention to the canzonettas of the *Scherzi*, largely because of their brevity, their apparently unambitious aim, and their perceived position in Monteverdi's canon as spin-offs from *Orfeo*. Brief as they may be, however, these pieces served Monteverdi as a useful laboratory for experimenting with text setting, melodic construction, and form. Chiabrera's virtuosity in handling poetic rhythm led Monteverdi to new ways of conceiving the relationship between music and text, ways that had little to do with interpreting a poem's affective content and everything to do with stripping the music–text relationship down to its essential components: rhythm, harmony, and the simplest melodic patterns.

The poems selected for the *Scherzi musicali* seem to have been chosen to

21. On the events leading up to the composition of *Arianna* see Fabbri, *Monteverdi*, 124–31.

22. "Il sommo di quanta fama può avere un uomo in terra," letter from Follino to Monteverdi, 24 September 1607, quoted in Fabbri, *Monteverdi*, 124. On Monteverdi's complaints about his treatment at court in 1608, see *Letters*, ed. Stevens, no. 6, 2 December 1608, pp. 55–61.

Table 3.2 Poetic types in the canzonettas of the *Scherzi musicali*

Canzonetta	Type of line	Meter
I bei legami	quinari piani	dattilici/giambici
Amarilli	ottonari piani	trocaici
Fugge il verno	ottonari and quaternari piani	trocaici
Quando l'alba	ottonari piani and sdruccioli	trocaici
Non così tosto	settenari piani	giambici
Damigella	ottonari and quaternari piani	dattilici/trocaici
La pastorella	endecasillabi sdruccioli	giambici
O rosetta	ottonari piani and tronchi	trocaici
Amorosa pupilletta	ottonari and quaternari piani	trocaici
Vaghi rai	ottonari and quaternari piani	trocaici
La violetta	quinari and settenari piani	dattilici/giambici
Giovinetta	quaternari and ottonari piani	trocaici
Dolci miei sospiri	senari piani	trocaici
Clori amorosa	quinari piani	dattilici/trocaici
Lidia spina	ottonari piani	trocaici

represent nearly the full panoply of metric forms that interested Chiabrera (table 3.2).[23] All are strophic and most consist of pure *ottonari* (eight-syllable lines) or pure *quinari* (five syllables); one is cast entirely in *senari* (six syllables). Several mix *quaternari* (four-syllable lines) and *ottonari*, and one combines *quinari* and *settenari* (seven syllables). Within these choices and possible combinations, Chiabrera allowed two basic meters, trochaic ‿– and iambic –‿. Each could take various forms according to the number of poetic feet present in a verse. As Fabri explains,

> Iambic verses can be made up of one, two, or three feet. Those made up of a single foot were not used by the ancients, and therefore we will not mention them; those that consist of two feet can be full, that is with both their feet complete, as in "Dolce per la memoria," or they are short [scemi], that is, with one syllable missing from the last foot, as in "Chiare fresche e dolci acque," or they are halved, having two fewer syllables in the second foot, as in "Che sia in questa città." Likewise, those that consist of three feet can also be full, as in "Tra l'isola di Cipri e di Maiolica," or short, as is "Con esso un colpo per le man di Artù." These, then, are iambic verses. Trochaic verses can also comprise one, two, or three feet. The ancients did not write any that consist of three feet, so we shall remain silent

23. See, for example, the list he gives at the beginning of the dialogue "Il Geri" (*Opere*, 571), as well as Lorenzo Fabri's introduction to *Le maniere de' versi toscani* (Chiabrera's *Opere*, 213–16), which summarizes Chiabrera's essential points in the dialogue.

about these. Those that are made up of two feet are full, as "Quando miro la rivera," or short, as "Io non l'ho perché non l'ho," or halved, as "Amore mi tiene." Verses consisting of a single foot could only be full: "E l'Amanza." In antiquity, trochaic verses had another variation: they could be augmented by one syllable, and then become hypermetric: Dante added this extra syllable to the single-footed form ("Non per mio grato"); Guittone added it to the first foot of a two-footed verse ("E chi non piange hai duro core"); and it can also be added at the end ("Chi vol bever, chi vol bevere"). From these examples one can gather that Tuscan verses can be of four, five, six, seven, eight, nine, ten, eleven, and twelve syllables: and all of these can be found in these pages.[24]

"Quando l'alba in oriente" exemplifies many of the features common to the rest of the *Scherzi*.[25] The poem consists of six stanzas of six lines each, all *ottonari trocaici*. The rhyme scheme ($a_8\, b_8\, b_8\, a_8\, c_8\, c_8$) is one of Chiabrera's standard patterns, mixing *piano* (lines 1 and 4) and the less common *sdrucciolo* endings (Fabri's *trocaici soprabbondanti*, lines 2–3 and 5–6).[26]

Quando l'alba in oriente
L'almo sol s'appresta a scorgere,
Giù dal mar la veggiam sorgere,
Cinta in gonna rilucente,
Onde lampi si diffondono
Che le stelle in cielo ascondono.

Rose, gili almi, immortali,
Sfavillando il crin adornano,
Il crin d'oro, onde s'aggiornano
L'atre notti de' mortali;
E fresche aure intorno volano
Che gli spirti egri consolano.

Nel bel carro a meraviglia
Son rubin che l'aria accendono;
I destrier non men risplendono
D'aureo morso e d'aurea briglia,

24. *Le maniere de' versi toscani (Opere*, 213–15). On Fabri's, as well as Chiabrera's, indebtedness to Gian Giorgio Trissino's *Poetica* (Vicenza, 1529) for this list, as well as on the misattribution of a number of the poems cited, see Turchi's annotations in the *Opere*, 213–16.

25. Chiabrera, *Opere*, 228.

26. W. Theodor Elwert, *Versificazione italiana dalle origini ai giorni nostri* (Florence: Le Monnier, 1982), pattern no. 5, p. 159.

E nitrendo a gir s'apprestano,
E con l'unghia il ciel calpestano.

Con la manca ella gli sferza
Pur con fren, che scossi ondeggiano
E se lenti unqua vaneggiano,
Con la destra alza la sferza:
Essi all'or, che scoppiar l'odono,
Per la via girsene godono.

Sì, di fregi alta e pomposa,
Va per strade che s'infiorano,
Va su nembi che s'indorano
Rugiadosa, luminosa;
L'altre dee, che la rimirano,
Per invidia ne sospirano.

È ciò ver; qual più n'apprezza
Per beltade a l'Alba inchinasi:
Non per questo ella avvicinasi
Di mia Donna alla bellezza,
I suoi pregi, Alba, t'oscurano;
Tutte l'alme accese il giurano.

> When in the East Dawn
> Is about to glimpse the life-giving Sun,
> We see her rising from beneath the sea,
> Clad in a resplendent gown,
> From which rays of light emanate
> That hide the stars in the heavens.
>
> Roses, beloved lilies, immortal,
> Sparkling adorn her hair,
> Her golden hair, by which
> Mortals' dark nights are illuminated;
> And fresh breezes fly around
> Consoling languishing souls.
>
> On the lovely chariot, marvelous
> To behold, rubies brighten the air,
> The horses are no less resplendent,
> With their golden bits and bridles,
> As, neighing, they prepare for their journey,
> Pawing the sky with their hooves.

With her left hand she whips them
To rein them in, so that they waver, shaken;
And if they should ever slow distractedly,
She raises the whip with her right:
They, upon hearing its snap,
Are eager to return to their course.

Thus, proud and tall with decorations,
She travels roads that bloom,
And rides clouds that turn to gold,
She is dewy, resplendent;
The other goddesses, admiring her,
Sigh with envy.

And this is true; those who most admire
Dawn's beauty, curtsy to her;
But this does not mean that she approaches
My Lady in beauty:
Her qualities, Dawn, outshine you;
All souls, enflamed by her, swear it is so.

Each stanza consists of a single continuous syntactic unit, with internal divisions occurring at various points in different stanzas: in the first, third, and sixth stanzas the first two lines form an introductory unit, and the rest forms a continuous phrase. In the second, fourth, and fifth stanzas, the pattern is reversed to match more closely the rhyme scheme, with the closing couplet forming a distinct syntactic element. As is typical of the *ottonario*, the internal caesura tends to fall most often after the fourth syllable (as in "Cinta in gonna | rilucente"), but other groupings can also occur: after the third syllable ("L'almo sol | s'appresta a scorgere" and "Giù del mar | la veggiam sorgere"), as well as more irregular ones ("Rose, | gili almi, | immortali").

Monteverdi's setting consists of six phrases that coincide with the verse structure but that seem to define an internal form only loosely reflective of the poem (example 3.1). The six phrases fall into two groups, defined by melodic shape: phrases 1–2; and 3–6. Phrase 2 is a transposed version of phrase 1, but with slight modifications that seem largely motivated by the different prosodic requirements of the *verso sdrucciolo*. Phrase 3 appears to be an extension of phrase 2, in that it occupies the same general range and shares with it some rhythmic features (the opening and closing rhythms); but harmonically it is quite distinct from those that precede it. Phrases 1 and 2 come to structural cadences on G and C; phrase 3 does not lead to a point of harmonic resolution

Ex. 3.1. "Quando l'alba in oriente"

but simply pauses on G before phrase 4 continues from G and finally closes with a strong cadence on G. The opening of phrase 4 introduces a new syncopated rhythm that characterizes each of the subsequent phrases; it also recalls the ornamental figure of the opening pair, and the *sdrucciolo* ending of phrase 2. Phrases 4–6, like the first two, are part of a rising sequence; and like phrases 3 and 4, phrases 5 and 6 form a continuous harmonic unit.

The brevity of the setting is reinforced by the concision with which a few elements are transformed from phrase to phrase to vary the melodic material. One ornamental figure (*a* and *a'* in example 3.1) takes on different connotations as part of a brief melismatic extension or as paired eighth notes.[27] Simple transposition, as we have seen, provides the basic structure of the first two and last three phrases. The rising opening motive of phrase 1 serves as the basic material for the opening of phrase 4 and is modified in phrase 5 with a falling third rather than an ornamental figure. The falling third, in turn, is expanded in phrase 6, where it is combined with the oranmental paired eighth notes. And the forced rhythmic ending of the *parole sdrucciole* ♩ ♪♪ characterizes all phrases from 2 on, including 4, where it is adapted to the *parola piana,* "rilucente."

The distribution of strong internal cadences (at the end of phrases 1, 2, and 4) appears to highlight the principal structural points of Chiabrera's syntax (which occur at the end of either the second or fourth verse). The motivation for the strong cadence at the end of the first phrase is unclear, since the poem never isolates the first line, and in the fourth strophe the first and second lines are joined by an enjambement that is contradicted by the setting ("Con la manca ella gli sferza / Pur con fren"). The closing couplet is strongly emphasized by the harmonic discontinuity that follows the cadence on G at "rilucente": the harmony shifts to F (none of the previous phrase transitions had been marked by such an abrupt harmonic disjunction), and the bass starts in a new high register. This is consistent with Chiabrera's practice of reserving the last two lines of most stanzas for a closing gesture, and indeed in the last stanza these lines encapsulate the point of the entire canzonetta.

Parallel phrase construction on a large scale is evident elsewhere in the *Scherzi:* the opening piece in the collection, "I bei legami," consists of five phrases; of these, only the first is significantly different from the others. The rest all open in the same way and are only slight variations of each other; the last

---

27. Some commentators have seen these paired eighth notes as evidence of the *canto alla francese* mentioned by Giulio Cesare in the "Dichiaratione." See, for example, Pirrotta, "Monteverdi's Poetic Choices," 292–93, 297, 311.

Ex. 3.2. "I bei legami," mm. 13–20

is a transposed repetition of the penultimate, which sets the closing couplet (example 3.2). As in "Quando l'alba in oriente," certain elements, such as the bridge between the first and second verses in the first phrase, and the motive at "strinse," recur to unify successive phrases. And as in "Quando l'alba," the closing section is isolated by the same harmonic disjunction: an F-major triad starts the last phrase following a cadence on G major, with the same registral shift in the bass.

Perhaps the most remarkable aspect of the *Scherzi*, especially when they are compared to the madrigals of the fourth and fifth books, with which they are contemporary, is their melodic construction. Monteverdi forsakes all text-expressive elements to focus on the poetic meter, from which he derives short rhythmic modules as building blocks for larger melodic units. Some extreme examples of modular construction can be found in the shortest of the *Scherzi*, "Dolci miei sospiri," "Giovinetta ritrosetta," and "Amorosa pupilletta." "Amorosa pupilletta" consists of six six-line stanzas, each divided into two symmetrical halves in which two *ottonari* frame a *quaternario* ($a_8 a_4 b_8 c_8 c_4 b_8$); all are *versi piani*, and the meter is trochaic throughout. The first and fourth verses emphasize the medial caesura; in the third and most of the sixth verses, an elision ("Folgorando‿in cor giamai") helps to soften the segmentation by emphasizing textual continuity. In most stanzas the syntactic structure coincides with the formal scheme, but Chiabrera does vary the pattern, creating tension between form and syntax: in the sixth stanza, for example, there is a strong enjambement across lines 3–4 that contradicts the main formal division. In the setting,

Ex. 3.3. "Amorosa pupilletta"

which underscores the bipartite structure of the strophe, this variation, slight as it may appear, wreaks havoc with the relationship between music and text.

Monteverdi highlights the formal aspects of Chiabrera's scheme rather than its syntactic continuity, setting the two three-line groups in two phrases (example 3.3), each of which consists of four units built from a single rhythmic module ♪♪♪♩ ♩ . The first three units correspond to the *quaternari* that make up the first and second verses; the fourth spans the entire *ottonario* of the third verse, where the caesura is softened by an elision ("sì soave‿al cor mi scocchi"). The only rhythmic variety is introduced in the third and sixth verses. In the third, two modules are combined, displacing the second in relation to the breve and creating a momentary syncopation; and in the sixth, Monteverdi makes his most significant departure from the pattern, establishing a sense of closure for the entire strophe.

Although it is an extreme case, "Amorosa pupilletta" illustrates the primarily formal nature of Monteverdi's response to Chiabrera's poetry. Rhyme scheme, verse structure, poetic meter, and word accentuation seem to have been of greater interest than either the syntax or the sometimes subtle but nevertheless affective qualities of the texts he set to music. In some cases, however, the expressive harmonic language of the madrigal did find its way into the *Scherzi*, and in surprising ways.

Sannazaro's "La pastorella mia spietata e rigida," written in hendecasyllabic *terza rima sdrucciola*, a verse form Monteverdi set only very rarely, may have been included to provide an example of its type; nevertheless it elicited from Monteverdi one of the most interesting, even if extremely brief, settings in the entire collection.[28] In the poem, a shepherd laments his beloved's cruelty in terms that approach those of Mirtillo's most impassioned outbursts in Guarini's *Il pastor fido*. The shepherdess is pitiless, hard, haughty, and colder than ice. Her victim weeps, and the surrounding countryside resounds with his laments; all of nature knows his sorrows, and even the trees speak of her.

If the affect and imagery of the text are conventional enough, the setting is not. In the space of only three phrases lasting a total of ten bars, Monteverdi encapsulates some of the more advanced harmonic developments associated with the madrigals of his fifth book. The most striking aspect of "La pastorella" is the shift in signature from *cantus mollis* to *cantus durus*—the only time this happens in the *Scherzi* and one of the very few occurrences of such a shift in Monteverdi's madrigals.[29] The new signature is introduced at the end of the third phrase, and its arrival coincides with the text "she remains haughty and

28. The only other examples of independent compositions in *terza rima* by Monteverdi are "O ciechi ciechi," from the *Selva morale*, and "Voglio di vita uscir," which survives in manuscript only (Naples, Biblioteca Capitolare dei Girolamini, MS S. M. IV-2-23-b, and Chapel Hill MS VM2.1 M1, f[38r–40v]). See Ossi, "*L'Armonia raddoppiata:* On Claudio Monteverdi's 'Zefiro torna,' Heinrich Schütz's 'Es steh Gott auf,' and Other Early Seventeenth-Century *Ciaccone*," *Studi musicali* 17 (1988), 225–52. When I wrote this article I was not aware of the Chapel Hill source; I have since checked it, and although it preserves the piece without attribution it does not depart from the Naples source in any way. Of the 48 cantatas, 36 are anonymous; the attribution to Monteverdi in the RISM Online catalog was made by me as cataloguer on the basis of Osthoff's publication.

29. On the *durus–mollis* shift in Monteverdi's madrigals see Eric Chafe, *Monteverdi's Tonal Language* (New York: Schirmer, 1992), 105ff. and 361–70.

Ex. 3.4. Closing sections of *(a)* "La pastorella" and
(b) "Ch'io t'ami," showing similar bass lines

colder than ice"; Monteverdi marks this point by breaking the uniform rhythmic pattern of whole–half with a dotted whole on a b-minor (or perhaps G^6) harmony—precisely the pitch affected by the new signature. The bass part, from the signature change onward, is identical to that found in "Ch'i' t'ami," from the fifth book, as are the insistence on the b in the bass and, with slightly more intense dissonances than are found in the madrigal (the struck d suspension over the e), the harmonic progression to the cadence. The contrast between *mollis* and *durus* in this canzonetta hints at the highly symbolic treatment of harmony emerging in the madrigals and in *Orfeo* (example 3.4).[30]

The harmonic language of "La pastorella" is the most extreme among the *Scherzi;* the rest of the canzonettas remain within a more limited range. All but two are in G ("Amorosa pupilletta" is in d-*durus,* and "Vaghi rai" is in C), and then primarily in the *durus* system; beside "La pastorella" only two others are in g-*mollis.* A few of the canzonettas in G-*durus* move, in one of their internal phrases, toward the sharp side, typically by cadencing on A (this is the case in "Amarilli," "Amorosa pupilletta," "Vaghi rai," "La violetta," and "Giovinetta"). Both of the *mollis* pieces veer briefly toward the two-flat hexachord. With the

---

30. On the significance of the *mollis/durus* shift in "Ch'io t'ami" see Chafe, *Monteverdi's Tonal Language,* 112–17. On the anomalous dissonances found in "La pastorella" and elsewhere in the *Scherzi,* see Kurtzman, "An Early 17th-Century Manuscript," 151–52, 155–59.

exception of "La pastorella," in which the harmonic plan is consistent with the affective content of the poem, the motivation for these more distant harmonic forays seems to reside less in the text than in the need for variety within the musical structure. Although it is possible to find some correspondences with textual cues (as in "Amarilli onde m'assale," in which the modulation to A coincides in the first stanza with "Di mio bene e di mio male" [of my good and of my harm] and in the second with "Ma dell'aspro tuo pensiero" [but of your harsh thoughts]), these are rarely carried out throughout the poem and invariably lose motivation as the poem progresses (in "Amarilli," for example, none of the remaining stanzas provide a suitable text for the fourth phrase). And in other pieces ("Giovinetta" and "La violetta," for example), the text never supports any kind of affective harmonic treatment at all.

Strophic forms are, by definition, open-ended: since there is no formal marker to suggest that the poem is coming to a close, the series of stanzas could continue indefinitely. The individual *Scherzi* take strophic form and combine it with instrumental ritornellos and vocal solos supported by the basso continuo to create a new, balanced structure. The "Avvertimenti" that introduce the 1607 volume reveal the formal balance created by juxtaposing the available ensemble combinations:

> Before beginning to sing, the Ritornello should be played twice. The Ritornellos should be played at the end of each stanza; the upper parts being played by two *violini da braccio*, and the bass by a chitarrone, harpsichord, or a similar instrument. The first Soprano part, the first stanza having been sung by the three voices with the two violins, can be sung solo, or at the lower octave, in the following stanzas, returning however to the three voices and violins for the last stanza. Where lines are drawn in place of the text, the notes that are found above the lines are to be played, and not sung.[31]

The form Monteverdi imparted to the *Scherzi* exploits the variety afforded by his instrumental and vocal forces, juxtaposing solo sections with *de facto* basso continuo, tutti ensembles with *colla parte* doubling, and purely instrumental elements that included not only ritornellos but also obbligato passages occurring within vocal sections.[32] Out of these elements Monteverdi constructed a balanced form consisting of two equivalent outer members for the

31. "Avvertimenti," *Scherzi* (1607).
32. They are in "Non così," "La violetta," and the *balletto*, "De la bellezza."

Fig. 3.1. Canzonetta structure as defined in the "Avvertimenti"

Ritornello x2 — instruments
Stanza 1 — a3 + instruments

Ritornello — instruments
Stanza 2 — a1 + continuo alone[a]
Ritornello — instruments
Stanza 3 . . .

Last stanza — a3 + instruments
Ritornello — instruments

---

a. In the two canzonettas that require obbligato instrumental passages within the vocal texture it can be assumed that the instruments would continue to participate even if solo performance were chosen.

entire ensemble framing a central section for solo voice, with regularly alternating instrumental and vocal sections (figure 3.1).

In the *Scherzi*, Monteverdi imposes formal balance (in the return of the tutti texture of the first strophe at the end) and transforms the canzonetta by giving it a sense of closure that the poem neither demands nor suggests. Furthermore, his indication that the middle strophes be performed by a solo voice in contrast to the full ensemble of the outer ones introduces an element of contrast between different performing forces that is not necessarily a part of strophic settings; and that is in keeping with Chiabrera's own preferences. In "Il Geri," in the course of a brief excursus on classical forms, Chiabrera addresses the question of predictability in musical settings. He recounts that

> In Rome, master musicians played for us a *strofe* sung to one air, and followed it by singing the *antistrofe* with the same air. But when the listeners expected to hear the same air a third time, they were deceived, because the *epodo* was set to a new air. And the deception gave marvelous delight, and with good reason, since variety almost always accompanies pleasure.[33]

The surprise with which the listener received the new air to which the *epodo* was set may not have been entirely appropriate, since, as Chiabrera explains in the second of his dialogues, "L'Orzalesi," in the *canzone a strofe, antistrofe ed epodo* the first two are of the same form, and the third is different — the sonnet,

33. *Opere*, 582.

for example, with its two quatrains (the *strofe* and *antistrofe*) followed by two tercets is an example of a *canzone* with two *epodi*. This would suggest that the setting itself might properly reflect the difference between the *epodo* and what precedes it. Nevertheless, the anecdote points to the fact that strophic settings carry a certain momentum of expectation, and that the composer's exploitation of that momentum by variation—presumably any kind of variation—was cause for delight. Monteverdi's rounded settings in the *Scherzi*, with their instrumental ritornellos, colla parte doublings, solo central sections, and instrumental passages interpolated in the vocal sections, must have had a similar pleasantly surprising effect.

The composer's basic devices—strophic form, ritornellos, and *colla parte* doublings—were not new: as Richard Hudson has suggested, the *Scherzi musicali* represent the first notated manifestations of a long-standing tradition in which vocal music was introduced and punctuated by improvised ritornellos, and the informal doubling of vocal music with instruments had probably taken place since time immemorial.[34] In the *Scherzi*, however, Monteverdi was the first to absorb these materials from the domain of performance practice into compositional practice, and he was also the first to adopt explicitly the ensemble of two violins and basso continuo that was to become common during the first half of the seventeenth century (although, as we saw earlier, Caccini's own *arie* were supposedly performed "to the accompaniment of an ensemble of string instruments").[35] With these elements he laid the foundations for the multifaceted *concertato* technique of his later madrigal books, operas, and sacred music.[36]

34. Richard Hudson, *Passacaglio and Ciaccona: From Guitar Music to Italian Keyboard Variations in the 17th Century*, Studies in Musicology, vol. 20 (Ann Arbor: U.M.I. Research Press, 1981), 12. See also James Haar, "Arie per cantar stanze Ariostesche," in *L'Ariosto, la musica, i musicisti: Quattro studi e sette madrigali Ariosteschi*, ed. M. A. Balsano (Florence: Olschki, 1981), 31–46.

35. See note 5 to this chapter.

36. Werner Braun, "Ritornello," in *Die Musik in Geschichte und Gegenwart* 8 (1998), cols. 343–48. Ritornellos, in the form of *passacagli*, had been published independently in Girolamo Montesardo's *Nuova inventione d'intavolatura per sonare li balletti sopra la chitarra spagniuola* (1606)—evidence that such patterns were part and parcel of the guitarist's repertoire, to be used whenever the situation called for them. See Hudson, *Passacaglio and Ciaccona*, 18–25.

Fig. 3.2. Structure of the *balletto* from the
"Favola di Endimione"

Aria 1: Tutti (all the instruments + stars).
Aria x: Duet + viole da brazzo
Aria 1: Tutti
Aria y: Duet + viole da brazzo
Aria 1: Tutti
Etc. until all combinations are exhausted.

Although his works in the new style were not published until 1607, the composer's correspondence bears witness to his self-conscious experimentation with new formal structures during the period between 1600 and 1607. In December 1604 he had written to the Duke of Mantua from Cremona concerning the now lost "Favola di Endimione."[37] Referring to one of the *balletti* to be included in the work, Monteverdi writes:

> I first set to work on the [ballet] for the stars [alone]. Having no instructions regarding the number of stars that were to dance in it, and wanting to build it from alternating [units], which seems to me new, beautiful, and enjoyable—that is, having first all the instruments play a short, cheerful air [*aria allegra et corta*] danced by all the stars and then, immediately after it, the instruments drop out and the five *viole da brazzo* come in with an air different from the first, to be danced by a pair of stars alone; following this the fist air returns, with all the instruments and stars, this pattern [*ordine*] being repeated until all the stars have danced in pairs—lacking the number [of stars], and this [information] being necessary (provided that Your Lordship likes this manner of invention with alternating [units] as I have described) I have postponed working on it, and have written to Giovanni Battista *ballarino* for the information.[38]

Monteverdi was proposing a form in which a fixed element, to be danced by all the stars (the *aria allegra et corta* for all the instruments), functions as a ritornello alternating with an ever-changing series of duets (the air for the *viole da brazzo*) (figure 3.2). The overall length of the piece is determined by the total number of stars—it is for this reason that Monteverdi had to postpone its composition while waiting for the information, apparently from the dancer in

---

37. See *Letters*, ed. Stevens, 44–47.
38. Letter no. 3, December 1604: *Lettere*, ed. De' Paoli, 24–25; *Letters*, ed. Stevens, 44–47.

charge of the choreography.[39] The pattern is an elaboration of the strophic ritornello form, and the composer uses the same structure at the end of the second act of *Orfeo*, where the chorus "Ahi caso acerbo" punctuates two laments, each sung by a pair of shepherds.[40] It is significant that in 1604 Monteverdi stresses not only the beauty of this arrangement, but also its novelty: the pattern, as he assures the Duke, was to be "novo, bello, et gustevole."

The same impulse toward formal clarity that governs the *Scherzi* is, as we have already seen, also in evidence in the continuo madrigals of 1605, all of which contain at least one section for solo or reduced ensemble. Although in those works the elements being combined are monody and ensemble madrigal, the availability of solo textures afforded by the presence of the basso continuo is as crucial to them as it is to the formal balance of the canzonettas. Monteverdi's use of monodic elements within the continuo madrigals was closely parallel to, and very likely contemporaneous with, the developments of the *Scherzi*. During the same years when he was distilling the Mantuan madrigal style into his own epigrammatic works, Monteverdi was already beginning to create the musical language and formal structures on which he was to found *Orfeo* and many of his later works.

Monteverdi's Other Canzonettas

Some twenty of Monteverdi's secular canzonettas have been preserved in publications after the *Scherzi musicali*. A number appeared in anthologies edited by others, like Carlo Milanuzzi's *Quarto scherzo delle ariose vaghezze*, published in Venice in 1624, and Alessandro Vincenti's *Arie di diversi* (1634). Most, however, were included in Monteverdi's own publications: the *Concerto* (1619), the second volume of *Scherzi musicali* (1632), the *Madrigali guerrieri et amorosi* (1638), and the posthumous *Madrigali e canzonette a due e tre voci: Libro nono* edited by Vincenti in 1651. These works fall into two categories: strophic ensemble canzonettas for two to four voices with continuo; and strophic arias for one voice (mainly soprano) and continuo.

---

39. On the uncertain identity of "Messer Gio. Batt. ballarino" see *Lettere*, ed. De' Paoli, 348, and *Letters*, ed. Stevens, 46. Stevens also proposes that the formal arrangement of the dance for the stars is the same as that of the *entrate* from the *Ballo delle ingrate* (p. 45 n. 6), but—aside from the fact that dancers are paired in both works—there is no evidence that the duets for the stars are based on the same bass line, or that each *entrata* was done to a different realization of the bass line given in the score. See Monteverdi, *Tutti le opere*, vol. 8, 332–37.

40. I am grateful to Professor Kerala Snyder for pointing out the parallel between the *balletto* and "Ahi caso acerbo."

Rigidly strophic settings did not lend themselves to the kinds of affective or formal subtleties that Chiabrera sometimes introduced in his poems. In the ensemble canzonettas, Monteverdi continued to explore the flexibility of the basic formal elements established in the *Scherzi musicali* of 1607. The two published in the seventh book, "Chiome d'oro" and "Amor, che deggio far?" explore increasingly sophisticated and varied formal designs and expand the expressive language of the genre (see table 3.3). The scheme of the *Scherzi*, in which the same ritornello is repeated throughout and formal closure is achieved by a symmetrical return to the sonority of the opening stanza, is altered to include three ritornellos, all of which are played twice at the beginning of the piece and are then heard in rotation between the strophes. In both pieces, the ritornellos and strophes use related but not identical bass parts against which the upper voices change for each repetition, creating an elaborate set of interlocking strophic variations (figure 3.3).

The rhythmic and melodic language of these canzonettas is also quite different from that of the *Scherzi*. In "Chiome d'oro" the modular construction of the earlier pieces, which was tied to the verse structure, is replaced by a more flexible declamation in which each stanza is articulated within a single statement of the strophic bass. There is little effort to underscore the verse structure, which is evident only in the melodic disjunctions that mark the beginning of the third and fourth verses. The distinction between *quaternario* and *ottonario*, frequently reflected in the modular construction of the *Scherzi*, is here blurred entirely. Phrases are articulated instead according to a musical, rather than poetic, logic: the modules of the *Scherzi* can still be seen in the three basic melodic units that make up each phrase, but the overall form of the strophe is not indebted to the text. The three units use the same components, a stream of even eighth notes punctuated by dotted rhythms, but in slightly different configurations each time so that the melodic shape of each is different from the others. A brief ornamental melisma divides the phrase into two unequal sections, the first of which consists of two units plus the ornamental extension, and the second of a single unit (example 3.5).

The middle strophe is extended, first by a second ornamental melisma at the end of the last line (marked "Adagio" in the score but without interruption of the strophic bass); and then by the repetition of the last phrase, "se ridete m'ancidete," over suddenly static harmonies (with the indication "presto onestamente," presumably a resumption of the original tempo). With the return of the walking bass the canzonetta resumes its previous character, and the

Table 3.3 Formal structure of "Chiome d'oro" and "Amor che deggio far"

"Chiome d'oro"

	R1	R2	R3	Stanza 1	R1	Stanza 2	R2	Stanza 3	R3	Stanza 4	R1	Stanza 5
Key:	C throughout											
Bass:	a			a'	a	a'	a	a' (with harmonic interruption)	a	a'	a	a' (with harmonic interruption)

"Amor che deggio far"

	R1	R2	R3	Stanza 1 (Canto), 2 (Tenor)	R1	Stanza 3 (2 C), 4 (TB)	R2	Stanza 5 (CCB)	R3	Stanza 6
Key:	C			C-E	C	C-E	C	C-E	C	C-E-C
Bass:	a			b	a	b	a	b	a	b for lines 1–3, free for lines 4–6

Fig. 3.3. Structure of the first two acts of *Orfeo*, excluding the
Messaggera's narrative

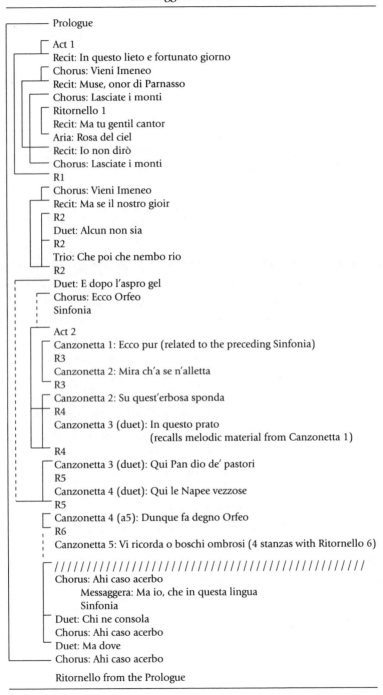

Prologue

Act 1
Recit: In questo lieto e fortunato giorno
Chorus: Vieni Imeneo
Recit: Muse, onor di Parnasso
Chorus: Lasciate i monti
Ritornello 1
Recit: Ma tu gentil cantor
Aria: Rosa del ciel
Recit: Io non dirò
Chorus: Lasciate i monti
R1
Chorus: Vieni Imeneo
Recit: Ma se il nostro gioir
R2
Duet: Alcun non sia
R2
Trio: Che poi che nembo rio
R2
Duet: E dopo l'aspro gel
Chorus: Ecco Orfeo
Sinfonia

Act 2
Canzonetta 1: Ecco pur (related to the preceding Sinfonia)
R3
Canzonetta 2: Mira ch'a se n'alletta
R3
Canzonetta 2: Su quest'erbosa sponda
R4
Canzonetta 3 (duet): In questo prato
            (recalls melodic material from Canzonetta 1)
R4
Canzonetta 3 (duet): Qui Pan dio de' pastori
R5
Canzonetta 4 (duet): Qui le Napee vezzose
R5
Canzonetta 4 (a5): Dunque fa degno Orfeo
R6
Canzonetta 5: Vi ricorda o boschi ombrosi (4 stanzas with Ritornello 6)

/ /
Chorus: Ahi caso acerbo
      Messaggera: Ma io, che in questa lingua
      Sinfonia
Duet: Chi ne consola
Chorus: Ahi caso acerbo
Duet: Ma dove
Chorus: Ahi caso acerbo

Ritornello from the Prologue

Ex. 3.5. "Chiome d'oro," mm. 1–5

fourth strophe follows the pattern set for the first and second. The last section again departs from the others in three respects: first, the ornamental melisma at the end of the second unit is missing, replaced by a sudden halt in melodic motion; second, the last phrase is repeated twice, the first time with an ornamental extension over the same static harmonies that had interrupted the walking bass in the third strophe; and third, the second time "o gradita mia ferita" is heard, the two voices are joined by the *obbligato* violins in a tutti ending.

The distribution of the ritornellos is also different from that of the *Scherzi.* Not only are there three of them, but the order in which they are distributed throughout the canzonetta—with the first ritornello being heard at the beginning, after the first strophe, and just before the last; and the others in reverse order—establishes an almost palindromic rounded form. The music seems to progress to the beginning, establishing a sense of closure that is reinforced by the new texture that closes the piece.

In the ensemble canzonettas, Monteverdi primarily explored the potential for formal and stylistic variety. The importation into the ensemble canzonetta of topoi characteristic of other genres, such as the *lamento* bass, the *ciaccona,* and the *genere concitato,* expanded the genre's expressive potential. At the same time, Monteverdi's use of complex strophic variations, *concertato* techniques, and the collage-like juxtaposition of stylistic elements made possible the transformation of the basic pattern established in the first volume of *Scherzi musicali* into a nearly limitless variety of designs.

Ex. 3.6. "Maledetto sia l'aspetto," vocal line

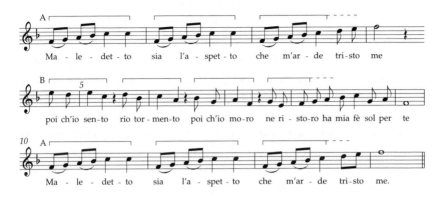

The strophic arias for solo voice are mostly miniatures, but they are characterized by the same concentration of material found in the canzonettas as well as by Monteverdi's interest in incorporating even in his smallest works elements derived from a variety of sources. To judge by the pieces that survive, Monteverdi seems to have come late to the solo aria, to have written only a few of them, and perhaps not to have valued very highly his own essays in this rather popular genre.[41] His earliest contributions came in 1624, when three of his arias were included in Carlo Milanuzzi's *Quarto scherzo delle ariose vaghezze.*[42] Aside from the four examples published in the second collection of *Scherzi musicali* (1632), none of his other arias appeared in his own publications, and the sum total of his output numbers only about half a dozen pieces.

All of these works follow in the footsteps of the first volume of *Scherzi musicali.* "Maledetto sia l'aspetto," from the *Scherzi* of 1632, is not unlike "Amorosa pupilletta" in the economy of its melodic construction: it uses two motivic units from which Monteverdi builds two contrasting phrases; the rising contour of the first phrase, which eventually spans an octave, is answered by a symmetrical fall in the second, which closes with a recall of the opening motive but quickly folds back to close on the lower F. The first phrase is then repeated to create a miniature A B A form (example 3.6). The contrasting phrases differ both in motivic material and in their harmonic content, so that the strong

41. This does not take into account the strophic arias for solo voice that make up large portions of *L'Orfeo.*
42. The three arias are "Ohimè ch'io cado ohimè," "La mia turca che d'amor," and "Sì dolce è il tormento," all either entirely strophic or strophic variations.

tonic–dominant relationships of the opening and closing phrases are juxtaposed to the ornamented falling third sequential pattern of the middle passage. As in "Amorosa pupilletta," the basic metric unit is the *quaternario;* the poem alternates *versi piani* and *tronchi,* and these are reflected in the rhythmic structure of the setting, which shows far greater flexibility than that of any of the pieces from 1607. In the first phrase the rhythmic units coincide with the breve—either two whole notes (for the two opening *quaternari piani*) or three (for the two *versi tronchi*), imparting to the declamation a foursquare effect; in the middle section the *versi piani* are set to three half notes and distributed across breve units, creating an unstable rhythm that drives toward the eventual harmonic resolution of the sequence. Monteverdi deals with the different number of verses in the middle section both by shortening the time allotted to each of the *versi piani* and by combining the last of them with the two *tronchi.*

The most complex of Monteverdi's arias, "Quel sguardo sdegnosetto" and "Ed è pur dunque vero," both from the collection of 1632, employ the strophic variation technique of "Chiome d'oro" and "Amor che deggio far." In "Quel sguardo," the bass pattern is based on the *ciaccona,* which only appears once in its original form as the second of the two bridges for the continuo part alone (because of their brevity they can hardly be called ritornellos) that link the three strophes. Although "Quel sguardo" matches the mocking tone of "Maledetto sia l'aspetto," and its formal plan is as straightforward as that of any of the strophic canzonettas, its highly virtuosic melismatic vocal style is unlike that of any other in Monteverdi's output. "Ed è pur dunque vero" is based, as are the two ensemble canzonettas from the seventh book, on a more complex double variation pattern. It has a fixed bass part for the sinfonia, which is scored for solo violin (the only instance in Monteverdi's works of a sinfonia or ritornello for one melody instrument), and another for the vocal sections. Against these fixed elements, the violin and the voice are given new material for each of their seven sections.[43] Both pieces set texts of either *settenari* ("Quel sguardo") or *settenari* mixed with *endecasillabi* ("Et è pur dunque"), and both emphasize flexibility over repetition of metric patterns. In "Quel sguardo," Monteverdi seems to seek out ways of placing accents so that they contrast with the regularity of the poetic meter. This is in part accomplished by the avoid-

---

43. The Malipiero edition (vol. 10, 82–90) gives a very odd repeat pattern, with a double bar placed after the fourth line of each six-line stanza. This establishes the form R1, lines 1-4 || R1, lines 1-6, R2, lines 7-10 || lines 4-6 (!), R2, lines 7-13, R3, lines 14-17 || lines 12-13 (!), R3, etc. Although the text is such that no serious violence is done to its coherence, the resultant form seems needlessly complicated.

ance of balanced phrases, in part by the odd syncopation ("ond'io tutt'ardo" in the first strophe, "io vi preparo il seno" in the third), and in part by the placement of melismas, which—even when they are justifiable as word painting—emphasize the "wrong" syllables: "Quel sguardo sdegnose*tto*, / lucente e minaccioso / quel dar*do* velenoso / *vo*la a ferirmi il petto / bellezze ond'io tutt'ar*do*."

Madrigal influence can also be felt in the occasional chromaticism that sets "Quel sguardo" and "Et è pur dunque vero" apart from the other arias of the *Scherzi musicali:* passages like "in fin ch'io venga meno" from "Quel sguardo" and "miei torbidi pianti" from "Et è" are unique in Monteverdi's treatment of the genre and can be found prominently in only one other work, the manuscript aria "Voglio di vita uscir." Although its attribution to Monteverdi has been questioned, it shares a number of characteristics with the two strophic arias from the *Scherzi:* a mocking text, melodic flexibility, free use of the *ciaccona* bass, and melodic chromaticism.[44]

The Canzonetta as Symbol and Formal Module

In *Orfeo,* Monteverdi expanded the formal model he had pioneered in the *Scherzi musicali* and adapted it to dramatic ends. In the process, the canzonetta assumed extramusical connotations that transcended its usefulness as a readily adaptable formal building block and turned into a symbol not only of celebration, but also of worldly pleasure. Thus, in *Orfeo* it becomes associated with the world of the living in contrast to the underworld, whose musical representation relies heavily on recitatives, and at the end of Monteverdi's career it resurfaces in *Poppea* to give voice to the frivolity of Seneca's followers.

I have discussed elsewhere in detail Monteverdi's use of the canzonetta to generate the formal structures on which the first one and one-half acts of *Orfeo* are based.[45] Building on the foundations established in the canzonettas of the *Scherzi musicali* and in other works, like the ballet for the stars in the *Favola di Endimione* (1604), he was able to combine a variety of ritornello-like structures to control both the tempo of the action and the grouping of singers throughout the celebrations that lead up to the arrival of the Messaggera in the second act. As figure 3.1 shows, ritornellos and canzonetta-like strophic sections define the structure in all its aspects, from the largest span, between the

44. On the problems posed by "Voglio di vita uscir," see my "L'Armonia raddoppiata," 240–53. Although I did not take a firm stand on the work's attribution at the time, its similarity to the two arias under discussion points toward Monteverdi as its author.

45. "Claudio Monteverdi's *ordine novo.*"

prologue and the ritornello at the end of act 2, to localized and self-contained units (labeled in the figure "a," "a'," "b"). Within the first unit—we might almost define it as a scene, since it focuses on a subgroup of revelers—Monteverdi gathers three different events: the large group singing "Vieni Imeneo"; the smaller chorus singing "Lasciate i monti"; and finally Orfeo and Euridice, the focal point of the opening celebrations, framed by the repetition of "Lasciate i monti." The return of "Vieni Imeneo" brings this action to an end before the focus shifts to a contrasting second group, which emphasizes more intimate, and also symmetrically arranged, duets and trios. Thus the first act is divided into two sections, each of which depends for its structure on symmetrical returning elements.

Recurring modules, such as a ritornello or a text-musical refrain, not only serve to frame an action or group of actions and give it internal coherence, but they can also link passages across such smaller units, creating a sense of continuity. And, at the largest level of organization, they provide the boundaries that organize the five acts of the opera into three overarching periods. For example, single statements of the ritornello from the prologue return at the end of the second and fourth acts, defining what appear to be the largest structural groups (acts 1 and 2, and 3 and 4); and each of the first four acts is also marked by a choral ending.[46] The closing chorus of act 1, "Ecco Orfeo," provides a link to the parallel "Dunque fa degno Orfeo" in the second, emphasizing the continuity of the celebrations across the two acts; similarly the Sinfonia that follows it provides an immediate link to the opening canzonetta of the second act, "Ecco pur."

The second act moves very quickly through a series of truncated canzonettas, each interrupting the preceding one and being itself interrupted by the one after it, in a crescendo of musical shifts—involving new vocal strophes, new ritornellos, new instrumentation, and new singers. The instability with which

46. The prologue itself is a series of strophic variations punctuated by a ritornello. The isolated occurrence of a ritornello seems a misnomer and may be the result of revisions undertaken between the performance of 1607 and the publication of the opera in 1609; although it is possible that this particular ritornello, having been heard several times in context at the beginning of the opera, is intended to discharge large-scale functions. Whenham's theory, that acts 1 and 2, and 3 and 4, are intended to be grouped into two units, each marked by its own scenery, offers a highly plausible explanation for the recurrence of this ritornello as a pause for changing sets. On the use of ritornellos at the end of acts, see Nino Pirrotta, "On Early Opera and Aria," in *New Looks at Italian Opera: Essays in Honor of Donald Jay Grout*, ed. William Austin (Ithaca: Cornell University Press, 1968), 88 n. 96, and "Monteverdi's Poetic Choices," 290 n. 43.

the second act begins can be likened to a series of cinematic cuts that, by their frequency, serve to propel the "action" to its proper goal, in this case Orfeo's celebratory "Vi ricorda o boschi ombrosi," where the spotlight can at last linger until the celebrations are suddenly brought to an end. A similar cinematic sequence takes place in the first act, starting with a large group scene, isolating a subgroup, and then closing in on the main protagonists before repeating the process in reverse and returning to the larger group, whose song may be seen as the continuation of what they had been singing at the beginning of the scene. Most importantly, throughout *Orfeo* the deployment of canzonetta-style sections is not an abstract element superimposed on the work's dramatic progress but serves to further the development of the plot.

In *Orfeo*, Monteverdi associates the canzonetta with the wedding celebrations and by extension with Orfeo; with his art as a singer; with his newly purposeful, structured, life after marriage; and with the world of the living in general. This symbolic function is made clear as soon as death intrudes on the shepherds' merrymaking. After the Messaggera's announcement of Euridice's death, the continuation of the second act as well as the remaining three acts are dominated by extended recitative sections in *genere rappresentativo*, with only three exceptions: in act 2, after Orfeo's "Tu se' morta" the entire group joins in a funerary lament, "Ahi caso acerbo"; and the third and fourth acts each contain one principal ritornello-based number ("Possente spirto" in the third, and "Qual honor di te sia degno" in the fourth).

In "Ahi caso," the chorus of nymphs and shepherds alternates with a tenor duet. The dirge-like chorus serves as a ritornello, providing a structural underpinning for the entire section, as the tutti passages had done in the *balletto* described in the letter of 1604, while the duets—although their openings are related—are free to develop along different lines. Orfeo's "Possente spirto," possibly the most celebrated passage in the entire opera, is cast as a set of strophic variations with ritornellos—actually a set of ornamental interludes of an improvisatory nature designed to represent the demigod's virtuosity.[47]

47. Monteverdi himself, as he noted on 9 December 1616 in a letter to Alessandro Striggio, regarded "Possente spirto" as the focal point of the entire work. In criticizing the libretto for *Le nozze di Tetide*, he wrote, "*Arianna* led me to a just lament, and *Orfeo* to a righteous prayer" [l'Arianna mi porta ad un giusto lamento; et l'Orfeo ad una giusta preghiera]: *Letters*, ed. Stevens, 117; *Lettere*, ed. De' Paoli, 87. John Whenham suggests that by calling on the principal classes of instruments for the ritornellos—bowed strings, winds, and plucked instruments—Orfeo calls on all of Music's resources in his attempt to mollify Charon ("Five Acts: One Action," in *Claudio Monteverdi: Orfeo*, ed. John Whenham [Cambridge: Cambridge University Press, 1986], 68).

In act 4, Monteverdi once more resorts to the canzonetta as the means for conveying happiness and the impending restoration of order. After Euridice's release, as Orfeo leads her upward toward the world of the living, he sings three strophes of a very jaunty canzonetta with an instrumental ritornello, "Qual onor di te sia degno," its brisk walking bass seeming the musical embodiment of the hubris that is his eventual downfall.[48] Orfeo's strophic variations are interrupted after the third strophe, as he is assailed by doubts: "Ma mentre io canto, ohimè, chi m'assicura ch'ella mi segua?" [But while I sing, alas, who can assure me that she follows me?] Monteverdi abruptly interrupts the major mode with a shift to a *molle* affect, dominated by falling tritones at "ohimè," whose growing anguish is reflected in a rising sequence. The stark contrast between the unrhymed recitative of "Ma mentre" and the regularly metric, rhyming canzonetta underscores Orfeo's second loss and recalls the withdrawal of order that had followed Euridice's death in the second act.

In each case, the form is based on that employed for the allegorical prologue, in which Music is represented by a set of strophic variations. In retrospect, the association of Music with this most organized and virtuosic form offers a key to the central allegory of the opera—the power of music to impart order, to tell stories, and to move the emotions. Heard against the backdrop of the surrounding recitatives, which are associated with death, loss, and the chaotic underworld, these highly structured passages serve as reminders of the order and harmony that had opened the opera and that Orfeo seeks to restore with his search for Euridice: "I am Music, who with sweet sounds am able to still every turbulent heart" [Io la Musica son, ch'ai dolci accenti so far tranquillo ogni turbato core].

In *Orfeo*, Monteverdi explores the potential of the canzonetta as a framework for building large-scale forms capable of conveying both dramatic action and meaning. The formal order of the celebrations mirrors the new-found order of Orfeo's world; the uncertainty of his quest in the remainder of the opera after Euridice's death finds musical expression in Monteverdi's avoidance of balanced formal structures in favor of open-ended recitatives. Most importantly, perhaps, the canzonetta fits into a multi-tiered system of musical representation, in which form and style serve expressive ends. In *Orfeo* the canzonetta is identified with real songs and dances, performed either as set pieces by the shepherds and by Orfeo, or sung as expressions of uncontained emotion.

Monteverdi himself makes clear the symbolic role of the canzonetta in a

48. *Tutte le opere*, vol. 11, 122.

letter written in January 1617 to Alessandro Striggio, in which he criticizes the libretto for *Le nozze di Tetide*, a *favola marittima* that the Mantuan court had wanted him to set to music as a set of *intermedii*. The composer found the conclusion wanting, and suggested a modification:

> In my opinion it does lack, at the very end after the last line, which reads, "Let heaven regain its serenity, and the sea its calm," a canzonetta in praise of the Most Serene princely bridal pair, the music of which could be heard in heaven and earth from the stage, and to which the noble dancers can dance, since a noble ending of this kind seems to me suitable to a noble scene such as I have proposed.[49]

As in many contemporary pieces, at the end the audience joins the performance with a *ballo* ("possano nobili ballarini far nobil danza"), and Monteverdi proposes a canzonetta probably because of its dual association with dance music and with nuptial celebrations.[50]

Unworthy though it may seem, the canzonetta could also be enlisted to convey moral messages. The *canzonetta morale* "Chi vol che m'innamori," from the *Selva morale e spirituale*, exploits the contrast between the *memento mori* of its text and the frivolous dance-like character of the setting. The anonymous text dwells rather conventionally on the ephemeral nature of earthly beauty — a flower's short-lived bloom, the soon-to-be extinguished radiance of enticing eyes, graying golden hair. These objects of secular love pale at the thought of death ("Death, alas, kills me . . . it engenders a terror that takes over my heart" [la morte, ohimè, m'ancide . . . produce terror che 'l cor m'ingombra]).

The setting is for three voices, homorhythmic, with a *basso seguente* and ritornellos for a pair of violins. The musical structure, however, is more fragmented than that of other canzonettas like it: after a conventional opening in which the phrase structure follows the poetic form, with regular cadences coinciding with the *versi tronchi* of the even lines, the third phrase interrupts this

49. *Letters*, ed. Stevens, no. 24, pp. 125–26; *Lettere*, ed. de Paoli, no. 24, p. 95–96. I have modified Stevens's translation slightly.

50. A number of contemporary accounts document the participation of the nobility in dances at the end of entertainments. See the various accounts cited in Robert Lamar Weaver and Norma Wright Weaver, *A Chronology of Music in the Florentine Theater, 1590–1750*, Detroit Studies in Music Bibliography, no. 38 (Detroit: Information Coordinators, 1978); also Nino Pirrotta, "The Orchestra and Stage in Renaissance *Intermedi* and Early Opera," in *Music and Culture in Italy from the Middle Ages to the Baroque* (Cambridge: Harvard University Press, 1984), 213.

pattern to emphasize "ah, che sian tosto spenti," which signals the change of affect for the second half of the stanza. Instead of continuing with the homorhythmic canzonetta texture, the setting shifts to a descending figure, suggesting the characteristic *lamento* bass of the "Lamento della ninfa," and a divided texture. The descending bass is not treated as an ostinato, however, but is extended into a scalar descent of almost two octaves, ending on an E major harmony. The contrast between sorrow and transitory happiness is then highlighted by the introduction of yet another stock bass pattern, the *ciaccona*, for "oggi si ride."

Happiness and its inevitable antithesis are reinforced by the direct juxtaposition of E major and the C major of the *ciaccona*.[51] This contrast is repeated twice more as the setting repeats the last pair of lines. A triple-meter dance-like ritornello for two violins and continuo, not heard at the beginning, separates the three strophes. Unlike the canzonettas of the *Concerto*, in "Chi vol che m'innamori" the violins do not join the voices for a tutti ending; rather, Monteverdi provides a second ritornello as a postlude. Like the canzonetta itself, this closing instrumental section contrasts two affects—the first part is in duple meter and is harmonically related to the *memento mori* lament of the vocal section; the second returns to the triple-meter *ritornello primo*.

As in *Orfeo*, Monteverdi's choice of genre in "Chi vol" relies on the immediate association of the canzonetta with the enjoyment of worldly, and even erotic, pleasures. By invoking the *lamento* bass and the *ciaccona* as well, he packs this diminutive piece chock-a-block with allusions to symbols of human frailty: the dance, emotions that shift, and the love song as a tool of seduction. To be sure, during the first half of the seventeenth century many secular elements, like the *ciaccona* bass and the strophic form with ritornello, found their way into sacred music without necessarily implying either an ironic stance toward the sacred context or a subversion of the religious texts. But in *Orfeo* and "Chi vol," the emblematic role of the canzonetta is clearly supported and even determined by its juxtaposition with the text.

Perhaps the clearest example of the canzonetta as emblem of worldly frivolity occurs in the third scene of act 2 of *L'incoronazione di Poppea*, during Seneca's leave-taking from his disciples. The symmetry of this scene is well known: Seneca opens and closes it with brief recitatives on the meaning of vir-

---

51. A similar shift occurs in "Zefiro torna e di soavi accenti," at the change from the *ciaccona* to the recitative section, where the G major of the ostinato is contrasted with the E major harmony at "Sol io."

tue and death; the main body of the scene is the reaction of his *famigliari*, who sing a canzonetta, "Questa vita è troppo dolce," preceded by their plea "Non morir Seneca" (set to a chromatic ascending line) and by an affirmation of their own distaste for death "Io per me morir non vo'" (set to a descending line).[52] After the canzonetta these two elements return in reverse order, creating a palindromic form that encompasses the entire scene.

"Questa vita" itself is quite remarkable: it is strophic, and its syncopated juxtaposition of 3/4 and 6/8 time recalls nothing so much as Orfeo's "Vi ricorda o boschi ombrosi."[53] The style jars both for its by now archaic character and for the contrast it establishes with the chromatic material that surrounds it as well as with Seneca's recitatives; more importantly, it jars because it is so completely out of place. The sudden contrast between the frivolity of the disciples' attachment to life in the face of their master's impending death and the philosopher's *gravitas* is utterly shocking: Seneca's measured response, "Itene tutti," underscores the gulf that separates him from his followers. Here the contrast is not so much between life and death, but between virtue and an uncomprehending lack of it—nowhere in Monteverdi's works had a canzonetta ever sounded so tawdry.

—❧—

Monteverdi's development around the turn of the century was not linear: his works from the first decade of the century suggest that he cast a wide net over the increasing variety of contemporary forms and expressive techniques, and that out of his haul he had begun to assemble a new language in which formal devices and madrigalian expression were brought into line for dramatic purposes. The canzonettas of the *Scherzi musicali* of 1607 served as the proving ground for some of the most important developments of Monteverdi's new

52. Tim Carter, in "Re-Reading *Poppea*: Some Thoughts on Music and Meaning in Early Seventeenth-Century Italian Opera" (paper presented at the Fifth Annual Conference of the Society for Seventeenth-Century Music, Tallahasee, 1997), points out the very close relationship between "Non morir Seneca" and the canzonetta "Non partir ritrosetta," which was published in the *Madrigali guerrieri et amorosi* (1638). The patterning of the *famigliari*'s plea for earthly life on an amorous canzonetta reinforces the fatuous and purely venereal connotations of the passage in *Poppea*.

53. Alan Curtis's realization of the missing upper parts of this ritornello emphasizes the similarity, which is of course clearly present in the bass part. See his edition of *L'incoronazione di Poppea* (London: Novello, 1989), 124ff.

style—*concertato* technique, schematic form, and a new rhythmic approach to text setting. In chapter 4 I turn to some of the most extreme examples of hybrid forms, including the canzonetta that provided the basic elements of the "Lamento della ninfa" from the eighth book. Like the absorption of improvised ornamentation into composition, which as Palisca has shown provides the foundation for the expressive dissonances of the "particelle" criticized by Artusi,[54] each component of the *Scherzi musicali* has its origins in Monteverdi's experience as performer and composer. Ritornellos, *colla parte* doublings, solo sections extracted from a polyphonic context, and the shifting flexible rhythms and declamation of the canzonettas—all were part of the informal language of the late sixteenth century that Monteverdi first experienced as a practical musician and then formalized, turning performance practice into compositional practice.

In spite of its apparent incongruity, then, Giulio Cesare's coupling of his "Dichiaratione" with Claudio's *Scherzi musicali* draws attention to the composer's varied interests around 1600. It is even possible that, by publishing the two together, he was seeking—however unsuccessfully—to broaden the terms of the debate with Artusi beyond the confines of contrapuntal propriety and toward the new concepts of rhythm, form, genre, and expression that were to become central to his brother's approach to text-setting for the remainder of his career.

54. Claude V. Palisca, "The Artusi–Monteverdi Controversy," in *The New Monteverdi Companion*, ed. Denis Arnold and Nigel Fortune (London: Faber and Faber, 1985), 130–34.

FOUR

The Blurring of Genres in Individual Madrigals

As we saw in chapter 2, the organization of the fifth book depends, at the largest and simplest level, on the progressive arrangement of madrigals for five, six, and nine voices and on the distinction between a cappella madrigals, madrigals with obbligato basso continuo, and the lone double-choir *concertato* madrigal at the end. "Questi vaghi concenti" is separated from the pieces that precede it by its instrumental sinfonia, which functions as much as a ritornello as it does as a means of creating discontinuity.

Congruent with these broad musical categories is, as we have seen, the division of the texts into two contrasting groups—the first dominated by dramatic excerpts taken from *Il pastor fido*, and the second consisting of short, independent *madrigali*. The latter group is organized into a narrative cycle that is imposed on the poetry, creating a measure of contrast—simultaneous, in this case—between structure and poetic genre. The large-scale tension between poetic type and architectural organization is reflected in the textual manipulations that create refrain structures from a refrainless genre and in the introduction of such text-independent structural devices as the strophic variation. On the most localized level, the juxtaposition of two different classes of composition, solo song and ensemble madrigal, provides the components for small-scale, contrast-based structures.

The fifth book bears witness to two simultaneous impulses, both of which gather strength over the next thirty-odd years of Monteverdi's career. The first is toward the creation of musical taxonomies; the second, toward the incorporation of text-independent formal paradigms (see table 1 in the prologue). Both contribute to the establishment of an aesthetic in which meaning is determined less by the Renaissance ideal of resemblance, in which the music is molded to the text, than by the simultaneous existence of independent textual and musical signs that, understood separately but interpreted together, lead the observer to their meaning.[1] In this equation, the relationship between *oratione* and *harmonia* is not between mistress and servant, but between two equals; and in this, perhaps, lies its true modernity.

The major works following the fifth book—*Orfeo*, the *Vespers*, and the sixth, seventh, and eighth books—attest to the growing importance of large-scale schematic organization. Although none of them returns to the narrative logic of the fifth book, all build on structural elements already present in the volume of 1605. In each work, Monteverdi arranges the individual components within a design that is based on scoring, genre, function, and character.

Perhaps the most celebrated aspect of the *Vespers* (1610) is the stylistic contrast between the *prima prattica* mass and the concertato techniques of the vespers proper; as in Book Five, the two styles are segregated into sections (table 4.1). The Vespers, the main body of the collection, are laid out in a double cycle in which four motets, for (in order) one, two, three, and six voices, are inserted between the large-scale psalm settings. The non-psalmodic cycle culminates in the "Sonata sopra Sancta Maria"; then, after the hymn "Ave maris stella," two versions of the Magnificat, one in *concertato* style with obbligato instruments and the other for voices and continuo, summarize the contrast between the styles that characterize the collection as a whole. The sixth book, like the fifth, contrasts groups of continuo and a cappella madrigals but organizes them into two roughly equivalent sections, each headed by a lament cycle (the polyphonic version of Arianna's lament in the first part, and the "Sestina: lagrime d'amante al sepolcro dell'amata" in the second; see table 2 in the prologue). As in Book Five, Monteverdi also juxtaposes different types of poetry— the dramatic *versi sciolti* of Rinuccini's *Arianna* with the strict forms of Petrarch's sonnets and Agnelli's Petrarch-inspired sestina. And the juxtaposition is further emphasized by the association of Petrarch with a cappella madrigals and Marino with highly schematic settings for contrasting solo voices and ensemble

1. On this point see Ellen Rosand, "The Descending Tetrachord: An Emblem of Lament," *Musical Quarterly* 65 (1975), 346–59; and, more recently, Gary Tomlinson, *Music in Renaissance Magic: Toward a Historiography of Others* (Chicago: University of Chicago Press, 1993), 189–246; and Tim Carter, "Resemblance and Representation: Toward a New Aesthetic in the Music of Monteverdi," read at the 1993 meeting of the Society for Seventeenth-Century Music (St. Louis). The point of departure for Tomlinson, Carter, and this chapter is the theories of Michel Foucault, *The Order of Things: An Archaeology of the Human Sciences* (New York: Vintage, 1970).

Table 4.1 Organization of the *Vespers* of 1610

Number and function	Scoring	Title	Text source
A. Mass			
1 *Missa ad imitationem*	6-part choir, with BC	*Missa da capella a sei voci fatta sopra il motetto 'In illo tempore' del Gombert*	Mass ordinary
B. Vespers			
2 Responsory	6-part choir, 6-part mixed instrumental ensemble, and BC	*Domine, ad adjuvandum*	
3 Psalm	6-part choir (with T solo), 6-part mixed instrumental ensemble, and BC	*Dixit Dominus*	Psalm 109
4 Motet	T and BC	*Nigra sum*	Song of Songs
5 Psalm	8-part choir (SS solo) and BC	*Laudate, pueri*	Psalm 112
6 Motet	SS and BC	*Pulchra es*	Song of Songs
7 Psalm	6-part choir and BC	*Laetatus sum*	Psalm 121
8 Motet	TTT and BC	*Duo seraphim*	
9 Psalm	*Cori spezzati*: 2 5-part choirs and BC	*Nisi dominus*	Psalm 126
10 Motet	T solo, with BC, and 6-part choir with BC	*Audi, coelum, verba mea*	
11 Psalm	7-part choir and BC	*Lauda, Jerusalem*	Psalm 147
12 Litany (invocation)	S solo and 8-part mixed instrumental ensemble with BC	*Sonata sopra 'Sancta Maria, ora pro nobis'*	
13 Hymn	*Cori spezzati*: 2 4-part choirs, 5-part mixed instrumental ensemble for the ritornelli, and BC	*Ave maris stella*	
14 Canticle I	7-part choir, 6-part mixed instrumental ensemble, and BC	*Magnificat*	Canticle of the Blessed Virgin
15 Canticle II	6-part choir and BC	*Magnificat*	Canticle of the Blessed Virgin

with continuo accompaniment. The lines of distinction are, however, not entirely without blur: Rinuccini's operatic monody is recast as an a cappella madrigal, and Marino is represented primarily by Petrarchan sonnets.[2]

In the seventh book, the taxonomic foundation of the structure is made apparent in the title, *Concerto: Settimo libro de madrigali a 1, 2, 3, 4 et sei voci, con altri generi de canti*,[3] and is reflected in the grouping of pieces according to scoring and genre (see table 3 in the prologue). Although the basic principle of organization according to scoring was common enough in modern madrigal books, the seventh book combines this with other conventions: works of a different type (the *romanesca*, monodies in *genere rappresentativo*, canzonettas) are grouped at the end, as was commonly done with instrumental works "appended" to vocal collections; and the entire volume is framed at the beginning by an operatic prologue with sinfonia and at the end by a *ballo*, following the practice of dramatic entertainments. Again, as with the sixth book, the order is blurred. The title refers to a madrigal for one voice, and it is not clear whether "Tempro la cetra" or "Con che soavità" is to be understood as that piece; neither is properly a madrigal, although "Con che soavità" fits the description more closely. Its apparently irregular placement after the madrigals for four voices parallels the equally odd insertion of "A quest'olmo," for six voices and instruments, after the first duet.[4] Finally, the eighth book combines the schemes Monteverdi tried out in the sixth and seventh (see table 4 in the prologue). The volume begins with a sinfonia, presumably the introduction to the entire collection, which comprises two parts: the *Madrigali guerrieri* and *Madrigali amorosi*. Each opens with two large-scale *concertato* settings of sonnets, introduces several works for smaller ensembles, including madrigalian duets and canzonettas, and presents a work in *genere rappresentativo* before concluding with a *ballo*.

Monteverdi's madrigal books attest to his increasing awareness of the distinctions between genres and between styles. This tendency toward categorization, which encompassed aspects of style, genre, and function, was to become

2. The choice of high forms may in part be related to the association, documented for at least one work in the collection, with Caterina Martinelli, the singer for whom Monteverdi intended the part of Arianna and who died while the opera was in preparation; see Edmond Strainchamps, "The Life and Death of Caterina Martinelli: New Light on Monteverdi's 'Arianna,'" *Early Music History* 5 (1985), 155–86.

3. Venice: Magni, 1619.

4. Because of its structure, poetic contents, and position within Monteverdi's output, the seventh book poses a wide range of problems, and I am currently working on a book-length study devoted entirely to it.

a central component of his final theoretical statement, the preface to the *Madrigali guerrieri et amorosi*. It also manifested itself in the juxtaposition of elements drawn from different genres within single pieces, and even in the superimposition of formal and stylistic characteristics, at times masking the distinction between the various categories. In this chapter, I discuss three works, the madrigal "Con che soavità" from the seventh book, the semidramatic "Lamento della ninfa" from the eighth, and the "Gloria a 7 concertata" from the *Selva morale*. Each presents a different aspect of Monteverdi's synthesis of compositional techniques: "Con che soavità" hovers between the "madrigali" that precede it and the "altri generi di canti" that follow it; the "Lamento" is a brilliantly disguised canzonetta; and in the "Gloria" a patchwork of *prima prattica* contrapuntal tutti sections, ostinatos, strophic variations, and canzonetta-like structures are combined into a large-scale structure of kaleidoscopic variety.

"Con che soavità"

Monteverdi's setting of Guarini's *madrigale* "Con che soavità" is unique among *concertato* madrigals published in the first half of the seventeenth century and ranks as one of his most unusual works. Perhaps its most striking aspect is its scoring, for solo *canto* and three instrumental *cori* requiring a total of 12 instruments, eight of which are assigned to a continuo role. No other concertato madrigal from the period calls for an ensemble of this size, and no other contemporary solo chamber work requires such a large complement of continuo instruments. But "Con che soavità" stands out for more than just its odd instrumental requirements: its style is an amalgam of monody and elements derived from vocal ensemble music; its sectional form is more closely allied with Monteverdi's large-scale *concertato* madrigals from the *Madrigali guerrieri et amorosi* (1638) than with the monodies it appears to resemble; and the composer's choice and distribution of the instrumental complement recalls the practices of dramatic music rather than those of genres destined primarily for chamber performance. "Con che soavità" is also one of only fifteen independent secular compositions by Monteverdi for solo voice; it is notable among them not only because of its scoring, but also because it is neither a kind of strophic *aria*, as are most of the others, nor a dramatic work in *genere rappresentativo*.[5]

---

5. Monteverdi's other works for solo voice are the arias "Ecco di dolci raggi," "Eri già tutta mia," "Et è pur dunque vero," "Maledetto sia l'aspetto," and "Quel sguardo sdegnosetto," all published in the second volume of *Scherzi musicali* (Venice: Magni, 1632); "Ohimè ch'io cado" and "La mia turca che d'amor," published in Carlo Milanuzzi, *Quarto scherzo delle ariose vaghezze* (Venice: Vincenti, 1624); "Pur lieto il guardo" and "Perché se m'odiavi," in *Arie di*

Monteverdi issued "Con che soavità" as the twenty-third composition in the *Concerto*. The seventh book seems to be both a madrigal collection after the latest fashion (the madrigals for one to six voices) and a more "public" program that opens with an allegorical prologue and closes with a *ballo*, as was often the case with dramatic entertainments.[6] Within the discernible organization of the volume, "Con che soavità" occupies an ambiguous position: it follows the orderly progression of madrigals for two, three, and four voices that forms the core of the book (nos. 4–16, 17–20, and 21–22, respectively) and precedes a section comprising what the composer terms *altri generi di canti—romanesca* variations, solo works in *genere rappresentativo*, canzonettas, and a *ballo*.[7] It is, perhaps pointedly, not placed at the beginning of the section devoted to the madrigals, where, as a solo setting of a madrigal text, it would seem to belong; and where, in a rather conspicuous reversal, Monteverdi instead put the madrigal "A quest'olmo" *a sei voci* and two obbligato instrumental parts (violins alternating with *flauti o fifare*).

Perhaps because it seems to find no counterpart in any of the composer's other works, "Con che soavità" has not been the object of extensive critical attention. Few writers have dealt with it, offering characterizations that class the work variously as an "arioso" offshoot from *Orfeo*, a dialogue for a single voice, or an aria with "orchestral" accompaniment.[8] Taking a cue from the title of the collection within which it appears, *Concerto*, some critics have found in the instrumental requirements of "Con che soavità," apparently too large for the resources of most private chamber music, evidence that Monteverdi intended the

---

diversi (Venice: Vincenti, 1634); the *partenza amorosa*, "Se pur destina e vole il cielo," and the *lettera amorosa*, "Se i languidi miei sguardi," in *genere rappresentativo*, both issued in the *Concerto*, to which should be added the "Lamento d'Arianna," which had a life independent of the opera from which it was extracted, and which was published in its monodic version in 1623 together with the two *lettere* from the *Concerto* (Venice: Magni); and finally the aria "Voglio di vita uscir" and the "Lamento d'Olimpia," in *genere rappresentativo*, both rare among Monteverdi's works in that they survive only in manuscript form. On "Voglio di vita uscir" see Ossi, "*L'Armonia raddoppiata*: On Claudio Monteverdi's 'Zefiro torna', Heinrich Schütz's 'Es steh Gott auf', and Other Early Seventeenth-Century *Ciaccone*," *Studi Musicali* 17 (1988), 225–53.

6. Nino Pirrotta, "Monteverdi's Poetic Choices," in *Music and Culture in Italy from the Middle Ages to the Baroque* (Cambridge: Harvard University Press, 1984), 305, and especially n. 98.

7. On the organization of the *Concerto*, see Pirrotta, "Poetic Choices," 305–9; and Paolo Fabbri, *Monteverdi* (Turin: U.T.E.T., 1985), 215–23.

8. See Fabbri, *Monteverdi*, 221; Nigel Fortune, "Monteverdi and the 'seconda prattica,'" in *The New Monteverdi Companion* (London: Faber and Faber, 1985), 186–88; Denis Arnold, *Monteverdi* (London: Dent, 1963), 85–86; Leo Schrade, *Monteverdi, Creator of Modern Music* (New York: Norton, 1950), 287 and 289; and Hans Redlich, *Claudio Monteverdi, Life and Works*, trans. by Kathleen Dale (London: Oxford University Press, 1952), 82–85.

entire book to furnish the music for a public concert, or at least to offer an abstract representation of such an event.[9] No documented performance has been associated with the *Concerto,* and Monteverdi's three brief references to the volume in his correspondence with Mantua shed no light on the question.[10] While these views are not entirely wrong, none addresses the problematic nature of "Con che soavità," and none fixes the position it occupies within Monteverdi's output. Most importantly, "Con che soavità" resists all attempts at a single categorization and is best explained as an amalgam of contrasts: between instrumentation and function; between instrumentation and style; between text-expressive, localized rhetoric and overall syntax; between single harmonic events and the overall harmonic layout. Conflict is inherent in Guarini's text, and Monteverdi emphasizes it throughout his setting.

I

The three instrumental *cori* (table 4.2) are distinguished from one another both by their function and by their composition. The first is made up of continuo instruments — two *chitarroni,* a *clavicembalo,* and a *spinetta.* The second

Table 4.2 Instrumental requirements of
"Con che soavità"

	Clef
Primo choro	
Duoi chitaroni	F4
Clavicembalo	F4
Spinetta	F4
Secondo choro	
Viola da brazzo	C1
Violino, Choro delle viole all'alta	C1
Choro delle viole da braccio	C3
Clavicembano	C4
Terzo choro	
Viola da braccio overo da gamba	C4
Basso da braccio overo da gamba	F4
Contrabasso	F4
Concerto, Terzo choro a4, Basso continuo	F4

9. Pirrotta, "Poetic Choices," 308.

10. Letters 35, 39, and 40, dated 13 December 1619, 16 January 1620, and 25 January 1620. See *The Letters of Claudio Monteverdi,* ed. and trans. by Denis Stevens (London: Cambridge University Press, 1980), 151–52 and 162–65; and *Claudio Monteverdi: Lettere, dediche e prefazioni,* ed. by Domenico De' Paoli (Rome: De Santis, 1973), 118–19 and 127–31.

consists of the uppermost instruments in the *viola da braccio* family—violin plus soprano and alto *viole da braccio*, accompanied by a single *clavicembalo*. Finally, the third *coro* consists of the lower instruments of both the *viola da gamba* and *viola da braccio* families—one tenor and one bass, each from either family, and one *contrabasso*—plus, again, a single unspecified basso continuo instrument. The overall distribution favors the continuo group—six *strumenti da corpo* and two bowed strings are all devoted to the bass line, and only four to the remaining parts.

The differences in instrumentation between the three groups also generate variety of texture. The quick attack and decay of the lutes and keyboard instruments of the first *coro* is juxtaposed with the sustained sound of the bowed strings, and the high and low tessituras of the two string ensembles produce contrasting colors. In addition to providing contrasts of texture and color, the three *cori* also serve different functions: the first and third are essentially continuo groups, although, while the first *coro* is left to play from the bass line, the ensemble of single-line instruments of the third *coro* plays at least a partial realization of the bass. The group of treble instruments, the second *coro*, is treated more flexibly than the others, at times reinforcing the voice in homorhythmic passages, and occasionally sharing in its melodic material.

Monteverdi's use of a large instrumental ensemble to accompany a work for solo voice is unusual, even in the context of concertato composition during the first twenty years of the seventeenth century. The preferred scoring for *concertato* madrigals (that is, madrigals with obbligato instrumental participation other than continuo) typically involved, in addition to the vocal ensemble, a pair of treble instruments—most often violins, occasionally cornettos or a combination of the two—plus continuo.[11] The treble instruments could either fulfill obbligato functions, as in Monteverdi's "A quest'olmo" from the *Concerto* or "Or che'l ciel e la terra" and the other large-scale madrigals of the *Madrigali guerrieri et amorosi*; or else they were assigned to the ritornellos that punctuated canzonettas like those of the *Scherzi musicali* (1607) or "Chiome d'oro" and "Amor, che deggio far?" from the seventh book.[12] The preponder-

---

11. On the instrumentation of the concertato madrigal between 1600 and 1650, see Ossi, "Claudio Monteverdi's Concertato Technique and its Role in the Development of his Musical Thought" (Ph.D. dissertation, Harvard University, 1989), especially chapters 1 and 5.

12. On Monteverdi's treatment of the canzonetta as a formal model in *Orfeo* and elsewhere, and on the importance of the first volume of *Scherzi musicali* for his development, see Ossi, "Claudio Monteverdi's *Ordine novo, bello et gustevole*: The Canzonetta as Dramatic Module and Formal Archetype," *Journal of the American Musicological Society* 45 (1992), 261–304.

ance of instruments assigned to the bass in "Con che soavità" is especially striking because it is entirely out of proportion with contemporary practice for chamber music, and especially for solo vocal pieces. Early seventeenth century continuo instrumentation falls into two broad categories: dramatic and semi-dramatic music, and vocal chamber music. For each, the continuo group acquired a distinct makeup, and Monteverdi's compositions generally reflect contemporary trends.[13]

All of Monteverdi's dramatic and semidramatic works employ more than one continuo instrument, often combining both *strumenti da corpo* and melodic bass instruments. The *Ballo delle ingrate*, first performed in 1608 and possibly revised for a performance in 1636, requires five *viole da brazzo*, a *clavicembalo*, and a *chitarrone*—at least three instruments are assigned to the bass line, and possibly more depending on the size of the room in which the work is to be performed.[14] The *ballo* "Tirsi e Clori," composed in 1615–16 and published at the end of the *Concerto*, requires a *chitarrone*, or a harp, to accompany Tirsi, and a harpsichord for Clori. In addition, the two soloists both play *chitarroni*, with which they double the continuo instruments assigned to them. For the *ballo* itself, the singers are doubled by an ensemble of viols, with a foundation complement consisting of a bass viol, a contrabass, and a *spineta arpata*.[15] *Il Combattimento di Tancredi et Clorinda*, like the *Ballo delle Ingrate*, requires an ensemble of *viole da brazzo*, one of which is assigned to the bass, and a harpsichord, plus a *contrabasso da gamba* doubling the bass line throughout ("che continuerà con il Clavicembano").[16]

Orfeo offers the greatest amount of information about Monteverdi's treatment of the continuo band in dramatic works. The following foundation instruments are required: two *contrabassi di viola*, three *bassi da gamba*, three *chitarroni*, an unspecified number of large citterns, a double harp, two

13. On continuo practices in seventeenth-century Italy, see Tharald Borgir, *The Performance of the Basso Continuo in Italian Baroque Music* (Ann Arbor: U.M.I., 1987).

14. Denis Stevens, "Madrigali guerrieri, et amorosi," in *The Monteverdi Companion*, ed. Denis Arnold and Nigel Fortune (London: Faber and Faber, 1968), 245.

15. Letter 18, 21 November 1615; *Letters*, ed. Stevens, pp. 107–8; *Lettere*, ed. De' Paoli, p. 80.

16. The instrumental forces required in the *Combattimento* are occasionally found also in semidramatic works published in madrigal books—as for example in Biagio Marini's "Ninfa," a dialogue scored for two voices and an accompanying ensemble of two violins, two viols (alto and tenor), and basso continuo, published in his *Concerto terzo delle musiche da camera* (1649). Marini's instrumental accompaniment consists largely of a simple realization of the harmonic implications of the bass and has no contrapuntal function, never interacting with the voice.

harpsichords, two organs, and a *regale*, totaling more than fourteen instruments.[17] Such a large band allows for a number of combinations, and Monteverdi makes varied use of the instruments to obtain a wide color range. The more colorful groupings, such as those using the *regale* or ensembles of wind instruments, are dictated by dramatic situations; this is the case with the chorus of souls in the underworld, which is accompanied by trombones, *regale*, and a complement of low strings; and with Charon's music, in which the *regale* alone is used. Choruses require the largest number of instruments: "Vieni Imeneo" was accompanied by all the instruments; "Lasciate i monti" by three *chitarroni*, two harpsichords, double harp, and *contrabasso di viola* in addition to five *viole da braccio* and a *flautino alla vigesima seconda* doubling the voices (at least eight players assigned to the bass, including both melodic and harmonic instruments). The norm for small vocal ensembles as well as for solo voice throughout *Orfeo* is a mixed pair of *strumenti da corpo* consisting of one keyboard instrument and one chitarrone, occasionally augmented with a bowed bass instrument: "In questo prato adorno," from the second act, is sung by two shepherds to the accompaniment of one *chitarrone* and one harpsichord; several solos and duets, including the celebrated "Possente spirto," call for one organ with wooden pipes and one *chitarrone*; and one solo passage, "Qual suon dolente" in act 2, is scored for harpsichord, *chitarrone*, and an unspecified *viola da braccio*.

The prints of vocal chamber music that began to appear after 1600, on the other hand, are much more modest in their instrumental specifications. Salomone Rossi's first book of madrigals for five voices, issued in 1600, includes some works to be sung in consort with a *chitarrone*;[18] Luzzasco Luzzaschi's *Madrigali per cantare et sonare*, also published in 1600, has a written-out accompaniment for a single harpsichord;[19] and similarly Giulio Caccini's *Le nuove musiche*,[20] which appeared the following year, assumes accompaniment

---

17. Instrumentation is reported in the 1609 score and is given in both Malipiero's edition and the facsimile editions. See also Jane Glover, "A List of Monteverdi's Instrumental Specifications," in *Orfeo*, ed. John Whenham (Cambridge: Cambridge University Press, 1986), 182–84, and Christoph Wolff, "Zur Frage der Instrumentation und des Instrumentalen in Monteverdis Opern," in *Claudio Monteverdi: Festschrift Reinhold Hammerstein zum 70. Geburtstag*, ed. Ludwig Finscher (Laaber: Laaber-Verlag, 1986), 489–98.

18. *Il primo libro di madrigali a cinque voci con alcuni di detti madrigali per cantar nel chitarrone, con la sua intavolatura posta nel soprano* (Venice: Amadino, 1600).

19. *Madrigali per cantare et sonare a uno, e doi, e tre soprani* (Rome: Verovio, 1600).

20. *Le nuove musiche* (Florence: Marescotti, 1601; repr. Florence: Studio Per Edizioni Scelte, 1983).

by a single *chitarrone*.[21] With increasing frequency, books of madrigals for five or more voices were issued with the generic rubric "accomodati da cantarsi nel [arranged so as to be sung with] Clavicembalo, Chitarone, Chitariglia, Arpicordo, et altri stromenti simili [and other similar instruments]." Rarely was more than one instrument, or a mixture of melodic bass instruments and *strumenti da corpo*, required.[22]

On especially festive occasions the continuo group for madrigals could be expanded, but not to the extent that it was for dramatic performances: Monteverdi himself, in describing a carnival concert in the Hall of Mirrors at Mantua, at which the entire court and more than one hundred gentlemen from the city were expected, writes:

> On a . . . splendid occasion I shall have the *chitarroni* played by the musicians from Casale, to the accompaniment of the wooden organ (which is extremely suave), and in this way Signora Adriana and her brother Giovanni Battista will sing the extremely beautiful madrigal "Ahi, che morire mi sento," and the other madrigal to the organ alone.[23]

For most of this repertoire, then, a single supporting instrument was typical, and even in extraordinary circumstances, when large audiences were in attendance and larger ensembles were warranted, musical considerations sometimes favored a softer, "extremely suave," single instrument for madrigals.[24]

Monteverdi's own publications reflect this general trend. He began exper-

21. It is mentioned in the introduction.

22. There are some exceptions, mostly involving the presence of a *chitarrone* or *tiorba* in addition to a basso continuo part. Whether the plucked instruments were used in a melodic function or actually realized the bass line is a matter of debate—see Borgir, *Basso Continuo*, especially 101–17, and Ossi, *The Italian Concertato Madrigal in the Early Seventeenth Century: An Anthology* (in preparation).

23. Letter 12, 22 June 1611. According to Stevens, the two *casaleschi* were probably Orazio and Giovanni Battista Rubini; the two madrigals were by Cardinal Ferdinando Gonzaga. See *Letters*, 85–86; *Lettere*, ed. De' Paoli, 58.

24. That the question of audibility may not have been particularly important in such large ceremonial gatherings is also evident from Thomas Coryat's account of a gathering of similar proportions for the feast of San Rocco, which he attended at the Scuola Grande di San Rocco in 1608. During the course of the music, which lasted for three hours beginning at five in the afternoon and included numerous works for large ensembles of mixed vocal and instrumental forces, "two singular fellowes played together upon Theorboes, to which they sung also, who yeelded admirable sweet musicke, but so still that they could scarce be heard but by those that were very neare them." *Coryat's Crudities* (Glasgow: MacLehose, 1905), 1, 390–91.

imenting with combinations of voices and instruments in chamber music around 1600, and the result of his early explorations, the volume of *Scherzi musicali* published in 1607, requires that the bass be played on a *chitarrone*, or a harpsichord, or a similar instrument.[25] Both his fifth and sixth books of madrigals, published in 1605 and 1614 respectively, make similar references to a single supporting instrument, to be chosen from the keyboard or lute families. His subsequent books dispense entirely with general instructions of this type, but occasionally individual works, like "Con che soavità," do make explicit demands. When he does specify the continuo instrument, Monteverdi requires only one — generally a keyboard, although occasionally a *chitarrone* is named, as in the canzonettas "Chiome d'oro" and "Chi vol aver felice e lieto il core" from the *Concerto*, which, like the *Scherzi* to which they are related, allow for either keyboard or *chitarrone*. The *contrabasso* appears, in addition to an unspecified *strumento da corpo*, in only two madrigals, both in the eighth book, and both for large choir: "Altri canti d'Amor" and "Vago augelletto." In the former it is part of an ensemble of *viole*; in the latter it reinforces the bass in tutti passages only.

Monteverdi's use of foundation instruments in "Con che soavità," then, is more closely allied with the scoring of *Orfeo* and other dramatic works than with the contemporary chamber repertoire, and this association is reinforced by the way the composer employs the lower *viole* to support the voice. Beginning at "che soave armonia fareste," the third *coro* plays full chords, accompanying the voice homorhythmically in what is essentially a simple realization of the continuo part. Several examples of this texture, in which four to six *viole* support the voice with simple chords, can be found in Monteverdi's *Orfeo*, the *Combattimento di Tancredi et Clorinda*, and the madrigal "Altri canti d'Amor" from the eighth book. In "Altri canti," an extended passage setting the text "Tu cui tessuta han di Cesare alloro" for solo bass is supported homorhythmically by a *spinetta* and an ensemble of two violins, two *viole* (alto and tenor), a tenor *viola da gamba*, and a *viola da contrabasso*. In the *Combattimento* the strings underscore with ever-rising sonorities, and again homorhythmically, Clorinda's dying words (at "Amico hai vinto" and "S'apre il ciel"); and in *Orfeo*, at the end of "Possente spirto" Orfeo's concluding appeal to Charon is supported by three *viole da braccio* and a *contrabasso de viola* playing simple realizations of the continuo harmonies in long sustained notes. In all three cases, it seems that Monteverdi intends that the instruments play only what is written, for he issues

25. *Tutte le opere*, vol. 10, "Avvertimenti."

specific performance instructions: the accompaniment to Clorinda's last words and to "Tu cui tessuta" is to be played with single bow strokes *(arcata sola)*, and for Orfeo's "Sol tu nobile dio" he specifies that the *contrabasso de viola* should play very softly ("tocchi pian piano").

The use of *accompagnato* technique in dramatic situations and in madrigals—particularly in "Con che soavità"—may well help to shed light on one of the composer's most celebrated works: Arianna's lament, "Lasciatemi morire." Monteverdi issued the lament twice: in 1614, arranged as a polyphonic madrigal cycle for five voices; and in 1623 as a monody, in a print pairing it with two other dramatic pieces, the "Lettere amorose." In all three the accompaniment consists only of an unspecified basso continuo line. While the isolated lament may well have been performed to the accompaniment of a single *strumento da corpo* by the amateurs who bought the print to sing the work as chamber music, it certainly does not reflect the way it was first performed as part of the opera. Contemporary sources unequivocally testify that Arianna sang her lament alone on stage, with the support of an offstage ensemble of "viole et violini." The Venetian ambassador, reporting on the Mantuan wedding, wrote of the performance:

> Then followed the commedia in musica . . . and all actors performed their parts very well, but best of all was the actress [who played] Arianna: it was the story of Arianna and Teseo, and in her lament, set to music and *accompanied by* viole *and* violini, she moved many with her sufferings [emphasis added].[26]

And Giovanni Battista Doni, in his *Trattato della musica scenica*, made reference to the kind of scoring used in the *Combattimento* and "Sol tu nobile dio" in criticizing Monteverdi's madrigal arrangement of the lament, apparently made at the request of a Venetian patron:

> Would it not have been better had the Venetian gentleman, instead of asking Sig. Claudio to arrange Arianna, truly the pride of his compositions, as [a cycle of] madrigals, asked for *an ensemble of four instruments to accompany as well as possible that lovely air for solo voice?* [emphasis added][27]

Doni's solution would not have altered the monody, as the madrigal version had done to the detriment of the original (in his opinion), and would have

---

26. In Angelo Solerti, *Gli albori del melodramma* (repr. Hildesheim: Olms, 1969), 1, 99. Also in Fabbri, *Monteverdi*, 138.

27. "Appendice," in *De' trattati di musica* (Florence: Gori, 1763), 61.

remained true to the dramatic purpose of the piece. Among recent commentators, only Gary Tomlinson has addressed the question of the relationship between the two surviving versions of the lament and the one heard at the first performance. Tomlinson proposes that both surviving versions are in fact arrangements of a semipolyphonic original, in which the instrumental ensemble played parts that approximated the texture of the madrigal without being quite so complex, but that also were not so chordally simple as a true continuo accompaniment would have been.[28] It was, to use his term, "pseudo-monody," the complexity of which made it necessary to restrict the singer's freedom of expression in the interest of coordinating the voice with the offstage instruments. But, given the evidence of *Orfeo*, the *Combattimento*, "Altri canti d'Amor," and, most importantly, of "Con che soavità," it is possible to imagine for "Lasciatemi morire" a string accompaniment that requires no alteration of the monodic vocal line, that realizes the existing continuo, and that does not sacrifice the expressive character of the music for practical reasons.[29] As "Con che soavità" demonstrates, the realization of a continuo bass line with a string ensemble allows considerable flexibility and expression — the one quality of the accompaniment that the official chronicler of the wedding, Federico Follino, found it worthwhile to mention: "The offstage instruments . . . matched their sound to every nuance of the music. [Arianna's lament] was represented with such *affetto* and in such a moving manner that there was no one in the audience who was not moved, and there was not a lady who did not shed a tear."[30] Considering that, according to Monteverdi, *Arianna* was in rehearsal for at least five months "after it was committed to memory," it seems likely that there had been ample time to work out whatever coordination was necessary between singer and instrumentalists.[31]

II

Battista Guarini included "Con che soavità" in the first collection devoted entirely to his own works, issued in 1598.[32] While settings of it had begun to appear as early as 1586 in Filippo di Monte's eleventh book of madrigals for

28. *Monteverdi*, 138–39.

29. On the possibility of ensemble realizations of the continuo line, see Gloria Rose, "Agazzari and the Improvising Orchestra," *Journal of the American Musicological Society* 18 (1965), 382–93.

30. Cited in Fabbri, *Monteverdi*, 133.

31. Letter 38, 9 January 1620. *Letters*, ed. Stevens, 159–61; *Lettere*, ed. De' Paoli, 124–26.

32. *Rime del molto illustre Signor Cavalier Battista Guarini* (Venice: Ciotti, 1598).

five voices,[33] it seems not to have been particularly attractive to composers—only nine settings of it are known in addition to Monteverdi's.[34] Within the *Rime*, "Con che soavità" (no. 77), titled "Words and kisses" [Parole e baci] by Guarini, closes a loosely organized group of poems dealing with various aspects of the kiss—the stolen kiss ("Bacio rubato," nos. 71 and 72); kissed lips ("Baciate labra," nos. 73 and 75); and the kiss as insufficient reward ("Un bacio è poco" [A kiss is not enough], no. 76).

In "Con che soavità," Guarini focuses on a single conceit, the mutual exclusivity of words and kisses: although both originate on the beloved's lips, they cannot be enjoyed simultaneously. The subject is developed in two stages, which function as an antecedent–consequent pair: the presentation of the problem (verses 1–6), and its fanciful solution (verses 7–11), which culminates in the paradoxical *concetto* of the last line ("Kissing words and discoursing kisses") (table 4.3).

The first half consists of three syntactic units: two declarative sentences distributed over three verses state the madrigal's premise; a more complex two-part question takes up the remaining three. The first group is unified by the combination of rhyme and syntax: the first, unrhymed, verse is followed by a rhymed couplet comprising two grammatically independent units, the second of which is subordinate to the first and depends on it for its meaning. Verses 4–6, like the preceding one (3), depend on the first two: the acts of kissing and listening are explicitly mentioned only in the first sentence of the premise, and are referred to only as "pleasures" [piacer] and "delights" [diletti] in the remainder

33. *L'undecimo libro delli madrigali a cinque voci* (Venice: Gardano, 1586).

34. In addition to Filippo di Monte's and Monteverdi's, they are: Benedetto Pallavicino, *Quarto libro de' madrigali a cinque voci* (Venice: Gardano, 1588); Girolamo Dalla Casa, *Il secondo libro de madrigali a cinque voci con i passaggi* (Venice: Amadino, 1590); Giovan Giacomo Gastoldi, *Concerti musicali con le sue sinfonie a otto voci: Comodi per concertare con ogni sorte de' stromenti* (Venice: Amadino, 1604); Giovanni Antonio Cirullo, *Il sesto libro de' madrigali a cinque voci* (Venice: Vincenti, 1609); Francesco Rognoni-Taeggio, *Il primo libro de' madrigali a cinque voci con il basso per sonar con il clavicembolo* [sic], *o chitarrone fatto per li sei penultimi, et per gli altri a beneplacito* (Venice: Vincenti, 1613)—"Con che soavità" is the second piece in the collection, and therefore not among those that require the basso continuo; Antonio Marastoni, *Madrigali concertati a due, tre, quattro et cinque voci per cantare et suonare nel clavicembalo o altro simile stromento* (Venice: Vincenti, 1619); Francesco Turini, *Madrigali a cinque cioè tre voci e due violini con un basso continuo duplicato per un chitarrone o simil istrumento: Libro terzo* (Venice: Vincenti, 1629); Orazio Tarditi, *Madrigali a doi, tre, e quattro voci in concerto per cantar e sonar' sopra il gravicembalo chitarone spinetta o altro simile istrumento: Con una Lettera amorosa in stile recitativo a voce sola: Libro secondo. Opera decima* (Venice: Vincenti, 1633). Of these, only the late settings by Marastoni, for three voices, Turini, for three voices and two violins, and Tarditi, for four voices, require basso continuo.

Table 4.3 Rhyme, meter, and translation of "Con che soavità"

Text	Rhyme	Meter	Translation
Con che soavità, labbra odorate,	A	11	With what sweetness, adored lips,
e vi bacio e v'ascolto!	b	7	I both kiss you and listen to you!
Ma se godo un piacer, l'altro m'è tolto.	B	11	But if I enjoy one pleasure, the other is denied me.
Come i vostri diletti	c	7	Why do your delights
s'ancidono fra lor, se dolcemente	D	11	kill one another, if my
vive per ambedue l'anima mia?	E	11	soul lives sweetly for both?
Che soave armonia	e	7	What delicate harmony
fareste, o cari baci, o dolci detti,	C	11	you would create, o dear kisses, o sweet words,
se foste unitamente	d	7	were you capable
d'ambedue le dolcezze ambo capaci:	F	11	of both sweetnesses at once:
baciando i detti e ragionando i baci.	F	11	kissing words and discoursing kisses.

of the first part. The restatement of the premise (verses 4–6) intensifies its meaning, both by reformulating it as a question and by using strongly contrasting language—the two pleasures "kill" [s'ancidono] one another, while the soul "lives sweetly" [dolcemente vive] for both. The antecedent–consequent construction of the question contrasts with the simpler declarative sentences that precede it, and its length is emphasized both by the caesura in the middle of verse 5 and by the two enjambements that bridge verses 4–5 and 5–6. After the question mark, which provides an open-ended articulation at the midpoint of the poem, comes the main body of the second part, which consists of a single conditional sentence that, spanning four verses and two clauses, is the longest unit in the poem. The overall division of the madrigal into two parts is emphasized by the redundant character of the second part, which, by repeating the premise of the poem, becomes almost independent of the first: words and kisses are mentioned in verse 8 for the first time since the opening sentence, almost implying a new beginning—indeed, verses 7–11 could almost stand alone as a five-line epigram.

Given the nearly symmetrical bipartite structure of the madrigal, the rhyme scheme lends flexibility to what could otherwise have become a routine formal arrangement, producing a pattern of shifting associations between content and structure. As we have seen, the opening three verses are grouped together by the rhyme scheme *(abb)*; after this opening unit, however, rhyme becomes independent of syntax and content. The remainder of the poem falls into two parallel groups *(cdee* and *cdff)* that straddle both the larger bipartite structure and its smaller syntactic components. The rhyme scheme also contrasts with the metrical organization, which alternates *settenari* and *endecasillabi* in two roughly equivalent symmetrical groups congruent with the two halves of the poem.

The expansive discursiveness of "Con che soavità" is quite removed from the epigrammatic directness of the Guarini texts Monteverdi selected for the fourth and fifth books of madrigals. Whether "Parole e baci" should be seen as falling short of an epigrammatic intent, as Tomlinson argues (the poem can almost be seen as a pair of semantically related epigrams),[35] it seems quite clear that it is not for its epigrammatic qualities that Monteverdi selected it. In setting "Con che soavità," in fact, the composer emphasized the expansive rhetoric of Guarini's poem, mirroring the formal ambiguities of the text with the interaction of several organizational plans, the most obvious of which hinges on

35. *Monteverdi*, 171–72.

Table 4.4 Formal plan of Monteverdi's setting of "Con che soavità"

Section		Measure	Verse	Cadence[a]	Texture	\ Scoring
A	a	1–6		[D]	monody	\ Ch. 1
	a	7–12	1–2	[E]		
	b	13–15		A		
	c	16–20	3	C		
	d	21–28[a]		A	ensemble	\ Ch. 2
	e	28–33			madrigal	\ Ch. 1 + 2
	f	33–37	4–6			
	e	37–40				
	f	40–47[a]		D		
B	g	48–54			acc. recit.	\ Ch. 3
	b″	55–60	7–8	G		\ Tutti
	g	61–67			acc. recit.	\ Ch. 3
	b″	68–72		A		\ Tutti
	g′	73–82		G	acc. recit.	\ Tutti
	h	82–85		C	madrigal	\ Ch. 1
	h	86–89	9–11	A		\ Ch. 2
	g′	90–99		G	acc. recit.	\ Tutti
	h′	99–102		C	madrigal	\ Ch. 2
	h′	103–6		A		\ Ch. 1
	g″	106–15[a]	11	D	madrigal	\ Tutti
	j	115–21		[Plagal extension]		

a. Principal structural cadences.

the distribution of the three instrumental *cori* (table 4.4). Related to the use of the instrumental ensemble is Monteverdi's juxtaposition of different stylistic elements, some derived from the a cappella madrigal and some from monody. On a larger scale, the transposed recurrence of melodic material and of stylistically related passages creates a series of internal correspondences that, like Guarini's rhyme scheme, cut across the larger formal divisions of the setting.

In "Con che soavità," scoring serves primarily as a rhetorical device. In the broadest of terms, Monteverdi's setting consists of two parts, which correspond to the principal divisions of Guarini's poem and, like them, stand in an antecedent–consequent relationship to one another (mm. 1–47 and 48–121). Within this larger framework, the distribution of the instrumental ensembles defines the principal rhetorical moments of the text (table 4.4).

The first entrance of each of the three *cori* establishes the way in which the instrumental ensembles are used to underscore the text. The piece opens with the voice accompanied by the *coro* of *strumenti da corpo* alone, stating the first two verses of the text. Monteverdi emphasizes the third verse, "Ma se godo un piacer, l'altro m'è tolto," by introducing it with a dramatic pause and shifting the texture from the plucked instruments of the first *coro* to the bowed *coro di viole* (m. 21), which is heard at this point for the first time. This crucial verse — the central paradox of the piece — is further highlighted by the fact that it is the only passage in the first forty-eight bars that is accompanied in its entirety by the second *coro* alone. A similar discontinuity of texture occurs at the beginning of the second part (m. 48), where, after the highly ornamented cadence at "l'anima mia" (m. 47) supported by the first and second *cori*, "Che soave armonia" is scored for the low strings and continuo of the third *coro*, an entirely new sound prepared, as had been "Ma, se godo" in measure 21, by the longest pause yet in the piece.

Monteverdi distinguishes the three ensembles not only by range and instrumentation, but also by the style of the music assigned to each: the first and third *cori* are primarily associated with monodic or recitative-like material, while the second *coro* is given a more active rhythmic profile than the others and behaves almost like a vocal group. The opening twenty measures are reminiscent of monodic madrigals in the vein of Caccini's *Le nuove musiche* — a vocal line over a relatively slow-moving harmonic bass that allows the singer several opportunities for ornamentation (at mm. 5, 11, 14, and 19, for example). At "Ma se godo un piacer" (mm. 21–28), the texture shifts to homorhythmic declamation with a faster harmonic rhythm (from bar or half-bar to quarter note) involving the ensemble of *viole all'alta*. After the cadence on the first beat of m. 28, the *canto*, again supported only by the *strumenti da corpo*, is isolated from the ensemble of *viole*, which follows the characteristic canzonetta-like rhythm of the vocal line at a one-measure interval and briefly echoes it without imitating it (mm. 32 and 39). This procedure is similar to one commonly found in ensemble madrigals, in which one voice (generally a tenor or a soprano) is singled out and presents material that is then imitated homorhythmically, either verbatim or in varied form, by the other voices.[36] When this texture returns at the end, setting the *concetto* (mm. 82–89), it does so with a similar rhythmic character. The relationship between soloist and chorus is also preserved in the *concetto*, but this time the ensemble repeats the phrase

36. See for example "Quel augellin che canta," from the fourth book, mm. 18–21 (*Tutte le opere*, vol. 4, 66).

presented by the canto in a responsorial texture that adumbrates the style of madrigals like "Vago augelletto," "Dolcissimo uscignolo," and "Chi vole aver felice e lieto il core," from the *Madrigali guerrieri et amorosi* (1638).[37]

Finally, the ensemble of bass and tenor instruments that enters at m. 48 to accompany, and to represent with its change of sonority, the text "che soave armonia fareste," supports the voice in what is essentially accompanied recitative, playing a simple triadic realization of the basso continuo. The lower instruments retain their harmonic role even in the more complex contrapuntal ending in which, unlike the violin and the soprano viola, they are never allowed to participate in the imitation of the vocal material but sustain the harmony in longer note values.

The only blurring of the otherwise distinct roles assigned to the three *cori* occurs at "o cari baci" and "o dolci detti" (mm. 55–60 and 68–72 respectively), where the three ensembles are brought together for the first time to support the text and all instruments participate briefly in the contrapuntal texture. These passages are particularly striking: Monteverdi writes two instrumental decrescendos by progressively reducing the ensemble from the initial tutti to only one part, the single continuo instrument that supports the third *coro*. This effect is more idiomatically instrumental than vocal, and it is achieved entirely by manipulating the instruments without involving the vocal line in the contrapuntal texture. Indeed, if the three instrumental groups were removed, retaining only the continuo from the third *coro* (the most complete of the continuo parts at this point), the essential elements of the passage—the vocal line and the bass progression—would not be significantly altered. Passages such as this provide a possible indication of the kind of flexibility that could be achieved in arranging an instrumental ensemble accompaniment for a work like the "Lamento d'Arianna" without altering its monodic nature while, as Follino wrote, "matching [the instrumental] sound to every nuance of the music."

Such a purely instrumental effect is particularly striking if it is compared to the way the ensemble is treated when the three *cori* are again brought together in m. 73. From this point until the end, the texture approximates the kind of broad choral homorhythmic declamation Monteverdi employed at the close of both parts of "Or che'l ciel e la terra" and of "Altri canti d'Amor." And in the final tutti restatement of the *concetto*, a classic madrigalian device, the instruments are regrouped giving the ensemble—especially the soprano *viola* and

37. *Tutte le opere*, vol. 8, 222, 271, and 280; this texture is also found in sacred works like "Nisi dominus" for three voices and two violins from the *Messa a quattro voci et salmi* (Venice: Vincenti, 1651). See *Tutte le opere*, vol. 16, 299.

violin — the function of interacting contrapuntally with the voice, as do the upper strings in "Or che'l ciel" and in the other large-scale *concertato* madrigals of the eighth book, while the rest of the ensemble functions as harmonic support. It is only in the last fifteen bars that the setting takes on a truly contrapuntal character, fully integrating the upper instrumental parts with the vocal line.

In addition to using the instrumental complement to underscore Guarini's rhetorical effects, Monteverdi mirrors the discursiveness of the poem and even exaggerates it, rather than attempting to overcome it in favor of a concise presentation. The disjunct presentation of the text is more characteristic of the episodic fragmentation found in late sixteenth century madrigals than of monodic settings: nearly every phrase is repeated (the pattern of repetitions is indicated with lower-case letters in table 4.4); several, including the opening, are interrupted; and one entire phrase is displaced in such a way that it interrupts the logical flow of the text ("come i vostri diletti s'ancidono fra lor, se dolcemente vive, *come i vostri diletti s'ancidono fra lor*, se dolcemente vive per ambedue," mm. 38ff.).

While the presentation of the text is subject to a process of fragmentation that at times negates its continuity, and at times responds to the localized impulses of its rhetoric (as at the emphatic disjunction that accompanies "Ma se godo"), the underlying harmonic plan is more directly congruent with the syntactic organization of Guarini's poem. Outwardly, the harmonic layout is centered around D and underscores the essential formal outline of the setting. D opens the piece and marks the articulation after the first six lines of the poem (m. 47), and it is on D that the last important cadence occurs (mm. 113–15) before the closing plagal extension. Predictably, A is also stressed at texually significant points (cadences at m. 15, "labbra odorate"; m. 28, "m'è tolto"; m. 72, "o dolci detti"; and m. 106, "ragionando i baci").

In keeping with the central conflict of the text, however, Monteverdi's use of transposition tends to create harmonic ambiguity from the very start. The opening progression wavers between G and D, depending on how the continuo player realizes the harmony over the A in bar 3, and on whether the word "labbra" is considered the end of the first phrase, making the D major chords dominant to G, or an incomplete extension of it beyond the cadence on D at "soavità," leaving it in suspended expectation of its syntactic continuation, "odorate."[38] The vagueness of the first phrase is reinforced by its upward

---

38. On the realization of harmonic basses at such an early date, see especially the rules given by Francesco Bianciardi in his *Breve regola per imparar a sonare sopra il basso con ogni sorte d'instrumento* (Siena: Falciani, 1607), excerpted and translated in F. T. Arnold, *The Art of*

transposition by a second (mm. 7–12), which turns the phrase toward E or possibly A. From a "functional" standpoint, the transposition and what follows it suggest that, at both mm. 5–6 and 11–12, "labbra" is an interruption, and that its proper resolution only comes with the cadential descent to A in mm. 13–15. However, "e vi bacio e v'ascolto," which completes the first gramatical unit of the poem, brings the piece to its first major rhetorical pause on C—reinforcing the harmonic ambiguity that characterizes the first twenty bars. The following "Ma se godo un piacer," emphasized both by the pause that precedes it and, as we have seen, by the change in scoring, continues from C and eventually ends with a cadence on A (m. 28) involving an ornamented preparation and a strong 3–4–3 figure in the voice—the first structural cadence in the setting. This cadence is, in turn, elided with another change of texture and style at "come i vostri diletti" (mm. 28–33), still on A. C returns again as a disjunctive harmonic element, when "come i vostri diletti s'ancidono" is repeated and transposed up a third (mm. 33–40), before the phrase "se dolcemente vive per ambedue l'anima mia," which begins on C, turns to D with the c-sharp at m. 43 and, with another structural cadence similar in ornamentation to the earlier "l'altro m'è tolto" (m. 25–28), concludes the entire first part on D at m. 47. The discontinuity of texture that takes place at mm. 20–21, then, emphasizes an element of tension within the longer harmonic span that coincides with the first formal unit of Guarini's text. In this sense, the conflict between texturally and stylistically determined groups on the one hand, and harmonic groups on the other, functions in a way that may be considered analogous to the displacement of the rhyme scheme relative to the syntactic structure of the poem. Both displacements generate tension and thus reflect the conflict with which the poem is concerned.

The process of repetition and incremental expansion set forth in the opening returns at the beginning of the second part. "Che soave armonia / fareste o cari baci o dolci detti" consists of two passages (mm. 48–60 and 61–72), the second of which repeats the first transposed—as at the beginning—up a second. The entire section, which returns to the declamatory style of the opening, is based on essentially the same harmonic layout as the first fifteen measures of the setting (example 4.1). As at the beginning, the upward transposition by a second represents, in harmonic terms, the tension between kisses (the subject of mm. 48–60) and words (transposed at mm. 61–72), while the radically

---

Accompaniment from a Thorough-Bass as Practised in the 17th and 18th Centuries (London: The Holland Press, 1961), 74–80. According to Bianciardi, the A in measure 3 would take a c-sharp, and measures 5–6 would therefore be considered extensions beyond the cadence on D.

Ex. 4.1. Parallel harmonic structures in "Con che soavità"

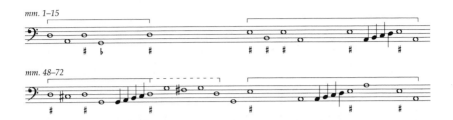

new sound to which both are treated underscores the utopian notion of "soave armonia." Indeed, the use of the same transposition in conjunction with the objects of conflict may be seen as representing the "explanation" for what seems, at the very opening of the piece, an odd harmonic procedure, almost a kind of "riddle" to which the solution is given as the piece progresses.

The harmonic and stylistic parallel between the opening of "Con che soavità" and its middle section is but one instance of a more extensive pattern of connections involving melodic material and, more generally, elements of style and texture. Perhaps the most significant example of melodic recurrence is Monteverdi's treatment of the descending cadential fifth that first appears at "labbra odorate" (mm. 13–15; see example 4.2a). It recurs prominently five times, at least once in each of the principal sections: a variation of it is used to set "ma se godo un piacer" (mm. 21–22 and 23–28, example 4.2b, the former in interrupted form, ending on a G-sharp, and the latter resolving to A); its falling fifth forms the cadence at "s'ancidono fra lor" (mm. 30–32, example 4.2c); and its last two occurrences coincide with the striking passages of instrumental decrescendo at "o cari baci" and "o dolci detti" (mm. 55–60 and 68–72 respectively, example 4.2d).[39] A smaller ornamental motive, in addition to the declarative homorhythmic texture, connects the second statement of "che soave armonia" and the later "se foste unitamente d'ambedue le dolcezze ambo capaci" (mm. 61–67 and 73–92)—as we have seen, the former is also based on the same harmonic progression that opens the piece. These recurring

39. Also used in "T'amo mia vita" from the fifth book, "Addio Florida bella" from the sixth, and at the opening of the *ballo* that concludes the *Concerto*, "Tirsi e Clori." See *Tutte le opere*, vol. 5, 90, vol. 6, 38, and vol. 7, 191. The descending linear progression from 5 to 1 can be seen as a stereotypical, harmonically driven line, which is therefore not useful as evidence of melodic connections between sections. The context in which it appears in "Con che soavità," however, in prominently exposed passages such as "labbra odorate," "o cari baci," and "o dolci detti," each time with similar rhythmic profiles, suggests that—in this instance at least—it carries a greater aural value than it might in other circumstances.

Ex. 4.2. Descending fifth motive in "Con che soavità"

elements, like Guarini's rhyme scheme, cut across formal divisions, blurring them and unifying what would otherwise be a highly fragmented design.

Like Guarini's, Monteverdi's "Con che soavità" is not an epigrammatic madrigal—indeed, the setting wears the label "madrigal" only with much qualification, for it is a complex amalgam of contrasting styles and techniques. The fragmented, repetitious presentation of the text recalls aspects of the vocal ensemble madrigal, and yet much of the setting employs elements of monodic technique. The choice of scoring suggests practices associated with dramatic or semidramatic works, while both the nondramatic text and the style of its presentation are more in keeping with music for the chamber. The instrumental complement is at times treated idiomatically, and at others almost like a vocal ensemble. Finally, harmonic ambiguity is generated by the conflicts that arise between the overarching harmonic layout, which tends to follow Guarini's syntactic scheme, and the localized rhetoric of the text-setting, which emphasizes the tensions inherent in the poet's favorite pleasures. It is perhaps because of its fundamentally ambiguous nature that it is assigned to a transitional role within the *Concerto:* it is likely the *madrigale a 1* of the title, but—part madrigal, part canzonetta, part monody, part dramatic piece—it belongs as much to the *altri generi di canti* that follow it as it does to the madrigals that precede it.

The "Lamento della Ninfa"

Monteverdi's preoccupation with achieving a synthesis of the compositional techniques available after the turn of the century, already evident in his first volume of *Scherzi musicali,* in the continuo madrigals of 1605, and in *Orfeo* and *Arianna,* also lies at the root of the "Lamento della ninfa," one of the most famous works of the *Madrigali guerrieri et amorosi.*[40] While this three-part "scena" in *genere rappresentativo* is well known for its descending tetrachord ostinato, its striking use of dissonance, and Monteverdi's brilliant manipulation of the text, it is not generally recognized that its formal outline is to a great extent a direct descendant of the *Scherzi musicali* of some thirty years earlier.[41]

The original text of the "Lamento," Ottavio Rinuccini's "Non avea Febo ancora," is a strophic poem in the vein of Chiabrera's French-influenced works.[42] Its structure is regular, consisting of four-line stanzas with refrain in which the rhyme scheme, *abab xx*, alternates *settenari piani* and *tronchi*. Four settings of it are known: three, by Antonio Brunelli, Giovanni Girolamo Kapsberger, and Giovanni Battista Piazza, were published before Monteverdi's, and an undated anonymous setting of the first stanza survives in a manuscript now in the Biblioteca Nazionale Centrale in Florence.[43] All but Monteverdi's are strophic

40. On the relationship between the madrigal and opera see Tomlinson, *Monteverdi,* chap. 5; "Rinuccini, Peri, Monteverdi, and the Humanist Heritage of Opera" (Ph.D. diss., University of California, Berkeley, 1979); and "Madrigal, Monody, and Monteverdi's 'via naturale all'immitatione,'" *Journal of the American Musicological Society* 34 (1981), 60–108.

41. The ostinato has been interpreted as representing the nymph's fixation with her lover. The descending tetrachord, variously labeled as passacaglia or—more rarely—*ciaccona*, became one of the traditional stock basses beginning in the 1630s: see Rosand, "Descending Tetrachord," 350.

42. It was published posthumously in *Poesie del S.r Ottavio Rinuccini*, an anthology assembled by the poet's son (Florence: I Giunti, 1622), p. 223.

43. Antonio Brunelli, *Scherzi, arie, canzonette, e madrigali a una, due, e tre voci per sonare, e cantare con ogni sorte di stromenti: Libro secondo. Opera decima* (Venice: Vincenti, 1614); Giovanni Girolamo Kapsberger, *Libro secondo di villanelle a 1. 2. et 3 voci* (Rome: Giovanni Battista

canzonettas, in which the text is set syllabically and the regularity of the verse structure is paralleled by the phrase structure of the music.

Non avea Febo ancora
Recato al mondo il dì,
Ch'una donzella fuora,
Del proprio albergo uscì.
Miserella ahi più no, no
Tanto giel soffrir non può.

Su'l pallidetto volto   7
Scorgeasi il suo dolor,
Spesso le venia sciolto
Un gran sospir dal cor.
    Miserella etc.

Sì calpestando i fiori   13
Errava or qua, or la,
E suoi perduti amori
Così piangendo va.
    Miserella etc.

Amor, diceva, e'l piè   19
Mirando il ciel fermò
Dove, dov'è la fe
Che'l traditor giurò?
    Miserella etc.

Fa che ritorni mio   25
Amor com'ei pur fu,
O tu m'ancidi, ch'io
Non mi tormenti più.
    Miserella etc.

Robletti, 1619); Giovanni Battista Piazza, *Libro secondo: Canzonette a voce sola* (Venice: Magni, 1633). Kapsberger's version is published in John Whenham, *Duet and Dialogue in the Age of Monteverdi*, Studies in British Musicology, no. 7 (Ann Arbor: U.M.I. Research Press, 1982), 2, 332–33; and Brunelli's can be found in Putnam Aldrich, *The Rhythm of Seventeenth-Century Italian Monody* (New York: Norton, 1966), 166. The anonymous setting is in Florence, Biblioteca nazionale centrale, Banco Rari 238, Magliabechiano xix.114, p. 10. The Florence manuscript carries the inscription "Monteverde, autografo da pag 2 a 35" on the inside cover, although at least three hands seem to have been involved in the compilation of the manuscript, the first on pp. 2–17, the second on pp. 18–35, and the third over the rest of the book. The repertoire consists mainly of monodies and includes a copy of the "Lamento d'Arianna" on pp. 18–34. On the possible early date of this manuscript, and on the relationship between the maunscript and the published version of the lament, see Fabbri, *Monteverdi*, 139.

Non vo' più ch'ei sospiri   31
Se non lontan da me,
No no ch'i suoi martiri
Più non dirammi a fe.
    Miserella etc.

Perché di lui mi struggo   37
Tutt'orgoglioso sta,
Che sì, che sì s'io'l fuggo
Ch'ancor mi pregherà?
    Miserella etc.

Se'l ciglio ha più severo   43
Colei, che'l mio non è,
Già non richiude in seno
Amor sì bella fe.
    Miserella etc.

Né mai sì dolci baci   49
Da quella bocca avrà,
Né più soave, ah taci,
Taci che troppo il sa.
    Miserella etc.

Sì tra sdegnosi pianti   55
Spargea le voci al ciel,
Così ne' cori amanti
Mesce Amor fiamma, e giel.
    Miserella etc.[44]

    Phoebus had not yet
    Brought daylight to the world
    When a damsel
    Came out of her dwelling.
    Poor wretch, alas, no longer
    Can she suffer such scorn.

44. A = Florence, Bibl. Naz. Centrale, Banco Rari 238 (olim Magliabechiano XIX.114), p. 10; M = Monteverdi; B = Brunelli; K = Kapsberger; P = Piazza.
3–4 A, B, K, P: Che dal suo albergo fuora (A, P: fora) / una donzella (P: donggela) uscì; after line 5, P inserts a new line: dicea dolente e mesta; 5–6 P: misera che farò / tanto gel non sofrirò; 9 M: le = gli; 13 M: calpestando fiori; 14 B: hor qua e là; 15 M: E = I, B: E i suoi; 19 K: piè = piede; 19–20 M: Amor, dicea, il ciel mirando il piè fermò; 21 K: fe = fede; 25 B, K: che = ch'ei; 31 M: No, non vò più sospiri; 33 M: che i martiri; 37 B: perché= poiché; 38

175

Her suffering was plain
On her face,
And frequently she let
Great sighs loose from her heart.
     Poor wretch, etc.

Thus trampling the flowers
She wandered here and there,
And her lost love
She thus wept.
          Poor wretch, etc.

Love, she said stopping
To look at the heavens,
Where, where is the faith
That the traitor swore to me?
          Poor wretch, etc.

Let my Love return
As he was,
Or else kill me, so that I
May no longer torment myself.
          Poor wretch, etc.

I don't want him to sigh
Except away from me,
I no longer want him
To confide his sufferings in me.
          Poor wretch, etc.

Because I suffer for him,
He is proud;
Will he beseech me
If I flee from him?
          Poor wretch, etc.

K: Di me (B: Dove) stima non fa; 39 M, K: s'io'l = se'l; 40 M: Ch'ancor = Ancor; 43 M: Se'l = Se; 44 K: Colei = colui; 45 B, K: rinchiuide = gl'alberga; 46 K: bella = nobil; 48 B: mai = più; 50 M: soave = soavi; B: ah = ai; 54 K: tra = fra; 55–56 B, K: Sfogava il suo dolor / Sì, de' gentili amanti; 57 K: Misto è col giel l'ardor; B: Misto è col gielo Amor.

     In B the stanzas are reordered: 1, 2, 3, 4, 8, 5, 9, 7, 6, 10; in K stanza 9 is not given.

She may have a haughtier
Brow than mine,
But even Love's breast
Does not harbor such beautiful constancy.
    Poor wretch, etc.

Never will he have such sweet kisses
From that mouth,
Nor sweeter—be still,
Be still, that he knows all too well.
    Poor wretch, etc.

Thus among scornful weeping
She scattered her laments to the sky;
Thus in lovers' hearts
Love mixes flame and ice.
    Poor wretch, etc.

Monteverdi departs radically from Rinuccini's original: he eliminates the regular recurrence of the refrain, allowing the narration to flow uninterrupted and gather momentum, and he groups the stanzas according to their poetic voice, consolidating the poem into three sections. The result shows the same classicizing tendencies already seen in the use of the chorus in *Orfeo*: in the opening and closing narratives, a male chorus is given the task of setting the stage and reflecting on the meaning of the tale, and in the middle section the young woman's first-person lament is punctuated by the chorus's narrative commentary, which is derived from the refrain.[45] While the objectivity of the choruses is underscored by the manner of their performance (they are to be sung to a steady pulse—"al segno della mano"), the woman's highly subjective lament is to follow the dictates of the heart ("sung to the tempo of the soul's emotions, and not to that of the hand" [cantato a tempo dell'affetto del animo, e non a quello della mano]). The overall frame within which the "scena" takes place also suggests a classicizing balance: two similar outer members for an ensemble of three male voices flanking a contrasting middle section dominated by the soprano.

45. There are considerable differences in the readings of the poem preserved in the four settings, quite apart from Monteverdi's formal manipulations. All depart significantly from the published version, although Monteverdi's is closest to it. In general, the readings preserved in the three *canzonette* are closer to one another than to Monteverdi's text.

Table 4.5 Comparison of the structures
of the "Lamento della ninfa" and the
canzonettas of the *Scherzi*

"Lamento della ninfa"	Scherzo*
Stanzas 1–3 a3 TTB + bc	1 a3 + instrs
Stanzas 4–8 S + bc (chorus a3)	2– . . . a1 + bc
Stanza 9 a3, TTB + bc	Last a3 + instrs

*See *Avvertimenti.*

Monteverdi's reworking seems to have left the original canzonetta far behind, but in fact the "Lamento" retains a number of important elements from its humbler beginnings. First, the overall form, with its contrast between outer tutti ensembles and soloistic inner strophes, parallels the symmetry of the *Scherzi musicali* (table 4.5). Second, the texture of the choruses recalls that of the canzonetta settings given to this poem by Monteverdi's contemporaries, with some important modifications. While Monteverdi retains the homorhythmic syllabicism of his colleagues, particularly in the first half of "Non avea," he does not slavishly follow Rinuccini's patterned versification. His first two phrases suggest a conventionally schematic approach, but their parallels are only superficial: Monteverdi emphasizes the *settenari tronchi* of the even-numbered lines and marks the others with internal caesuras only. His treatment of rhythm in the opening chorus of the lament is much more varied than that of his contemporaries (example 4.3). The two subsequent phrases travel even further afield from the model of the canzonetta, introducing extreme dissonances (at "il suo dolor"), and setting off "un gran sospir dal cor" with sighing rests, recalling in both passages traditional madrigalian topoi. The second half of the opening chorus, beginning at "sì calpestando i fiori," relies on a madrigalesque pictorialism, recalling with its disjunct motion the confused trampling of the parting lovers in "Addio Florida bella," another miniature dramatic *scena* with narration from the sixth book of madrigals (example 4.4). The final chorus, "Sì tra sdegnosi pianti," returns to the homoryhthmic texture of the opening, but the text-expressive settings of "sdegnosi," with its disjunct profile, and "voci" and "fiamma," which contain the only melismas given to the tenors, again inject a madrigalian element into the canzonetta.

The middle section, "Amor," makes use of techniques of mixed-mode narrative that Monteverdi had already tested in "T'amo mia vita," one of the continuo madrigals published in 1605: the woman's first-person utterances, like those of the unseen lover in "T'amo," are set against a background of homorhythmic

Ex. 4.3. Rhythmic treatment of the first four lines of "Non avea Febo ancora"

Ex. 4.4. *(a)* "Addio Florida bella," mm. 42–48;
(b) "Non avea Febo ancora," mm. 18–24

Ex. 4.5. *(a)* "T'amo mia vita," mm. 1–11; *(b)* "Amor, dicea," mm. 1–8

low voices (example 4.5). While in the earlier madrigal the repeated utterances of the soprano had served as a kind of ritornello against which the narrative developed, in "Amor" it is the male chorus that takes over the function of punctuating the narrative. Monteverdi then overlays this madrigal-inspired texture onto the ostinato bass pattern.

The "Lamento della ninfa" is outstanding among contemporary settings, for no canzonetta-style strophic setting can match it in emotional impact and formal balance, but its aesthetic premises are not anomalous in Monteverdi's output. The work belies the brilliant transformation of its text by blending madrigalian elements from the fifth and sixth books of madrigals, newly

(b)

developed ostinato techniques, and canzonetta textures, all within the formal scheme the composer had first developed in the *Scherzi musicali*.[46]

46. The date of ca. 1632, proposed by Ellen Rosand in "The Descending Tetrachord" and endorsed by Tomlinson in *Monteverdi*, 214 n. 34, agrees with the rise in popularity of vocal variations based on ostinato basses. See also Ossi, "*L'Armonia raddoppiata.*"

"Gloria a 7 concertata"

Scholars have found the *locus classicus* of Monteverdi's tendency toward technical and formal synthesis in the famous "Beatus Primo" from the *Selva morale,* in which the composer transforms the structural components of the canzonetta "Chiome d'oro" (ostinato patterns, ritornellos, and even large-scale harmonic plan) into a much larger and less rigidly patterned work.[47] This tendency is particularly apparent in the large-scale works of the late collections, such as the *Selva morale et spirituale* (1640) and the posthumous *Messa et Salmi* (1651), although it is already present in the *Vespers* of 1610, particularly in the transformation of the *toccata* from *Orfeo* in the first movement, "Domine, ad adjuvandum."

The "Gloria" is different from the two cases already discussed in this chapter because in it Monteverdi, rather than superimposing (and therefore blurring) different formal and stylistic models, sets them up in a collage-like structure that capitalizes on the sectional nature of the text and maximizes variety (the formal plan is given in table 4.6).[48] The setting is framed by the opening chorus ("Gloria in excelsis deo," mm. 1–33), which returns at the end ("In Gloria Dei Patris. Amen," mm. 272–98) and also in the middle ("propter magnam gloriam tuam," mm. 128–38). This material is cast in highly melismatic, virtuosic lines of a decidedly instrumental character, which contrast individual vocal parts either singly (the first tenor and *canto* at the opening, for example) or in smaller combinations (such as the two tenors at m. 5, or the two *canti* and the second tenor at m. 13) with the full ensemble and with the two obbligato violin parts. The entire section is built on the free alternation of two bass modules (example 4.6a and b; the bass modules are labeled a and a' in the structural diagram). Against this material, Monteverdi juxtaposes sections in different styles. The most abrupt of these contrasts occurs at "Et in terra pax hominibus bonae voluntatis," which is cast in a cappella choral style. In this section the violins, rather than contrast with the voice groupings, are integrated into the contrapuntal vocal texture as independent lines, and the first violin is consistently assigned the highest sonorities in the section, well above the two *canti.* In their three principal occurrences (at the beginning, mid-point, and end), the "Gloria" and "Et in terra" styles are always paired, and they are centered in G,

47. John Steele, "The Concertato Synthesis: Monteverdi's Beatus Primo," in *Claudio Monteverdi: Festschrift Reinhold Hammerstein zum 70. Geburtstag,* ed. Ludwig Finscher (Laaber: Laaber-Verlag, 1986), 427–34.
48. Fabbri, *Monteverdi,* 316–17, gives a brief description of this piece, identifying some of its formal and stylistic elements, and also a slightly different formal diagram.

Table 4.6 Formal plan of the "Gloria a7 concertata"

mm.	Text	Cadences	Bass pattern	Comments
1–33	Gloria	G–D	a, a', b	instrumental character, virtuoso lines
34–52	Et in terra	G	free	A cappella style
53–121	Laudamus te	G, C	c	ostinato; 89–119 in triple meter
122–28	Gratias	–	free	A cappella style
128–40	Propter	d, G, C, G	b, a	see 1–33 and 272–98
141–72	Domine deus	a	d, b" (×3)	first set of strophic variations; d: duet variations; b": choral interjections (Tutti)
172–234	Qui tollis	d	e, f (×3)	second set of strophic variations; e: ritornello; f: duet/trio variations
235–36	Quoniam	G	free	A cappella style
237–64	Tu solus	a, G	g, h (×3)	third set of strophic variations; g: duet, always in a; h: ritornello always in G
265–72	Tu solus	G	free	A cappella style
272–98	In gloria	d, G	b, a	recap. of 1–33; "Amen" in a cappella style like 34–52

the final of the work as a whole. Within the larger architecture of the "Gloria," they function similarly to the "Beatus, beatus vir" ritornello of the psalm setting—their recurrence serves as a frame within which are cast contrasting internal sections. The "Gloria" text does not necessarily suggest the kind of ritornello structure that Monteverdi imparts to his setting: the composer seizes on the three occurrences of the word "gloria," each in a different syntactic context, as the pretext for the form of his setting.

In the internal sections, Monteverdi deals with the repetitive sections of the text, the exhortations of the first part ("Laudamus te. Benedicimus te. Adoramus te. Glorificamus te.") and the rogations of the second ("Domine Deus . . . qui tollis . . ."). The first consists entirely of a four-note ostinato (example 4.6c; both in duple and triple meter) over which a series of duets develops freely, exchanging material between the various voice-pairs and the two violins. The steady, highly rhythmic half-note motion of the ostinato, together with the prevailing parallelism and short phrases of the duets, recalls the canzonetta texture of "Chiome d'oro"; the setting, however, does not adopt the canzonetta's formal structure. As he does in the "Beatus vir" and in the "Laetatus sum" from the *Messa et Salmi,* Monteverdi shifts from duple to triple meter without changing the ostinato pattern. Unlike those works, however, in which the

Ex. 4.6. Bass patterns in the "Gloria a7 concertata"

triple meter section becomes the central member of a large ABA structure, in the "Gloria" it is only the second half of a smaller internal division and does not assume larger structural significance.

For the supplications that follow the central recurrence of the ritornello material, Monteverdi turns to another organizational principle: the strophic variation. The text develops in three phases, the first consisting of threefold epithets ("Domine Deus, Rex caelestis . . ."), the second of the three parallel rogations ("Qui tollis . . ."), and the third another set of epithets ("Tu solus Altissimus . . ."). Each stage is set as a group of three strophic variations; the

three groups focus on contrasting finals (a, d, and a/G), reserving the introduction of the greatest harmonic variety for what is roughly the second half of
the piece. The structural elements of the variations are different in each case as
well. The first set is entirely given to the two *canti* and contrasts a short, almost
improvisatory, duet with tutti interjections built on a slightly modified form
of the bass module (example 4.6b) from the "Gloria" ritornello. The second
("Qui tollis") alternates an instrumental ritornello (derived from that of the
prologue in *Orfeo*) with extensive vocal sections devoted to different vocal
combinations (two *canti* and bass, tenor duet, and bass duet). The bass is not
repeated exactly for the second and third rogations; the second half is modified
slightly each time. The final set consists, again, of vocal duets alternating with
an instrumental ritornello; the character of the vocal line, however, is once
more different, invoking the canzonetta with its mainly syllabic style and short
phrases, and, with its paired eighth-note declamation, the style of smaller
works, like the "Nisi dominus," that are labeled "alla francese." [49]

In its vocal and instrumental requirements, as well as in its large scale, the
"Gloria a 7" recalls such *concertato* madrigals as "Or che'l ciel e la terra" and
"Altri canti di Marte" of the *Madrigali guerrieri et amorosi*. And indeed for a
number of reasons the *Selva morale* has been associated with Monteverdi's last
madrigal book. The two collections seem to cover roughly similar periods of
compositional activity and were published within two years of one another.
Both bear dedications to the Austrian imperial house; the *Madrigali* were
originally meant for Ferdinand II, and the *Selva* is dedicated to his second wife,
Eleonora Gonzaga, daughter of the Mantuan Duke Vincenzo I, whom the
composer served, as he remembers in his dedication, for twenty-two years. [50]
Furthermore, as its counterpart does for secular music, the *Selva* covers the full
range of stylistic and technical resources available to a church composer, from
a cappella contrapuntal technique in the style of the *prima prattica* to large-scale
concertato settings to sacred madrigals, canzonettas, and even the dramatic
monody of the "Pianto della Madonna" based on the lament from *Arianna*.
Finally, in such works as the "Gloria," the "Beatus vir," and, as we saw in

49. Nino Pirrotta sees in the paired eighth notes possibly one of the identifying traits of
the elusive "alla francese" style of such compositions as the "Nisi" and the madrigals "Dolcissimo uscignolo" and "Chi vol aver felice e lieto il core." See "Monteverdi's Poetic Choices,"
292–93. Another element shared by all these pieces is the responsorial exchange between a
soloist and the larger ensemble; in the "Gloria" this is hinted at in the echo of the vocal line
that opens the ritornellos.

50. See Schrade, *Monteverdi*, 335, and Fabbri, *Monteverdi*, 313.

chapter 3, the *canzonetta morale* "Chi vol che m'innamori," Monteverdi makes use of a highly stylized language based on the existence of distinct categories of genre and style in which each musical element carries its own independent significance. The interaction of these elements with one another and with the text imparts meaning to the composition as a whole. It is precisely this interaction, and the classification system that makes it possible, that forms the core of Monteverdi's *seconda prattica*. And that is the subject of the preface to the *Madrigali guerrieri et amorosi*.

F I V E

The Public Debate, II:
The Philosopher's *Seconda Prattica*

"Non faccio le mie cose a caso"

By 1633–34, the philosophical lan-
guage that Giulio Cesare Monteverdi had introduced in the "Dichiaratione"
had become the foundation for Claudio Monteverdi's theory. The treatise itself
was to be divided into three sections corresponding to the components of
Plato's "melodia," and, according to the composer, it had been by reading Plato
that he had found, albeit in an indirect way, the "via naturale all'immitatione"
("through one of his hidden lights, so much so that I could barely [discern]
from a distance with my feeble sight what he was showing me").[1] Monteverdi's
writings make clear that his exploration of the compositional principles
underlying the *seconda prattica* had focused as much on the purpose of music—
on the goals of the new expressive language—as on the means by which expression could be achieved. This concern involved not only practical experimentation, from which Monteverdi seems never to have strayed too far, but
also abstract speculation and observation—of nature in general and human
nature in particular. Indeed, in his second letter to Doni, the composer maintained that his efforts had been sustained not by musical treatises, but, in terms
that suggest the Aristotelian concept of "ars imitatur naturam," by the "principles of the best philosophers to have investigated nature." He wrote:

No earlier than two weeks ago I read Your Worship's first letter, most cour-
teous and most helpful, from which I gathered the most kindly advice, all

1. Letter no. 122, 22 October 1633; *Lettere*, ed. de Paoli, 321. Monteverdi's choice of image recalls Plato's simile of the Cave (*Republic*, 517b).

189

of it worthy of my careful consideration; and for this I am sending you my infinite thanks. I have however seen the Galilei[2]—not just now, but rather twenty years ago—the part where he mentions the inadequate practice of ancient times. I valued seeing it then, perceiving in that same part how the ancients used their practical signs in a different way from ours, but I did not try to go further in understanding them, being sure that they would have come out as very obscure ciphers, or worse, since that ancient practical manner is completely lost.

Whereupon I turned my studies in another direction, basing them on the principles of the very best philosophers to have investigated nature. And because, in accordance with my reading, I notice that the results agree with those reasonings (and with the requirements of nature) when I write down practical things with the aid of those observations, and really feel that our present rules have nothing to do with those requirements, I have for this basic reason given my book the title of Second Practice. . . . I keep well away, in my writings, from that method upheld by the Greeks with their words and signs, employing instead the voices and characters that we use in our practice, because my intention is to show by means of our practice what I have been able to extract from the mind of those philosophers for the benefit of good art, and not for the principles of the First Practice, which was only harmonic.[3]

It is not surprising that Doni should have recommended Galilei's writings as necessary background reading for anyone concerned with the theoretical issues raised by modern music. He himself had made a career of studying the practices of ancient Greek theater and relating them to modern dramatic music, following in the footsteps of the Florentine Camerata;[4] among all of Monteverdi's compositions, he most admired the "Lamento d'Arianna," which he saw as embodying the Camerata's classicizing ideals.[5] Monteverdi's dismissal of the *Dialogo*, however polite, must have come as a surprise and as something of a provocation, since it also distanced the composer from the Camerata's

---

2. *Dialogo della musica antica e della moderna*, 1581, 1602.

3. Monteverdi, *Lettere, dediche e prefazioni*, ed. Domenico De' Paoli (Rome: De Santis, 1973), no. 123, 4 October 1634, pp. 325–26; *The Letters of Claudio Monteverdi*, ed. and trans. by Denis Stevens (London: Cambridge University Press, 1980), no. 124, pp. 414–15.

4. The second volume, *De' trattati di musica di Gio. Batista Doni: Tomo secondo* (Florence: Stamperia Imperiale, 1763), contains several *Lezioni* delivered by Doni at the home of Cardinal Francesco Barberini in 1624 and before the Accademia della Crusca.

5. Doni describes the "Lamento d'Arianna" as "forse la più bella composizione, che sia stata fatta a' tempi nostri in questo genere." See "Trattato della musica scenica," 23, in *De' trattati*.

concern with bringing modern music into line with the models of Greek antiquity. It was probably this letter that led Doni to disparage the composer's learning and to deny Monteverdi credit for the effectiveness of his "Lamento d'Arianna." "As for Monteverdi," he wrote to Mersenne in 1638,

> he is scarcely a man of letters — no more than any other modern musician — but he excels at a kind of pathetic melody, thanks to the long practice he had in Florence with the lofty spirits of the Accademie, and to signor Rinuccini . . . who, although he knew nothing of music, contributed more than Monteverdi himself to the beauty of the "Lamento d'Arianna." I have been assured that he [Monteverdi] is at work on a large study of music, in which he discusses the music of all peoples, and in which he disagrees with me on numerous occasions. . . . I am surprised that he has not written to me since I sent him a copy of my book . . . since in the past he had written to me several times . . .[6]

There is no evidence to support Doni's assertion that Monteverdi had "long practice in Florence with the lofty spirits of the Accademie," in spite of Doni's insistence in the *Trattato della musica scenica* that much of the credit for the musical success of the "Lamento d'Arianna" belonged to Rinuccini:

> Monteverdi received great help from Rinuccini [in composing] *Arianna*, although the poet did not know music (a *lacuna* for which he compensated with his excellent judgment and his exacting ear, both of which can be discerned in the quality and texture of his poetry). With great willingness, and attention, these three musicians [Peri, Caccini, and Monteverdi] followed his useful teachings, which those noblemen [Jacopo Corsi and Ottavio Rinuccini] passed on to them, constantly imparting excellent thoughts, and highly refined precepts, which were necessary in such a new and valuable endeavor.[7]

Furthermore, Doni was not a good reporter of facts — he had written in 1634 to Mersenne that Monteverdi's book would be titled "Nouvelle ou seconde

6. Letter to Marin Mersenne, 7 July 1638, *Correspondance du p. Marin Mersenne religieux minime*, ed. C. De Waard, V (1960), 17–18. Quoted in Paolo Fabbri, *Monteverdi* (Turin: E.D.T., 1985), 293.

The book Doni must have sent to Monteverdi was his *Compendio del trattato de' generi e de' modi della musica*, recently published (Rome: Fei, 1635).

7. *Trattato*, 25. Tomlinson credits this passage with greater reliability than I have allowed and argues that evidence of its veracity may be found in the congruence of musical and poetic rhetoric in the "Lamento." See "Madrigal, Monody, and Monteverdi's 'via naturale all'immitatione,'" *Journal of the American Musicological Society* 34 (1981), 86–96.

practique de musique," which suggests that he had missed the substance of Monteverdi's title, "Melodia overo seconda pratica musicale," and the explanation the composer had given of it in his first letter of 1633. It is therefore hard to evaluate his new report on the progress of the book, especially regarding Monteverdi's disagreements with him—perhaps he only imagined that the composer would not understand his writings and therefore would disagree with them, but perhaps he had heard rumors to that effect, conveyed by the same grapevine that had brought the two men together in 1633. If that were the case, then Doni's comments would suggest that in the early 1630s Monteverdi had been discussing his ideas not only with Doni, but with others as well, and that his interest in the treatise, which had begun as a forced reaction to Artusi's criticism, had continued as an independent project long after the controversy had died down.

In spite of his comments to Doni, however, Monteverdi's attitude toward antiquity was not one of complete indifference. Unlike the composers of the Florentine Camerata, he was not seeking to revive ancient music, whose terminology he saw only as vestiges of an era beyond reconstruction; nevertheless, both his letters and the preface to the *Madrigali guerrieri et amorosi* of 1638 make it clear that classical thought had fueled much of the development of the *seconda prattica*. Indeed, the most important innovation after *Arianna*, the *genere concitato* of the *Combattimento di Tancredi et Clorinda* of 1624, was conceived with the intent of restoring to modern music the expressive range ascribed to it by Plato and was constructed using elements derived from classical poetry.[8]

The preface to the eighth book represents Monteverdi's last and most extensive theoretical discussion and as such occupies a central position in early seventeenth century musical aesthetics. In it, Monteverdi identifies perhaps the most important issue to have emerged from the debate over the two *prattiche*, the relationship between the style of a composition and its function, and focuses attention on the end purpose of music rather than on the details of

---

8. Nino Pirrotta, "Monteverdi's Poetic Choices," in *Music and Culture in Italy from the Middle Ages to the Baroque* (Cambridge: Harvard University Press, 1984), 312–13, has suggested that Monteverdi arrived at his theoretical framework for the *genere concitato* ex post facto, and that the elements that constitute it were arrived at "spontaneously and madrigalistically." Although it is impossible to argue either way, the process for developing them, as Monteverdi describes it to Doni, seems entirely plausible: keen observation of human nature, of what imitates it most effectively, and musical experimentation tested against observation. That this process may have been bolstered along the way by readings in Plato and Aristotle also seems entirely plausible.

compositional technique. His organization of musical language into categories defined by function and style had wide-ranging influence, extending into
the second half of the century in the writings of Marco Scacchi and Angelo Be-
rardi, and echoing in the controversy between Giulio Cesare Arresti and Maurizio Cazzati.[9]

Monteverdi imparts a distinctive structure to his essay: it opens abruptly,
with a statement that emphasizes personal observation; this is then followed
by a rigid pattern of symmetrical orderings that form the backbone of his theoretical system. From the very beginning, he establishes a series of threefold
classifications: for the affects of the soul ("ira, temperanza et umiltà o supplicatione"), for the nature of the human voice ("alta, bassa et mezzana"), and for
music ("genere concitato, molle et temperato"). On these fundamental principles, and on the premise that the purpose of music is to move the emotions,
the composer then bases his invention of the *genere concitato*, the only one of
the expressive categories listed by Plato in the *Republic* for which he could find
no example in the music of the composers of the *prima prattica*. After explaining his derivation of the new *genere*, giving its history, and establishing its importance in fulfilling the expressive potential of music, "which without it has
been, one can state with good reason, until now imperfect, having had only the
two *generi, molle* and *temperato*," Monteverdi adds a cautionary note to performers which concerns the *genere concitato* in particular but which is also
applicable to all kinds of music. Players should remember that the principles
of good playing "are of three kinds—*oratoria, armonica,* and *retmica,*" and ad-
just their performance accordingly by observing the *genere*, whether *concitato,
molle,* or *temperato*, of the music they are performing. Finally, the composer
turns to the functional classification of music with yet another triad of labels:
music is used in princely households for the theater, the chamber, and the

---

9. On the legacy of Monteverdi's ideas, particularly in Marco Scacchi's *Breve discorso sopra
la musica moderna* (Warsaw, 1649), see Claude V. Palisca, "The Artusi–Monteverdi Controversy," in *The New Monteverdi Companion,* ed. Denis Arnold and Nigel Fortune (London: Faber
and Faber, 1985), 155–58, as well as his "Marco Scacchi's Defense of Modern Music," in
*Words and Music: The Scholar's View (A Medley of Problems and Solutions Compiled in Honor of
A. Tillmann Merritt by Sundry Hands),* ed. Laurence Berman (Cambridge: Harvard University,
Department of Music), 189–235; and Barbara Russano Hanning, "Monteverdi's Three Genera: A Study in Terminology," in *Musical Humanism and Its Legacy,* ed. Nancy Kovaleff Baker
and Barbara Russano Hanning (Stuyvesant, N.Y.: Pendragon Press, 1992), 148 n. 4. On the dispute between Cazzati and Arresti see Ursula Brett, *Music and Ideas in Seventeenth-Century Italy:
the Cazzati–Arresti Polemic* (New York: Garland, 1989).

ballo. This last passage concludes with an ambiguous segue: having established the three functions of music, Monteverdi continues by stating that "thus [perciò] in this work I have adumbrated the three aforementioned *generi* within the title as *guerriera, amorosa,* and *rappresentativa.*"

Threefold classifications were not, of course, new with Monteverdi, nor were they limited to Aristotle; they were common currency in aesthetic writings throughout the sixteenth century and earlier. In the preface, Monteverdi cites Boethius and Plato; and as Barbara Russano Hanning has shown, he could have derived at least a general methodology, if not the specific language of his system, from such widely read theorists as Cleonides, Aristides Quintilianus, and Manuel Bryenius.[10] Furthermore, such late Renaissance music theorists as Zarlino, Mei, and Galilei all refer to threefold orderings of the voice, of emotions, and of rhythm.[11] In his first letter to Vincenzo Galilei of 8 May 1572, for example, Girolamo Mei touched on several of Monteverdi's key concepts. "It is clear that other people's affections are moved by representing before them either as an object, or as a memory, those affects that these appearances are meant to conjure," he wrote.

> With the voice, this can only be achieved through its qualities, be it low, high, or moderate, since it has been provided with them by nature to this end, so that it may generate a sound that is appropriate and natural to the emotion to which it wants to move others. Similarly, it is well known that moderate sounds, between the extremes of high and low, are appropriate for demonstrating a quiet and moderate affect, and those that are too high reflect a soul that is moved and *sollevato,* while those that are too low reflect subdued thoughts and habit. In the same way, a middle speed between fast and slow denotes a quiet soul, a fast one excitement [concitato], and a slow speed a lethargic and lazy soul. Taken together, it is evident that all the qualities of harmony and number have as their proper nature the ability to move those affections that are similar to themselves. Therefore pitches that are too high or too low were rejected by the Platonists, the ones for being too lament-like, and the others too lugubrious; only pitches in the middle were accepted, as was also the case with numbers and rhythm. Moreover, all contrasting qualities, be they natural or acquired, will be weakened when mixed or confused together, and in a

---

10. See "Monteverdi's Three Genera," 152–53.

11. Ibid., 157–68. Recently, Eric Chafe has argued that Monteverdi could have derived some of his ideas from Doni's own *Compendio del trattato de' generi e de' modi,* in which the theorist sets up similar tripartite correspondences between emotions and musical generi. See *Monteverdi's Tonal Language* (New York: Schirmer, 1992), 237–38.

certain sense they blunt each other's strength if they are equal, or reduce it proportionately according to the power and vigor each has. The result is that when mixed with different ones, each will operate either imperfectly, or very little.[12]

Mei's conclusions, however, were very different from Monteverdi's: ancient music, in order to achieve its effect, used only those characteristics that were able to arouse the passions intended, and it avoided mixing them with elements that might defeat their purpose. This led to homophony ("medesime parole . . . medesima aria . . . medesima qualità di tempo et con la medesima qualità di numero et ritmo") even in the largest choruses.[13] Monteverdi never renounced counterpoint, and, as I shall argue, he sought out the mixture of contrasting elements as the best means for generating strong emotions—not confusion—in his listeners.

Perhaps closest to Monteverdi, as we saw in chapter 1, Artusi himself concisely encapsulates these concepts in the second of his books on modern music:

> And melody is made up of Text [Oratione], Rhythm [Ritmo], and of Harmony [Armonia] together, as Plato so defines it in the *Republic*. And those qualities that are joined within it, as the highness, lowness, and equality of the voices, are to be considered as part of Harmony.[14] The slowness, quickness, and movement [in general], belong to Rhythm. The length or brevity of the words belongs to meter, that is to say to the Text.[15]

And already in 1607 Giulio Cesare had picked up Doni's reference to Plato in the "Dichiaratione," expanding on its meaning and, seizing on a comment not cited by Artusi, making Plato's premise that mode and rhythm should be suited to the words into the banner of the *seconda prattica*:

> My brother notes that he does not go about his business haphazardly. His intention therefore was (in this kind of music) to make sure that the text [oratione] be the mistress of the music [armonia] and not its servant. Accordingly, his compositions should be judged in the entirety of their *melodia*. In this regard Plato writes the following: "Melos consists of three things, text, harmony, and rhythm," and a little further on, "and so of the

---

12. Claude V. Palisca, *Girolamo Mei: Letters on Ancient and Modern Music to Vincenzo Galilei and Giovanni Bardi*, Musicological Studies and Documents 3 (Neuhausen-Stuttgart: American Institute of Musicology, 1960), 92–93.

13. Ibid., 93.

14. Artusi's interpretation of Plato's statement (*Republic*, 398c) comes close to the implications of "harmoniai" (see chapter 1, n. 7).

15. *L'Artusi, parte seconda*, 23.

apt and the unapt, if the rhythm and the harmony follow the words, and not the words these," and (in order to give greater weight to the text) he continues, "Do not the manner of the diction and the words follow and conform to the disposition of the soul?" and then "indeed all the rest follows and conforms to the diction."[16]

The fundamental difference between these earlier constructs and the preface to the *Madrigali guerrieri et amorosi* is that Monteverdi establishes a set of generalized iconic categories (to use Jeffrey Kurtzman's term for them) to which the composer can then refer in the course of a composition.[17] The distinctions between these categories are made along taxonomic lines—that is, each is characterized by a particular configuration of its components, the three elements of Plato's *melos:* text, harmony, and rhythm. The preface is the first text to take these threefold groupings and turn them into an analytical and constructive tool, giving a composer the means to create a particular effect in response to observed emotions or natural effects.

Partly because of its brevity, the preface poses a number of problems of interpretation, the most vexing of which concerns the way in which the various threefold definitions are intended to fit within a unified system.[18] Perhaps the most important difficulties arise when matching the functional categories listed in the essay (theater, chamber, and *ballo*) to those in the title, *Madrigali guerrieri et amorosi: Con alcuni opuscoli in genere rappresentativo, che saranno per brevi Episodi fra i canti senza gesto: Libro ottavo.* Both essay and title refer to only two general types of music: nondramatic pieces (chamber, or *senza gesto*) and works requiring some degree of gesture (*genere rappresentativo*)—both *musica da teatro* and *musica da ballo* are encompassed within this category.[19] Similarly,

16. "Dichiaratione," in *Lettere*, ed. de Paoli, p. 396.

17. See Jeffrey Kurtzman, "A Taxonomic and Affective Analysis of Monteverdi's 'Hor che'l ciel e la terra,'" *Music Analysis* 12 (1993), 170–72. The concept of an independent musical symbol, capable of standing alone as a referent, was first explored in relation to Monteverdi's music by Ellen Rosand in "The Descending Tetrachord: An Emblem of Lament," *Musical Quarterly*, 65 (1979), 346–59.

18. On the structure of the preface, see Hanning, "Monteverdi's Three Genera," 146–47. It is not entirely clear that Monteverdi's space was indeed limited by practical considerations, such as a hypothetical printer's restriction to a single typset page, and that this may account for the lack of connecting material between the various parts of the system. The skeletal presentation of the preface is not entirely out of character with Monteverdi's expository style in the preface to the fifth book of madrigals and in his letters.

19. The essay does touch briefly on sacred music, but it does not include it in its classifications. The oversight is rather surprising in light of Monteverdi's employment at St. Mark's but can be explained in terms of the secular context in which the preface appears.

the designations "canti guerrieri" and "canti amorosi" are applied not just to the *canti senza gesto* but to the whole of the two parts including both *canti senza gesto* and *opuscoli in genere rappresentativo*, in spite of the fact that Monteverdi in the essay had seemed to draw a distinction between them with his confusing statement that "I have adumbrated the aforementioned *generi* with the designations *guerriera, amorosa,* and *rapresentativa*" [ho accennato gli detti tre generi con la intitulatione guerriera, amorosa, et rapresentativa]. The problem is that categories based on function and on expression are independent of one another, and that Monteverdi, at the end of the essay, appears to draw a confusing direct correlation between them. Presumably Monteverdi meant that *concitato, molle,* and *temperato* are somehow reflected in the title, but although it is possible to match the *madrigali guerrieri* of the title with *genere concitato,* and *amorosi* with either *genere molle* or *temperato* or both, *opuscoli in genere rappresentativo* cannot be made to square with any of the other three *generi.* In the eighth book, and elsewhere in his output, Monteverdi had always used *"genere rappresentativo"* to distinguish a category of pieces such as the *Combattimento* and the central portion of the *"Lamento della ninfa"* from the *"canti senza gesto"* that make up the remainder of the collection. This fourth *genere,* which originates outside the logical flow of the preface, muddles things up. In spite of the apparent clarity of its beginning, and of each successive section in turn, the sum total of the preface is clouded in terminological confusion that undermines its perception as a complete system and fuels speculation that the composer may have exceeded his grasp as an abstract thinker, or that he may have resorted to pseudo-theoretical language only to please a humanistically inclined audience.[20]

But there is evidence that classical sources served as more than a mere intellectual veneer for Monteverdi's compositional experiments. The preface contains an unlikely but highly suggestive factual error: while correctly attributing the sentence "take that harmony that would fittingly imitate the utterances and the accents of a brave man who is engaged in warfare" to Plato, the composer mistakenly ascribes it to the third book of a treatise on rhetoric that the philosopher never wrote;[21] the proper reference is to the third book of the

---

20. Andrew Dell'Antonio has suggested, in a paper titled "Monteverdi's Ruse? Toward a Deconstruction of the *Seconda Pratica,"* read at the fifty-eighth annual meeting of the American Musicological Society (1992), that Monteverdi's proposed treatise was in fact a ruse intended to satisfy just such an audience and therefore promote his aims.

21. The error is not discussed in Strunk, *Source Readings in Music History from Classical Antiquity through the Romantic Era* (New York: Norton, 1950); Fabbri, *Monteverdi,* 299–302; Chafe,

Republic.[22] The error can be explained by the obviously rhetorical frame of the essay and by the alliterative nature of the substitution; that it has gone largely unremarked is ascribable to Monteverdi's shaky reputation for learning. But the misattribution turns out not to be the result of ignorance: rather, it is a telling slip of the pen that offers an unexpected key to an important and un-acknowledged aspect of the intellectual background of the essay, as well as to some of its thornier logical and structural problems.

The mixup points to another text—Aristotle's *Rhetoric*—that plays a central role in determining the substance and form of the preface.[23] A comparison be-tween Monteverdi's essay and the opening section of the third book of the *Rhetoric* shows that the composer modeled the style, methodology, and struc-ture of his argument on Aristotle's, closely paraphrasing his model for impor-tant concepts. This explains Monteverdi's error: it was a classic Freudian slip—he was quoting from the third book of one classical source, and at the same time following the structure of the corresponding part of another.

The third book of Aristotle's *Rhetoric* is concerned with style: with the man-ner in which ideas are delivered, and with the character that the elements of delivery impart to them. This fits within an overall scheme by which Aristotle analyzes oratory:

> There are three things which require special attention in regard to speech: first, the sources of proofs; secondly, style; and thirdly, the arrangement of the parts of the speech. . . . We have therefore next to speak of style; for it

---

Monteverdi's Tonal Language, 234–36; or Palisca, "The Artusi–Monteverdi Controversy." Han-ning, "Monteverdi's Three Genera," 151 n. 10, notes the error without comment and gives the correct citation to Plato's *Republic.*

22. The section on music is found in 398c–400c; the passage Monteverdi cites is at 399d.

23. Plato dealt with rhetoric elsewhere, most prominently in the *Gorgias,* in which he at-tempts to define with what elements the art of rhetoric concerns itself. The conclusion is that the rhetorician is a "craftsman of belief-inspiring" rather than a teacher, for rhetoric bypasses knowledge and learning in order to persuade. Those who are persuaded cannot, in turn, per-suade others, for they do not know or understand the subject matter underlying the argu-ments that persuade them. Rhetoric appears evil in the *Gorgias* precisely because it divorces form (speech) from content. In the course of his argument, Socrates touches on music, and particularly on the relationship between music and tragedy, and the rhetorical nature of trag-edy. See George Kimball Plochmann and Franklin E. Robinson, *A Friendly Companion to Plato's Gorgias* (Carbondale and Edwardsville: Southern Illinois University Press, 1998), 23–49 and 175; also Plato, *Gorgias and Phaedrus,* trans. by James H. Nichols, Jr. (Ithaca: Cornell Univer-sity Press, 1998), 501e–503a.

Although this passage is interesting for what it conveys about Greek theater and its aes-thetic aims, it is not generally referred to by sixteenth-century writers on music, possibly be-cause it puts music and tragedy in a negative light, associating their appeal to emotion and

is not sufficient to know what one ought to say, but one must also know how to say it, and this largely contributes to making the speech appear of a certain character. In the first place, following the natural order, we investigated that which first presented itself—what gives things themselves their persuasiveness; in the second place, their arrangement by style; and in the third place, delivery, which is of the greatest importance, but has not yet been treated by any one.[24]

Aristotle notes that the art of delivery originated with those poets who recited their tragedies, and that it later became the domain of tragic actors and of politicians—those whose business it is to influence opinion. The study of this art is concerned with the expressive qualities of the voice:

> Now delivery is a matter of voice, as to the mode in which it should be used for each particular emotion; when it should be loud, when low, when intermediate; and how the tones, that is shrill, deep, and intermediate, should be used; and what rhythms are adapted to each subject. For there are three qualities that are considered—volume, harmony, rhythm.[25]

After establishing those elements that properly pertain to style, Aristotle reflects on contemporary oratorical practice and on the reasons why a subject previously considered vulgar has been rendered necessary. Only after these justifications have been set forth does he turn to the analysis of the various parts of a speech and to how the voice is best used in each situation. Central to the thesis of the entire book is the notion that "a different style [of delivery] is suitable to each kind of rhetoric" and that the right effect can only be obtained by matching the delivery to the given text; a mismatch defeats the orator's purpose.[26] Monteverdi's preface reflects Aristotle's treatment of delivery and its components, as well as his emphasis on the intrinsic connection between the style of delivery and the style of the text. It is in expressing these concepts that the composer matches his model most closely.

First, just as the *Rhetoric* establishes connections between the physical

---

sense with rhetorical persuasion rather than teaching. For the use of Plato in Renaissance music theory and scholarship, see Ann E. Moyer, *Musica Scientia: Musical Scholarship in the Italian Renaissance* (Ithaca: Cornell University Press, 1992), and Palisca, *Girolamo Mei*, as well as his *The Florentine Camerata* (New Haven: Yale University Press, 1989) and *Humanism in Italian Renaissance Musical Thought* (New Haven: Yale University Press, 1985).

24. The *"Art" of Rhetoric*, ed. and trans. by John Henry Freese (New York: Putnam, 1926), 345.

25. Ibid., 347.

26. 3.12; *"Art" of Rhetoric*, 419.

properties of the voice, the emotions given in the text, and the speech-rhythms used to express them, so the preface draws parallels between emotions, levels of the voice, and the three musical *generi*. Second, Monteverdi addresses the relationship between the substance of a composition (its *"genere"*) and the means by which performers execute it, just as Aristotle turns to the problem of delivery as a separate component of the orator's art but one that must nevertheless take its cues from the content of the speech. Aristotle's general premise that "a different style [of delivery] is suitable to each kind of rhetoric" echoes throughout Monteverdi's admonitions to those who perform his new *genere concitato*, as does his breakdown of delivery into its three components, volume, harmony, and number,[27] which in Monteverdi's preface becomes "the manners of playing must be of three kinds — oratorical [text-related], harmonic, and rhythmic." Monteverdi's instructions recall the passage on delivery quoted earlier from the *Rhetoric*: "Thus I recommend," he wrote,

> that the basso continuo and the accompanying parts [of the *genere concitato*] must be played *according to the manner and form of the genere in which it is written* [nel modo et forma in tal genere che sta scritto]. In it [the basso] are similarly contained all the directions that are to be followed in the works written in the other *generi*, because the manners of playing must be of three kinds — oratorical [voice- or text-related], harmonic, and rhythmic [emphasis added].[28]

In addition to relying on Aristotle for the concepts at the core of the preface, Monteverdi also imitates the tone and general plan of the *Rhetoric*. The rather abrupt declarative opening sentence, *"Avendo io considerato le nostre passioni od affettioni del animo essere tre le principali . . ."* [having considered that three among our emotions are preeminent], parallels both the beginning of Aristotle's discussion, which in Annibale Caro's sixteenth-century Italian translation reads *"Essendo tre le cose de le quali s'ha da trattare intorno a l'arte del dire"* [there are three things which require special attention in regard to speech], as well as his later *"onde che tre sono le cose, che si considerano circa la*

---

27. 3.1. "Onde che tre sono le cose che si considerano circa la recitazione. La grandezza, l'armonia, e'l numero." *Retorica d'Aristotele fatta in lingua toscana*, trans. by Annibale Caro (Venice: Salamandra, 1570). Bernardo Segni's translation, *Retorica et poetica d'Aristotele tradotte di Greco in lingua fiorentina* (Florence: Torrentino, 1549; reprinted in Venice, 1551), has "la grandezza, l'armonia, e'l ritmo, o ver numero."

28. Monteverdi, Preface to Book Eight.

recitazione" [since there are three things that must be considered regarding delivery].[29] And both essays have in common the rhetorical strategy of beginning by establishing the fundamental components of their subject, continuing with a justification of their topic, and then dealing with its practical applications. Whereas Aristotle continues the third book with a detailed discussion of rhetorical performance practice, Monteverdi closes his essay by sketching his functional classification of music. The distinctive structure and tone of the preface, then, can be ascribed in large part to the model chosen for it.

The significance of Monteverdi's imitation of Aristotle is twofold. First, above and beyond what can be learned from his overt quotations from Boethius and Plato, the presence of a hidden model clarifies the relationship between Monteverdi's ideas and the process of reading and experimentation that he had described to Doni in 1633 as having required "not a little study and effort" [non poco mio studio et fatica]. The composer's absorption of Aristotle's text is fully consistent with his earlier accounts to Doni of the arduous process of discovery that had begun with the composition of *Arianna* and continued into the 1630s. In his first letter to the theorist he had written:

> I found out in practice that when I was about to compose the "Lamento d'Arianna"—finding no book that could show me the natural way of imitation [la via naturale all'immitatione], not even one that would explain what an imitator ought to be (other than Plato, in one of his shafts of wisdom, but so hidden that I could hardly discern from afar with my feeble sight what little he showed me)—I found out . . . what hard work I had to do in order to achieve the little I did do in the way of imitation, and I hope [the book] will not be displeasing.[30]

And in the second letter, a few months later, after mentioning that he had seen one of Galilei's treatises "twenty years ago" (and therefore sometime in the first decade or so of the century), Monteverdi had expanded on the course his hard work had taken, connecting his continued investigations with the *seconda prattica* of nearly thirty years earlier:

> I turned my studies in another direction [from Galilei's], basing them on the principles of the best philosophers to have investigated nature. And because, in accordance with my reading, I notice that the results agree with those reasonings (and with the requirements of nature) when I write

29. *Retorica*, trans. by Caro, 3.1.
30. Italian original in appendix, ad chapter 1 n. 8.

down practical things with the aid of those observations, and really feel that our present rules have nothing to do with those requirements, I have for this reason given my book the title of *Seconda Prattica*.[31]

Several elements in this passage adumbrate the 1638 preface. First, in both, Monteverdi refers to having read the "best philosophers." Second, the letter to Doni describes a process of experimentation in which principles are derived from classical texts and from observation, are then put into practice in compositions, and finally are checked against both philosophical sources and nature. This is also Monteverdi's method for investigating the *genere concitato* and validating its effects. Third, the confrontation of practice against principle lies at the root of the composer's criticism of the *prima prattica:* it has nothing to do with the requirements of nature and the reasoning of philosophers. Finally, he frames his method and musical system within an essay whose logical structure originates in a Classical philosophical text.

In addition to providing a link with the Doni correspondence, the Aristotelian model offers a text against which the contents of the preface can be read. In Aristotle's *Rhetoric,* oratory or delivery is treated as subservient to subject matter, which includes the emotional character of an argument.[32] Delivery pertains to the voice, which must reflect the content of a speech, and which is divided into three elements that a skillful orator can manipulate to match his text: "volume"; tone, or "harmony"; and rhythm. For the first two he provides three general categories, loud or high, low or deep, and intermediate. He offers none for rhythm.

Music is at once a manner of delivery (of the poetic text being set by the composer), and a text to be delivered (by the performers). Monteverdi divides his topic into two parts: first, the application of rhetoric to the setting of the text (the making of a *melodia*), and second the manner in which this *melodia* must be delivered by the performers, the "maniera di suonare." The *genere concitato* itself serves as a practical demonstration of Monteverdi's application of Plato's threefold breakdown of *melodia*. It consists of three elements: an appropriate "oratione contenente ira et sdegno"; a slow-moving harmonic component, which corresponds to the "tempo spondeo tempo tardo;" and finally a fast surface rhythm, the "tempo piricchio, che è tempo veloce" (example 5.1).

31. Italian original in appendix, and chapter 5 n. 3.
32. In this respect it is different from Plato's *Gorgias,* which is concerned with defining rhetoric and in which separating delivery and its emotional appeal to the audience is considered a negative quality, in that it presupposes that the rhetor is not concerned at all with content, and especially not with moral content.

Ex. 5.1. *Il combattimento di Tancredi e Clorinda,* mm. 168–76

D'or in or più si me - sce e più ri - stret - ta si fa la pu - gna e

Qui si lascia l'arco, e si strappano le corde con duoi diti

spa - da o-prar non gio-va; dan-si con po-mi e in-fel-lo-ni-ti e cru-di

Tempo piricchio (tempo veloce): surface

Tempo spondeo (tempo tardo): harmony

These, when heard simultaneously, generate in the listener the powerful emotions of Plato's "brave man on military service or any dangerous undertaking." In addition, since, as Monteverdi admits, "the vocal part cannot follow with its metric feet the speed of the instrument" [l'oratione non seguitasse co' piedi la velocità del instromento], the instrumental component becomes integral to the new *genere*—indeed, it becomes the vehicle for its most distinctive characteristic, the repeated-note figurations. Thus, with the *genere concitato, concertato* technique, which had occupied Monteverdi since the beginning of the century, is fully integrated into the composer's theoretical system. That Monteverdi turned to classical metric feet for the building blocks of the new *genere*, together with his explanation that the inspiration for it came from Plato's account of the modes suitable for inclusion in his ideal state, is also significant. Although references to Greek philosophers had begun to appear as early as Giulio Cesare's "Dichiaratione" of 1607, it is only in the preface to the *Madrigali guerrieri et amorosi* that Monteverdi first claims the "discovery" of something that had already existed in antiquity (*"la ritrovata da me di qual genere"*).

Monteverdi's premise behind the formulation of the *genere concitato*, that the mixing of opposites causes the greatest reaction in the listener, is remarkable because it runs counter to the well-established wisdom that the mixing of contrary affects cancels the two extremes and causes confusion in the listener. Galilei drew on this commonly held view when he criticized modern contrapuntal practices:

> It is possible to argue that modern contrapuntal composers have understood very poorly that famous precept that mandates that the voices of a composition move in contrary motion. The opposite is manifestly true: that they are better able to express a uniform feeling through similarities rather than differences, and that happiness or sadness, together with the other emotions, can be generated in the listener not only with high or low sounds, or with fast or slow movement, but with the different quality of intervals as well. Thus an ascending fifth is sad . . . and a descending one is happy; conversely, an ascending fourth is happy, and sad when it is descending. The same holds true for the semitone and the rest of the intervals.[33]

The simultaneous combination of ascending and descending intervals can only be effective if their qualities are similar; contrasting qualities cancel each

33. Vincenzo Galilei, *Dialogo della Musica Antica et della Moderna: A Facsimile of the 1581 Florence Edition*, Monuments of Music and Music Literature in Facsimile, Second series, Music Literature 20 (New York: Broude, 1967), 76.

other. Galilei expands this concept to include rhythmic motion as well as the mixture of intervals:

> To the difficulties caused by the diversity of sounds and voice-leading we can add those, no less important, that result from the disparity in the [rhythmic] motion of the parts. These result from the fact that often the Soprano barely moves in lazy note-values, while the Bass, at the opposite extreme, flies along, and the Tenor and Alto move slowly.[34]

Following Aristotle's premise, Monteverdi then establishes a system in which delivery (*maniera di suonare*) is suited to a work's content (the *generi*). He is less specific about the particulars of the three "maniere di suonare," but his three elements closely resemble Aristotle's: "armonica" is a transformation of Aristotle's "tone" into musical terms, and "retmica" matches "rhythm." "Oratorica" has more complex connotations. First, it directs the performers' collective attention to the text, from which they take their expressive cues. The components of the "maniera di suonare" must be combined into configurations that are peculiar to each *genere*. The continuo players whom Monteverdi castigates for failing to play the repeated notes of the pyrrhic meter and exposing only the "tempo spondeo" transgress against the principles of good "maniera di suonare" and deprive the "oratione concitata" of its "similitudine." Second, it can also be seen as pertaining to the properties of Aristotle's "voice," since it is the performer's voice that delivers the text of the composer's "oration." And indeed it is only for the voice that Monteverdi applies the levels given by Aristotle to their corresponding emotions: high to "ira"; middle to "temperanza"; and low to "umiltà o supplicatione." We can of course assume that the text the composer transmits to the performer presumably already takes into account, in its distribution of pitches, Aristotle's three levels of the orator's voice and therefore conditions the performer's rhetoric with its own—the composer, not the performer, is the "prime rhetorician."[35] The three elements of the "maniera di suonare" also parallel the three parts of the treatise Monteverdi had outlined to Doni ("oratione," "armonia," and "la parte Ritmica"), and therefore the components of Plato's *melodia* as well.

Monteverdi's three functional categories of music can be grouped, according to the presence or absence of "gesture," into "canti senza gesto" and "opuscoli

---

34. *Dialogo*, 82. The source of Galilei's ideas on the way affects work to cancel each other is Girolamo Mei's letter of 8 May 1572. See Palisca, *Girolamo Mei*, 97.

35. I am grateful for this particularly apt characterization to Barbara Russano Hanning, who used it in her response to my paper at the Montreal AMS in 1993.

in genere rappresentativo." How this final stage is viewed in the continuum from content to delivery varies according to the importance one accords to "gesture"—whether it is intrinsic to the composition and therefore properly classed as "content" [*genere*], or whether it is another attribute of "delivery" [*maniera*]. We may find a clue to this in Monteverdi's confusing use of the term "genere rappresentativo": unlike his contemporaries, who almost uniformly adopted "stile recitativo," Monteverdi consistently used *"genere* rappresentativo" for works that are either directly associated with staging and action or imply it to some degree.[36] This is the designation he used for the "Lettera amorosa" and the "Partenza amorosa" of the seventh book, and again for the "Lamento d'Arianna" when he issued it in 1623 with the two "Lettere," and for the *Combattimento,* the *Ballo delle ingrate,* and the middle section of the "Lamento della ninfa" of the *Madrigali guerrieri et amorosi.* In most cases— *Arianna,* the *Ballo,* the *Combattimento*—action is explicitly required, and in the others—the "Lettere" and the "Lamento della ninfa"—it can be inferred with relative ease. This consistent usage for a limited repertoire suggests that for Monteverdi "gesto" was not "maniera" but indeed "genere."[37]

Finally, there remains the problem of the two *prattiche.* While in the first of his two letters to Doni, Monteverdi still maintains the chronological distinction between the two ("second when considered in relation to the modern one, first in order of antiquity" [seconda . . . considerata in ordine alla moderna, prima in ordine all'antica . . .]), in the second he draws distinctions between the two based on philosophical criteria: the first practice was unable to meet the requirements of nature and of the principles established by classical authorities; the second was invented to agree with these ancient criteria. In the preface, Monteverdi discusses more explicitly the deficiencies of the first practice: having only two expressive *generi,* it was imperfect ("[it] can rightly be said to have been *until now* imperfect" [emphasis added]). With the invention of the third, modern music (the *seconda prattica*) had, by extension, transcended its imperfection. This could only be if, at the same time, it had retained the

36. The title to the 1632 collection of *Scherzi musicali,* which includes "madrigali in stil recitativo," is almost certainly not Monteverdi's own, but the publisher's.

37. This has obvious implications for performance practice; concert performances of the *Combattimento,* for example, lack the elements of surprise and theatrical immediacy that were clearly part of the composer's plan; and this is true of other works, like the *ballo* "Tirsi e Clori," for which Monteverdi has left very specific instructions regarding staging. A similar position toward gesture can be found in Marco Scacchi's distinction between "stile semplice recitativo," which does not involve gesture, and "stile recitativo," which does. See Palisca, "The Artusi– Monteverdi Controversy," 157.

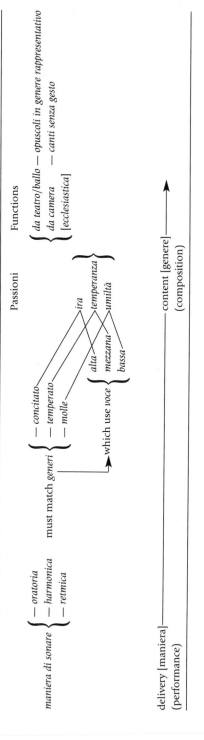

Fig. 5.1. Organization of the preface to the *Madrigali guerrieri et amorosi*

ability to express the other two—the *seconda prattica* includes not only the third *genere*, but all of them. At this point, there are two possible and conflicting interpretations of Monteverdi's view of the relationship between the two *prattiche*. One maintains that the *seconda prattica* offers a new way of expressing all three *generi* and is totally independent of the *prima;* the other, that the *seconda prattica* is an extension of the *prima*, adding to it new expressive devices and subsuming it, as a kind of dialect, within a language that has been made complete. The latter view deemphasizes the conflict between the different stylistic possibilities available to composers after the turn of the century and explains Monteverdi's apparently easy transition between the "Lamento d'Arianna" monody (in *genere rappresentativo*) and its madrigal version, his continued interest in the techniques of the classical madrigal even in such later volumes as the sixth and seventh books of madrigals, and his mixture of them within single works and collections.

In summary, the systematic outline of the *seconda prattica* that Monteverdi lays out in the preface to the *Madrigali guerrieri et amorosi* establishes a rhetorical continuum between content, or *genere*, and delivery, or *maniera* (figure 5.1). The central element of the system consists of the three *generi*, together with the emotional content of the text, which the music must match. Each *genere*, of course, is made up of a unique configuration of the three components—text, harmony, and rhythm. The *prima prattica*, represented by the two *generi, temperato* and *molle*, which already existed in the music of earlier composers, is subsumed within the expanded threefold expressive range of modern music. As the works of the eighth book demonstrate, and as the composer relates in his preface, all three *generi* can be deployed in works belonging to the various functional categories: "musica rappresentativa," "canti senza gesto," and "musica ecclesiastica." The latter does not figure in Monteverdi's classification system, but he does mention it in the body of the preface as a distinct genre—one in which he had applied his newly invented *concitato* technique. It seems to follow from his treatment of "musica rappresentativa" and "canti senza gesto" that Monteverdi regarded the absence or presence of gesture as not merely a matter of optional performance practice, but rather as pertaining to the intrinsic content of the works themselves—so that performers who left out the visual and pantomimic aspects of the "Combattimento," for example, were not performing it "nel modo et forma *in tal genere che sta scritto*"—*genere rappresentativo* as well as *concitato*, in this case. At the other end of the spectrum, the performers must pay heed to the particular dictates of the *generi* that are present in a composition, taking their cues for the proper "maniera di suonare" from the work's text, its rhythm, and its harmony. The voice occupies a particular position within the system, because it is the closest embodiment of the classical orator, declaiming the "compound text" made up of the poet's verses and the composer's setting of them.

By bringing together practice and reason and fulfilling after a fashion the composer's promise made in 1605 in the introduction to the fifth book of madrigals, the preface appears to mark a point of arrival for the aesthetic and philosophical journey Monteverdi claimed to have begun with the composition of *Arianna*. It brings full circle his assertion of thirty years earlier that, Freudian slips and editorial carelessness notwithstanding, "I don't go about my business haphazardly [non faccio le mie cose a caso]."

S I X

The *Genere Concitato*

"What does Your Lordship want the music to be able to do?"

"Arianna moved us because she was a woman, and similarly Orfeo be-cause he was a man. . . . *Arianna* led me to a just lament, and *Orfeo* to a righteous prayer." Thus Monteverdi held his earlier operas, and their characters, as benchmarks by which to judge Scipione Agnelli's libretto of *Le nozze di Tetide*, which had been sent to him from Mantua in 1616. Agnelli's *favola* lacked verisimilitude: among its other problems, it required winds, which do not speak, to sing; the composer doubted their efficacy. "How, my dear Sir, will I be able to imitate the speech of winds if they do not speak!" he demanded.

> How will I be able to move the emotions [of the audience] through them! Arianna moved us because she was a woman, and similarly Orfeo because he was a man, not a wind. Harmony [le armonie] can imitate, without any words, the noise of winds and the bleating of sheep, the neighing of horses and so on and so forth; but it cannot imitate the speech of winds because no such thing exists.[1]

But the most fundamental problem of all was that the story did not move the composer (he claimed that he could not even understand it), and that it did not lead to "an end that moves me," as had *Orfeo* and *Arianna*. In the end,

---

1. Monteverdi, letter 21, 9 December 1616; *The Letters of Claudio Monteverdi*, ed. and trans. by Denis Stevens (London: Cambridge University Press, 1980), p. 117; *Lettere, dediche e prefazioni*, ed. Domenico De Paoli (Rome: De Santis, 1973), p. 87.

Monteverdi left Striggio with what was for him the most fundamental of questions: "So what does Your Lordship want the music to be able to do?"

Monteverdi's own answer was that music, with text, could imitate the emotions of the characters; without text, it could imitate those natural sounds that do not require words. This is an important point, because it shows that in 1616, just as in the "Dichiaratione" and in the preface to the *Madrigali guerrieri et amorosi*, Monteverdi felt that emotions could be conveyed only when all the components of Plato's *melos* were present; instrumental music alone could not express affect. The *genere concitato*, even as it recognized the necessary presence of the instruments to achieve its effect, did not legitimize instrumental music as an independent category in Monteverdi's system of *generi* and functions. In this regard Monteverdi, even in his most advanced theoretical formulation, differs from Zarlino's view of instrumental music, that it could at best provide pleasant entertainment, only to the extent that he accords *concertato* composition equal status with the a cappella music of the *prima prattica*.[2] Purely instrumental composition has no real place in his system.[3]

Verisimilitude, at any rate, must govern both texted and untexted music, for it alone could ensure that the overall effect would have a chance to move the emotions of the audience. In order to be effective, a play's action must move toward its end in a natural way.[4] These concerns are reflected in Monteverdi's justification for choosing the duel between Tancredi and Clorinda from Tasso's *Gerusalemme liberata*:

2. This, when the very *genere concitato* upon which rested the perfection of modern music was finding its place in the affective instrumental compositions of such composers as Monteverdi's fellow Venetian, Dario Castello, who employed it in the middle section of his "Sonata xvi à 4," published in *Sonatae concertate . . . libro secondo* (1629).

3. This had long-range implications, as neither Scacchi nor Bernhardt allows for purely instrumental composition in their systems, although Scacchi specifically includes concertato composition. See Claude V. Palisca, "The Artusi–Monteverdi Controversy," in *The New Monteverdi Companion*, ed. Denis Arnold and Nigel Fortune (London: Faber and Faber, 1985), 157–58.

4. Monteverdi's impression was that *Le nozze di Tetide* was to be an independent theatrical production, and he critiqued it from that perspective. When he discovered that it was actually meant to be a set of intermedii, to be staged between the acts of a play, he adjusted his assessment accordingly and pronounced it "degna cosa et nobilissima" (letter of 6 January 1617; *Letters*, ed. Stevens, p. 125; *Lettere*, ed. De Paoli, p. 95). On the quality of librettos in relation to their function, see Silke Leopold, *Monteverdi: Music in Transition* (Oxford: Clarendon Press, 1991), 192. Taking his cue from Monteverdi's suggestion that perhaps one solution to the problems posed by *Tetide* might be to let each singer write his or her own part, Lorenzo Bianconi reads Monteverdi's critique of the libretto in ironic terms. See *Il Seicento* (Turin: E.D.T., 1982), 38–39.

I took up the divine Tasso, as a poet who expresses with his words naturally and with all propriety those passions he wishes to describe, and I found the description he gives of the battle between Tancredi and Clorinda, so as to have the two contrasting emotions to set to music—war, that is [cioè] prayer and death.[5]

Monteverdi's account focuses on the two emotional poles of the narration: death, which we may construe as the purpose of all the violent actions that lead to Clorinda's fatal wounding; and prayer, Clorinda's request for baptism and her eventual transformation in death. Taken together, these two elements make up his "guerra." Unlike *Le nozze di Tetide*, in the *Combattimento* the purpose of music is clear: it is to move the emotions of the spectators by juxtaposing the two extreme affects and imitating the essence of Tancredi's and Clorinda's psychological states. In addition, it imitates a panoply of external sounds that illustrate and govern the actions that take place in the pantomime, such as the motions of the combatants and of the horse, the sound of swords clashing and the crashing of armor, and Tancredi's and Clorinda's wrestling. Like Monteverdi's first two operas, the *Combattimento* leads to a natural focal point, and like Orfeo and Arianna its protagonists move the audience (almost to the point of tears, as Monteverdi recounts in the brief introduction to the work in the eighth book) because they are a man and a woman.[6] As with the *Pastor fido* excerpts of the fifth book, the emotional impact of the *Combattimento* originates at least in part in its placement within the work from which it is drawn.

The encounter between Tancredi and Clorinda is one of the crucial moments of the *Gerusalemme liberata*, bringing together the themes of concealed identity, recognition, love, and Christianity. It takes place in canto 12, after Clorinda and Argante have set fire to the Christian siege tower and have been chased back toward the city gate. The main events of the *canto* unfold in the arc of a single night, beginning at nightfall with Clorinda's plans to raid the tower and ending with her death just as dawn is breaking. The first part of the *canto* sets up both the dramatic situation and the main theme of the episode: Clorinda plans the excursion, and Argante insists on joining her; realizing that her life may be in danger, the Muslim eunuch Arsete, who had raised her, reveals

5. Preface to the eighth book.
6. Giovanni Getto underscores the intense humanity of the entire episode, "situazioni contrastanti della condizione umana, illusioni che sfiorano l'anima e la deludono proprio in quelle che sono le certezze credute più salde e destinate invece a non aver compimento." "Tancredi e l'immagine dell'amore," in *Nel mondo della Gerusalemme* (Florence: Vallecchi, 1968), 155.

to Clorinda that she is of Christian origin.[7] Her mother, wife of Senapo, king of Ethiopia, horrified at having given birth to a white child (both she and her husband being black) and fearing her jealous husband's wrath, entrusts her to Arsete, asking him to take her away and have her baptized.[8] Having raised her as pagan, Arsete, now that she is in danger, counsels her to embrace her parents' faith, and perhaps to lay down her arms. She responds that she would rather follow the only faith she has known and leaves with Argante to burn the tower.

In the skirmish that follows their successful attack, she and Argante repair to the walls of Jerusalem, where Suleyman's forces repel the pursuing Christians. Clorinda, who has stopped to return a blow dealt to her from behind, is left outside as Argante regains the safety of the city and the doors are closed. In the fray, he does not notice her absence, and even the Christians are not aware that she is left among them. Before the raid, in order to gain access to the heavily guarded tower, she had exchanged her own armor for an old rusty suit, and in the confusion beneath the walls she goes unnoticed by all except Tancredi. As she searches for another way back into the city, he follows her without knowing who she is.

It is at this point that the *Combattimento* picks up the story. The two confront and challenge one another and begin their duel. The fight, which is interrupted by a brief respite in which Tancredi asks for Clorinda's name and meets with her defiant refusal, is fierce, the finer points of combat having been rendered useless by darkness and the combatants' own violent ire. The duel is devoid of Tasso's customary interest in the mechanics of combat; rather, the emphasis is on its violence and on the emotions of the participants. Clorinda is wounded, and Tancredi gives her no quarter until she falls and asks to be baptized, offering her forgiveness and asking for his. In order to baptize her,

---

7. On the significance of Clorinda's history (she is the only character whose past Tasso explores), and on its sources in Vergil and Heliodorus, see Antonella Perelli, "La 'Divina' Clorinda," *Studi Tassiani* 39 (1991), 45–76.

8. Clorinda's "monstrous" birth is caused by her mother's looking at a painting of St. George in which a white virgin struggles in the clutches of a dragon while the knight attacks the beast with his lance. The woman's image becomes imprinted on the child. Regarding the significance of Clorinda's multiple nature (she is the child of Christian parents, but is raised as a Muslim warrior; she is perceived as either a wild beast or a man by her opponents, but not as a woman; she herself aims to transcend her nature as a woman by deeds more appropriate to her male comrades), see Marilyn Migiel, "Clorinda's Fathers," *Stanford Italian Review* 10 (1991), 103–7. Migiel convincingly interprets Tancredi's killing of Clorinda as a parallel to the St. George story, in which he kills the "monster" (Clorinda's physical form), saves her virginity, and restores her true nature.

Tancredi removes her helmet and at that point recognizes her, realizing that he has killed the woman he secretly loves. He finishes the sacrament, and she dies offering her hand. After her death he faints from exhaustion, and the two are found by a party of French crusaders who take them back to camp, where he is revived and she is prepared for burial. The remainder of the canto is taken up by Tancredi's lamentations on Clorinda's death, which are repeatedly interrupted by the ministrations of his companions.

Two themes dominate canto 12: Clorinda's Christianity—her knowledge of it, its reflection in her character, and her conversion on the point of death; and Tancredi's pathological, obsessive, and hopelessly alienated love for her, which as Giovanni Getto has noted reflects a conception of love as "a terrible and untamed force that subjugates man . . . a love that approaches death."[9] Just as canto 12 divides the epic almost exactly in half (the *Gerusalemme liberata* spans a total of twenty cantos), the duel divides the *canto* into two not quite symmetrical halves. The first, consisting of fifty-one *ottave*, is devoted to Clorinda's actions, history, and character. This is the first time since her appearance in canto 3 that she is seen as an independent agent; throughout her trajectory in the epic she appears opposite Tancredi, whose obsessive interest in her gives her character life.[10] The second, which comprises the last thirty-five, focuses on Tancredi and his reactions to her death. The *Combattimento* occupies the middle eighteen ottave and serves as a pivot for the overlapping lives of the two warriors, the one about to come to an end and the other about to be set on a new course.

The symbolic importance of their encounter reaches backward from the confines of this canto to the first time Tancredi sees Clorinda, in canto 3, when he meets her on the battlefield. Tasso constructs the beginning and the end of their relationship around parallel motives. Tancredi falls in love with Clorinda when, struck by a blow from his lance, she loses her helmet and "her golden hair blowing in the wind / the young woman appeared in the middle of the field" [le chiome dorate al vento sparse, / giovane donna in mezzo 'l campo apparse], leaving Tancredi awestruck at her sudden apparition.[11] In canto 12, the helmet again hides her face, and again Tancredi removes it and is struck dumb

9. "Tancredi," 137. The psychological dimension of Tancredi's fixation on his unattainable love for Clorinda and its reflection of Tasso's own "vita passionale acuta e strana" is discussed by Eugenio Donadoni, *Torquato Tasso*, 6th ed. (Florence: La Nuova Italia, 1967).

10. Getto, "Tancredi," 133.

11. On the importance of the helmet, see Giovanni Getto, "Clorinda ed Erminia e l'immagine dell'amore," in *Lezioni di letteratura italiana* (Turin: Giappichelli, 1967), 158–59.

at the sight: "he saw her, and knew her, and was struck / dumb and paralyzed. Alas, such a sight! Alas, such knowledge!" [la vide e la conobbe, restò senza / e voce e moto. Ahi vista! ahi conoscenza!]

The two situations are linked by other structural parallels that go beyond the moment of sudden discovery. In the third canto, following the shock of seeing her for the first time, Tancredi cannot continue to fight ("When hit, the knight does not hit back" [Percosso, il cavalier non ripercote]) and backs off as she pursues and aims her blows at him. Finally, he draws her out of the crowded battle and challeges her to a separate duel; once they are alone, he offers his naked breast for her to remove his heart, wounded not by her hand's blows but by the more accurate ones delivered by her eyes. Before the situation can be resolved, however, their encounter is interrupted by the fight around them, which encroaches on them and separates them. The *Combattimento* is their first opportunity to meet face to face after canto 3 and is in a sense a continuation and conclusion of the earlier duel. Just as the passages Monteverdi had selected from *Il pastor fido* for the fifth book of madrigals encapsulate the principal characters and situations of the play, the *Combattimento* fulfills a synoptic function within the *Gerusalemme liberata:* by joining two distant points in the epic, it collapses into its brief span the histories of the two characters.

The significance of this canto lies first in its theological implications, which fit into the notions of piety that pervade the entire epic, and second in the way it defines Tancredi's character for the remainder of the narrative. Clorinda's origins as a character are subservient to Tancredi, and she is seen as the object of his obsession, just as her friend Erminia exists to complete, with her own pursuit of Tancredi, a triangle of star-crossed lovers. But in canto 12 Clorinda takes on a life of her own; her independence can be seen as a function of her eventual fate, which is driven by the knowledge of her Christianity and finds resolution in her dying conversion. In the economy of this narrative, her spiritual life eclipses her prior "reflected" life; the true piety of her character takes precedence over her fierceness (returning her to a more properly feminine role); and even her encounter with Tancredi, for all its vivid immediacy, is secondary to the outcome it is intended to bring about.

The rather scant iconographic evidence for this episode supports the notion that the actual duel is not representative of the canto as a whole or even of this particular encounter between Tancredi and Clorinda. The artists who provided visual synopses of canto 12 for illustrated editions of the *Liberata* generally showed various combinations of events, including the burning of the tower, the skirmish at the city gates, Tancredi's pursuit of Clorinda, the baptism, Clorinda dying in Tancredi's arms, and the return of the two bodies to the Christian encampment, but not the combat itself (figure 6.1). And, in perhaps the best-known representation of the protagonists of the *Combattimento*, Jacopo and Domenico Tintoretto's *The Baptism of Clorinda* focuses on Tancredi administering the sacrament, representing not only the piety of the episode, but its underlying eroticism as well (figure 6.2).[12]

Monteverdi's own description of the substance of the *Combattimento*—that it conveyed the two emotions he was looking for, "war, that is, prayer and death" [guerra, cioè preghiera et morte], not "anger" [ira], or "anger and supplication" [ira et supplicatione]—is consistent with the interpretation of this canto as Clorinda's apotheosis rather than as a battle scene.[13] The composer focused not on the *genere concitato* alone, but on the larger emotional conflicts that give the action its verisimilitude. Taken in isolation, the *genere concitato* does not represent Monteverdi's conception of the power of the *Combattimento;* it is the contrast between "morte" and "preghiera," between the "ira" of the *genere concitato* and the "umiltà o supplicatione" of the *genere molle*, that brings the action "with a natural progression to an end that moves" [con ordine naturale ad un fine che . . . mova]. Like his contemporaries, Monteverdi did not see the essence of his text in the duel but found it instead in the pathos of the larger emotional conflicts of Tasso's "guerra."[14]

Tasso's poetry provided Monteverdi with a text that is fundamentally unlike that of any other libretto. It is a narrative with interpolated passages of dialogue; it is set in a fixed pattern of hendecasyllabic *ottave rime*, with frequent enjambements that undercut the rhyme scheme; it relies on vivid description of light and scenery to make its impact; and it offers none of the structural elements that Monteverdi was accustomed to exploiting to create large-scale pieces, such as a variety of refrain and strophic forms. As a result, the architecture of the *Combattimento* is unlike that of any of his other extant compositions.

12. Houston, Museum of Fine Arts. On the pictorial fortune of the Tancredi–Clorinda story, see Rensselaer W. Lee, *Poetry into Painting: Tasso and Art* (Middlebury, Vt.: Middlebury College, 1970), 19–20. Also, Lorenzo Bianconi, "I Fasti musicali del Tasso nei secoli xvi e xvii," in *Torquato Tasso tra letteratura, musica, teatro, arti figurative*, ed. Andrea Buzzoni (Bologna: Nuova Alfa, 1985), 143–50, and, in the same volume, Alessandra Chiappini, "Le Edizioni illustrate delle opere di Torquato Tasso."

13. Eric Chafe interprets this passage as referring to three separate emotions, "guerra," "preghiera," and "morte," but this reading disregards Monteverdi's syntax. *Monteverdi's Tonal Language* (New York: Schirmer, 1992), 239.

14. Love and death are juxtaposed elsewhere in the *Liberata:* in canto 20, the conclusion of the story of Gildippe and Odoardo, war and love culminate in death. On this point, see Luigi Malagoli, *Seicento italiano e modernità* (Florence: La Nuova Italia, 1970), 28.

Fig. 6.1. Bernardo Castello's illustration for canto 12 of Tasso's
La Gerusalemme liberata, 1590.

Fig. 6.2. Jacopo and Domenico Tintoretto, *The Baptism of Clorinda.*
(Houston, Museum of Fine Arts)

Monteverdi selected sixteen stanzas from canto 12, nos. 52–62 and 64–68. He left out stanza 63, which, as the battle draws to a close, compares its ebb and flow to a storm on the Aegean Sea. This *ottava* introduces a problematic passage of purely descriptive material that can be neither mimed nor effectively imitated; furthermore, the narrator's voice becomes impersonal to a greater extent than anywhere else in the *Combattimento*. Finally, *ottava* 63 stands between the excitement of the fight and Clorinda's fall, interrupting the momentum of the action. The composer also stopped short of Clorinda's actual death, described in *ottava* 69, which would have provided one last opportunity for affective pantomime as she, on point of death, offers Tancredi her hand. In spite of its obvious dramatic potential, it would have closed the *Combattimento* with the narrator's account of the events rather than with Clorinda's final words and the ethereal *morendo* sonority that accompanies them.

In Monteverdi's setting, the sixteen *ottave* fall into eight units (figure 6.3). The first is introductory, comprising the setting of the scene and the combatants' challenges; the second corresponds to the narrator's apostrophe to Night; the third consists of the first *guerra*, which is followed in the fourth by the lull in the fighting. The duel resumes in the fifth, and in the sixth Clorinda is wounded and Tancredi pursues her until she falls; her prayer asking for and granting forgiveness and her request to be baptized make up the seventh; the last consists of Tancredi's recognition of her, the baptism, and her final words.

Thus organized, the action divides the text in a symmetrical three-part arrangement. The first section comprises the first two units; the middle includes the two *guerre*, separated by the lull in the fighting, and Clorinda's fall; and the conclusion, framed by the *accompagnato* texture that characterizes her words, begins when she asks to be baptized. The distribution of the poetic material reinforces this symmetry, with the three sections comprising, respectively, the first three, middle ten, and final three *ottave*. Thus the elimination of *ottava* 63, in addition to preserving the momentum of the narrative, ensures the symmetrical distribution of the poetic material.

The harmonic plan underscores the narrative structure (table 6.1). The center for the whole work is D, alternating between *durus* and *mollis;* as Chafe has shown, much of the *Combattimento* hinges on the juxtaposition of major and minor harmonies as well as of sharp and flat regions.[15] The narrative opens in d minor (no. i in table 6.1), then shifts to major for the *moto del cavallo,* and finally to G major when Tancredi and Clorinda provoke one another to battle.

---

15. *Monteverdi's Tonal Language,* 240–45.

Fig. 6.3. Structure of the *Combattimento*

Sets stage	| "Notte"	| Guerra	Rest	Guerra	Clorinda wounded	| "Amico hai vinto"	| Baptism	"S' apre il ciel"
I	II	III	IV	V	VI	VII	VIII	
	**	**	**	**	**	♭	♮	
♭		|						
d G	|g mollis	|G	g mollis	G	To E, A, D	| mollis	| D, with flat infl.	
(cavallo)			(to D, A, G, D)					

Introduction   Battle   Baptism and Death (Conclusion)

** = *genere concitato*

Tempo piricchio (tempo veloce): surface   + *Text (anger and scorn)*

Tempo spondeo (tempo tardo): harmony

Monteverdi set "Notte" (no. ii) in g minor, separating it from the preceding music with a change of signature to one flat. For the continuation of the hostilities (no. iii), Monteverdi changes the signature back to the *durus* system and returns to G major, which, with C major, is the predominant key for the *genere concitato*, not only in the *Combattimento* but in other pieces as well. The lull in the fighting (no. iv) is introduced by another juxtaposition of G *durus* and g *mollis*, which signifies the exhaustion of the combatants. After the description of their physical degradation, this central section is harmonically wide-ranging, with cadences on A, G, and D. G major again marks the duel (no. v); the resolution of the fight after the most violent exchange of blows (no. vi) introduces another area of wide harmonic breadth, ranging as far as B, E, A, and eventually D, as Clorinda struggles to remain standing after being fatally wounded and as her soul succumbs to her native faith.[16] Her request for baptism (no. vii) is harmonically open-ended; Monteverdi again changes the signature to one flat and sets her words to two phrases that focus on g minor but that emphasize harmonic disjunction and end on an unresolved A major harmony.[17] After she has spoken, another signature change back to the *durus* system (no. viii) marks Tancredi's preparations for the sacrament and remains in force throughout the remainder of the piece.

In addition to providing a set of harmonic contrasts between the various sections, this large-scale tonal plan reinforces the formal symmetry that frames the work as a whole. The signature changes identify five main sections, alternating between the *durus* and *mollis* systems. These, in turn, coincide with the three main periods that make up the largest articulation of the piece. The introduction and the conclusion move, respectively, from *durus* to *mollis* and from *mollis* to *durus*; the two *mollis* sections frame the central battle, which is entirely in *durus* (with brief affective contrasts with *mollis*). Thus the opposition of the two harmonic regions governs the largest structure of the *Combattimento*, and some of its more localized affective passages reflect the structural role of this opposition. For example, the resolution of the two characters' actions suggests the opposition of *durus* and *mollis* harmonic areas, as well as the double function of their encounter in the *Liberata*. Tancredi is last mentioned as he baptises Clorinda; this part of the narration closes with a cadence to A major (m. 429). Clorinda's "the heavens open: I die in peace" [s'apre il ciel, io vado in pace] ends on a D major harmony introduced by one last move toward the flat side.

---

16. On this passage, see Chafe's excellent commentary in *Monteverdi's Tonal Language*, 243.
17. Ibid., 244–45.

This "bifocal close," which contrasts Clorinda's apotheosis with Tancredi's tragedy (and the continuation of his suffering in the rest of the epic), encapsulates the opposition of polarized emotions that drives the *Combattimento* and that provides the underpinning for the aesthetic system Monteverdi laid out in the preface to the eighth book.

Within this larger structure, Monteverdi uses three elements, distinct from what precedes and follows them, to mark the principal formal divisions. "Notte," the narrator's address to the fight's silent witness, closes the opening section, preparing the way for the events that follow; the three brief dialogues between Tancredi and Clorinda propel the drama toward its resolution (which is reached with Clorinda's closing words); and the two *guerre* shape the hostilities of the central section. The narrator's meditation on the duel that is about to take place is the only part of the *Combattimento* that is constructed according to a closed formal plan. Its structure is by now familiar: it consists of a pair of strophic variations introduced by a sinfonia and a brief pantomime *(passeggio)* and separated by the return of the *passeggio*. To make the symmetry of "Notte" possible, Monteverdi inverts the order of the first four lines of *ottava* 54, distorting the syntax of the strophe. Tasso's original did not lend itself to a bipartite division but instead encompassed three syntactic units: an opening pair of verses commenting on the greatness of the deeds the narrator is about to witness, a four-line clause, and finally the closing couplet. Both of the latter address Night and would have made a logical six-line unit. Monteverdi chose to follow the organization of this stanza found in the *Gerusalemma conquistata*, which allows for a break after the fourth line and makes a considerably stronger rhetorical opening with its direct apostrophe to Night, which would otherwise have been buried within the stanza.[18]

Liberata:

> *Degne d'un chiaro sol, degne d'un pieno*
> *teatro, opre sarian sì memorande.*
> *Notte, che nel profondo oscuro seno*
> *chiudesti e ne l'oblio fatto sì grande,*
> *piacciati ch'io ne 'l tragga e 'n bel sereno*
> *a le future età lo spieghi e mande.*
> *Viva la fama loro; e tra lor gloria*
> *splenda del fosco tuo l'alta memoria.*

---

18. Monteverdi achieves a similar effect in the opening verse, which in the original read "Vuol ne l'armi provarla: un uom la stima / degno a cui sua virtù si paragone." The change al-

Worthy of the clear light of day, of a full
Theater, are such memorable actions.
Night, since in your deep dark breast
And in oblivion you enclose such a great event,
Allow me to retrieve it, and in clear light
To explain it and transmit it to future ages.
Let their fame remain alive; and by means of their glory,
Let the lofty memory of your darkness shine brightly.

Conquistata and *Combattimento:*

Notte, che nel profondo oscuro seno
chiudesti e ne l'oblio fatto sì grande,
degne d'un chiaro sol, degne d'un pieno
teatro, opre sarian sì memorande,
piacciati ch'io ne 'l tragga e 'n bel sereno
a le future età lo spieghi e mande.
Viva la fama loro; e tra lor gloria
splenda del fosco tuo l'alta memoria.

Night, since in your deep dark breast
And in oblivion you enclose such a great event,
Worthy of the clear light of day, of a full
Theater, are such memorable actions.
Allow me to retrieve them, and in clear light
To explain them and transmit them to future ages.
Let their fame remain alive; and by means of their glory,
Let the lofty memory of your darkness shine brightly.

It should come as no surprise that Monteverdi chose to set this section as a pair of strophic variations: his treatment of it recalls not only the strophic variations of the prologue to *Orfeo*, in which Music introduces the opera and establishes herself as the agent that gives the work its order and its power, but also those of "Tempro la cetra," sung by the singer-poet-composer at the open-

---

lows him to start his narration at this point (*ottava* 52 has its antecedents in 51 and cannot otherwise be separated from it), and to begin with the much more emphatic and economical "Tancredi, che Clorinda un uomo stima, / vuol ne l'armi provarla al paragone." On Monteverdi's conflation of the two versions of the *Liberata*, the *Liberata* and its later revision the *Conquistata*, see Nino Pirrotta, "Monteverdi's Poetic Choices," in *Music and Culture in Italy from the Middle Ages to the Baroque* (Cambridge: Harvard University Press, 1984), 288 and 433–34 n. 37, where he lists the composer's modifications. As Pirrotta notes, Monteverdi's editorial judgment was such that the result is greater than the sum of its parts.

ing of the seventh book. Significantly, "Notte" is the only part of the work in which Monteverdi allows virtuoso ornamentation: as in Orfeo's "Possente spirto," the vocal display is symbolic of the bard's rhetorical proficiency. The orderliness of the structure and the virtuosity it demands (from both composer and performer) associate the narrator, who speaks for the poet as he brings order to the epic, with the composer, whose musical rhetoric shapes the events on the stage. In character, tone, and structure—indeed, in all but placement—"Notte" functions as the prologue of the *Combattimento*. Its role in Tasso's epic has been likened to a proscenium arch that frames the action in the virtual theater of the reader's imagination (Tasso refers to the deeds he is about to tell as being "degne d'un pieno teatro").[19] In Monteverdi's staged setting, it serves as a kind of double frame, distancing the audience from the pantomime and establishing the dichotomy between the narrator's words and the "real" actions of the protagonists.

Monteverdi could have taken "Notte" out of sequence and used it to open his setting, as a proper prologue would have done. As it stands, the narrator's interlude is a song within the sung drama—one that is not motivated by the dictates of the action and that shifts attention away from the protagonists in mid-pantomime. It stops time, holding the fighters poised to attack but motionless, as if in a stop-action sequence. As such, it has the potential to rob the narrative of its momentum; instead, the pause it introduces creates more tension than it dissipates. Two elements help to sustain the drama and explain its placement *in medias res* rather than at the beginning. First, just before the sinfonia, Monteverdi introduces for the first time the *genere concitato*, for the line "quai due tori gelosi e d'ira ardenti," and interrupts it, heightening the sense of foreboding that is established in the introduction. Second, by interpolating the *passeggio*, the composer draws the observer's attention back to the suspended action, reinforcing the tension between characters and narrator and between dramatic and narrative time.

The narrator occupies an ambiguous position in the *Combattimento*: although he is an impartial observer of the events he describes, it is through his words and the emotions he projects that the audience "feels" Tancredi's shock when he recognizes Clorinda as she lay wounded and dying, or "sees" the setting in which the action takes place. His mediation introduces an important extra layer in the relationship between audience and characters, one that was not present in *Arianna* and *Orfeo*, whose protagonists were able to speak di-

19. Getto, "Tancredi," 149.

rectly to their listeners. He is undoubtedly a character—arguably the most important character in the work—but speaks as such only when he steps out of his role to interrupt the flow of his own narrative. He is, of course, prescient, and this poses particular demands on his own emotions as he narrates. When he is overwhelmed by his insight into the characters and their fate, as he is when Tancredi, seeing Clorinda wounded, swells with vainglorious pride that will soon turn to grief, his role changes almost imperceptibly from narrator to participant, and he takes center stage. In both the break in the fight and in "Notte," his commentaries suspend time, holding the characters poised on the brink of violence and creating a moment of high tension at the beginning of the scene, and moralizing midway through the battle while setting the stage for the tragic resolution of the conflict.

The brief exchanges between Tancredi and Clorinda embedded within the narration provide three crucial moments of dramatic immediacy, one in each of the major sections (the introduction, duel, and conversion scene). The first comes at the beginning, when they challenge one another; the second, during the lull in the duel, when Tancredi asks to know his opponent's identity and is enraged by Clorinda's defiant reply, "whoever I may be, you see in front of you one of the two who burned the great tower" [chiunque io mi sia, tu inanzi vedi un di quei due che la gran torre accese], which spurs him on to resume the fight and eventually kill her; and the third occurs at the end of the battle, when Clorinda speaks to pardon her opponent and ask for his forgivenss and baptism. In these places, Monteverdi bridges the gap between the primarily narrative form of the piece, in which the protagonists' pantomime illustrates the narration and is secondary to it, and real drama, in which the action becomes almost independent of the narrative. As the focus changes, so does the audience's perspective, which oscillates between passive reception of the narrative and first-hand observation of the action. In places, Tasso blurs the distinction between these levels, as when he makes the reader a participant in the narrative ("*Hear* the swords clashing horribly in mid-blade" [*Odi* le spade orribilmente urtarsi a mezzo il ferro]), when he has the narrator enter his own narrative space and address his characters directly in the first person ("Wretch, why do you gloat?" [Misero, di che godi?]), and when he mixes first person speech with the narrator's own imagining for Clorinda's closing "S'apre il ciel." [20]

The dialogues also help shape the drama, driving its events forward and toward their eventual resolution, which comes with Clorinda's final apotheosis

---

20. On the narrator's interjection during the break in the fight, see Getto, "Tancredi," 151.

as her words seem to float upward in the eventual direction of her soul. As the culmination of the entire *scena*, her closing "The heavens open, I die in peace" [S'apre il ciel, io vado in pace] offers one last opportunity for blurring the distinction between what appears to take place directly before the audience and what is mediated by the narrator. These words are not truly hers; rather, they are only "fictional," in that according to the narrator she only *looks* as if she might have spoken them. In assigning them to her rather than to the narrator, Monteverdi leaves his audience with one last deception.

Just as "Notte" frames the entire *Combattimento* within a virtual proscenium arch, and as the dialogues provide dramatic impulse for the action, Monteverdi deploys the *genere concitato* to frame the fighting. The label "concitato" has been applied to a wide variety of music involving martial texts and either triadic, fanfare-like figurations or rapid syllabic text declamation on a single pitch.[21] Monteverdi's own definition of the *genere*, however, limits it, as we have seen, to three elements—a text containing "ira et sdegno," a slow, rhythmic element representing the spondaic foot and coinciding with the whole note (the harmonic rhythm corresponds to this), and the division of the whole note into sixteen *semicrome*. Although it is clear that, particularly after the *Combattimento*, the various components of the *genere* are often used by themselves as iconic substitutes for it, it is useful in analyzing the *Combattimento* to separate the *genere* as Monteverdi defined it from the mimetic devices that surround it. In its archetypal form, it appears only five times: after the combatants challenge one another and are enflamed like "two jealous bulls, burning with anger" [due tori gelosi e d'ira ardenti]; in the middle and at the end of the first round of fighting; at the beginning of the resumption of the fight, when "anger returns to their hearts" [torna l'ira nei cori]; and at the climactic moment of the

---

21. On this point, see Pirrotta, "Monteverdi's Poetic Choices," 312–13. As the discussion in this chapter makes clear, I favor a more restrictive use of the term than does Pirrotta, whose list of examples, which includes "Sì ch'io vorrei morire" from the fourth book, "Addio, Florida bella" from the sixth, and "A quest'olmo" and "Eccomi pronta ai baci" from the seventh, is rather broadly inclusive. Rather than to a particular style of composition, his examples point to the affective performance manner advocated by Aquilino Coppini, who sent his three collections of sacred contrafacta, *Il [primo, secondo e terzo] libro della musica di Claudio Monteverde e d'altri autori a cinque voci* (1608), to Hendrik van der Putten with a cover letter in which he recommended that Monteverdi's pieces "require, in execution, broader pauses and a somewhat irregular beat, at times speeding up or slowing down, and even rushing . . . they have a marvellous ability to move the emotions." Original in Paolo Fabbri, *Monteverdi* (Turin: E.D.T., 1985), 152–53. Similarly, Chafe has argued that "the *concitato* genus cannot be limited to the repeated-sixteenth-note style" on the grounds that "other, equally prominent emblematic devices [are] often inseparable from it." Like Pirrotta, Chafe finds antecedents for the

duel, when the two are wounded to the point of collapse and the *guerra* itself comes to a close as Clorinda is mortally wounded. In none of these situations is the instrumental texture (repeated sixteenth notes and stationary harmonies) associated with either actions or noises: it has no descriptive purpose and coincides with the narrator's use of the words "ira" and "sdegno" to describe the characters' emotions. The only instance in which this is not strictly true occurs at the end of the first part of the duel, when, after wrestling with one another, Tancredi and Clorinda separate and take up their swords, inflicting such wounds that "both are blood-tinted" [e l'un e l'altro il tinge di molto sangue].[22] The text is strictly descriptive and does not mention specific emotions; rather than represent the swordthrusts themselves, the instruments convey the blind rage that drives the combatants.

The separation between the text and the other components of the *genere* can be accounted for by the general context in which this passage takes place; it is preceded by Tancredi's wrestling with Clorinda, holding her in "the grip of a powerful enemy, and not of a lover" [nodi di fier nemico e non d'amante], which emphasizes, by negating the erotic potential that is the subtext of the encounter, the hatred that grips the two.[23] Furthermore, the independent role of the instruments is carried over into the continuation of this moment, where the instruments, changing abruptly from G major to g minor and from *genere concitato* to *genere molle*, anticipate the narrator's description by projecting, with descending melodic figures over static *molle* harmonies and slow quarter-note rhythms (that reveal the spondaic component of the *concitato*), Tancredi's and Clorinda's emotional and physical state (mm. 201–4, example 6.1). Monteverdi's strategy for deploying the *genere concitato*, then, is to use it as a formal

---

genere as far back as the fourth book of madrigals and links it, as does Fabbri (*Monteverdi*, 252), with the "Lamento d'Arianna" (*Monteverdi's Tonal Language*, 240). For other examples of excited sixteenth-note declamation, see Orfeo's "s'arman forse ai miei danni con tal furor le furie" (act 4), discussed in Gary Tomlinson, "Madrigal, Monody, and Monteverdi's 'via naturale all'immitatione,'" *Journal of the American Musicological Society* 34 (1981), 70–72. For a more recent discussion of this problem, see Robert Holzer, "'Ma invan la tento et impossibil parmi,' or How *guerrieri* are Monteverdi's *madrigali guerrieri*?" in *The Sense of Marino: Literature, Fine Arts, and Music of the Italian Baroque*, edited by Francesco Guardiani (Ottawa: Legas, 1994), 443. I proposed a literal reading of the *genere concitato* in chapter 6 of "Claudio Monteverdi's Concertato Technique and its Role in the Development of His Musical Thought" (Ph.D. diss., Harvard University, 1989).

22. Migiel, "Clorinda's Fathers," 96–98, draws attention to Tasso's particularly arresting visual descriptions of blood, wounds, and mutilation, especially in relation to Clorinda.

23. On the erotic dimension of the duel see Giovanna Scianatico, *L'arme pietose: Studio sulla Gerusalemme liberata* (Venice: Marsilio, 1990), 89–91.

Ex. 6.1. *Il combattimento di Tancredi e Clorinda*, mm. 201–4

tor - na-no al fer - ro e l'un e l'al - tro il tin - ge di mol - to san-gue

boundary and as an emotional signal for the audience: the combatants blaze with fury before the fight, and the spectators are left in suspense throughout the narrator's address to night; their ire carries them to the first climax of the battle and jars with the pitiful image of their blood-stained armor as they separate to rest; contempt and anger drive them to resume their duel; and, finally, sapped of all strength and driven only by their scorn for one another, they reach the resolution of the fight.

At the opposite end of the spectrum from the *genere concitato* is the varied array of illustrative devices with which Monteverdi controls the pace of the pantomime. The horse's motion, the measured steps with which Tancredi and Clorinda approach one another, the *passeggio* inserted between the strophes of "Notte," the pizzicatos that imitate the clashing swords, and the syncopations that mark the combatants' wrestling—all of these illustrate particular moments of the narrative that have no independent emotional content. They are sound effects, Monteverdi's own version of Tasso's descriptive arsenal.[24]

The distinction between the *genere concitato* and the variety of madrigalian devices that illustrate the fight is not, however, absolute. Just as Tasso's descriptive language links the mechanics of the fight to the protagonists' emotional state, so that the growing confusion and brutality of the battle is an outward reflection of their inner fury, Monteverdi mediates between the two types of musical expression by manipulating rhythmic motion in such a way that the music flows from one to the other without obvious interruption.

The first of the two *guerre* is illustrative of his technique. It can be divided into twelve stages, each of which projects a different level of rhythmic intensity (table 6.1). The instrumental accompaniment begins with the relatively static rhythms and sparse texture that correspond to the halting blows that open

24. On Tasso's contrast-based imagery, see Malagoli, *Seicento italiano e modernità*, 19–20.

Table 6.1 *Combattimento*: Phases of the first guerra

Phase	Measures	Text	Musical characteristics
i	133–38	"Non schivar"	*(musical notation)*
ii	139–46	Non danno i colpi	*(musical notation)*
iii	147–54	Odi le spade	*(musical notation)*
iv	155–58	sempre il piè fermo	*(musical notation)*
v	159–62	né scende taglio	*(musical notation)*
vi	163–69	l'onta irrita lo sdegno	*(musical notation)* concitato in the voice; in strings
vii	169–74	stimol novo s'aggiunge	*(musical notation)* → *(musical notation)* (concitato)
viii	175–76	dansi con pomi	*(musical notation)* Pizz.
ix	177–81	cozzan con gli elmi	*(musical notation)*
x	182–87	Tre volte	*(musical notation)*
xi	186–98	e altretante poi	*(musical notation)*
xii	199–202	tornano al ferro	*(musical notation)* (concitato)

the fight (phases i–ii in table 6.1) and gradually increases to the cascading sixteenth-note figures that represent the slashing cuts that bring the encounter to its first high point (iii–vi). The most violent blows lead directly to the repeated sixteenth notes of the *genere concitato* at the point when "offence enflames scorn to vengeance" (vii).

In spite of the seamless progression of musical figures, however, there are signs that make it clear that with phase vii the setting has slipped into a different expressive mode. Phase vi ends with a cadence, the first of this section; at the beginning of phase vii the instruments suddenly change register, shifting down one octave; and after the cadence the narrator finds himself struggling to keep control of his own words. After this high point, the battle degenerates as Tancredi and Clorinda hammer at each other with shields and sword hilts (sections viii–x) and finally forgo their weapons entirely to wrestle one another (xi). The rhythmic activity loses its momentum and becomes a confused tangle of syncopations before frustration drives the two back to their swords and once more the *genere concitato* marks the emotional and dramatic climax of the section (xii).

Two moments stand out in this first *guerra*. The first occurs when the narrator becomes involved in his own story to the point that he takes over the repeated sixteenth-note figures of the *genere concitato*. The introduction of the new *genere* in the vocal part draws attention to the narrator's voice and coincidentally illustrates rather convincingly Monteverdi's point that the text cannot follow the rapidity of the instruments. That it cannot, of course, is what makes its employment here effective. The second is the continuation of this passage, in which the alto viola enters with repeated-note *concitato* figurations while the two violins illustrate the blows being exchanged. In the superimposition of the two devices, action and emotion are fully integrated; and, seen in this context, the *genere concitato* becomes one component of an expressive continuum in which the two form an interrelated whole.

In turning to Tasso and the *Gerusalemme liberata* to experiment with the new *genere*, Monteverdi returned to the poet who, more than any other before Rinuccini, had helped to shape his attitude toward text setting.[25] Tasso's lyric poetry had already appeared in the first and second books of madrigals, and in the third the composer had set two cycles of *ottave* from the *Liberata*, "Vattene pur crudel con quella pace," Armida's angry response to being abandoned by Rinaldo (canto 16 nos. 59, 60, and 63), and "Vivrò fra i miei tormenti e le mie cure," from Tancredi's lament on Clorinda's death (canto 12, *ottave* 77–79).[26] Tasso's importance for Monteverdi was in part the result of the composer's contact with the madrigals of Jaches de Wert, the *maestro di cappella* at the Mantuan court, whose settings from the *Liberata* continue to resonate in Monteverdi's works as late as the fifth book.[27]

Echoes of Wert's choral declamation can be heard throughout the recitative of the *Combattimento* and distance it from the "Lamento d'Arianna" and other monodies. Monteverdi set Tasso's narrative in a more economical way than he had Rinuccini's libretto: the *Combattimento* makes fewer concessions to the recitative as a melodic style, favoring instead a manner of delivery that emphasizes the precise rhythmic realization of Tasso's poetry and subordinates melody to prosody. Simply put, most of the text is recited rather than sung; as Tomlinson has noted of the "Lamento d'Arianna," Monteverdi's score is less a "setting"

---

25. Tasso's central place among the poets set by Monteverdi before 1600 has long been recognized: see Leo Schrade, *Monteverdi, Creator of Modern Music* (New York: Norton, 1950), 135–48; Pirrotta, "Monteverdi's Poetic Choices," 279–83; Fabbri, *Monteverdi*, 37–39; and Tomlinson, "Madrigal, Monody, and Monteverdi's '*via naturale all'immitatione*,'" 69 n. 12 and 70–75.

26. A third madrigal pair in the third book, on the sonnet "'Rimanti in pace' a la dolente e bella" by Livio Celiano (Angelo Grillo), takes as its point of departure *ottava* 56 from canto 16.

27. Tomlinson, "Madrigal, Monody, and Monteverdi's '*via naturale all'immitatione*,'" 71 n. 16, makes the point that Monteverdi actually avoided setting any of the *ottave* set by his mentor, even turning to the *Conquistata* for "Piagn'e sospira" (the last piece in the fourth book), which occupies the same position in the revised epic as "Sovente, allor che sugli estivi ardori," set by Wert in his eighth book, does in the *Liberata*. Wert's penchant for homorhythmic or staggered textures is evident, for example, in the choral declamation that pervades Monteverdi's settings of *Il pastor fido* in the fifth book.

Ex. 6.2. *Il combattimento di Tancredi e Clorinda*, mm. 1–9

than a realization of the "rhetorical and assonant music inherent in the text."[28] This is evident from the very beginning: in the first four lines Monteverdi emphasizes Tasso's speech-rhythms, declaiming the text on a reciting tone and using melodic inflections only for cadential formulas (mm. 1–9, example 6.2).

The first thirty-eight bars consist of a steady rhythmic buildup leading to the first point of high excitement, when the sound of Tancredi's armor alerts Clorinda to his presence. The propulsive rhythm of the "motto del cavallo" is adumbrated in the regularity of the opening; Clorinda's urgent search for a way back into Jerusalem is marked by the quickening of the pulse from whole notes to half notes, and—in one of only two vocal madrigalisms of the first part—by the rising melodic contour that underscores "the craggy summit" [alpestre cima]. Monteverdi emphasizes the regular construction of the first four lines, whose function is introductory, by setting the rhyming pair *paragone-dispone* to nearly identical cadential formulas; aside from "Notte" this is the only example of parallel phrase construction in the *Combattimento*. A further quickening of the rhythm coincides with "eagerly, he follows her" [segue egli impetuoso]; as in previous phrases, Monteverdi paces the declamation around principal stresses (Tancredi, *stima*, provarla, paragone, *cima*, porta, dispone, segue, avien, *armi*), setting the rest to even note values and repeated pitches. The only departure from this plain setting coincides with the second madrigalism, which occurs at "so that his weapons clang" [che l'armi suone], where triadic motion

28. On the musical rhetoric of the "Lamento d'Arianna," see Tomlinson, "Madrigal, Monody, and Monteverdi's *'via naturale all'immitatione,'*" 86–96.

and text repetition (another rarity in the *Combattimento*) depicts the clanging of Tancredi's weapons. The forward motion of the entire section comes to a standstill with the shift back to duple meter for "so that she turns and calls out" [ch'ella si volge e grida] and a broadening in the rhythmic structure of the dialogue that follows.

To a great extent, it is the presence of the ensemble of *viole* that frees the voice from having to both declaim and illustrate the text. With its entrance in m. 10, the ensemble takes the lead in depicting the action and continues to do so throughout the section, so that when the voice imitates the sound of Tancredi's weapons it merely confirms what the audience has already been hearing. This separation of functions continues throughout the two *guerre:* there as well the voice is largely reduced to a reciting tone, deriving its rhythmic vigor from the prosody of Tasso's poetry while the musical focus shifts to the instrumental illustration of the fight.

The distance between the stark recitation of the *Combattimento* and monodies such as the "Lamento d'Arianna" and the two "Lettere" is bridged somewhat by the passages in which the ensemble of *viole* falls silent—the lull in the fight and the last part of the battle beginning with Clorinda's wounding. Even in these sections, however, the musical rhetoric is distinguished by the parsimony with which Monteverdi deploys his melodic material. From "e stanco ed anelante" (m. 205) to "e sè non tanto offeso" (m. 234), inflected recitation remains the rule, and the significance of such subtle devices as the upward leap of a third for "albor," in the brief description of breaking dawn, and the rising line at "del suo nemico" is enhanced in light of the restrained declamation that surrounds them. Similarly, the narrator's sudden impassioned outburst ("Oh, our mind's folly / which exaggerates any sign of fortune!" [O nostra folle mente / ch'ogni aura di fortuna estolle!]) stands out for its melodic variety, from the urgency of the two brief sequences that introduce it ("he gloats, and swells with pride" [ne gode e insuperbisce]), to the parallel exclamations that govern its structure, to the drop in pitch level that marks the parenthetical "should you remain alive" [s'in vita resti] (example 6.3).

In *ottave* 64 and 65, Monteverdi expands the melodic and expressive range of the recitative, matching his musical rhetoric to the climactic events of Tasso's narrative. Clorinda's fall comprises three large-scale periods, each of which cadences, as Chafe has noted,[29] on successively less sharp degrees (E, A, and D): in the first she is wounded (mm. 317–40); in the second and third

29. *Monteverdi's Tonal Language*, 243–44.

Ex. 6.3. *Il combattimento di Tancredi e Clorinda*, mm. 235–47

(mm. 341–54 and 355–64), her spirit is transformed by her until now latent Christian faith. Within this larger structure, however, Monteverdi establishes a pattern of shorter phrases that alternate between rising and falling contours, as well as between the sharp and flat regions. In the four phrases of the first period, the focus shifts between Clorinda and Tancredi. Her faltering strength is mirrored in the generally static melodic lines associated with her and in their generally falling melodic and harmonic profile (example 6.4, phrases 1 and 3). Tancredi's victorious pursuit, as he drives home the fatal blow, is just the opposite: "he pushes the blade's point into her lovely breast" [spinge egli il ferro nel bel sen di punta] rises through a seventh and moves from G to A, ending on an interrupted D^6 harmony with "and greedily drinks her blood" [e'l sangue avido beve] (example 6.4, phrases 2 and 4). The fourth phrase starts where the second leaves off, returning to the spilling of blood ("drains her of a warm river" [l'empie d'un caldo fiume]) and extending the upward sequence to the e" of "fiume." Clorinda's fall (phrase 5) is then reflected in the descent to the cadence on E an octave below the climactic note and in the B-flat harmony that underscores "and her foot falters" [e'l piè le manca].[30]

30. Chafe's point that the sharp–flat juxtapositions in this passage reflect the struggle between the pagan and Christian sides of Clorinda's soul is marred by his observation that "the sharp/flat shift that accompanies the juxtaposition of *morirsi* (B) and *pie* (B-flat) recalls Monteverdi's reference to *passioni contrarie*, suggesting perhaps that he had this particular passage in mind," in which he appears to have misread "piè" in "e'l piè le manca" [and her foot falters] as "pie" [pious]. There is no syntactic support for his reading (indeed, it makes no sense), and Monteverdi's shift is better seen as an illustration of Clorinda's failing strength than as the

Ex. 6.4. *Il combattimento di Tancredi e Clorinda,* mm. 317–40

Rising sequences again accompany Tancredi's pursuit in the first phrase of the second period, and again a turn toward the flat side and falling melodic contour introduce Clorinda's "weakened voice" [voce afflitta]. Her conversion, however, returns to the sharp region (through E major, A minor, and A major),

---

origin of Monteverdi's "morte" and "preghiera." Chafe's description of the *Combattimento* is inaccurate in other respects: Monteverdi provides the indication "questa ultima va in arcata morendo" over the last note of the violin, not in the preface, as Chafe maintains (241); and at the first climax in the duel Tancredi does not strike Clorinda three times as Chafe would have him do (241), but holds her ("tre volte il cavalier la donna stringe"). Monteverdi is quite precise in depicting this with syncopations, whereas the confused blows that precede the wrestling ("dansi con pomi, e infeloniti e crudi cozzan con gli elmi insieme e con gli scudi") are represented by the increasing rhythmic irregularity that culminates in the meter change.

as well as to the rising sequential fragmentation that drives the second period to its cadence (from "last words" [parole estreme] onward) and, inverted to mirror the finality of the events to which it refers, pervades the third as well. For the moment when Tancredi discovers Clorinda's identity ("and he uncovered her. He saw her, *he saw her* and he knew her" [e la scoprio. La vide, *la vide* e la conobbe]), the emotional climax of the narrator's part, Monteverdi returns to the urgent sequential fragmentation he had employed for the resolution of the conflict, and his empathy for Tancredi is expressed by recalling the exclamations that accompanied his commentary on the protagonist's misplaced pride ("Ahi vista! ahi conoscenza!"), intensifying them with a dissonant setting that recalls "Ahi caso acerbo," the shepherds' lament on Euridice's death in *Orfeo*.

In contrast with the economy of the narrator's part, Tancredi's and Clorinda's lines are characterized by a considerably greater degree of melodic activity. This is already evident in the triadic motion of their first exchange and is intensified in the dialogue that leads to the second part of the duel, where the disjunct profile of Clorinda's reply to Tancredi's more measured request is in keeping with the ferocity of character that is her hallmark until her death (example 6.5).

The restraint with which Monteverdi treats the narrative, when compared with the relative freedom of the other parts, emerges as the chief musical ingredient in the composer's subtle rendering of the interaction between narrative and drama that pervades the *Combattimento*. The distinction that is highlighted is that between the first-person expression of a character like Arianna or Clorinda, whose words are direct reflections of personal emotions, and the narrator's objective delivery of a given text — and, most importantly, of a well-known and almost revered literary icon. The ambiguity of the narrator's persona — part poet, part first-hand observer of the events, part reader of the poet's text, part composer — is captured by Monteverdi's highly nuanced recitative, which moves between the opposite extremes, sometimes (as at the beginning) distancing him from the action, and at times endowing him with the rhetorical powers reserved for the protagonists.

The *Combattimento* was Monteverdi's *locus classicus* for the innovations introduced in the preface to the *Madrigali guerrieri et amorosi*. In it, he took on Tasso's heroic genre and demonstrated that his music could indeed match, without apology, the best examples of rhetorical high style, and that "speech alone has great power, but it has even more when it is joined to music" [gran forza ha da se stesso il parlare, ma molto più ha forza, quando è congiunto

Ex. 6.5. *Il combattimento di Tancredi e Clorinda,* mm. 273–77 and 285–91

all'armonia], as Zarlino writes.[31] Perhaps conscious of this achievement, he conferred on it the distinction of being the only one of his works to which was specifically attached an aesthetic manifesto, doing so not because he was forced into it, but because he intended to put it there. And, indeed, his setting married theoretical principles and practical application to a greater degree than any of his other works. Whether theory preceded practice, or vice versa, is of little consequence: in the *Combattimento* the two come together as a practical demonstration of the symbiotic relationship between philosophical speculation and practical application that the composer had described to Doni in 1634.[32] This was the closest Monteverdi ever came to fulfilling the promise he had made in 1605 to justify his practice in terms that satisfied both reason and the senses.

As the practical demonstration of the composer's aesthetic premises, the

---

31. Zarlino, *Istitutioni harmoniche,* 72.

32. Pirrotta saw the preface as "a theorization *ex post facto* for manners and movements that Monteverdi must have found spontaneously and madrigalistically." "Monteverdi's Poetic Choices," 312.

Combattimento was the first (and, again, the only one) of Monteverdi's works to be clothed in an overtly classicizing garb, and this is not limited to the materials from which Monteverdi fashioned the *genere concitato*. The structure of the *Combattimento*—indeed its very genre, with its hybrid of narration, pantomime, and sound effects—recalls that of another ancient Greek model known to sixteenth-century writers on music. In the *Istitutioni*, Zarlino described the *Certame Pithico*, an elaborate representation of the battle between Apollo and the serpent. This had already been set to music, with obvious classicizing intent, by Luca Marenzio as the third of Giovanni Bardi's *intermedii* for Girolamo Bargagli's play *La pellegrina*, the centerpiece of the celebrations for the wedding between Grand Duke Ferdinando I of Florence and Christine of Lorraine in 1589.[33]

According to Zarlino, the battle between Apollo and the serpent was

> divided into five parts, of which the first was called *Rudimento overo Esploratione;* the second *Provocatione;* the third Iambic; the fourth *Spondeo;* and the fifth and last *Ovatione,* or *Saltatione.* . . . In the first part was acted the way in which Apollo studied and explored the place of the battle, to see if it was suitable or not; in the second, the way in which he provoked the serpent to battle; in the third, the battle [*combattimento*] itself, and this part contained a particular way to sing to the accompaniment of a flute, called *Odontismos,* because the serpent's teeth clattered whenever he was struck with an arrow. The fourth recounted Apollo's victory, and the fifth told how Apollo celebrated his victory with dance and mime [*balli, et salti*]. It should not surprise that the Ancients mimed and danced [*avessero saltato, et ballato*], when this *legge* was acted, since they used to mime and dance in their tragedies and comedies, and had developed a particular manner for each type. . . . As we can see from what we have said, Music had several components: Harmony, Rhythm, Meter, and Instrumentation (for this last it was called *Organica*). There was also Poetry and Mime; and these parts were at times all present in a composition, and at other times most of them were.[34]

Zarlino's description of the *Certame Pithico* contains a number of significant parallels with Monteverdi's *Combattimento*. The representation was a mixture of narrative and pantomime in which the story was told ("si raccontava,"

---

33. See D. P. Walker, *Musique des intermèdes de "La Pellegrina": Les fêtes de Florence, 1589* (Paris: Editions du Centre National de la Recherche Scientifique, 1986).

34. *Istitutioni,* 66–67.

Table 6.2 Comparison of the structures of the *Combattimento* and the *Battle between Apollo and Python* as described by Zarlino

	Apollo and Python	Combattimento
I	Rudimento (Esplorazione)	Setting of stage, pursuit, circling
II	Provocatione	Challenge
III	Iambico (combattimento) (Odontismos)	Battle (sound effects)
IV	Victory (Spondeo)	Clorinda's fall
V	Saltatione (Ovatione)	Baptism and Clorinda's last words

"si dichiarava,") as well as acted out. As in the *Combattimento*, the encounter progressed through five well-defined stages (table 6.2). It began with Apollo's reconnaisance of the location; in the *Combattimento*, Clorinda wanders around looking for an entrance into Jerusalem and Tancredi pursues her. The first part of the confrontation consists of Apollo provoking the serpent to battle, just as Tancredi and Clorinda challenge one another (not once, but twice, since the resumption of the battle is motivated by their second exchange). After the confrontation, the main body of the representation consists of miming the battle itself. Finally, Apollo offers a dance of thanksgiving for slaying the serpent; his closing celebration is replaced in Tasso's text by Clorinda's baptism and Christian death, a sacramental celebration that is joyful even *in extremis*. In the tragic plan of the *Liberata*, Tancredi's victory, which is both the cause and the result of his misguided pride, is of course negated by his realization that his slain enemy is the object of his unspoken desire.

In the *Certame Pithico*, the actors moved only according to the directions established by tradition, which did not allow for any modification of the established pattern. Monteverdi's instructions to his singers were just as strict: Tancredi and Clorinda "will conform their steps and actions to the way the text states them, and nothing more nor less, following diligently the timing, the blows, and the steps" [faranno gli passi et gesti nel modo che l'oratione esprime, et nulla di più nè meno, osservando questi diligentemente gli tempi, colpi et passi]. According to Zarlino, the proper representation of the classical *combattimento* required the presence of an instrumental accompaniment, which was employed to heighten the effect of the pantomime by supplying the sounds made by the serpent as it fought. Monteverdi's offstage viola ensemble fulfilled an identical role. Finally, Zarlino comments on his own purpose for describing such classical representations: "So that it may be seen that they consisted of measured verse, and that they aimed to move [the emotions], and to generate in the soul different passions."[35] Such is the purpose behind the *Combattimento*.

The cumulative effect of dramatic action as the means for conveying a character's psychological condition is also evident in Monteverdi's plans for the never-completed (and perhaps never even begun) setting of Giulio Strozzi's *Licori finta pazza innamorata d'Aminta*.[36] Monteverdi discussed the libretto in a series of letters to Alessandro Striggio in 1627, and his comments on the play's content and musico-dramatic potential are consistent with the ideas he put forth in his critique of *Le nozze di Tetide* and subsequently elaborated in the *Combattimento*.[37] Almost all of Monteverdi's observations concern the character of Licori, who feigns madness in her pursuit of Aminta; this is the play's central conceit, and the composer's aim is to enhance the effect of her antics as much as possible, since "it will, on stage, turn out to be new, varied, and pleasing" [riuscirà in sena et più nova et più varia et più dilettevole].

As a character, Licori's attraction derived from the sudden and unpredictable changes in her behavior and moods. Monteverdi emphasized that the music must match the character's repertory of affects at every turn. "The imitation must have as its foundation the words," he wrote,

> and not the sense of the sentences, so that when she speaks of war the music must imitate war, when of peace, peace, and when of death, death, and so on. And since the shifts from one [image] to the other will have to take place within a short time of one another, as will the imitations, the singer assigned to this most important part (which must move to both laughter and compassion) must forget about any other kind of imitation except for the immediate imitation of the words.[38]

---

35. *Istitutioni*, 66.

36. On Monteverdi's reluctance to undertake the *Licori* project for Mantua, see Gary Tomlinson, "Twice Bitten, Thrice Shy: Monteverdi's 'finta' *Finta pazza*," *Journal of the American Musicological Society* 36 (1983), 303–11.

37. The connection between the *Combattimento* and *Licori* is reinforced by the fact that, according to Monteverdi, Strozzi had written this short play to be performed at the palazzo of Girolamo Mocenigo, where the *Combattimento* had been staged, and where *Armida abbandonata* (excerpted—like the *Combattimento*—from Tasso's *Gerusalemme liberata*, 16.40) was almost certainly performed (in letter 118 of 4 February 1628 Monteverdi tells Striggio that *Armida* is in Mocenigo's hands; *Letters*, ed. Stevens, p. 389; *Lettere*, ed. De' Paoli, p. 304). For Mocenigo, Monteverdi also composed *Proserpina rapita*, which was produced on the occasion of the wedding between Giustiniana Mocenigo and Lorenzo Giustiniani in 1630. See Fabbri, *Monteverdi*, 282–83.

38. Letter of 7 May 1627; *Letters*, ed. Stevens, p. 315; *Lettere*, ed. De' Paoli, p. 244.

As in the *Combattimento*, the instruments were supposed to be offstage, to heighten the surprise, and as in the *Combattimento* mimetic sounds played an important part in the overall effect. Licori's feigned madness placed her within a fictional world, and the function that Monteverdi envisioned for the accompaniment was similar to that which he had given to the instruments in parts of the *Combattimento:* to bring that world before the audience by letting them hear the swords, the horse, and the clashing of shields. This was the focus of some of the passages from Licori's part that he singled out as likely to be successful: "my goal," he wrote,

> is that every time that she comes onto the stage she is to introduce new entertainment with fresh variations. Three places, I think, will have good effect: the first where she sets up camp, and from offstage are heard sounds and crashing noises similar to the ones being imitated by her words. In my opinion this will come off well. The other is when she feigns death, and the third when she pretends to be asleep, when the music must employ harmonies that imitate sleep. In certain other places, however, where the words do not imitate gestures, or noises, or where some other manner of imitation cannot be brought forth, I fear that [the lack of opportunities for effects] will weaken the material that precedes and follows them.[39]

Monteverdi's first example, "where she sets up camp, and from offstage are heard sounds and crashing noises similar to the ones being imitated by her words," is particularly telling in this regard. The off-stage music must imitate those sounds described by her words, making them seem real and therefore appearing to blur the distinction between the imaginings of a woman who is pretending to be mad and the "real" sounds the audience hears from offstage. The entire play hinges on the character's versatility and on the composer's ability to mold the music to fit her part, creating an ambiguous sound world that mediates between reality and dream. Indeed, the overall character of the work was that of a fantastic kaleidoscope: the *balletti* that the composer requested be inserted in each of the acts had to be "all different and fantastic" [tutti diversi l'un da l'altro et bizzarri]. Monteverdi therefore felt that those places where Licori failed to introduce new effects that lent themselves to musical realization might not be effective and might detract from the rest of the play. To this end he recommended not only that her part be revised, but also that her

39. Letter of 24 May 1627; *Letters*, ed. Stevens, pp. 320–21; *Lettere*, ed. De' Paoli, pp. 251–52.

appearances in the play be limited and involve new ideas each time, so as to maximize the impact of her deception.[40]

In the context of *Le nozze di Tetide* and the *Combattimento*, Monteverdi's aims in *Licori* seem clear.[41] Like the *Combattimento*, *Licori* is described in affective terms — it must move to laughter and compassion. Like the *Combattimento*, its success derives less from individual effects than from the sum total of all the affects and images introduced by its lead character's volatility. Finally, like the three *generi* of the preface to the *Madrigali guerrieri et amorosi*, its premise, that madness is best represented by disconnecting the present from both the past and the future, stems from Monteverdi's astute observation of human nature. His emphasis on individual words at the expense of syntax derives not from his disregard for context but from his expanded view of it: the context in *Licori* is not the text but the condition of (feigned) madness. And *that* is the subject of the composer's *immitatione*.

---

40. Letter of 5 June 1627; *Letters*, ed. Stevens, p. 323; *Lettere*, ed. De' Paoli, p. 254.

41. Monteverdi's intentions for *Licori* have engendered conflicting interpretations. Tomlinson has seen in the composer's apparent disregard for syntax in favor of individual words evidence that his fascination with mimetic depiction had led him to abandon the rhetorical premises that lay behind the works of the fourth and fifth madrigal books in favor of a "pictorial conception of the joining of text and music." *Licori* would have been the most extreme representation of this tendency, "Marinist drama par excellence" (*Monteverdi*, 205). Tomlinson takes Monteverdi's emphasis on the imitation of camp sounds, feigned death, and feigned sleep as evidence of his preoccupation with pictorial mimesis, on the grounds that the examples the composer cites are extrinsic to Licori's madness. In fact, Monteverdi makes it clear that the camp sounds are in imitation of Licori's words, and the context of the whole passage leaves little doubt that her feigned sleep and death are also part of her antics. For Lorenzo Bianconi, Monteverdi represents Licori's madness precisely by abandoning logic and syntax in favor of a fragmented setting that focuses on individual words without regard for their context (in Monteverdi's words, "solo che nel presente e non nel passato e nel futuro"). As such, Bianconi takes *Licori* as evidence of the rhetorical foundations of Monteverdi's art (*Il Seicento*, 39). On this point see also Chafe, *Monteverdi's Tonal Language*, 139.

EPILOGUE

After the *Combattimento,* Monteverdi continued to employ the new *genere* and to explore its potential: "Having seen that it was effective in imitating anger," he recounts in the preface to the *Madrigali guerrieri et amorosi,* "I continued to experiment with it, renewing my study of it, and used it in a variety of compositions, for both church and chamber."[1] This is an important point, because it makes clear that the theoretical formulation of the *genere concitato* applies to the *Combattimento* more specifically than it does to the rest of the collection, which Monteverdi assigns at least in part to a later creative expansion of the premises established in the preface. The variety of works in which the *genere concitato* is found bears out Monteverdi's claim of continued experimentation and attests to the flexibility with which it could be treated. Various manifestations of *concitato* affect appear in such different works as "Altri canti d'Amor," "Altri canti di Marte," "Or che'l ciel e la terra," the encomiastic "Io che nell'otio nacqui" (the *seconda parte* of "Ogni amante è guerrier"), the duet "Armato il cor," and the humorous canzonetta "Gira il nemico insidioso amore," all included in the eighth book. *Concitato* passages figure as well in Latin motets like the setting of "Laudate Dominum" for solo voice published in the *Selva morale,* where the new *genere* is employed side by side with another of Monteverdi's favorite emblematic devices, the *ciaccona.*

Critics have found, and will undoubtedly continue to find, that Monteverdi's "maggiori studi" produced his most challenging compositions. "Or che'l ciel" and the rest of the eighth book have drawn the most ambivalent critical

1. Monteverdi, Book Eight, Preface.

reception of any of the composer's works and have been the subject of debate.[2] It is by now a commonplace that, aside from the *Combattimento*, the *Madrigali guerrieri et amorosi* are not particularly "guerrieri," and that this can also be said of most of the other pieces in which the *genere concitato* is employed, when they are measured against Monteverdi's original theoretical formulation.[3] *Concitato*-derived passages rarely accompany texts expressing "ira et sdegno"; rather, they serve as aural cues whenever any kind of martial imagery is involved, and the various components of the new *genere* are pressed into service, even when no warlike text is present, to convey a range of agitated emotions.

Both aspects are evident in the large-scale *concertato* madrigal "Ardo, avvampo, mi struggo, ardo: accorrete," from the *Canti guerrieri*, where eighty-four bars of breathless martial triplets blast forth a text that, in spite of its urgent conflagration, is conspicuously lacking a smoking gun. As Pirrotta has noted, beyond the Petrarchan imagery of its opening there lurks a comic intent, and Monteverdi realizes it, first by unleashing its unsustainably long opening tirade, and then by following it with a full arsenal of madrigalistic arrows.[4]

An accounting of the role of humor in Monteverdi's works has never been attempted and lies beyond the scope of this study.[5] Some of the madrigals of the eighth book, however, are clearly comic in character, and in them Monteverdi exploits the pseudo-military imagery invoked by the arsenal of sound effects derived from the *Combattimento* for purposes that could not be further

2. Among modern critics, Leo Schrade saw the eighth book as "the fulfillment, the final answer to the constant search which gave meaning to his artistic life" (*Monteverdi, Creator of Modern Music* [New York: Norton, 1950], 335). More recently, Gary Tomlinson has voiced a less enthusiastic assessment: "These sonorous, grandiloquent, but after all hollow works are not, perhaps, a gratifying summation of a madrigalian career that had witnessed the wonders of 'Ecco mormorar l'onde,' 'Vattene pur crudel,' 'Ohimè se tanto amate,' and the *Sestina*" (*Monteverdi and the End of the Renaissance* [Berkeley and Los Angeles: University of California Press, 1987], 210).

3. On this point see Nino Pirrotta, "Monteverdi's Poetic Choices," in *Music and Culture in Italy from the Middle Ages to the Baroque* (Cambridge: Harvard University Press, 1984), 309–11, and more recently Robert Holzer's insightful discussion in "'Ma invan la tento et impossibili parmi,' or How *guerrieri* Are Monteverdi's *madrigali guerrieri*," in *The Sense of Marino: Literature, Fine Arts, and Music of the Italian Baroque*, ed. Francesco Guardiani (Ottawa: Legas, 1994), passim.

4. Pirrotta ("Monteverdi's Poetic Choices," 310) found "Ardo, avvampo" the most successful of the *Canti guerrieri*, and Holzer ("'Ma invan la tento,'" 436 n. 15) concurs, noting the Ovidian origins of the text's imagery. Pirrotta's judgment, however, can only be sustained in light of his interpretation of the work as a joke.

5. I presented a preliminary study of humor, "'Excuse me, but your teeth are in my neck': Of (Love)bites, Jokes, and Gender in Claudio Monteverdi's 'Eccomi pronta ai baci' and Other Madrigals," at the 1996 annual meeting of the Society for Seventeenth-Century Music.

removed from "ira et sdegno." One such work is the setting of Giulio Strozzi's canzonetta "Gira il nemico insidioso Amore," which develops the siege imagery that lies at the heart of "Ardo, avvampo." Each of the six stanzas follows the same form: two sets of paired lines, of which the first is always an *endecasillabo* and the second either a *settenario* (line 2) or a *quinario* (line 4).[6] In all six, the first pair describes the movements of the assailant, Love, and his forces; the second reports the inept preparations being made by the defenders to repel his attack. The struggle is of course perfunctory, and the outcome never in doubt; the futile rushing back and forth within the embattled citadel is therefore comic to the point of slapstick.

Gira il nemico insidioso Amore
la rocca del mio core.
Su presto, ch'egli è qui poco lontano,
armi alla mano!

Nol lasciamo accostar, ch'egli non saglia
sulla fiacca muraglia,
ma facciam fuor una sortita bella;
butta la sella!

Armi false non son, ch'ei s'avvicina
col grosso a la cortina.
Su presto, ch'egli è qui poco discosto,
tutti al suo posto!

Vuol degl'occhi attaccar il baloardo
con impeto gagliardo.
Su presto, ch'egli è qui senz'alcun fallo,
tutti a cavallo!

Non è più tempo, ohimè, ch'egli ad un tratto
del cor padron s'è fatto.
A gambe, a salvo chi si può salvare
all'andare!

Cor mio, non val fuggire, sei morto e servo
d'un tiranno protervo,
che'l vincitor, ch'è già dentro alla piazza,
grida: "Foco, ammazza!"

6. As preserved in Monteverdi's setting, the last lines of stanzas 5 and 6 do not fit the pattern: the first contains only four syllables, and the second has six. See Stanley Appelbaum, preface to *Madrigals, Books IV and V,* by Claudio Monteverdi (New York: Dover, 1986).

That insidious enemy, Love, circles
The fortress of my heart.
Come quickly, for he's nearby,
To arms!

Let's not allow him to get near, so that he will not
Climb our sagging walls,
Let us put on a good show with a nice sortie,
Saddle up!

His are not fake weapons, for he nears
Our defensive line with his main army.
Come quickly, for he draws near,
To your posts!

He wants to attack the bulwark around my eyes
With a daring charge.
Come quickly, for he is here without fail,
Onto the saddle!

There is no longer time, alas, for suddenly
He is master of the heart.
Run, it's every man for himself,
Flee!

My heart, fleeing is pointless and you are enslaved
By an arrogant tyrant,
For the victor, who has reached the main square,
Hollers: "Burn and kill!"

Monteverdi retains the three-voice texture and stanzaic structure of the can-zonetta and invokes the trademark regularity of the genre in other ways as well. The distribution of voices varies from section to section but does so in a way that emphasizes the three-part design of the first volume of *Scherzi musicali*. The voices rotate throughout the solo sections in a scheme that is reminiscent of "Amor che deggio far"; in "Gira," however, there is no recourse to other uni-fying elements, such as the strophic variation technique of the *Concerto* or the literal repetition of the *Scherzi*. The first stanza uses the entire ensemble through-out, as do the last two; the middle strophes open with declarative solo passages (for tenor, alto, and bass, respectively) in arioso style that are contrasted with the martial music, which is always scored for three voices. The use of solo voices to impart variety to the setting and to help delineate its form dates back to the *Scherzi*, as does the placement of the fullest textures at the beginning and at the end.

As in other canzonettas, like "Chi vol che m'innamori" from the *Selva morale*, each of the sections comprises two contrasting units, a duple-meter opening followed by a section in triple meter that sets the warlike images of Strozzi's mock battle. The recurrence of the triple-meter *concitato*-like sections functions as a kind of refrain, even if the poem itself lacks a fixed textual return. Strozzi's only refrain-like text ("su presto . . . "), which opens the second half of the first, third, and fourth strophes, elicits parallel (although not identical) humorously fragmented settings; Monteverdi uses its falling third figure, which recalls that for "la morte" in "Chi vol," to set "sei morto" in the last stanza, creating an ironic juxtaposition of lively animation and defeat. The comic effect of the "battle" sequences (all bloodless, since the defenders never actually engage the enemy) is heightened by the combination of exaggerated text repetitions, war cries, and madrigalistic depiction.

Monteverdi's harmonic language, as in "Chi vol che m'innamori," underscores the changing affect of the text. Whereas the first four strophes, in which the defenders seek in vain to hold the enemy at bay, are firmly in C major, the fifth, in which Love sets them to flight, dwells for the first time on A and D before closing with an ironic return to C major for the battle music that summons all to a speedy retreat. The closing section, in which the poet recognizes his utter defeat, juxtaposes an E major chord, the most remote harmony of the setting, to the C major that closes the fifth part. E major then leads to A for the line "e servo d'un tiranno protervo," underscoring the harmonic implications of the A minor sonority that had announced the breach at the opening of the *quinta parte*— the fortress is now under a new master. After the A major cadence the victor's rampage through the ranks of the defeated remains in sharp fifth-related keys (D, G, and A) and only touches on C in passing; the middle passage ("che'l vincitor già dentro alla piazza grida 'foco, ammazza'") comes to an abrupt halt on an E major chord before returning, once more in an ironic tone, to C for the final triple-meter section, in which the conqueror "borrows" the rallying cry of his quarry for his own assault.

Not all of the *Madrigali guerrieri et amorosi* are so far removed from the high rhetorical style of the *Combattimento*. "Or che 'l ciel e la terra" has long been read as evidence of Monteverdi's continued capacity for intense emotion, and in it, as in the setting of Tasso's epic, the *genere concitato* (in its sixteenth-note form) is deployed to highlight the poet's internal war, not to illustrate some exterior skirmish.[7] Similarly, the *concitato* passages of "Io che nell'otio nacqui," again in sixteenth-note form, emphasize the terror felt by the emperor's enemies ("the Orient, filled with panic and terror, will hear the sound of war trumpets" [[udrà] pien di spavento e di terrore l'Oriente sonar belliche squille]) and mark the climactic lines of the entire encomium ("As you gather up your spoils, O Great Ferdinand Ernest, they will bow before your unconquered sword, offering up their crowns and kingdoms" [Carco di spoglie O Gran Fernando Ernesto t'inchineranno alla tua invita spada vinti cedendo le corone e i regni]). It is highly unlikely that here, in light of both his position toward the empress and his pursuit of support from the imperial court, Monteverdi could have intended the *genere concitato* to be heard as anything less than heroic.[8] And the vivid imagery of the parallel "Altri canti" madrigals elicits a form of *concitato* that closely resembles the more intense passages from the *Combattimento*.[9]

Rather than ambivalence toward the new *genere* and the viability of the heroic mode, the *Madrigali guerrieri et amorosi* offer a multi-faceted exploration of its potential, from the "memorable deeds" [opre sì memorande] of the *Combattimento* to the low comedy of "Gira il nemico" and "Ardo, avvampo." For all the variety with which the often ambiguous martial imagery of the eighth book is treated, Monteverdi's approach to the *genere concitato* remained in fact remarkably true to his original theoretical formulation. The further the text strays from a "text containing anger and scorn" [oratione contenente ira et sdegno], the more the music emphasizes the merely mimetic devices introduced in the *Combattimento*—triadic fanfare figurations, battle cries, trotting horses. When the text veers toward war as a metaphor for emotional conflict, the music returns to the superimposition of pyrrhic and spondaic meters, the keys to the listeners' own passions.

Later uses of the *genere concitato* indicate that Monteverdi continued to

7. Partly because of the personal significance that in his view Petrarch held for Monteverdi, Pirrotta sees "Or che 'l ciel" as a departure from the "detached or sentimental half-committment" that he finds pervasive in all of Monteverdi's works after the continuo madrigals of the sixth book ("Monteverdi's Poetic Choices," 313).

8. In "New Light on the Genesis of Monteverdi's Eighth Book of Madrigals" (paper presented at the annual conference of the Society for Seventeenth-Century Music, 1994), Steven Saunders argues, on the basis of newly discovered documents, that Monteverdi's dedication of the *Madrigali guerrieri et amorosi* to the Habsburg emperor was likely linked to his petition for support from the court in his pursuit of a canonry in Cremona. I am grateful to Professor Saunders for providing me with a copy of an expanded version of his talk.

9. For a different assessment of the *concitato* passage in "Altri canti d'Amor," "Or che 'l ciel," and "Ogni amante è guerrier," see Holzer, "'Ma invan la tento,'" 443.

reserve its original form for situations where the music needs to reflect a character's most excited state. Thus, in *Poppea* it marks the high point of Nerone's anger during his confrontation with Seneca in the first act; whereas triadic motion had occurred in both Seneca's and Nerone's parts at other points in their altercation (for example, in conjuction with Nerone's mention of war), the telltale sixteenth-note figurations occur only in conjunction with Nerone's "you push me to scorn" [mi sforzi allo sdegno]. Even then, the full *concitato* texture is not invoked until the second time the words are uttered and the emperor's temper has flared out of control.[10]

With the invention and theoretical justification of the *genere concitato*, Monteverdi brought to fruition the realignment, begun with the works that had precipitated Artusi's attacks, of the principal elements of composition. After the turn of the century, Monteverdi's concept of *oratione* shifted its focus from the surface of the text—its individual words, their meaning, and their syntactic organization—to its emotional and psychological content. This new, fundamentally dramatic, approach to the text is evident in the cyclic organization of the *Pastor fido* excerpts of the fifth book, in Monteverdi's imposition of a narrative ordering on the continuo madrigals at the end of the same volume, in his emphasis on rhythm and form to evoke the delicate moods of Chiabrera's poetry, in the transformation of genre and form of the "Lamento della ninfa," and in the dazzling rhetorical subtlety of the *Combattimento*. In light of Monteverdi's progress after 1600, the *seconda prattica* emerges as an ongoing process in which Giulio Cesare's benchmark definition of it, as an approach to composition in which "the text is the mistress of the harmony and not its servant," remained the composer's guiding principle. At its root lay a paradox that did not become obvious until the separation between the instrumental and vocal parts of the *Combattimento* made it so, but that was already evident in the juxtaposition of the "Dichiaratione" and the *Scherzi musicali:* that, in order for music to truly serve the text, it first had to become independent of it. Only after acquiring a symbolic language of its own could music participate equally in conveying the substance of the text. By the time Monteverdi formalized their

---

10. On this point see Ellen Rosand, "Seneca and the Interpretation of *L'Incoronazione di Poppea*," *Journal of the American Musicological Society* 38 (1985), 62–63. This scene has been much discussed: for a recent structural and tonal analysis, see Eric Chafe, *Monteverdi's Tonal Language* (New York: Schirmer, 1992), 324–28; on its philosophical underpinnings, see Iain Fenlon and Peter N. Miller, *The Song of the Soul: Understanding Poppea*, Royal Musical Association Monographs 5 (London: Royal Musical Association, 1992), 68–69.

relationship in the preface to the eighth book, it was only at this deeper dramatic level that music remained subordinate to its mistress.

Monteverdi as "Modernist"

"L'oracolo della musica"—thus Benedetto Ferrari characterized Monteverdi in an encomiastic sonnet published with the libretto of *Arianna* for its Venetian revival at the Teatro S. Moisè in 1640. An innovator, showing his contemporaries the way to new musical ideas and a new musical language; perhaps sometimes a confusing figure, cryptic and challenging—thus the identification with the ancient oracles whose wisdom was delivered in riddles to be interpreted and pondered.

The publication of Ferrari's praise in conjunction with *Arianna* highlights an important historic convergence: in 1640, Monteverdi had two works playing in Venice, the second being *Il ritorno di Ulisse in patria*. Two near-beginnings, we might say: *Arianna* showed the way to the realistic representation of a character's emotions and psychological workings, sending Monteverdi deeper into his quest for the language of the *seconda prattica*; *Ulisse* marks the start of his last great creative outburst, his operas for the Venetian stage, which culminated in *L'incoronazione di Poppea*, completed shortly before his death in 1643.

Beyond its immediate significance, however, Ferrari's description of Monteverdi as an "oracle" highlights the composer's own conception of himself, bringing us back to the point in his career where this book began: the Artusi–Monteverdi controversy. For it was Giulio Cesare, in his "Dichiaratione" of some 35 years earlier, who first identified his brother as a widely imitated pathbreaker.

The Monteverdi brothers, as I argued in chapter 3, may have adopted their "avant-gardist" stance as a strategy to solidify Claudio's position at court against a rising tide of fashionable "foreigners," mostly Florentines, in imitation of Gabriello Chiabrera, then a frequent visitor to Mantua and a self-styled literary "discoverer" who compared himself to Columbus. He, after all, flaunted his association with Giulio Caccini, who had set his spectacular "opera" *Il rapimento di Cefalo*, the piece that had played opposite *Euridice* during the Florentine wedding celebrations in 1600. Moreover, they may have been forced to do so, at least in part, by Giovanni Maria Artusi's public excoriation, which made Claudio, willy-nilly, into a highly visible symbol of the most recent excesses of the younger generation. Monteverdi's early responses suggest that perhaps he may not have been entirely comfortable with this role, partly because he did in fact know how to write good old-fashioned counterpoint and continued to do so for the rest of his life (and we may read the didactic nature of the Missa "in Illo tempore" from the Vespers of 1610 as staking a public claim to the compositional traditions of the *prima prattica*).

Regardless of what external pressures may have been at work, however, once the "avant-garde" label had been pinned on, Monteverdi wore it proudly for the rest of his career. As we saw in chapter 3, as early as 1604 he referred to the *balletto* for *Endimione* as being "novo, bello et gustevole," giving novelty pride of place. Thirty years later, he was not afraid to claim, as he did to Doni, that "I would rather be moderately praised for the new style than greatly praised in the ordinary. And for this presumption I ask fresh pardon." "Presumption" or not, the need to advance the limits of musical language in response to fresh challenges seems to have been the main driving force behind his approach to composition, even when he masked it with conventional self-deprecation ("omne principium est debile"). The centrality he accorded the composition of Arianna's lament for his own development as a composer seems to bear testimony to this basic impulse.

Along with this tendency toward identifying himself with the "new" in music, Monteverdi held in sceptical regard the musical achievements of Classical antiquity. To modify Doni's negative assessment of the composer as "not a man of letters, no more so than any of his contemporaries," it seems clear that Monteverdi was not a "humanist" in the sense that the term applied to Zarlino, or even Artusi; such was not his background, and in a sense the lack of humanistic preparation may just have served him perfectly. It freed him from the burden of having to reject the recent past in favor of antiquity, an attitude which one senses all too often in Vincenzo Galilei's writings. Fittingly, the only theory book we have proof that Monteverdi owned is a copy of Zarlino's *Istitutioni harmoniche* now at Yale University that bears his signature. His assessment of ancient music as "poca cosa" is certainly more blunt than Zarlino's balanced view of it as appropriate to its time in the same way that modern music was appropriate to his own, but the refusal to view the present as a corruption of a glorious past, and the pragmatic need to make music for the present, are certainly common to both. Whether Monteverdi derived his view from Zarlino or from some other source, it prepared him for the intellectual climate of Venice, where pragmatism in the present tense, as Bouwsma has argued, overshadowed the dictates of classical humanism.[11]

11. William J. Bouwsma, *Venice and the Defense of Republican Liberty: Renaissance Values in the Age of the Counter Reformation* (Berkeley and Los Angeles: University of California Press, 1968), 83–94.

Although it is hard to prove, it is likely that Monteverdi's self-conscious "modernism" played a part in his compositional decisions. Logically, such a deliberately chosen (or adopted, once it had been imposed on him) aesthetic stance conformed to what were for him probably natural tendencies toward certain kinds of problems: dramatic music; the psychological nature of characters; the expressive potential of different genres and styles; and the need to transcend the madrigal and other sixteenth-century forms to create large-scale musical structures. To what degree these tendencies were sharpened by his public persona we may never know, but the fact that so many of his works seem to defy characterization—as do for example "Con che soavità," the *Combattimento*, the "Lamento della ninfa," and the continuo madrigals of the fifth book—supports this notion.

Modern scholars, like his contemporaries, cannot escape Monteverdi's "oracular" voice. He is both "creator of modern music" and "end of the Renaissance." In this study, I have emphasized his "modernism," but also his all-encompassing ear for the shades of meaning inherent in all the styles available to him, from improvised practices to highly disciplined counterpoint to the imaginative brilliance of the monodists. To borrow a cliché from the other end of the Baroque, Monteverdi's approach to composition, like Bach's, was fundamentally encyclopedic; his works reflect all the music of his age, and more importantly also the fluidity and constant searching that propel the making of a new musical language.

EPITAPH

O tu che in nere spoglie
del gran padre de' ritmi e dei concenti
l'essequie rinovelli e le mie doglie,
segui gli uffici tuoi dolenti e mesti,
ma pian, sì che no' l desti:
ch'egli estinto non è, come tu pensi,
ma stanco dal cantar dà al sonno i sensi.

> As, clad in black,
> You recite the funeral rite and give voice to my grief
> For the great father of rhythms and harmonies,
> Perform your woeful mournful office,
> But do so softly, so as not to wake him,
> For he is not dead, as you believe,
> But, tired from singing, he has surrendered his senses to sleep.
>
> Leonardo Quirini
> On Monteverdi's death
> (*I marinisti*, in Ferrero, ed., *Marino e i marinisti*, 988)

APPENDIX OF
ORIGINAL TEXTS

The paragraphs in this appendix are keyed to footnote numbers accompanying the translations of these passages.

Chapter One

8. "Sappia dunque come che è vero ch'io scrivo ma però sforzatamente; essendo che l'accidente che già anni mi spinse a così fare, fu di così fatta natura che mi tirò non accorgendomi a promettere al mondo quello che dopo avvedutomene non potevano le debil forze mie. . . . Il titolo del libro sarà questo: Melodia, overo seconda pratica musicale. Seconda (intendendo io) considerata in ordine ala moderna, prima in ordine all'antica. Divido il libro in tre parti della Melodia, nella prima discorro intorno al oratione nella seconda intorno all'armonia, nella terza intorno alla parte Ritmica; Vado credendo che non sarà discaro al mondo, posciachè ho provato in pratica che quando fui per scrivere il pianto del Arianna, non trovando libro che mi illuminasse che dovessi essere immitatore, altri che Platone per via di un suo lume rinchiuso così che appena potevo di lontano con la mia debil vista quel poco che mi mostrava; ho provato dicco la gran fatica che mi bisognò fare in far quel poco ch'io feci d'immitatione." *Lettere*, ed. De' Paoli, no. 122, 22 October 1633, pp. 320–21; *Letters*, ed. Stevens, no. 123, p. 410.

12. "Ha detto prattica e non Teorica perciocché intende versar le sue ragioni intorno al modo di adoperar le consonanze e dissonanze nel atto prattico, non ha detto *Istitutioni melodiche*, perciocché egli confessa non essere soggetto di così grande impresa, ma lascia al Cavalier Ercole Bottrigari e al Rev. Zerlino il componimento di così nobili scritti." Giulio Cesare Monteverdi, "Dichiaratione della lettera stampata nel quinto libro de' suoi madregali," in Monteverdi, *Lettere*, ed. De' Paoli, p. 399.

25. "Ha fatto sapere al mondo mio fratello questa voce essere sicuramente sua, acciochè si sappia, e si concluda che quando l'aversario disse nel secondo Artusi queste parole; *seconda prattica* che si può dire con ogni verità essere la feccia della prima, che ciò disse per dir male de le opere di mio fratello e che fu nel anno 1603, nel qual tempo propose mio fratello, d'incominciar a scrivere per diffendersi dal oppositore, che apena questa voce *seconda prattica*, ei si era lasciato uscir di bocca, indicio vero, che vorrebbe potere l'aversario lacerare nella istessa aria, nonché in iscritto, le parole di mio fratello, e le sue note insieme." "Dichiaratione," in Monteverdi, *Lettere*, ed. De' Paoli, pp. 401–2.

27. "Questi promettono cose grandi, dispute di filosofia, nove regole difese con l'autorità di Aristosseno, Tolomeo, Zarlino, et Galilei, allargano il campo alli artificiosi contraponti, et vado vedendo, che invece di abbellirlo, lo insporcheranno." *Seconda parte*, 4–5.

31. "Che d'altra prattica il Rever. Zarlino non s'intende trattare come bene afferma dicendo : non fu mai, né anco è mia intentione di scrivere l'uso de la prattica, secondo il modo de li antichi, o Greci, o Latini, se bene a le fiate la vò adombrando, ma solamente il modo di quelli, che hanno ritrovato questa nostra maniera, nel far cantare insieme molte parti, con diverse modulationi e diverse arie, specialmente secondo la via e il modo tenuto da Messer Adriano; sicché dunque l'istesso Rever. Zarlino confessa, non essere quel una verità? e sola de la pratica la sua insegnata." Monteverdi, *Lettere*, ed. De' Paoli, p. 400.

35. "Si trasgrediscono le buone regole, parte fondate nella esperienza madre di tutte le cose; parte speculate dalla natura; et parte dalla demostratione demostrate: bisogna credere che siano cose deformi dalla natura, et proprietà dell'armonia propria." *L'Artusi*, 39v.

37. "Tutto vi concedo che sia vero; ma ditemi se questa scienza si può con nuovi modi di dire accrescere: perché non volete, o non vi piace, o non vi pare che sía bene augmentarla? il campo è largo, ogn'uno s'affatica intorno alle cose nuove, devono ancora li musici dilettarsi, ché il fare le cantilene tutte ad un modo, genera nausea e fastidio all'udito." *L'Artusi*, 42.

39. "Dai sapienti regolate, et di ciascuna ci sono stati lasciati i primi elementi, le regole, et li precetti, sopra le quali sono fondate, affin che non deviando da i principii, et dalle buone regole, possi uno intendere, quello che dice, o fa, l'altro." *L'Artusi*, 41v.

40. "Essendo questa modulatione nova, per trovar con la novità sua novi concenti, et novi affetti, né discostandosi in niuna parte dalla ragione, se bene s'allontana in un certo modo dalle antiche tradittioni d'alcuni eccellenti musici." *Seconda parte dell'Artusi*, 5.

43. "Et quanto a quello, che ella dice non esser né Pittore, o Scultore, né Poeta, overo Oratore, che non cerchi d'imitare gli Antichi, e massime gl'eccellenti. A questo io rispondo, che ve ne sono, et saranno sempre, quelli massime che stimano più la inventione, che la imitatione, nella qual parte, in questi suoi Madrigali esso Signor Etc. si ha fatta particolare professione, come che nella Musica questa sii di gran lunga più lodata di quella, oltra che in questa facoltà non s'ha d'attendere alla imitatione de gl'Antichi, essendovi massimo campo con la inventione, et con questa nova modulatione d'avanzarli." *Seconda parte*, 19.

53. "Prima prattica intende che sia quella che versa intorno alla perfetione del armonia; cioè che considera l'armonia non comandata, ma comandante, e non serva ma signora del oratione, e questa fu principiata, da que' primi che ne' nostri caratteri composero le loro cantilene a più di una voce, seguitata poi, e ampliata, da Occheghem, Josquin des Pres, Pietro della Rue, Iouan Motton, Crequillon, Clemens non Papa, Gombert, e altri di que' tempi perfettionata ultimamente da Messer Adriano con l'atto prattico, e dal Eccellentissimo Zerlino con regole giudiciosissime." "Dichiaratione," in Monteverdi, *Lettere*, ed. De' Paoli, p. 399.

58. "Ma se l'intelletto può errare alle volte discorendo, come veramente erra; quando maggiormente il senso potrà ingannarsi? però vi dico, che il senso senza la ragione, e la ragione senza il senso non può dar giudizio, che vero sia di qualunque oggetto si voglia scientifico; ma sì bene quando accompagnati, et uniti sono." *L'Artusi*, 12.

59. "Lo Eccellente sensibile corrompe il senso, il che altro non vuol dire, senonché l'altre parte tutte occupano l'udito di tal maniera, che non puote udire intieramente l'offesa fattale, come farebbe se fosse la cantilena a due, overo a tre voci; ma la ragione,

che conosce, e discerne il buono dal cattivo, molto bene giudica che è un inganno fatto al senso, che non riceve la materia, se non in un certo modo confuso, se bene vecino al vero." *L'Artusi*, 41v.

60. "Dicovi adunque, che nelle cose attenenti alla facoltà armonica vi sono due giudici; il senso dell'udito per il primo; et la ragione per il secondo . . . il senso giudica quelle cose che versano intorno alla materia: et la ragione s'affatica intorno alla forma; dalle quali parole sì cava che sí come riceve perfettione la materia dalla forma, così il giudizio che fa il senso d'alcuna cosa, viene fatto perfetto dalla ragione. Il proprio del senso è di ritrovare almeno da sé il più vicino, e dalla ragione ricevere la perfettione; ma dalla ragione accade il contrario; imperocché riceve dal senso il più vicino, et da sé stessa; riceve la perfettione: et quello che il senso nella instabile materia confusamente conosce; la ragione in astratto, e lontano dalla materia spogliato, lo giudica; per la qual cosa concludono, non solamente questi Teorici Moderni ma gli Antichi ancora, che il giudizio dell'Armonia, non solo appartenga al senso dell'udito, ma alla ragione ancora . . . Il senso dell'udito è necessario, perché è il primo a ricevere in sé stesso tutte le cose a lui appartenente, e senza di lui la ragione non può fare il suo offitio: ma è poi imperfetto, perché se la ragione non le pone aiuto, si vede, che è manco, et debile et totalmente instabile." *L'Artusi*, 44–44v.

61. "L'eccellente sensibile, che corrompe il senso . . . gl'accompagnamenti si potrà dire, che facciano effetto d'offuscare il senso, come sempre ho detto, et confermo." *Seconda parte*, 37.

62. "Di sé stessi innamorati, che le pare di poter corrompere, guastare et rovinare quelle buone Regole, che di già hanno lasciate tanti Teorici, e Musici Eccellentissimi . . . tutto il loro pensiero, è di sodisfare al solo senso; poco curandosi, che la ragione, entri qua a iudicare le loro Cantilene." *L'Artusi*, 42–43.

"Per propria ambizione studiandosi tutti a gara di compiacere sommamente a le orecchie, senza tenere più altro conto del intelletto; essendo che questo nuovo allettamento cominciò a sviare l'animo da la attenzione de' concetti e d'altre imitazioni degli affetti, quasi snervandolo con queste soperchie delicatezze." Palisca, *Girolamo Mei*, 114.

64. "Fuori dalla ragione, e lontani dalla esperienza già fatta da' nostri passati, e ridotta in regole certe dal senso abbracciate, et dall'intelletto confirmate." *Seconda parte*, 8v.

"Veggo per il fine del ultima vostra che voi avete oppinione che la musica debba avere per suo oggetto il dilettar l'orecchio con l'armonia . . . Or se voi intendete il diletto che nasce dal aria del cantare, la quale bene accomodata esprimendo acconciamente il concetto et facendo con l'aiuto suo ben comparirne l'affetto, non può essere se non gioconda all'udirsi." Palisca, *Girolamo Mei*, 115.

65. "Se lo affetto è una passione, overo un moto dell'animo, o come disse Cicerone nel 2. de Inventione. Est animi, aut corporis ex tempore aliqua de causa commutatio." *Seconda parte*, 10.

67. "Come sarebbe che l'uomo allegro per qualche causa diventasse melanconico, et di mite iracondo; overo di sano che s'appartiene al corpo infermo, et simili cose; sarà forse vero che la musica del etc. abbi operato, overo operi nell'animo de gl'uomini questi effetti, et queste mutationi? eccene qualche autentica probatione? Ha forse questa sorte di musica fatto qualche miracolo come già si lesse che facevano quei musici antichi, et eccellenti? Non l'ha fatto; adunque non può fare novi affetti, come V. S. mi dice; bene come ho detto ella sollecita l'udito, et aspramente, et duramente lo percuoterà." *Seconda parte*, 10.

70. "Però crederei (e sia detto senza offesa di V. S.) che avrebbe detto meglio, se detto avesse; novo disconcento; nova aria, nova sollecitudine dell'udito, sollecitato, e percosso dalla prestezza, e tardanza del moto or soavemente, et or aspramente, secondo

l'aria, che il etc. ha dato alle parti della cantilena, e la disposizione delle consonanze, et dissonanze. Et questa è la novità che aporta questa sorte di Musica. Et in somma nuova confusione." *Seconda parte,* 9.

72. "Cessino adunque questi novi Maestri di portare all'udito cose dispettose, aspre, dure, insoportabili, et apportino cose armoniose, et soavi, che più facilmente lo inchineranno a quell'effetto, che si proponeranno di moverlo." *Seconda parte,* 52.

78. "Farà bene in alcuni secondo la dispositione loro, l'aria nova, e la nova modulatione un certo effetto di desiderare sentire più d'una volta quella cantilena, quella dico che sarà piena di vaghezza, bellezza, gravità, artificiosi contraponti; ma non per questo si potrà dire, che questo sia novo affetto in specie, perché più, e più volte è nato questo desiderio d'udire compositioni da valente Compositore composte. . . . Questo desiderio si può intendere in due maniere, overo che nasce nell'uomo, perché l'udito ne sente infinito piacere, e l'intelletto ne gode . . . overo che l'udito le desidera per sentirne un certo modo piacevole, che induce l'uomo alle risa, et a burlarsene. . . . È ben vero, che le due cose, che siano contrarie l'una all'altra, non si possino udire nel medesimo fine; il gusto non brama all'istesso modo, et con lo istesso desiderio il dolce, et l'amaro." *Seconda parte,* 26.

79. "Si ricercano cose naturali, che siano conformi alla natura, a volere che la natura si mova, et faccia effetti naturali, ma ci vuole di più che il soggetto sia disposto a ricevere così fatta passione. Ma questi effetti non saranno poi anco novi effetti in specie, anzi effetti altre volte, et ben mille operati. Et quando pur col mezo delle moderne Musiche si vedessero operare simili effetti, nascerebbono forse per così fatti intervalli, et con il mezo d'altre cose usate contra natura? Nascono dall'armonia, dal numero, dal ritmo che sono servi dell'oratione, et queste operano nel soggetto secondo ch'egli è disposto a ricevere cotali passioni, come a lungo ne ha ragionato, e dimostrato il Rever. Zarlino nelle Institutioni di sopra citate, et nel cap. 8. del lib. 8. de Sopplementi." *Seconda parte,* 31.

86. "Essendo adunque le Armonie et li Numeri simili alle passioni dell'animo; sì come afferma Aristotele: possiamo dire, che lo assuefarsi alle Armonie et alli Numeri, non sía altro, che uno assuefarsi et disporsi a diverse passioni et a diversi Habiti morali et costumi dell'animo: perciocché quelli, che odono le Armonie et li Numeri, si sentono trammutare secondo la dispositione dell'animo, alcuna volta nell'amore; alcuna volta nell'ira; et alcuna volta nell'audacia: il che da altro non aviene . . . che dalla simiglianza, che si trova tra le sopradette passioni con le armonie." *Istitutioni,* 88.

88. "È da considerare che le passioni et affetti naturali sono tutti senza molta fatica, come quelli che nascono tutti da inclinazioni e principi nati con essi noi, e tutti accommodati a quelli; et per ciò agevoli ad imitarsi et esprimersi, et conseguentemente a commoversi, né hanno bisogno se non di attititudine et disposizione conveniente a quello che le sono." Letter of 8 May 1572 to Vincenzo Galilei, in Palisca, *Girolamo Mei,* 101.

91. "Si deve adunque sapere, che le Affettioni o Costumi sono stati da gli Antichi chiamati *ethoi;* perciocché col mezo loro si veniva ad indricciare et conoscer le umane Costitutioni o Qualità; le quali se ben le volessimo chiamar Passioni dell'Animo, non sarebbe questo mal detto, dei quali erano (come dissi) Tre i Generi loro; et il Primo era quello, che chiamavano *sustaltikon,* overo l'Intervallare, nel quale col mezo del Parlare si recitava et dimostrava in esso alcuna cosa detta o fatta magnificamente con animo forte et virile; com'erano le cose dette et fatte da gli Eroi; intorno al quale s'affatica sopr'ogn'altra cosa la Tragedia. . . . Il Secondo nominavano *hesuchastikon;* cioè Ristretto o Contratto, et era quello, nel quale narrando alcun fatto presente, o già accaduto, si dimostrava l'animo ridotto et ritirato nella umiltà, et sottoponendosi effeminatamente ad alcuna passione o affettione, lo dipingevano poco virile, et senza nervo alcuno. . . . Ma

il Terzo, che chiamavano *hexukastikon*, o Quieto, era quello, nel quale accommodavano cose quiete et libere, et le pacifiche dispositioni dell'animo, con la moderanza della mente." *Sopplimenti*, 270–71.

92. "Le nenie, i lamenti, i pianti, i gemiti, i sospiri, et altre cose simili; del che ne sía essempio il quarto dell'Eneide di Virgilio intorno a quello ch'ei recita di Didone . . . gli Inni, gli Imenei, gli Esodi, le lodi, i consigli, et altre cose simili . . . trasportatione de gli intervalli, nei toccamenti (per dirsi così) et per le percussioni delle corde, che sono numerabili; ma etiando per i varii offici et administrationi, che in esse intravenivano; onde s'aveano varie sorti di cantilene." *Sopplimenti*, 271.

94. "Le quali accompagnate insieme nelle compositioni, secondo il Soggetto che conterà la Oratione, possino insieme nel Composto della Melodia muovere l'Animo, et ridurlo in diversi costumi et passioni." *Sopplimenti*, 270.

95. "Cagionerà bene affetto, cioè desiderio con la novità della sua modulatione d'udir bene spesso simil sorte di concento, più atto a mover l'animo nostro con la novità sua in questa nova pratica, che nella passata come quella che con più efficacia ferisce il senso." *Seconda parte*, 17.

96. "Come accento, e come inganno, overo come dissonanza sì, ma raddolcita dallo accompagnamento delle altre parti; senza dubbio non solo farà buono effetto, ma come cosa nova sarà di maggior diletto all'udito, che non sarebbe stata l'ottava suposta; et perché ella ne desidera la dimostratione; da ottimo poeta accordi la metafora al proposito, et così in vece di settima ponghi l'ottava, che ne la trarrà facilissima." *Seconda parte*, 16.

Chapter Three

4. "Il canto alla francese in questo modo moderno che per le stampe da tre o quattro anni in qua si va mirando, or sotto a parole de motetti, or de madregali, or di canzonette, e d'arie, chi fu il primo di lui che lo riportasse in Italia di quando venne da li bagni di Spà, l'anno 1599? e chi incominciò a porlo sotto ad orationi lattine e a volgari nella nostra lingua, prima di lui? non fece questi scherzi all'ora?" "Dichiaratione," in Monteverdi, *Lettere*, ed. De' Paoli, 402.

5. "Onde . . . considerato che altresí in quei tempi si usavano per i musici alcune canzonette per lo più di parole vili, le quali pareva a me, che non si convenissero, e che tra gli uomini intendenti non si stimassero; mi venne anco pensiero per sollevamento tal volta de gli animi oppressi, comporre qualche canzonetta a uso di aria per poter usare in conserto di più strumenti di corde; e comunicato questo mio pensiero a molti gentiluomini della Città fui compiaciuto cortesemente da essi di molte canzonette di misure varie di versi, sì come anche appresso dal Signor Gabriello Chiabrera, che in molta copia, et assai diversificata da tutte l'altre ne fui favorito, prestandomi egli grande occasione d'andar variando, le quali tutte composte da me in diverse arie di tempo in tempo, state non sono poi disgrate eziandio a tutta Italia." Caccini, *Le nuove musiche*, [v].

6. "Ne tacerò, ch'avendo i versi lirici speciale riguardo ad essere cantati, i musici con maggiore altri diletto, e loro minor fatica, variano le note sui versi, i quali non sempre sono gli stessi; e di ciò fa prova Giulio Romano, a cui hassi da prestar fede, perché l'Italia tutta quanta l'ammira." Lorenzo Fabri, in Chiabrera, *Opere*, 215.

9. "Vincenzo Gonzaga, duca di Mantova, pure si valse di lui, e nelle nozze di Francesco suo figliuolo il chiamò, e lasciò a lui i pensieri di ordinar macchine e versi per intermedi sulla scena. Da questo signore fu in tal guisa sempre onorato, sempre alloggiato e spesato in suo palazzo, e sempre udillo colla testa coperta; ed andando a pescare sul lago, ve lo condusse sulla propria carrozza sua, e pescando, fece entrarlo nel suo proprio navicello, e desinando, tennelo seco a tavola; poi, spedite quelle allegrezze, rimandollo a Savona, e volle che, senza obbligo di niuna servitù, pigliasse un onorevole stipendio

sulla tesoreria di Monferrato, e così fu; ed ogni volta che Gabriello fu a quella corte sempre accarezzollo." Chiabrera, *Opere*, 517–18.

12. "Sia un giovinetto, ovvero una donzella innamorata, nel cui petto sia passione, e la non si regga con franca ragione, né con specolazioni da scuola de' filosofi. Che cantassero eglino? Certamente tutto quello che sentiranno dentro del core, e tutto ciò non fia altro che affetto lieto o dolente, di cui gli uomini amando sono naturalmente ripieni. Io per me stimo, che di cento i novanta lascieranno a dietro ciò che Socrate divinamente insegnò a Fedro, e tutto ciò che Platone fa discorrere con tanta altezza nel dialogo del suo Convito. . . . Credo che per voi si leggano poesie francesi: ponetevi in memoria quei loro vezzi amorosi, quelle lusinghe, quelle tenerezze, le quali ogni donna ed ogni uomo può e sa esprimere, e ciascuno, quando sono espresse, le intende agevolmente; non pigliate voi sollazzo in vedere così amorosamente reppresentati sì fatti scherzi, a quali intendere non fa mestiere, né commento, né chiosa? D'altra parte cantate ad un drappello di vergini una canzone di Dante o di Petrarca, e poi chiedete a loro ciò che hanno ascoltato. Mi direte, è vero, quelle son poesie sovraumane, e vogliono uditori di sottilissimo ingegno, e di qui meritano ammirazione. Io non voglio contrastarvelo, ma infra la generazione umana trovansi degl'ingegni assottigliati ed anco de' materiali, e ciascuno dee poter cantare, e però si vuole dar loro versi che abbiano buon riguardo alle materie che da loro sogliono e possono recitarsi." Chiabrera, *Opere*, 573–74.

24. "I versi giambici o sono monometri, o dimetri, o trimetri; i monometri non furono usati dagli antichi, e però se ne tace, i dimetri o sono pieni, cioè con le due loro misure compiute; come "Dolce per la memoria"; o sono scemi, cioè con una sillaba meno all'ultima misura, come: "Chiare fresche e dolci acque"; o sono ammezzati cioè con due sillabe meno all'ultima misura, come: "Che sia in questa città." I trimetri similmente o sono pieni, come: "Tra l'isola di Cipri e di Maiolica"; o sono scemi, come "Con esso un colpo per le man di Artù"; e così fatti sono i versi giambici. I trocaici similmente sono monometri, dimetri, e trimetri, i trimetri non furono usati dagli antichi, e però anco di questi se ne tace; i dimetri o sono pieni, come: "Quando miro la rivera"; o sono scemi, come: "Io non l'ho perché non l'ho," o sono ammezzati, come: "Amore mi tiene." I monometri furono usati pieni, e non altrimente, come: "E l'Amanza." Ancora i versi trocaici hanno presso gli antichi una varietà; cioè che loro si giunge una sillaba, e fansi essere soprabbondanti; al monometro giunsela Dante alla prima misura, come: "Non per mio grato"; al dimetro giunsela Guittone alla prima, come: "E chi non piange hai duro core"; ed ancora gli si giunge all'ultima, come: "Chi vol bever, chi vol bevere." Di qui con esempio si raccoglie, che il verso toscano può essere di quattro, di cinque, di sei, di sette, di otto, di nove, di dieci, di undici, e di dodici sillabe: e di sì fatti leggerassene in questi fogli." Fabri, *Le maniere de' versi toscani* (*Opere*, 213–15).

31. "Prima che si comincia a cantare, si dovrà sonare due volte il ritornello. I ritornelli dovranno esser sonati in fine d'ogni stanza nei soprani da due violini da braccio, & nel basso dal chitarrone, o clavicembalo, o altro simile instrumento. Il primo soprano, cantata, che sia la prima stanza a tre voci con i violini potrà esser cantato solo, o vero all'ottava bassa nelle stanze che seguono, ripigliando però l'ultima stanza con l'istesse tre voci; e i violini stessi. Dove si vedranno tirate alcune linee nella sede delle parole, a quelle note che sono ad esse linee sopraposte dovranno esser sonate, ma non cantate." Monteverdi, *Scherzi*, "Avvertimenti."

33. "In Roma i maestri di musica ci hanno fatto sentire una strofe cantante con un'aria, e l'antistrofe pure con la medesima aria: ma quando l'uditore aspettava che di nuovo si ritornasse all'aria stessa la terza volta, egli si ritrovava ingannato, perciocché udiva un'aria novella formata sopra l'epodo; ed allo inganno maravigliosamente si dilettava,

ed a ragione, conciassiacché la varietà è quasi sempre compagna del diletto." Chiabrera, *Opere*, 582.

38. "Mi posi per far prima quello delle stelle, ma non trovando nella instrutione quante di numero hanno ad essere nel ballarlo, volendolo fare intercalato come mi pare che sarebbe stato novo, bello et gustevole, cioè facendo sonare prima da tutti li ustrimenti un aria allegra et corta, et danzata da tutte le stelle parimenti dipoi in un subito le cinque viole da brazzo pigliando un aria diversa da la detta fermandosi li altri ustrimenti ballandola solamente due stelle restando le altre et nel fine di detta partita a due di novo ripigliar la prima aria con tutti li ustrimenti et stelle, seguitando questo ordine sino che avessero ballato a due a due tutte le dette stelle; ma non avendo avuto il ditto numero, et questo essendo di necessario il saperlo (piacendo però alla A. V. S. in tal maniera d'inventione intercalata come ho detto) pertanto sino ch'io lo sappia ho tralassato il farlo et per saperlo ho scritto a Messer Gio. Batt. ballarino." Letter no. 3, December 1604; *Lettere*, ed. De' Paoli, 24–25; *Letters*, ed. Stevens, 44–47.

49. "Manca però al mio parere per conclusione del tutto dopo l'ultimo verso che dice "Torni sereno il ciel, tranquillo il mare" qui manca dico una canzonetta in lode de' Seren.mi Prencipi sposi, l'armonia de la quale possa essere udita in cielo et in terra de la sena et alla quale possano nobili ballarini far nobil danza che così nobil chiusa mi par convenire a così nobile vista proposta." Letter no. 24; *Letters*, ed. Stevens, pp. 125–26; *Lettere*, ed. de Paoli, pp. 95–96.

Chapter Four

23. "Con tal bella occasione farò sonare li chitaroni a li casaleschi nel organo di legno il qual'è soavissimo et così canterà la Sig.ra Andriana et Don Gio. Batt.a il madregale bellissimo Ah che morir mi sento, et l'altro madregale nell'organo solamente." Monteverdi, Letter 12, 22 June 1611.

26. "Si fece poi la commedia in musica . . . et tutti i recitanti ben vestiti fecero la loro parte molto bene, ma meglio di tutti Arianna comediante: et fu la favola d'Arianna et Teseo, che nel suo lamento in musica accompagnato da viole e violini fece piangere molti la sua disgrazia." Solerti, *Gli albori del melodramma*, vol. 1, 99. Also Fabbri, *Monteverdi*, 138.

27. "Quanto era dunque meglio che quel gentiluomo veneziano invece di far ridurre al Sig. Claudio quell'Ariadna, la gioia veramente delle sue composizioni, in madrigali gli avesse fatto fare un concento a quattro voci instrumentali nel miglior modo che si fosse potuto per accompagnare con essi quella bellissima aria ad una voce sola?" Doni, "Appendice," in *De' Trattati di musica*, 61.

30. "L'armonia degli stromenti collocati dietro la scena, che l'accompagnavano sempre e con la variatione della musica variavano il suono . . . [il] lamento che fece Arianna . . . fu rappresentato con tanto affetto e con sì pietosi modi, che non si trovò ascoltante alcuno che non s'intenerisse, né pur fu una dama che non versasse qualche lagrimetta al suo bel pianto." Cited in Fabbri, *Monteverdi*, 133.

Chapter Five

1. "Per via di un suo lume rinchiuso così che appena potevo di lontano con la mia debil vista quel poco che mi mostrava." Letter no. 122, 22 October 1633; *Lettere*, ed. de Paoli, 321.

3. "Lessi quindici giorni fa et non prima la cortesissima et virtuosissima prima lettera di V. S. Rev.ma da la quale ne cavai affettuosissimi avisi et degni tutti da essere molto considerati da me; per lo ché glie ne vengo a rendere infinite gratie, ho però visto non

prima d'ora anzi venti anni fa il Galilei colà ove nota quella poca pratica antica, mi fu caro all'ora l'averla vista, per aver visto in questa parte come che adoperavano gli antichi gli loro segni praticali a differenza de' nostri, non cercando di avanzarmi più oltre ne lo intenderli, essendo sicuro che mi sarebbero riusciti come oscurissime zifere, et peggio, essendo perso in tutto quel modo praticale antico; per lo ché rivoltai gli miei studi per altra via appoggiandoli sopra a fondamenti de' migliori filosofi scrutatori de la natura, et perché secondo ch'io leggo, veggo che s'incontrano gli affetti con le dette ragioni et con la soddisfatione de la natura mentre scrivo cose praticali con le dette osservationi, et provo realmente che non ha che fare queste presenti regole con le dette sodisfationi; per tal fondamento ho posto quel nome di seconda pratica in fronte al mio libro, et spero di farla veder così chiara, che non sarà biasimata bensì considerata dal mondo; Lassio lontano nel mio scrivere quel modo tenuto da Greci con parole et segni loro, adoperando le voci et gli caratteri che usiamo ne la nostra pratica; perché la mia intentione è di mostrare con il mezzo de la nostra pratica quanto ho potuto trarre da la mente di que' filosofi a servitio de la buona arte, et non a' principii de la prima pratica, armonica solamente." *Lettere*, ed. De' Paoli, no. 123, 4 October 1634, pp. 325–26; *Letters*, ed. Stevens, no. 124, pp. 414–15.

6. "Pour Cl. Monteverde il n'est pas homme de grandes lettres, non plus que les autres musiciens d'aujourdhuy, mais il excelle à faire del melodies pathetiques, merci de la longue pratique qu'il a eu à Florence de ces beaux esprits des Academies, mesme du sieur Rinuccini . . . lequel . . . encores qu'il n'entendist rien en la musique, contribua plus que Monteverde à la beauté de ceste Complainte d'Ariadne, composee par lui. On m'asseure qu'il travaille depuis longues années sur une grande ouvrage de musique où il traicte des chants de toutes le nations, où il me contredict en beaucoup de choses. . . . Je suis bien escandalizé de luy en tant qu'il ne m'a jamais escrit depuis que je luy envoyay mon livre . . . au lieu qu'auparavant il m'escrivoit aucunes fois." Letter to Marin Mersenne, 7 July 1638, *Correspondance du p. Marin Mersenne religieux minime*, ed. C. De Waard, 5 (1960), 17–18. Quoted in Fabbri, *Monteverdi*, 293.

7. "E parimente grandissimo aiuto ricevè il Monteverde dal Renuccini nell'Arianna, ancorché non sapesse di musica (supplendo a ciò col suo giudizio finissimo, e con l'orecchia esattissima, che possedeva; come anco si può conoscere dalla qualità, e tessitura delle sue poesie) poiché con molta docilità, e attenzione questi tre musici ascoltarono sempre gli utilissimi insegnamenti, che quei gentiluomini gli somministravano, instruendogli di continuo si' pensieri eccellenti, e dottrina esquisita, quale si richiedeva in cosa sì nuova, e pregiata." Doni, *Trattato*, 25.

12. "È cosa chiara che le affezzioni si muovono negli animi altrui rappresentandonsi loro quasi innanzi o per obbietto, o per memoria que' tali affetti che da queste tali apparenze sono fatte lor apparire. Or questo con la voce altramente far non si può che con quelle qualità di lei, sia ella, o grave, o acuta, o mezzana che da la natura l'è stata appropriata [proveduta] per questo effetto, e che è nota propria e naturale di quello che altri vuol commuovere nel uditore. Simigliantemente è cosa notissima che de' tuoni i mezzani tra l'estrema acutezza e l'estrema gravità sono atti a dimostrare quieta e moderata disposizione di affetto: e i troppo acuti sono da animo troppo commosso e sollevato: e i troppo gravi, da pensieri e abbietto rimesso; nel modo medesimo che il numero mezzano tra la velocità e la tardanza mostra animo posato; e la velocità, concitato; e la tardanza, lento e pigro: et insieme è chiaro che tutte quelle qualità così de l'armonia, come del numero hanno per propria natura facoltà di muovere affezzioni simiglianti ciascuna a sé. Onde i tuoni troppo acuti e troppo gravi furono da' Platonici rifiutati ne la loro Republica [Palisca's note: *Republic*, iii, 398c]: quelli per esser lamentevoli; e questi, lugubri: e solamente ricevuti quelli di mezzo. Così come ancora fu fatto da' medesimi circa i

numeri e ritmi. Di più tutte le qualità contrarie, o naturali, o acquistate che le si siano nel mescolarsi e confondersi insieme indeboliscono, et in un certo modo spuntan le forze l'una a l'altra se le son pari, del pari, se non son pari, proporzionatamente a la potenza et vigore di ciascuna; onde ne nasce che ciascuna di esse mescolata con altra diversa da sé opera quanto a lei o imperfettamente, o pochissimo." Palisca, *Girolamo Mei*, 92–93.

15. "Et la melodia si compone di oratione, di ritmo, et d'armonia insieme così dichiarata da Platone De Repubblica et quelle qualità, che in essa vi concorrono, come è l'acutezza, la gravità, et equalità delle voci, si considerano nella armonia; la tardità, e la velocità, et il movimento, s'appartiene al ritmo. La lunghezza, e brevità della parola s'appartiene al metro, overo alla oratione." *L'Artusi, parte seconda*, 23.

16. "Dice mio fratello che non fa le sue cose a caso; atteso che la sua intentione è stata (in questo genere di musica) di far che l'oratione sia padrona del armonia e non serva; e in questo modo, sarà la sua compositione giudicata nel composto della melodia, del che parlando Platone, dice queste parole, 'Melodiam ex tribus constare, oratione, harmonia, Rithmo,' e poco più a basso 'Quin etiam consonum ipsum et dissonum eodem modo, quando-quidem Rithmus et Harmonia orationem sequitur non ipsa oratio Rithmum et Harmoniam sequitur,' dopo (per dare più forza all'oratione seguita con queste parole): 'quid vero loquendi modus ipsaque oratio non ne animi affectionem sequitur?' e poi, 'orationem ver cetera quoq; sequuntur.'" "Dichiaratione," in *Lettere*, ed. De Paoli, p. 396.

28. "Perciò aviso dover essere sonato il basso continuo con gli suoi compagnamenti nel modo et forma in tal genere che sta scritto, nel quale si trova parimente ogni alto ordine che si ha da tenere nelle altre compositioni d'altro genere, perché le maniere di sonare devono essere di tre sorti, oratoria, armonica, et retmica." Monteverdi, Preface to Book Eight.

33. "Si può fare argumento, quanto sia stato male inteso quel precetto così famoso appresso delli moderni contrappuntisti, quando hanno detto che le parti della cantilena devono procedere per moto contrario; vedendosi manifestamente per l'opposito, che con maggiore efficacia son' atte ad esprimere l'istesso affetto col simile, che col diverso; et che l'allegrezza et la mestitia insieme con l'altre passioni, possono esser cagionate nell'uditore non solo con il suono acuto et grave, et col veloce e tardo movimento; ma con la diversa qualità delli intervalli: anzi con l'istesso portato verso il grave, o verso l'acuto. Imperocché la quinta, nell'ascendere è mesta . . . et nel discendere è lieta, e per il contrario la quarta è tale nel salire, e d'altra qualità nel discendere; et l'istesso si vede accadere al semituono, e alli altri intervalli." Galilei, *Dialogo*, 76.

34. "Aggiunghiamo appresso questi impedimenti che cagionano la diversità de' suoni et la varietà delle voci, quelli che nascono dall'inugualità del moto delle parti, non meno de' primi importanti. Et questi sono che molte volte la parte del Soprano a mala pena si muove per la pigritia delle sue note, quando per contrario quella del Basso con le sue vola, et che quella del Tenore et del Contralto se ne vanno passeggiando con lento passo." Galilei, *Dialogo*, 82.

Chapter Six

1. "Come caro Sig.^re potrò immitare il parlar de' venti se non parlano! et come potrò io con il mezzo loro movere li affetti! Mosse l'Arianna per esser donna, et mosse parimenti Orfeo per essere uomo et non vento; le armonie imittan loro medesime e non con l'oratione et li streppiti de venti e il bellar de le pecore, il nitrire de cavalli et via discorrendo, ma non imitano il parlar de' venti che non si trovi." Letter 21, 9 December 1616; *Letters*, ed. Stevens, p. 117; *Lettere*, ed. De Paoli, p. 87.

5. "Diedi di piglio al divin Tasso, come poeta che esprime con ogni proprietà et

naturalezza con la sua oratione quelle passioni che tende a voler descrivere, et ritrovai la descrittione che fa del combattimento di Tancredi con Clorinda, per aver io le due passioni contrarie da mettere in canto, guerra cioè preghiera et morte." Monteverdi, Preface to the eighth book.

34. "Divisa in cinque parti, delle quali la prima nominavano Rudimento, overo Esploratione; la seconda Provocatione; Iambico la terza; la quarta Spondeo; et la quinta et ultima Ovatione, o Saltatione. La rapresentatione . . . era il modo della pugna di Apollo col Dragone: et nella prima parte si recitava, in qual modo Apollo investigava et contemplava il luogo se era atto alla pugna, over non: nella seconda si dichiarava il modo che teneva a provocare il Serpente alla battaglia: nella terza il combattimento: et questa parte conteneva un modo di cantare al suono del Piffero, chiamato O'dontismos: conciosia che il Serpente batteva li denti nel saettarlo: nella quarta si raccontava la vittoria di Apollo: et nella ultima si dichiarava, come Apollo faceva festa con balli et salti, per la ricevuta vittoria. Non sarebbe gran maraviglia, se gli Antichi avessero saltato et ballato, quando si recitava cotal legge: perciocché usavano anco di saltare et ballare nelle loro Tragedie et Comedie; et a ciascuna aveano accommodato il suo proprio modo . . . Potiamo ora vedere da quello, che si è detto, che la Musica avea più parti: l'Armonia, il Ritmo, il Metro, et lo Istrumento: dal quale questa parte si diceva Organica. Eravi etiandio la Poesia et la Saltatione; et queste parti alle volte concorrevano tutte in una compositione; et tallora la maggior parte di esse." Zarlino, Istitutioni, 66–67.

35. "Acciò si possa vedere, che erano composte di verso numeroso, accommodate a commovere, et generare ne gli animi diverse passioni." Istitutioni, 66.

38. "La imitatione dovendo aver il suo appoggiamento sopra alla parola et non sopra al senso de la clausula, quando dunque parlerà di guerra bisognerà inmitar di guerra, quando di pace di pace, quando di morte di morte, et via seguitando, et perché le trasformationi si faranno in brevissimo spatio, et le immitationi; chi dunque avrà da dire tal principalissima parte che move al riso e alla compassione, sarà necessario che tal donna lassi da parte ogni altra immitatione che la presentanea che gli somministrerà la parola che avrà da dire." Letter of 7 May 1627; Letters, ed. Stevens, p. 315; Lettere, ed. De' Paoli, p. 244.

39. "Il mio fine tende che ogni volta che sia per uscire in scena sempre abbi ad aportare diletto novo con le variationi nove; tre lochi bensì penso sortirassi l'effetto, l'uno di quando forma il campo che sentendosi dentro la scena gli soni et gli strepiti simili alle immitationi de le sue parole, mi pare non farà mal riuscita; l'altro di quando finge essere morta et terzo di quando ella finge dormire, dovendosi in tal loco adoperare armonie imitanti il sonno, ma in certi altri che le parole non ponno aver imitatione di gesti, o de strepiti o altro modo d'immitatione che salti fuori, dubito che languidirebbe o il passato o il futuro." Letter of 24 May 1627; Letters, ed. Stevens, pp. 320–21; Lettere, ed. De' Paoli, pp. 251–52.

Epilogue

1."Veduto riuscire alla immitatione del ira, seguitai ad investigarlo maggiormente con maggiori studi, et ne feci diverse compositioni altre così ecclesiastiche come da camera." Monteverdi, Book Eight, Preface.

BIBLIOGRAPHY

Aldrich, Putnam. *The Rhythm of Seventeenth-Century Italian Monody.* New York: W. W. Norton, 1966.

Anfuso, Nella, and Annibale Gianuario. *Preparazione alla interpretazione della poiesis monteverdiana.* Florence: Otos and Centro Studi Rinascimento Musicale, 1971.

Appelbaum, Stanley. Preface and new literal translations of the texts of *Madrigals: Books IV and V,* by Claudio Monteverdi, ed. Gian Francesco Malipiero. New York: Dover, 1986.

Aristotle. *The "Art" of Rhetoric.* Edited and translated by John Henry Freese. New York: Putnam, 1926.

———. *Retorica d'Aristotele fatta in lingua toscana.* Translated by Annibale Caro. Venice: Salamandra, 1570.

———. *Retorica et poetica d'Aristotele tradotte di Greco in lingua fiorentina.* Translated by Bernardo Segni. Florence: Torrentino, 1549. Reprint, Venice, 1551.

Arnold, Denis. *Monteverdi.* London: J. Dent, 1963.

Arnold, F. T. *The Art of Accompaniment from a Thorough-Bass as Practised in the 17th and 18th Centuries.* London: The Holland Press, 1961.

Artusi, Giovanni Maria. *L'Artusi, overo Delle imperfettioni della moderna musica.* Venice: Vincenti, 1600. Reprint, Bibliotheca Musica Bononiensis, sezione 2, no. 36. Bologna: Forni, 1968.

———. *Discorso secondo musicale di Antonio Braccino da Todi per la dichiaratione della lettera posta ne' Scherzi Musicali del Sig. Claudio Monteverdi.* Venice: Vincenti, 1608. Reprint, Bibliotheca Musica Bononiensis, sezione 2, no. 36. Bologna: Forni, 1968.

———. *Seconda parte dell'Artusi, overo Delle imperfettioni della moderna musica.* Venice: Vincenti, 1603. Reprint, Bibliotheca Musica Bononiensis, sezione 2, no. 36. Bologna: Forni, 1968.

Austin, William. ed. *New Looks at Italian Opera: Essays in Honor of Donald Jay Grout.* Ithaca: Cornell University Press, 1968.

Bianconi, Lorenzo. "I Fasti musicali del Tasso nei secoli xvi e xvii." In *Torquato Tasso tra letteratura, musica, teatro, arti figurative,* edited by Andrea Buzzoni, 143–50. Bologna: Nuova Alfa, 1985.

———. *Il seicento.* Turin: E.D.T., 1982.

Bieber, Margarete. *The History of Greek and Roman Theater.* Princeton: Princeton University Press, 1961.

Bibliography

Bonino, MaryAnn Teresa. "Don Severo Bonini (1582–1663), His *Discorsi e Regole.*" Ph.D. diss., University of Southern California, 1971.

Borgir, Tharald. *The Performance of the Basso Continuo in Italian Baroque Music.* Ann Arbor: U.M.I., 1987.

Bouwsma, William J. *Venice and the Defense of Republican Liberty: Renaissance Values in the Age of the Counter Reformation.* Berkeley and Los Angeles: University of California Press, 1968.

Boyden, David. "Monteverdi's 'violini piccoli alla francese' and 'viole da brazzo.'" *Annales Musicologiques* 6 (1958–63), 387–401.

Braun, Werner. "Ritornello." In *Die Musik in Geschichte und Gegenwart,* ed. Ludwig Finscher, 8 (1998), cols. 343–48. Kassel: Bärenreiter.

Brett, Ursula. *Music and Ideas in Seventeenth-Century Italy: the Cazzati–Arresti Polemic.* New York: Garland, 1989.

Buzzoni, Andrea, ed. *Torquato Tasso tra letteratura, musica, teatro, arti figurative.* Bologna: Nuova Alfa, 1985.

Caccini, Giulio. *Le nuove musiche.* Florence: Marescotti, 1601. Reprint, Florence: SPES, 1983.

Canal, Petro. "Della musica in Mantova: Notizie tratte principalmente dall'archivio Gonzaga." *Memorie del R. Istituto veneto di scienze, lettere e arti* 21 (1881), 655–774.

Carter, Tim. "Artusi, Monteverdi, and the Poetics of Modern Music." Paper presented at the national meeting of the American Musicological Society, Oakland, Calif., 7–11 Nov. 1990, as "The Artusi-Monteverdi Controversy Revisited: Print Culture and the *Seconda Prattica.*"

———. "A Florentine Wedding of 1608." *Acta Musicologica* 55 (1983), 89–107.

———. "Re-Reading *Poppea*: Some Thoughts on Music and Meaning in Early Seventeenth-Century Italian Opera." Paper presented at the annual meeting of the Society for Seventeenth-Century Music, Tallahassee, 1997.

———. "Resemblance and Representation: Toward a New Aesthetic in the Music of Monteverdi." Paper presented at the annual meeting of the Society for Seventeenth-Century Music, St. Louis, 1993.

———. Review of *The New Monteverdi Companion,* edited by Denis Arnold and Nigel Fortune, and *Monteverdi,* by Paolo Fabbri. *Music and Letters* 67 (1986), 169–72.

Chafe, Eric. *Monteverdi's Tonal Language.* New York: Schirmer, 1992.

Chiabrera, Gabriello. *Canzonette, rime varie, dialoghi.* Edited by L. Negri. Turin: U.T.E.T., 1952.

———. *Opere di Gabriello Chiabrera e lirici non marinisti del Seicento.* Edited by Marcello Turchi. Turin: U.T.E.T., 1973.

Chiappini, Alessandra. "Le Edizioni illustrate delle opere di Torquato Tasso." In *Torquato Tasso tra letteratura, musica, teatro, arti figurative,* edited by Andrea Buzzoni. Bologna: Nuova Alfa, 1985.

Cope, Jackson I. *The Theater and the Dream: From Metaphor to Form in Renaissance Drama.* Baltimore: The Johns Hopkins University Press, 1973.

Coryat, Thomas. *Coryat's Crudities.* 2 vols. Glasgow: MacLehose, 1905.

Curtis, Alan, ed. *Claudio Monteverdi: L'incoronazione di Poppea.* London: Novello, 1989.

Cusick, Suzanne G. "Gendering Modern Music: Thoughts on the Monteverdi-Artusi Controversy." *Journal of the American Musicological Society* 46 (1993): 1–25.

———. "'There was not one lady who failed to shed a tear': Arianna's Lament and the Construction of Modern Womanhood." *Early Music* 21 (1994), 21–41.

Dell'Antonio, Andrew. "Monteverdi's Ruse? Toward a Deconstruction of the *Seconda*

Pratica." Paper presented at the 58th annual meeting of the American Musicological Society, Urbana, Ill., 1992.

Disertori, Benvenuto. *Le frottole per canto e liuto intabulate da Franciscus Bossinensis.* Milan: Ricordi, 1964.

Donadoni, Eugenio. *Torquato Tasso.* 6th ed. Florence: La Nuova Italia, 1967.

Doni, Giovanni Battista. *De' trattati di musica di Gio. Batista Doni: Tomo secondo.* Florence: Stamperia Imperiale, 1763.

———. *Lyra Barberina.* Florence: Typis Caesareis, 1763. Facsimile edition, Bibliotheca Musica Bononiensis, Sezione II, 151. Bologna: Forni, 1974.

Einstein, Alfred. *The Italian Madrigal.* Translated by Alexander H. Krappe, Roger H. Sessions, and Oliver Strunk. Princeton: Princeton University Press, 1971.

Elwert, W. Theodor. *Versificazione italiana dalle origini ai giorni nostri.* Florence: Le Monnier, 1982.

Fabbri, Paolo. *Monteverdi.* Turin: E.D.T., 1985.

Feldman, Martha. "Venice and the Madrigal in the Mid-Sixteenth Century." Ph.D. diss., University of Pennsylvania, 1987.

———. *City Culture and the Madrigal at Venice.* Berkeley and Los Angeles: University of California Press, 1995.

Fenlon, Iain. "Franzoni, Amante." In *The New Grove Dictionary of Music and Musicians,* ed. Stanley Sadie; executive editor, John Tyrrell. 2d ed., 9, 213. New York: Grove, 2001.

———. "The Mantuan Stage Works." In *The New Monteverdi Companion,* ed. Denis Arnold and Nigel Fortune, 251–87. London: Faber and Faber, 1985.

Fenlon, Iain, and Peter N. Miller. *The Song of the Soul: Understanding Poppea.* Royal Musical Association Monographs, 5. London: Royal Musical Association, 1992.

Ferrero, Giuseppe Guido, ed. *Marino e i marinisti.* Milan: Ricciardi, 1954.

Florio, John. *Queen Anne's World of Words.* London: Bradwood, 1611. Facsimile, Menston: The Scholar Press, 1968.

Fortune, Nigel. "Monteverdi and the 'seconda prattica' ii: From Madrigal to Duet." In *The New Monteverdi Companion,* ed. Denis Arnold and Nigel Fortune, 198–215. London: Faber and Faber, 1985.

Fubini, Enrico. *A History of Musical Aesthetics.* Translated by Michael Hatwell. London: Macmillan, 1991.

Foucault, Michel. *The Order Of Things: An Archaeology of the Human Sciences.* New York: Vintage Books, 1970. French original, 1966.

Galilei, Vincenzo. *Dialogo della musica antica et della moderna: A Facsimile of the 1581 Florence Edition.* Monuments of Music and Music Literature in Facsimile, series 2, Music Literature, 20. New York: Broude Brothers, 1967.

Gallico, Claudio. "Emblemi strumentali negli 'Scherzi' di Monteverdi." *Rivista Italiana di Musicologia* 2 (1967), 54–73.

Getto, Giovanni. "Gabriello Chiabrera poeta barocco," in *Barocco in prosa ed in poesia,* 137–42. Milan: Rizzoli, 1969.

———. "Tancredi e l'immagine dell'amore." In *Nel mondo della Gerusalemme.* Florence: Vallecchi, 1968. Previously published as, "Clorinda ed Erminia e l'immagine dell'amore." In *Lezioni di letteratura italiana,* ed. Riccardo Massano. Turin: Giappichelli, 1967.

Gianuario, Annibale. "Proemio all'"Oratione di Monteverdi.'" *Rivista Italiana di Musicologia* 4 (1969), 32–47.

Giustiniani, Vincenzo. "Discorso sopra la musica de' suoi tempi," in *Le origini del melodramma,* ed. Angelo Solerti, 122–23. Turin, 1903. Translated by Carol MacClintock

Bibliography

in *Il Desiderio, or Concerning the Playing Together of Various Musical Instruments, [by]*
Hercole Bottrigari, [and] Discorso sopra la musica, [by] Vincenzo Giustiniani, p. 77. Musicological Studies and Documents, 9. Rome: American Institute of Musicology, 1962.

Glover, Jane. "A List of Monteverdi's Instrumental Specifications." In *Claudio Monteverdi:*
Orfeo, ed. John Whenham, 182–84. Cambridge: Cambridge University Press, 1986.

Greene, Thomas. *The Light in Troy: Imitation and Discovery in Renaissance Poetry.* New
Haven: Yale University Press, 1982.

Grout, Donald Jay. *A Short History of Opera.* 3d ed., with Hermine Weigel Williams.
New York: Columbia University Press, 1988.

Guarini, Battista. *Rime del molto illustre Signor Cavaliere Battista Guarini.* Venice:
Ciotti, 1598.

———. *Opere.* Edited by Marziano Guglielminetti. Turin: U.T.E.T., 1971.

Haar, James. "Arie per cantar stanze Ariostesche." In *L'Ariosto, la musica, i musicisti:*
quattro studi e sette madrigali Ariosteschi, ed. M. A. Balsano, 31–46. Florence: Olschki,
1981.

Hanning, Barbara Russano. "Monteverdi's Three Genera: A Study in Terminology," in
Musical Humanism and Its Legacy, ed. Nancy Kovaleff Baker and Barbara Russano
Hanning. Stuyvesant, N.Y.: Pendragon Press, 1992.

———. *Of Poetry and Music's Power: Humanism and the Creation of Opera.* Ann Arbor:
UMI Research Press, 1980.

Hathaway, Baxter. *The Age of Criticism: The Late Renaissance in Italy.* Ithaca: Cornell
University Press, 1962.

Heller, Wendy. "Arcangela Tarabotti and Busenello's Octavia: Defending Women in
The Opera in Venice." Paper presented at the annual meetings of the Society for
Seventeenth-Century Music, St. Louis, 1993, and the American Musicological Soci-
ety, Montreal, 1993.

Holzer, Robert. "'Ma invan la tento et impossibil parmi,' or How *guerrieri* are
Monteverdi's *madrigali guerrieri?*" In *The Sense of Marino: Literature, Fine Arts,*
and Music of the Italian Baroque, ed. Francesco Guardiani, 429–50. Ottawa: Legas,
1994.

———. "'Sono d'altro garbo . . . le canzonette che si cantano oggi': Pietro della Valle
on Music and Modernity in the Seventeenth Century." *Studi Musicali* 21 (1992),
253–306.

Hudson, Richard. *Passacaglio and Ciaccona: From Guitar Music to Italian Keyboard*
Variations in the 17th Century. Studies in Musicology. Ann Arbor: U.M.I. Research
Press, 1981.

Kristeller, Paul Oskar. *Renaissance Thought and the Arts.* Princeton: Princeton University
Press, 1990.

Kurtzman, Jeffrey. "An Early 17th-Century Manuscript of *Canzonette e Madrigaletti*
Spirituali." *Studi Musicali* 8 (1979), 149–71.

———. *Essays on the Monteverdi Mass and Vespers of 1610.* Rice University Studies 64,
no. 4 (Fall 1978). Houston: Rice University, 1979.

———. "A Taxonomic and Affective Analysis of Monteverdi's 'Hor che'l ciel e la terra.'"
Music Analysis 12 (1993), 170–72.

La Via, Stefano. "Cipriano de Rore as Reader and as Read: A Literary-Musical Study of
Madrigals from Rore's Later Collections (1557–1566)." Ph.D. diss., Princeton University, 1991.

Lee, Rensselaer W. *Poetry into Painting: Tasso and Art.* Middlebury, Vt.: Middlebury College, 1970.

Leopold, Silke. *Monteverdi: Music in Transition.* Translated by Anne Smith. Oxford: Clarendon Press, 1991. German original, 1982.

Mac Clintock, Carol. "New Sources of Mantuan Music." *Journal of the American Musicological Society* 22 (1969), 508–11.

Malagoli, Luigi. *Seicento italiano e modernità.* Florence: La Nuova Italia, 1970.

Malipiero, Gian Francesco. *Claudio Monteverdi.* Milan: Treves, 1929.

Mann, Brian. *The Secular Madrigals of Filippo di Monte, 1521–1603.* Studies in Musicology, 64. Ann Arbor: U.M.I. Research Press, 1983.

McClary, Susan. "Constructions of Gender in Monteverdi's Dramatic Music." In *Feminine Endings: Music, Gender, and Sexuality,* 35–52. Minneapolis: University of Minnesota Press, 1991.

Migiel, Marilyn. "Clorinda's Fathers," *Stanford Italian Review* 10 (1991), 93–121.

Mirollo, James V. *The Poet of the Marvelous: Giambattista Marino.* New York: Columbia University Press, 1963.

Monteverdi, Claudio. *Lettere, dediche e prefazioni.* Edited by Domenico De' Paoli. Rome: De Santis, 1973.

———. *The Letters of Claudio Monteverdi.* Edited and translated by Denis Stevens. London: Cambridge University Press, 1980.

———. *La selva morale e spirituale.* 2 parts. *Opera Omnia,* vol. 15, edited by Denis Stevens Cremona: Fondazione Claudio Monteverdi, 1998.

———. *Tutti le opere.* Edited by Gian Francesco Malipiero, 2d ed. Vienna: Universal, 1954–68.

Moyer, Ann E. *Musica Scientia: Musical Scholarship in the Italian Renaissance.* Ithaca: Cornell University Press, 1992.

Muscetta, Carlo, ed. *La letteratura italiana: storia e testi.* Bari: Laterza, 1970–80.

Nemerow, Linda Gail. "The Concept of 'Ut Pictura Poesis' in Giambattista Marino's 'Galeria' and the 'Dicerie Sacre' with a Translation of 'La Pittura.'" Ph.D. diss., Indiana University, 1980.

Neri, A. "Chiabrera e la corte di Mantova," *Giornale storico della letteratura italiana,* 7 (1886), 317–75.

Newcomb, Anthony. *The Madrigal at Ferrara, 1579–1597.* Princeton, N.J.: Princeton University Press, 1980.

Ossi, Massimo. "*L'Armonia raddoppiata:* On Claudio Monteverdi's 'Zefiro torna,' Heinrich Schütz's 'Es steh Gott auf,' and Other Early Seventeenth-Century *Ciaccone.*" *Studi Musicali* 17 (1988), 225–52.

———. "Between Madrigale and Altro genere di canto: Elements of Ambiguity in Claudio Monteverdi's Setting of Battista Guarini's 'Con che soavità.'" In *Guarini, la musica, i musicisti,* ed. Angelo Pompilio, 13–29. Lucca: L.I.M., 1997.

———. "Claudio Monteverdi's Concertato Technique and Its Role in the Development of His Musical Thought." Ph.D. diss., Harvard University, 1989.

———. "Claudio Monteverdi's *Ordine novo, bello et gustevole:* The Canzonetta as Dramatic Module and Formal Archetype." *Journal of the American Musicological Society* 45 (1992), 261–304.

———. "*Dalle macchine . . . la meraviglia:* Bernardo Buontalenti's *Il Rapimento di Cefalo* at the Medici Theater in 1600." In *Opera in Context: Essays on Historical Staging from the Renaissance to the Time of Puccini,* ed. Mark Radice, 15–35. Portland: Amadeus Press, 1998.

———. "'Excuse me, but your teeth are in my neck': Of (Love)bites, Jokes, and Gender in Claudio Monteverdi's 'Eccomi pronta ai baci' and Other Madrigals." Paper presented at the annual meeting of the Society for Seventeenth-Century Music, Wellesley, Mass., 1996.

———. *The Italian Concertato Madrigal in the Early Seventeenth Century: An Anthology*. In preparation.

———. "L'ordine novo e la via naturale all'immitatione: Struttura e rappresentazione nei madrigali concertati del Quinto Libro di Monteverdi." In *Claudio Monteverdi: Studi e prospettive: Atti del convegno, Mantova, 21–24 Ottobre 1993*, ed. Paola Besutti, Teresa M. Gialdroni, and Rodolfo Baroncini, 113–31. Florence, Olschki, 1998.

———. "Lamento." In *Die Musik in Geschichte und Gegenwart, Sachteil*, vol. 5, cols. 903b–11a. Kassel: Bärereiter, 1996.

Owens, Jessie Ann. "Music Historiography and the Definition of 'Renaissance.'" *Notes* 47 (1990), 305–30.

Palisca, Claude V. "The Artusi–Monteverdi Controversy." In *The New Monteverdi Companion*, Ed. Denis Arnold and Nigel Fortune, 127–58. London: Faber and Faber, 1985.

———. *The Florentine Camerata*. New Haven: Yale University Press, 1989.

———. "Galilei's Counterpoint Treatise: a Code for the 'seconda prattica.'" *Journal of the American Musicological Society* 9 (1956), 81.

———. *Girolamo Mei: Letters on Ancient and Modern Music to Vincenzo Galilei and Giovanni Bardi. A Study with Annotated Texts*. Musicological Studies and Documents, 3. Neuhausen-Stuttgart: Hänssler Verlag for the American Institute of Musicology, 1977.

———. *Humanism in Italian Renaissance Musical Thought*. New Haven: Yale University Press, 1985.

———. "Marco Scacchi's Defense of Modern Music." In *Words and Music: The Scholar's View (A Medley of Problems and Solutions Compiled in Honor of A. Tillmann Merritt by Sundry Hands)*, ed. Laurence Berman, 189–235. Cambridge: Harvard University, Department of Music, 1972.

Perelli, Antonella. "La 'Divina' Clorinda." *Studi Tassiani* 39 (1991), 45–76.

Pieri, Marzio. *Fischiata xxxiii: Un sonetto di Giambattista Marino*. Parma: Pratiche, 1992.

Pirrotta, Nino. "Monteverdi's Poetic Choices." In *Music and Culture in Italy from the Middle Ages to the Baroque*, 271–316. Cambridge: Harvard University Press, 1984.

———. "On Early Opera and Aria." In *New Looks at Italian Opera: Essays in Honor of Donald Jay Grout*, ed. William Austin, 39–107. Ithaca: Cornell University Press, 1968.

———. "The Orchestra and Stage in Renaissance *Intermedi* and Early Opera." In *Music and Culture in Italy from the Middle Ages to the Baroque*, 210–16. Cambridge: Harvard University Press, 1984.

———. "Scelte poetiche di Monteverdi." *Nuova rivista musicale italiana* 2 (1968), 10–42, 226–54.

Pirrotta, Nino, and Elena Povoledo. *Music and Theatre from Poliziano to Monteverdi*. Translated by Karen Eales. Cambridge: Cambridge University Press, 1982.

———. *Li due Orfei da Poliziano a Monteverdi*. Turin: Einaudi, 1975.

Plato. *Complete Works*. Edited by John M. Cooper, various translators. Indianapolis: Hackett, 1997.

———. *Gorgias and Phaedrus*. Translated by James H. Nichols, Jr. Ithaca: Cornell University Press, 1998.

———. *The Republic*. Edited by G. R. F. Ferrari, translated by Tom Griffith. Cambridge: Cambridge University Press, 2000.

———. *Republic*. Translated by Robin Waterfield. Oxford: Oxford University Press, 1993.

Plochmann, George Kimbell, and Franklin E. Robinson. *A Friendly Companion to Plato's Gorgias*. Carbondale and Edwardsville: Southern Illinois University Press, 1998.

Pozzi, Mario, ed. *Trattatisti del cinquecento*, vol. 2. Milan: Ricciardi, 1996.

Prunières, Henry. "Monteverdi and French Music," *The Sackbut* 3 (1922), 98–110.

———. "Monteverdi e la musica francese del suo tempo." *Rassegna Musicale* 2 (1929), 483–93.

———. *Monteverdi: His Life and Work*. Translated by Marie D. Mackie. Dent's International library of books on music. London: J. Dent, 1926. Reprint, Westport, Conn.: The Greenwood Press, 1974. French original, 1926.

Quint, David. *Origin and Originality in Renaissance Literature: Versions of the Source*. New Haven: Yale University Press, 1983.

Redlich, Hans. *Claudio Monteverdi, Life and Works*. Translated by Kathleen Dale. London: Oxford University Press, 1952.

Reiner, Stuart. "Preparations in Parma—1618, 1627–28." *Music Review* 25 (1964), 272–301.

Rinuccini, Ottavio. *Poesie del S.r Ottavio Rinuccini*. Florence: I Giunti, 1622.

Roche, Jerome. "Dognazzi, Francesco." In *The New Grove Dictionary of Music and Musicians*, 1st ed., 5, 521–22. London: Macmillan; New York: Grove's Dictionaries, 1980.

Rosand, Ellen. "The Descending Tetrachord: An Emblem of Lament." *Musical Quarterly* 65 (1979), 346–59.

———. *Opera in Seventeenth-Century Venice: The Creation of a Genre*. Berkeley and Los Angeles: University of California Press, 1991.

———. "Operatic Ambiguities and the Power of Music." *Cambridge Opera Journal* 4 (1992), 75–80.

———. "Seneca and the Interpretation of *L'Incoronazione di Poppea*." *Journal of the American Musicological Society* 38 (1985), 34–71.

Rose, Gloria. "Agazzari and the Improvising Orchestra." *Journal of the American Musicological Society* 18 (1965): 382–93.

Saslow, James M. *The Medici Wedding of 1589: Florentine Festival as Theatrum Mundi*. New Haven: Yale University Press, 1996.

Saunders, Steven. "New Light on the Genesis of Monteverdi's Eighth Book of Madrigals." *Music and Letters* 77 (1996), 183–93.

Schrade, Leo. *Monteverdi, Creator of Modern Music*. New York: W. W. Norton, 1950.

Scianatico, Giovanna. *L'arme pietose: Studio sulla Gerusalemme liberata*. Venice: Marsilio, 1990.

Sendrey, Alfred. *Music in the Social and Religious Life of Antiquity*. London: Associated University Presses, 1974.

Solerti, Angelo. *Gli albori del melodramma*. 3 vols. Repr. Hildesheim: Olms, 1969.

———. *Le Origini del melodramma*. Rome: Bocca, 1903.

Steele, John. "The Concertato Synthesis: Monteverdi's Beatus Primo." In *Claudio Monteverdi: Festschrift Reinhold Hammerstein zum 70. Geburtstag*, ed. Ludwig Finscher, 427–34. Laaber, Germany: Laaber-Verlag, 1986.

Stevens, Denis. "Madrigali guerrieri, et amorosi," in *The Monteverdi Companion*, ed. Denis Arnold and Nigel Fortune, 227–54. London: Faber and Faber, 1968.

Strainchamps, Edmond. "The Life and Death of Caterina Martinelli: New Light on Monteverdi's 'Arianna.'" *Early Music History* 5 (1985), 155–86.

Strunk, Oliver. *Source Readings in Music History from Classical Antiquity through the Romantic Era*. New York: Norton, 1950.

Tasso, Torquato. *La Gierusalemme liberata: Con le figure di Bernardo Castello; e le annotationi di Scipio Gentili e di Giulio Guastavini*. Genoa: Girolamo Bartoli, 1590. Reprint edited by Roberto Peliti, with an introduction by Giuseppe Piersantelli, Rome: Stabilimento Tipografico Julia, 1966.

Tesauro, Emmanuele. *Il cannocchiale aristotelico*. Turin: Bartolomeo Zavatta, 1670. Facsimile, Savigliano: Artistica Piemontese, 2000.

Tomlinson, Gary. "Madrigal, Monody, and Monteverdi's 'via naturale all'immitatione.'" *Journal of the American Musicological Society* 34 (1981), 60–108.

———. *Monteverdi and the End of the Renaissance*. Berkeley and Los Angeles: University of California Press, 1987.

———. *Music in Renaissance Magic: Toward a Historiography of Others*. Chicago: University of Chicago Press, 1993.

———. "Rinuccini, Peri, Monteverdi, and the Humanist Heritage of Opera." Ph.D. diss., University of California, Berkeley, 1979.

———. "Twice Bitten, Thrice Shy: Monteverdi's 'finta' *Finta pazza*." *Journal of the American Musicological Society* 36 (1983), 303–11.

Turchi, Marcello, ed. *Opere di Gabriello Chiabrera e lirici del classicismo barocco*. Genoa: U.T.E.T, 1974.

Vogel, Emil. "Claudio Monteverdi." *Vierteljahrsschrift für Musikwissenschaft* 3 (1887), 315–440.

Walker, Daniel Patrick. *Musique des intermèdes de "La Pellegrina": Les fêtes de Florence, 1589*. Paris: Editions du Centre National de la Recherche Scientifique, 1986.

Weaver, Robert Lamar, and Norma Wright Weaver. *A Chronology of Music in the Florentine Theater, 1590–1750*, Detroit Studies in Music Bibliography, 38. Detroit: Information Coordinators, 1978.

Weinberg, Bernard. *A History of Literary Criticism in the Italian Renaissance*. 2 vols. Chicago: University of Chicago Press, 1961.

Whenham, John. *Duet and Dialogue in the Age of Monteverdi*. 2 vols. Studies in British Musicology, 7. Ann Arbor: U.M.I. Research Press, 1982.

———. "Five Acts: One Action." In *Claudio Monteverdi: Orfeo*, ed. John Whenham, 42–77. Cambridge Opera Handbooks. Cambridge: Cambridge University Press, 1986.

———. "The Later Madrigals and Madrigal-Books." In *The New Monteverdi Companion*, edited by Iain Fenlon and Nigel Fortune, 216–47. London: Faber and Faber, 1985.

Wolff, Christoph. "Zur Frage der Instrumentation und des Instrumentalen in Monteverdis Opern." In *Claudio Monteverdi: Festschrift Reinhold Hammerstein zum 70. Geburtstag*, ed. Ludwig Finscher, 489–98. Laaber, Germany: Laaber-Verlag, 1986.

Zarlino, Gioseffo. *The Art of Counterpoint. Part Three of Le Istitutioni Harmoniche, 1558*. Translated by Guy A. Marco and Claude V. Palisca. New Haven and London: Yale University Press, 1968.

———. *Dimostrationi harmoniche*. Venice: Francesco dei Franceschi, 1571. Facsimile, Ridgewood, N.J.: The Gregg Press, 1966.

———. *Istitutioni harmoniche*. Venice: n.p., 1558. Facsimile, Ridgewood, N.J.: The Gregg Press, 1965.

———. *Sopplimenti musicali: Terzo volume*. Venice: Francesco dei Franceschi, 1588. Facsimile, Ridgewood, N.J.: The Gregg Press, 1966.

INDEX